Takane & Hana

8

STORY AND ART BY

Yuki Shiwasu

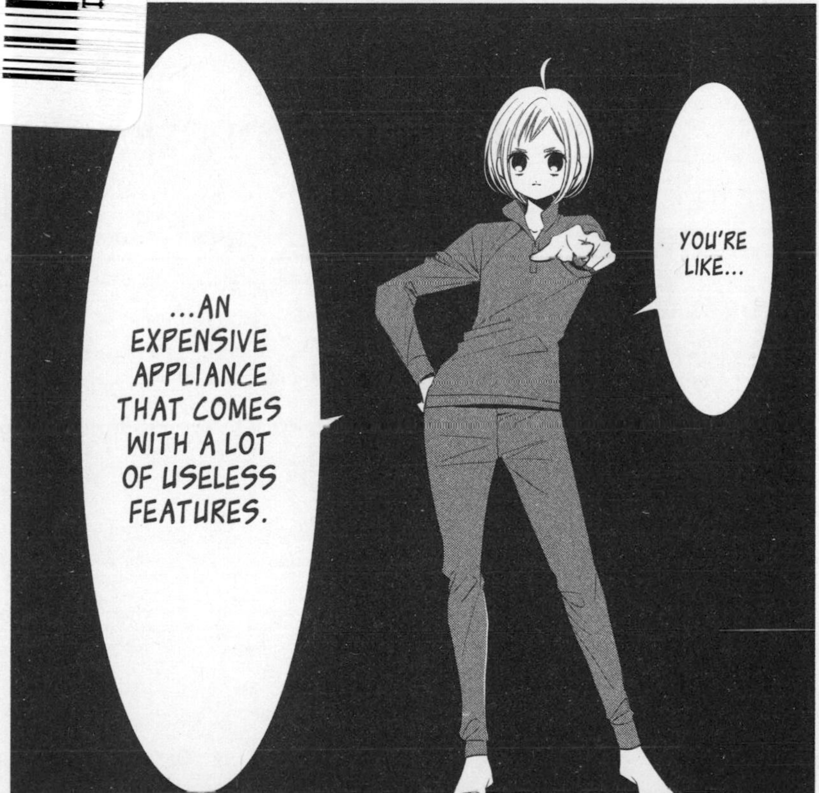
YOU'RE LIKE...
...AN EXPENSIVE APPLIANCE THAT COMES WITH A LOT OF USELESS FEATURES.

Takane & Hana

8

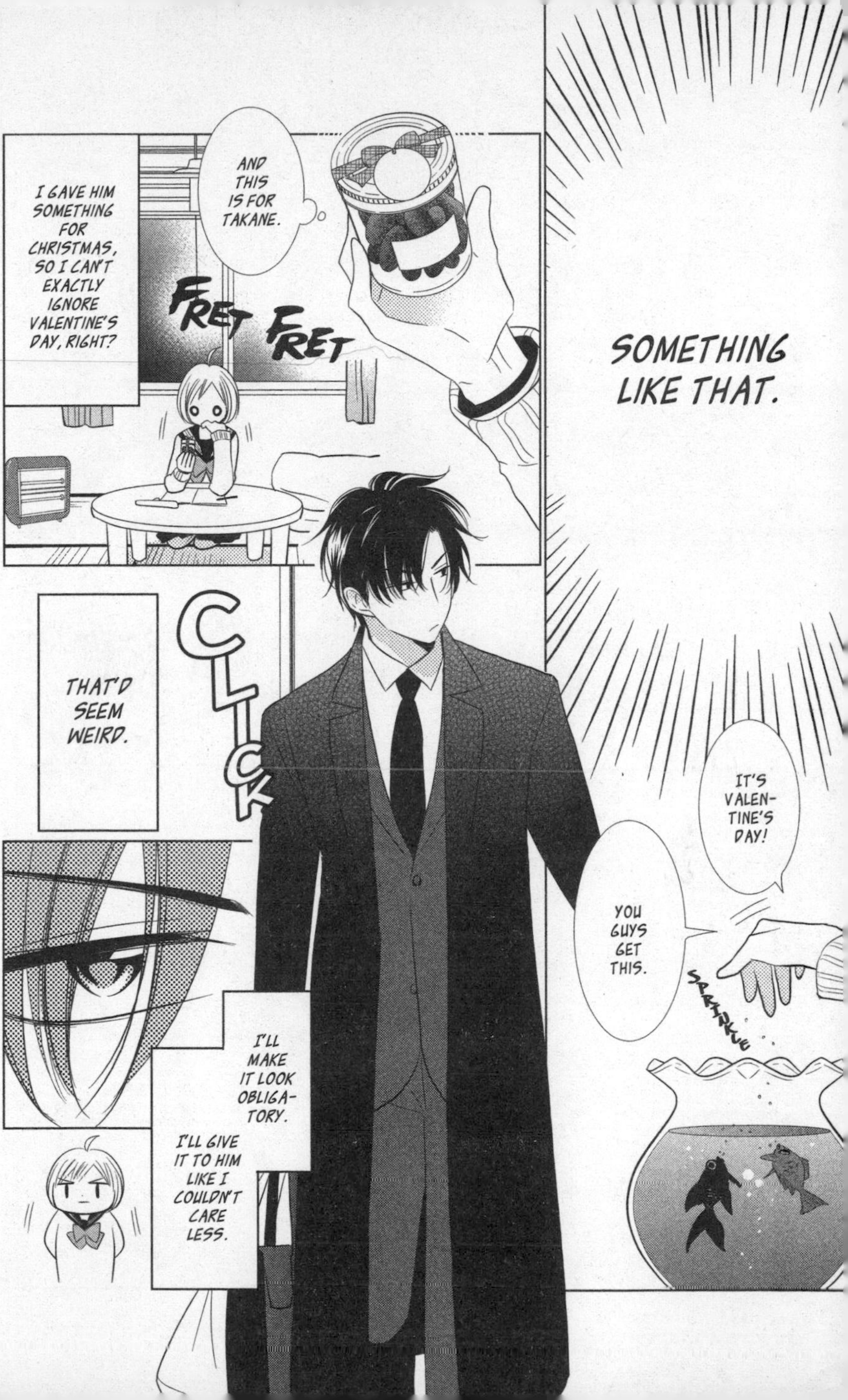
SOMETHING LIKE THAT.
IT'S VALENTINE'S DAY!
YOU GUYS GET THIS.
SPRINKLE
AND THIS IS FOR TAKANE.
I GAVE HIM SOMETHING FOR CHRISTMAS, SO I CAN'T EXACTLY IGNORE VALENTINE'S DAY, RIGHT?
FRET FRET
CLICK
THAT'D SEEM WEIRD.
I'LL MAKE IT LOOK OBLIGATORY.
I'LL GIVE IT TO HIM LIKE I COULDN'T CARE LESS.

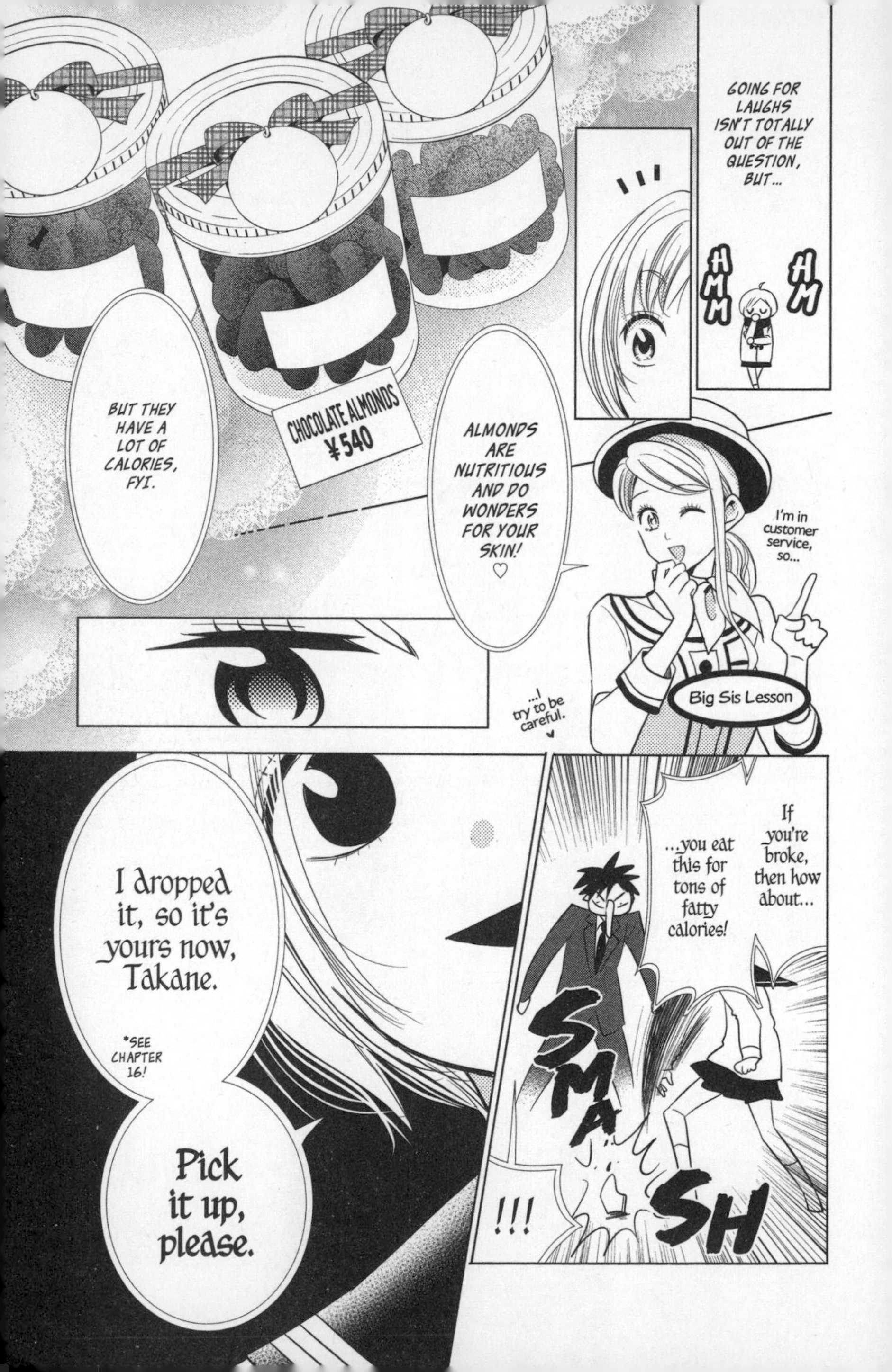
GOING FOR LAUGHS ISN'T TOTALLY OUT OF THE QUESTION, BUT...
HMM
HM
ALMONDS ARE NUTRITIOUS AND DO WONDERS FOR YOUR SKIN! ♡
I'm in customer service, so...
...I try to be careful.
Big Sis Lesson
CHOCOLATE ALMONDS ¥540
BUT THEY HAVE A LOT OF CALORIES, FYI.
If you're broke, then how about...
...you eat this for tons of fatty calories!
SMASH
!!!
I dropped it, so it's yours now, Takane.
*SEE CHAPTER 16!
Pick it up, please.

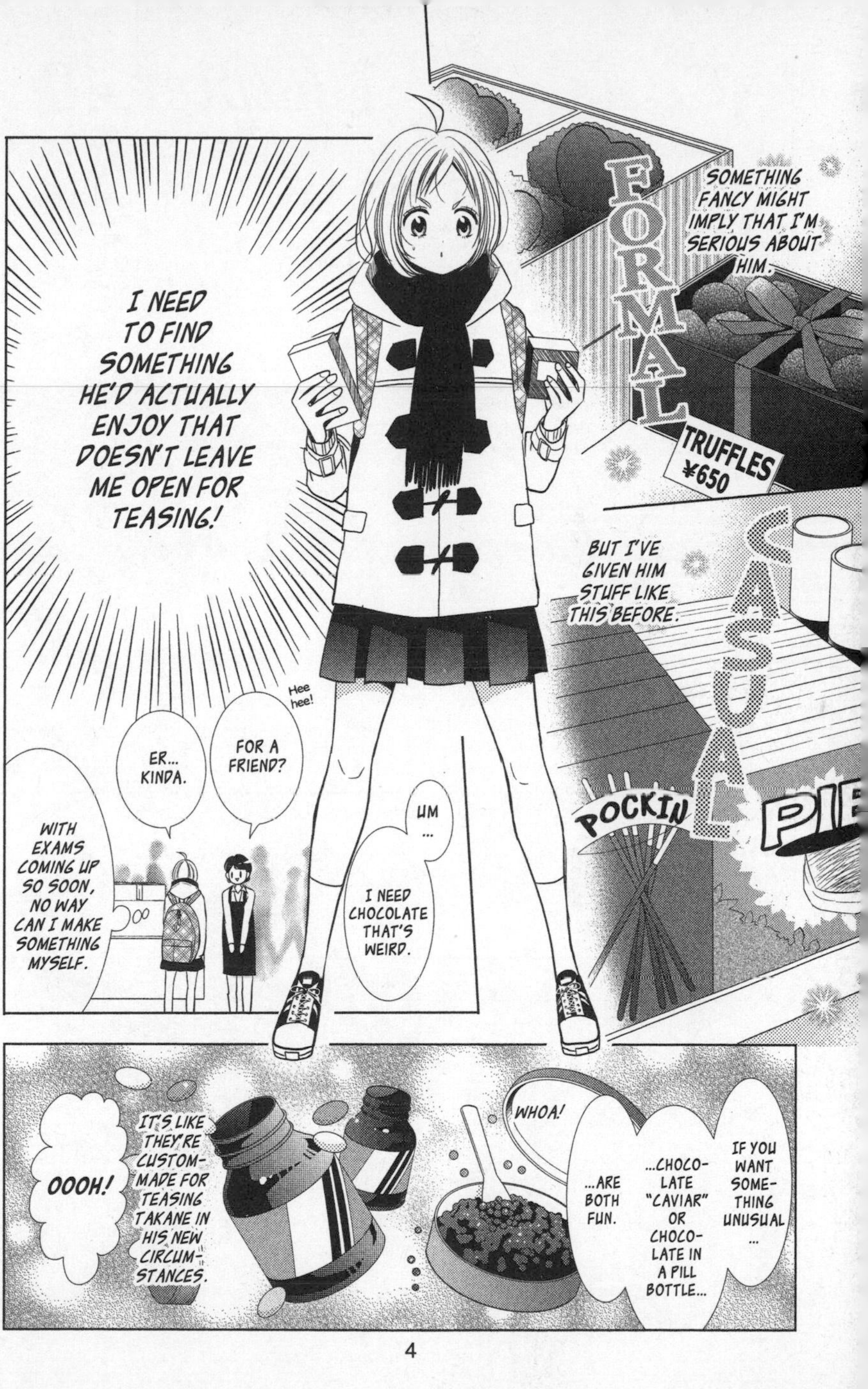
SOMETHING FANCY MIGHT IMPLY THAT I'M SERIOUS ABOUT HIM.
FORMAL
TRUFFLES ¥650
CASUAL
BUT I'VE GIVEN HIM STUFF LIKE THIS BEFORE.
POCKIN
PIE
I NEED TO FIND SOMETHING HE'D ACTUALLY ENJOY THAT DOESN'T LEAVE ME OPEN FOR TEASING!
UM ...
I NEED CHOCOLATE THAT'S WEIRD.
Hee hee!
FOR A FRIEND?
ER... KINDA.
WITH EXAMS COMING UP SO SOON, NO WAY CAN I MAKE SOMETHING MYSELF.
IF YOU WANT SOMETHING UNUSUAL ...
...CHOCOLATE "CAVIAR" OR CHOCOLATE IN A PILL BOTTLE...
...ARE BOTH FUN.
WHOA!
IT'S LIKE THEY'RE CUSTOM-MADE FOR TEASING TAKANE IN HIS NEW CIRCUMSTANCES.
OOOH!

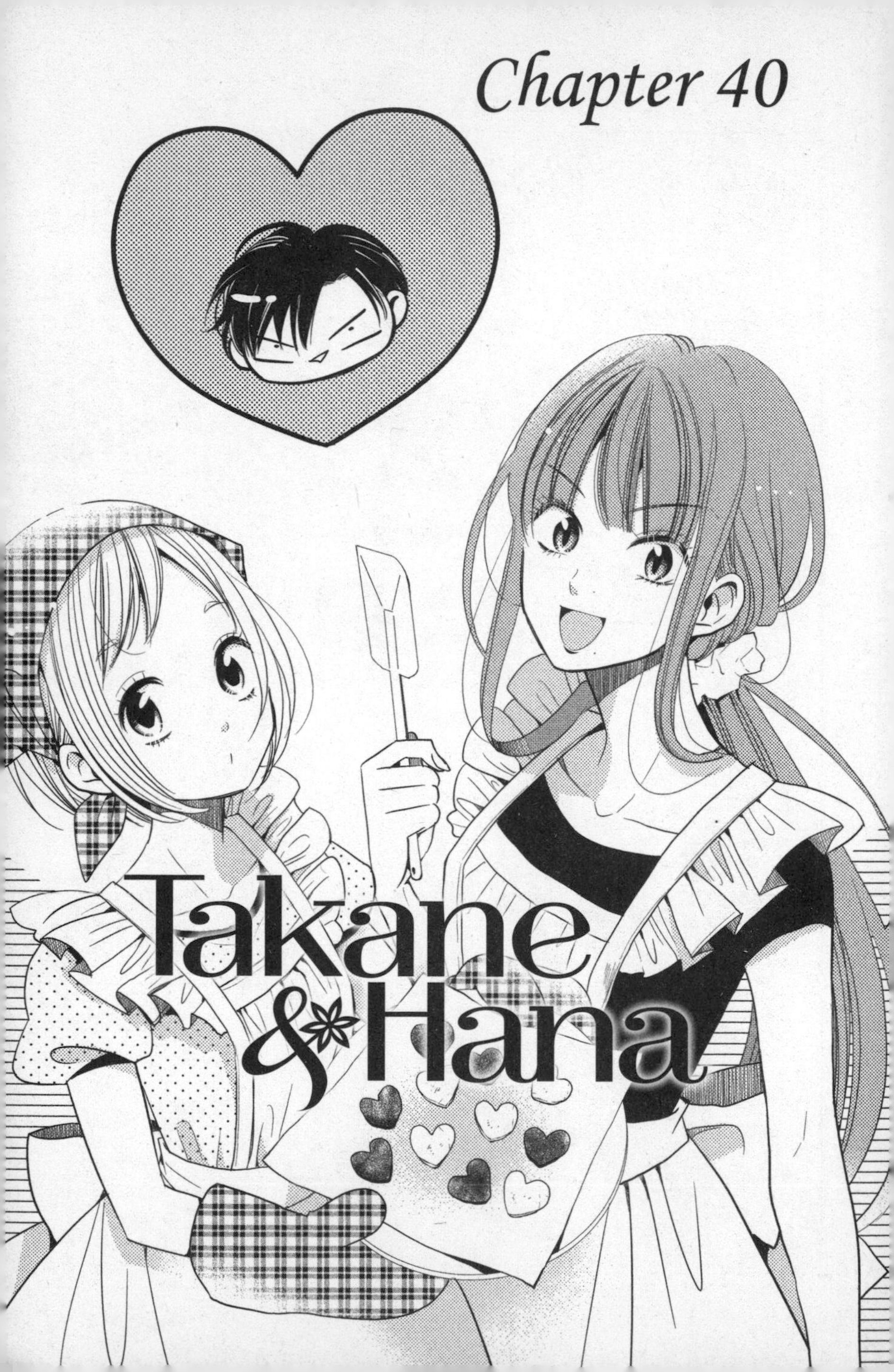
Chapter 40
Takane & Hana

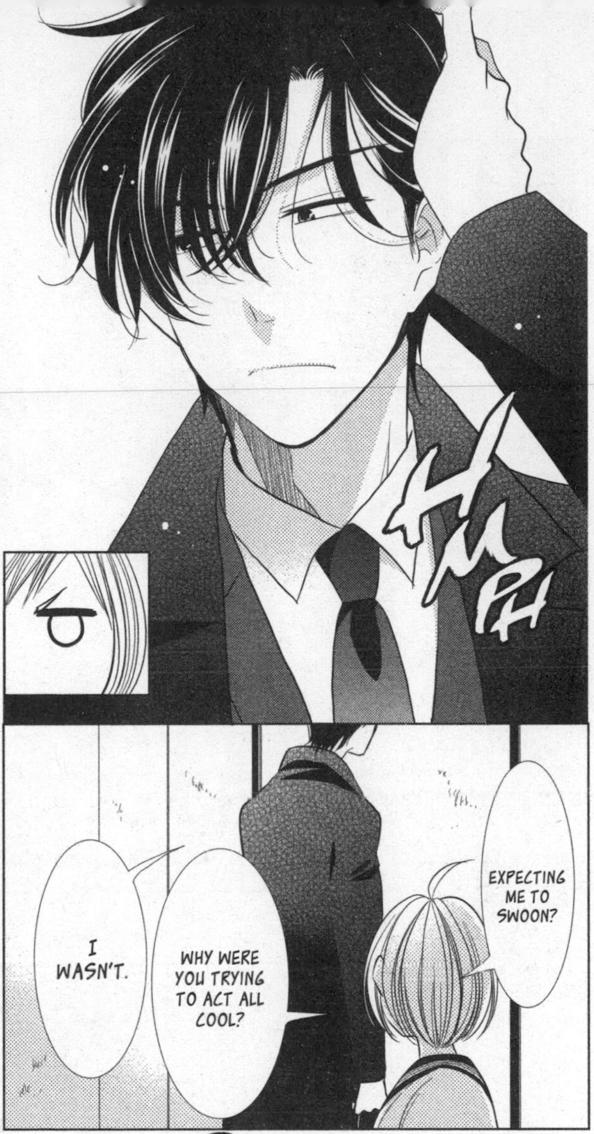
HMPH
EXPECTING ME TO SWOON?
WHY WERE YOU TRYING TO ACT ALL COOL?
I WASN'T.
KLK
MAYBE HE DIDN'T GET ANY CHOCOLATE AT WORK?
BOO BOO
CAN'T SHE PLAY ALONG AND SAY "SQUEE~! ♡" OR SOME-THING?
Honestly.
HE'S SULK-ING.

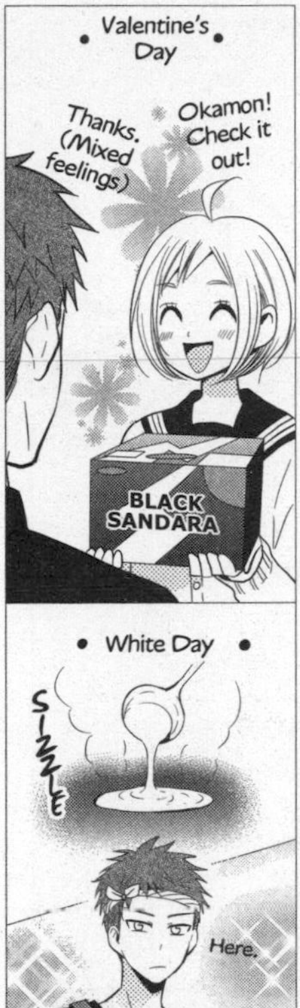
• Valentine's Day •
Okamon! Check it out!
Thanks. (Mixed feelings)
BLACK SANDARA
• White Day •
SIZZLE
Here.
STEAM
STEAM
CREPE ♥
My childhood friend is unreal...!!
Okamonnn...!

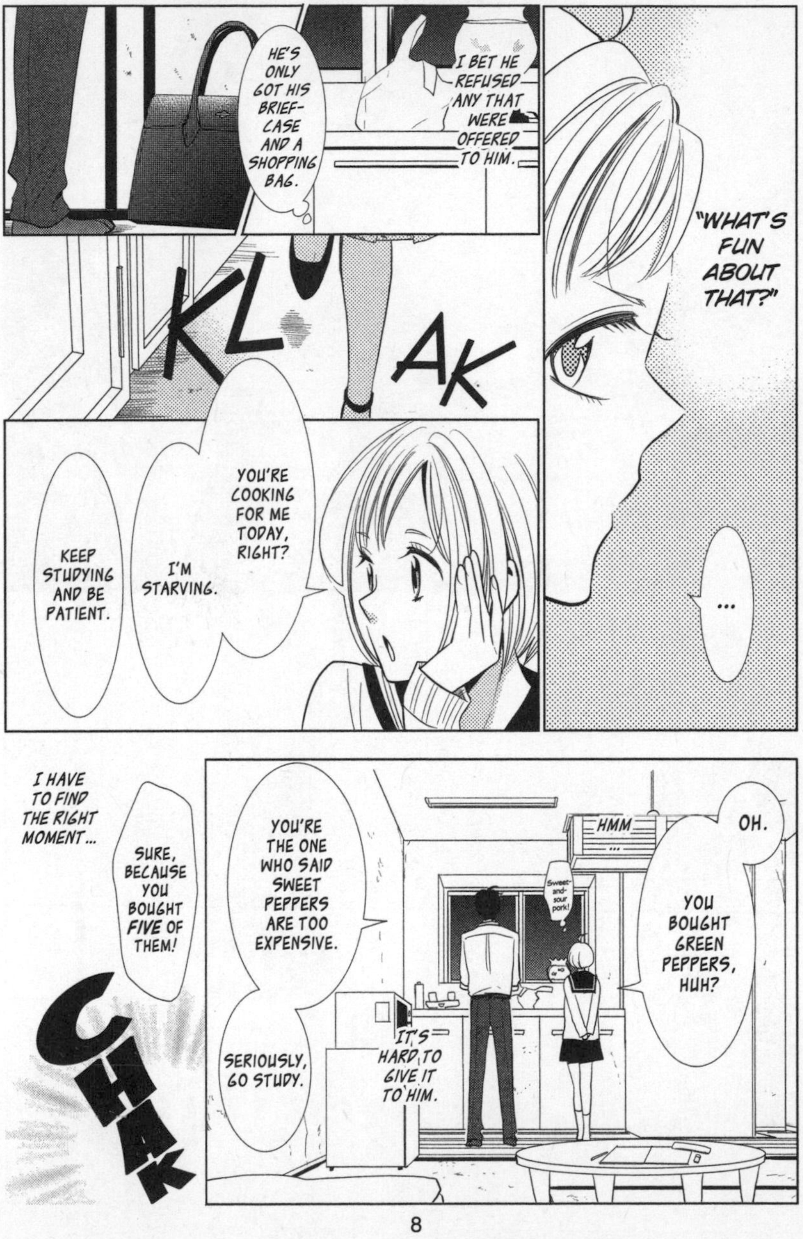
"WHAT'S FUN ABOUT THAT?"
...
HE'S ONLY GOT HIS BRIEF-CASE AND A SHOPPING BAG.
I BET HE REFUSED ANY THAT WERE OFFERED TO HIM.
KLAK
YOU'RE COOKING FOR ME TODAY, RIGHT?
I'M STARVING.
KEEP STUDYING AND BE PATIENT.
OH.
YOU BOUGHT GREEN PEPPERS, HUH?
HMM...
Sweet-and-sour pork!
YOU'RE THE ONE WHO SAID SWEET PEPPERS ARE TOO EXPENSIVE.
SURE, BECAUSE YOU BOUGHT *FIVE* OF THEM!
IT'S HARD TO GIVE IT TO HIM.
SERIOUSLY, GO STUDY.
I HAVE TO FIND THE RIGHT MOMENT...
CHAK

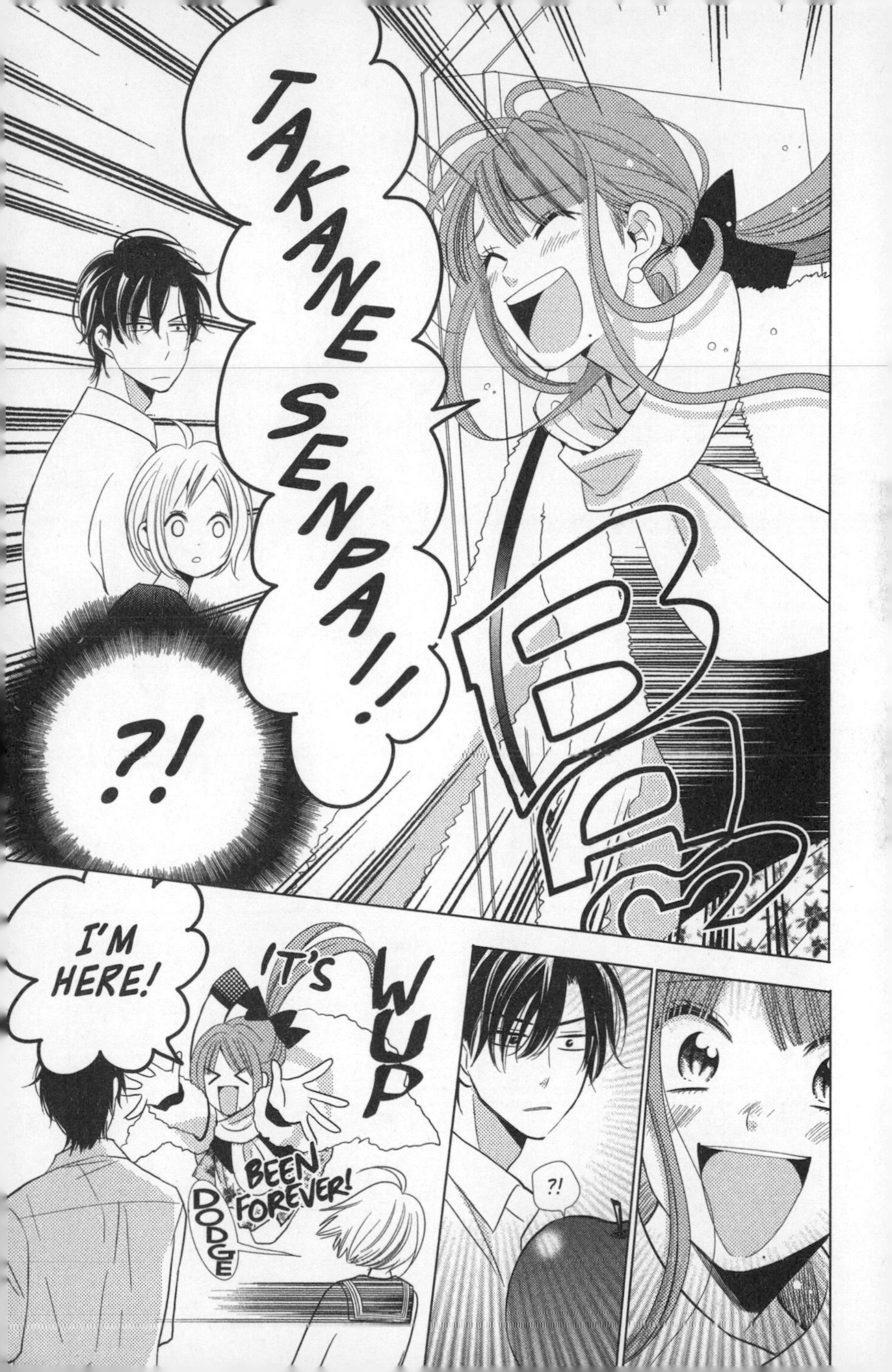
TAKANE SENPAI!!
?!
?!
WUP
IT'S BEEN FOREVER!
I'M HERE!
DODGE

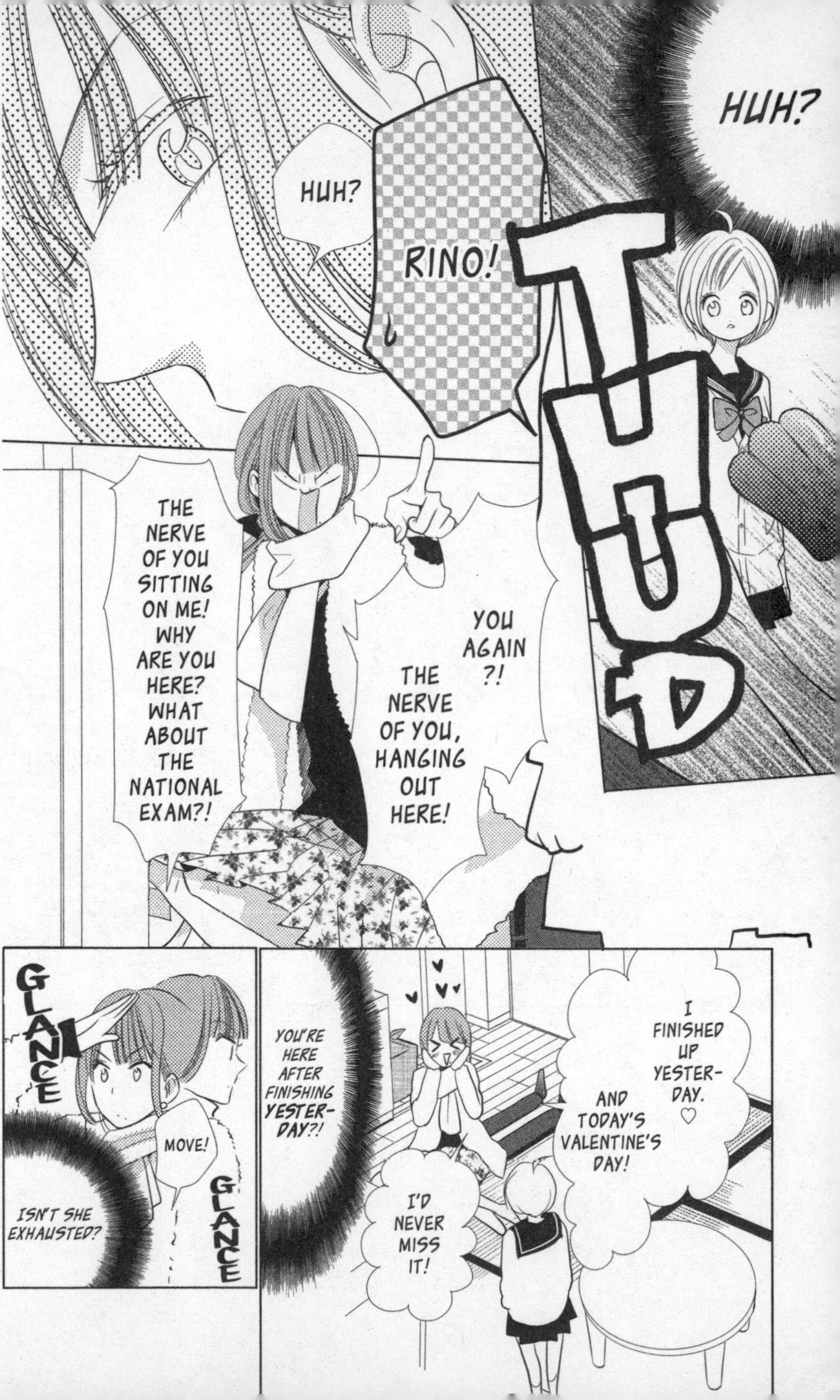
HUH?
THUD
HUH?
RINO!
YOU AGAIN?!
THE NERVE OF YOU, HANGING OUT HERE!
THE NERVE OF YOU SITTING ON ME! WHY ARE YOU HERE? WHAT ABOUT THE NATIONAL EXAM?!
I FINISHED UP YESTER-DAY. ♡
AND TODAY'S VALENTINE'S DAY!
I'D NEVER MISS IT!
YOU'RE HERE AFTER FINISHING YESTER-DAY?!
GLANCE
GLANCE
MOVE!
ISN'T SHE EXHAUSTED?

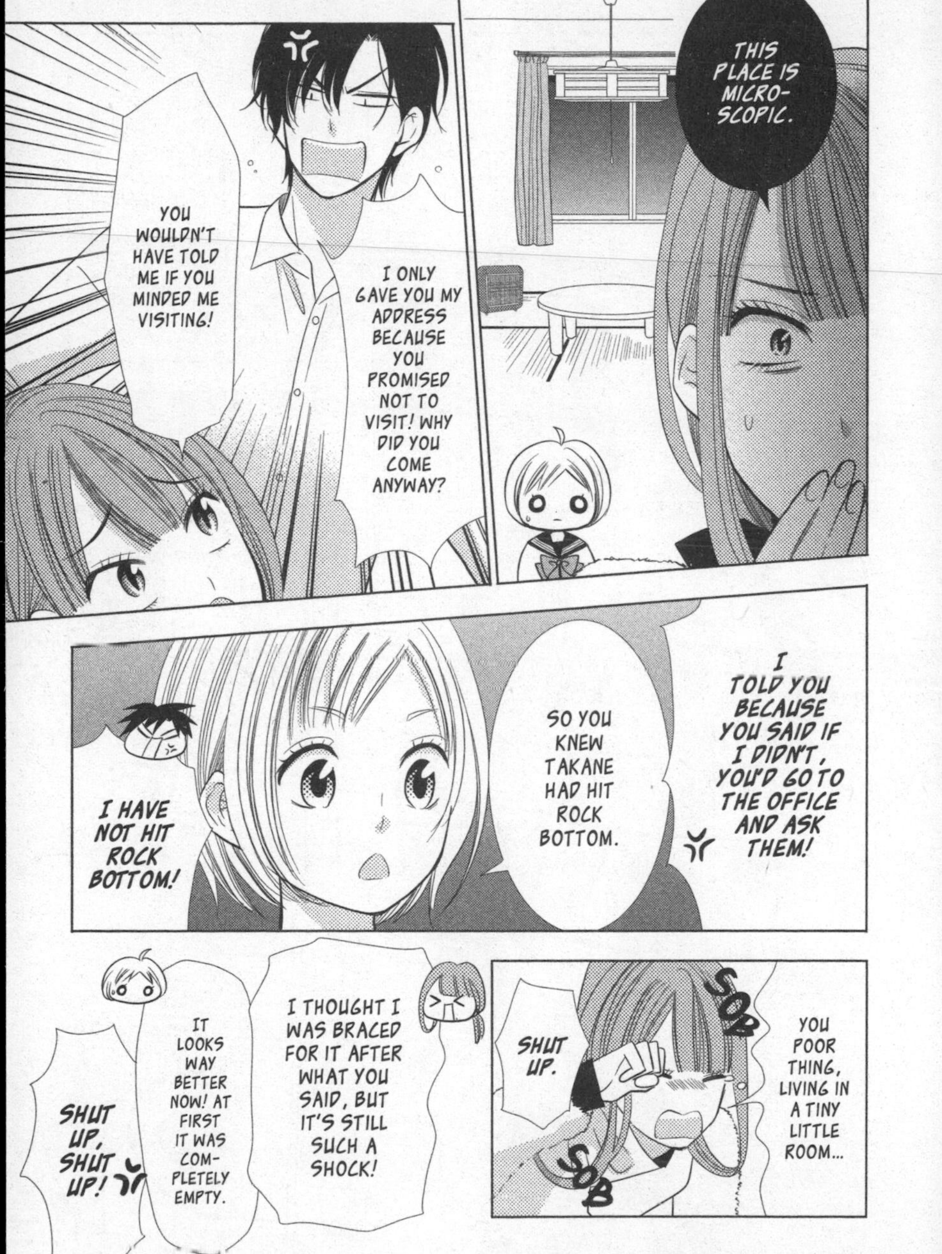
THIS PLACE IS MICRO-SCOPIC.
I ONLY GAVE YOU MY ADDRESS BECAUSE YOU PROMISED NOT TO VISIT! WHY DID YOU COME ANYWAY?
YOU WOULDN'T HAVE TOLD ME IF YOU MINDED ME VISITING!
I TOLD YOU BECAUSE YOU SAID IF I DIDN'T, YOU'D GO TO THE OFFICE AND ASK THEM!
SO YOU KNEW TAKANE HAD HIT ROCK BOTTOM.
I HAVE NOT HIT ROCK BOTTOM!
YOU POOR THING, LIVING IN A TINY LITTLE ROOM...
SOB
SHUT UP.
SOB
I THOUGHT I WAS BRACED FOR IT AFTER WHAT YOU SAID, BUT IT'S STILL SUCH A SHOCK!
IT LOOKS WAY BETTER NOW! AT FIRST IT WAS COM-PLETELY EMPTY.
SHUT UP, SHUT UP!

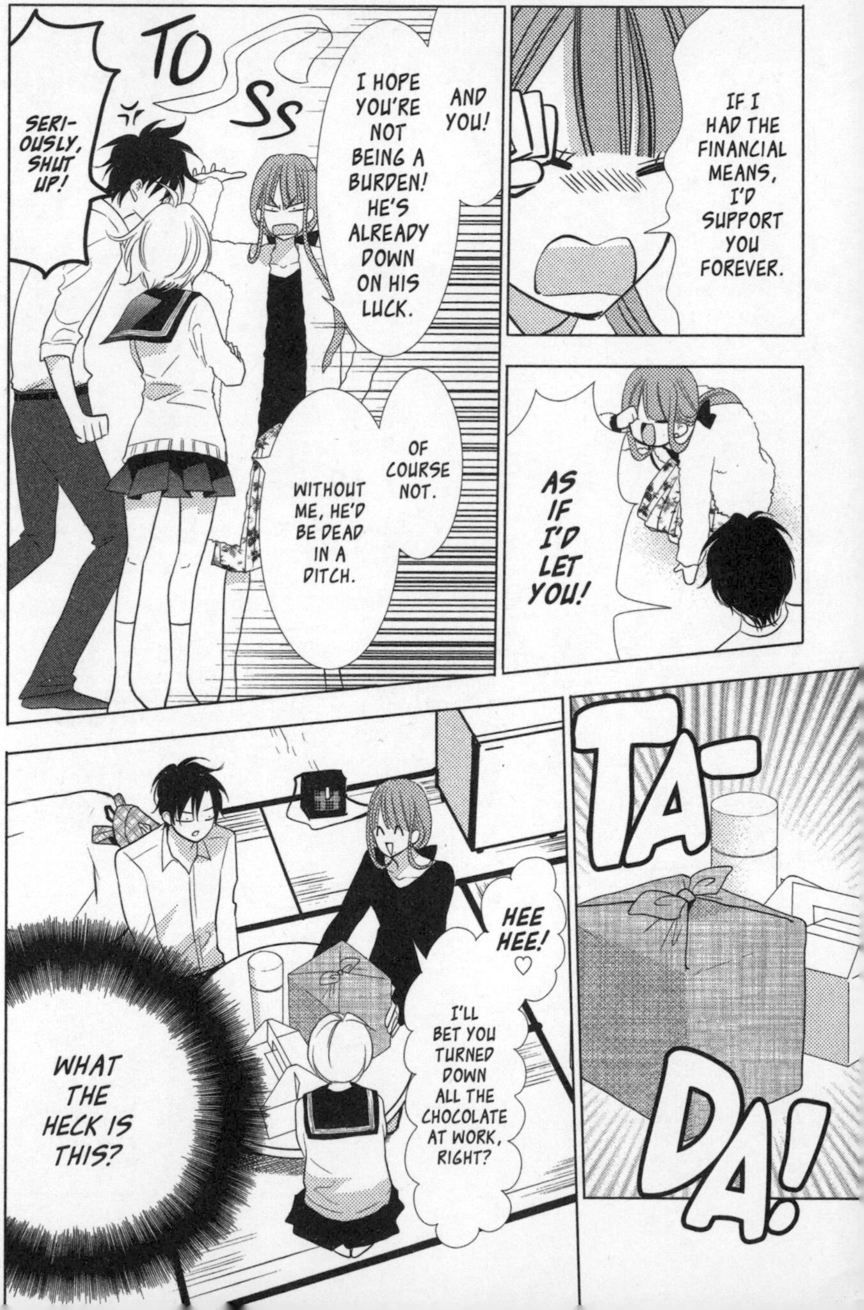
IF I HAD THE FINANCIAL MEANS, I'D SUPPORT YOU FOREVER.
AS IF I'D LET YOU!
AND YOU!
I HOPE YOU'RE NOT BEING A BURDEN! HE'S ALREADY DOWN ON HIS LUCK.
TOSS
SERI-OUSLY, SHUT UP!
OF COURSE NOT.
WITHOUT ME, HE'D BE DEAD IN A DITCH.
TA-DA!
HEE HEE! ♡
I'LL BET YOU TURNED DOWN ALL THE CHOCOLATE AT WORK, RIGHT?
WHAT THE HECK IS THIS?

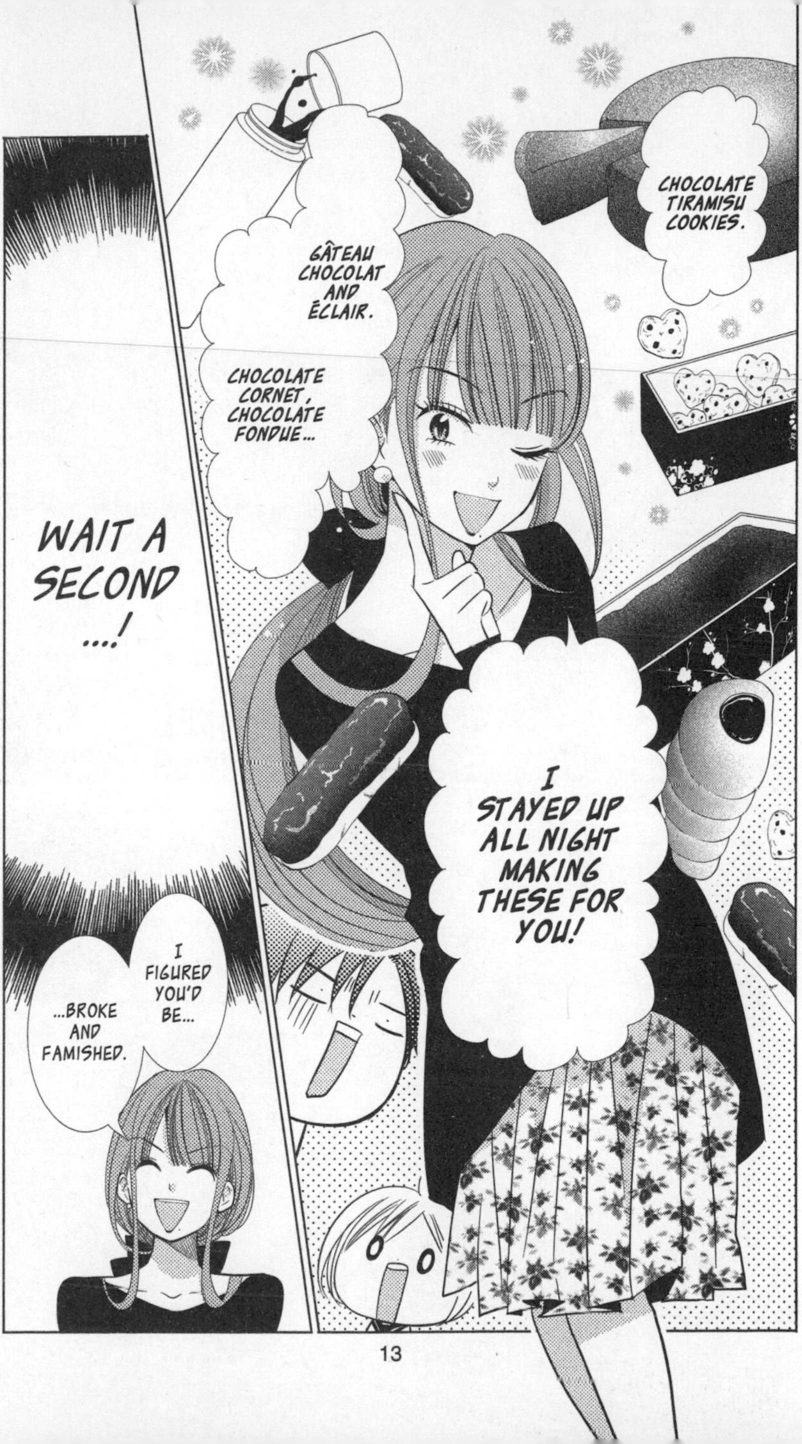
CHOCOLATE TIRAMISU COOKIES.
GÂTEAU CHOCOLAT AND ÉCLAIR.
CHOCOLATE CORNET, CHOCOLATE FONDUE...
I STAYED UP ALL NIGHT MAKING THESE FOR YOU!
WAIT A SECOND ...!
I FIGURED YOU'D BE...
...BROKE AND FAMISHED.

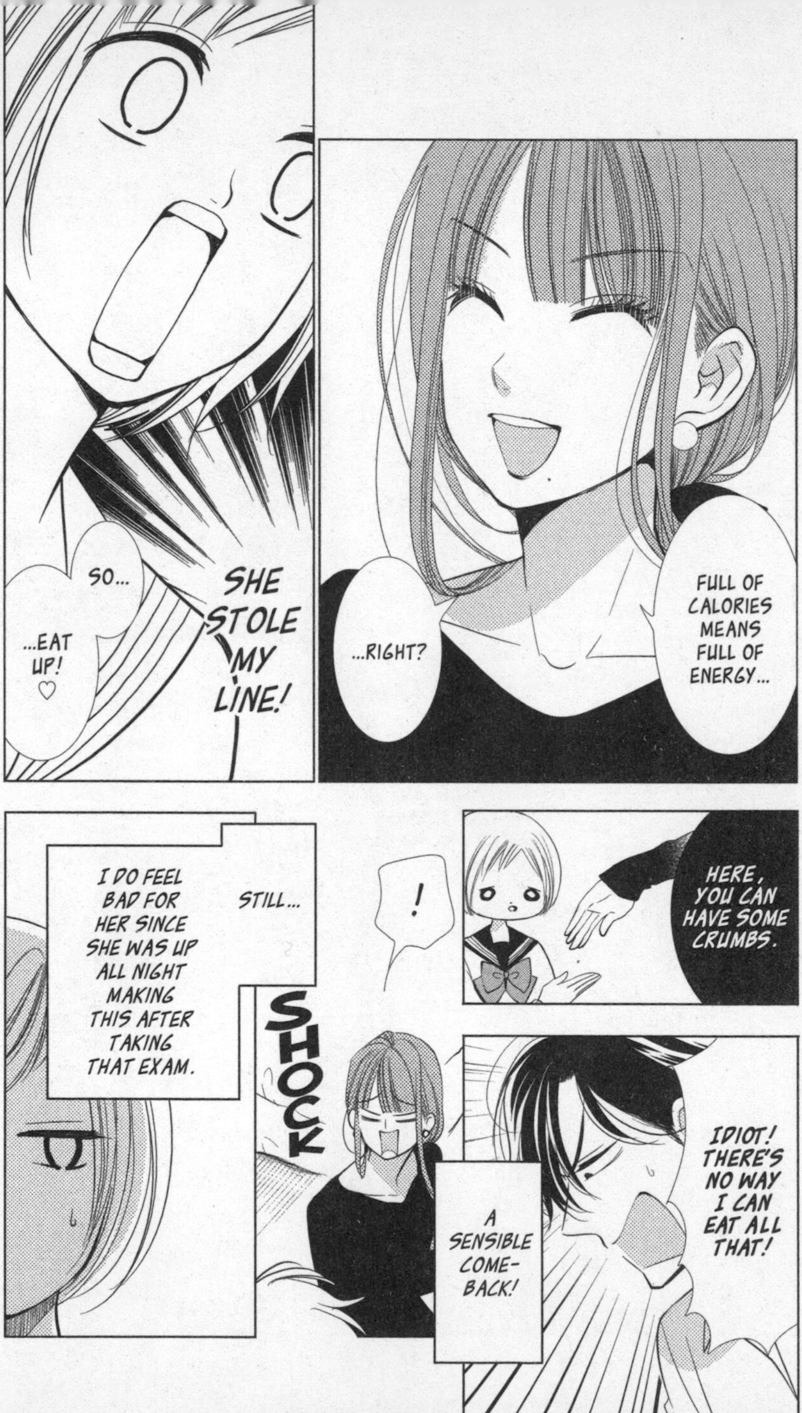
FULL OF CALORIES MEANS FULL OF ENERGY...
...RIGHT?
SHE STOLE MY LINE!
SO...
...EAT UP! ♡
HERE, YOU CAN HAVE SOME CRUMBS.
!
IDIOT! THERE'S NO WAY I CAN EAT ALL THAT!
A SENSIBLE COME-BACK!
SHOCK
STILL...
I DO FEEL BAD FOR HER SINCE SHE WAS UP ALL NIGHT MAKING THIS AFTER TAKING THAT EXAM.

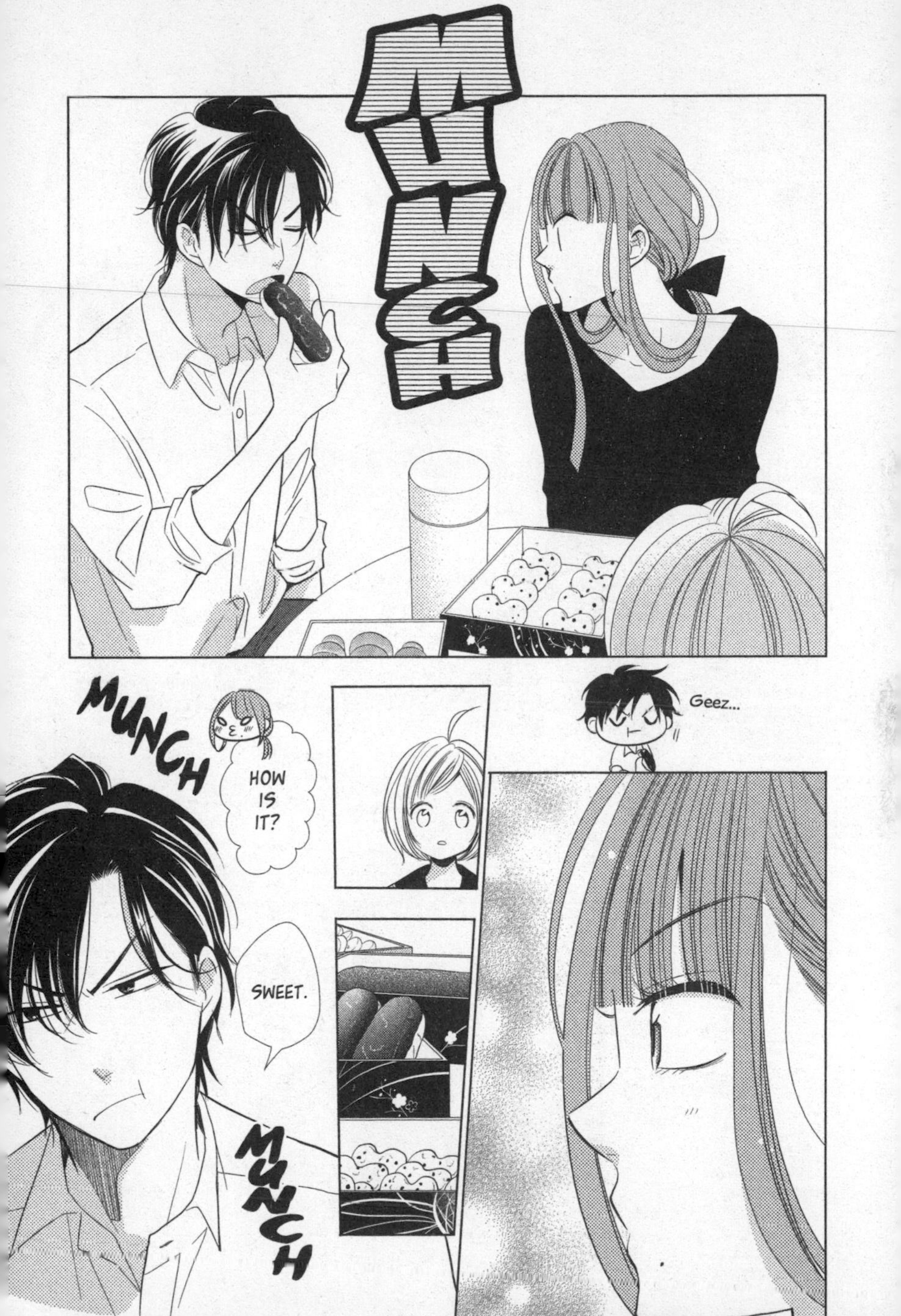
MUNCH
Geez...
MUNCH
HOW IS IT?
SWEET.
MUNCH

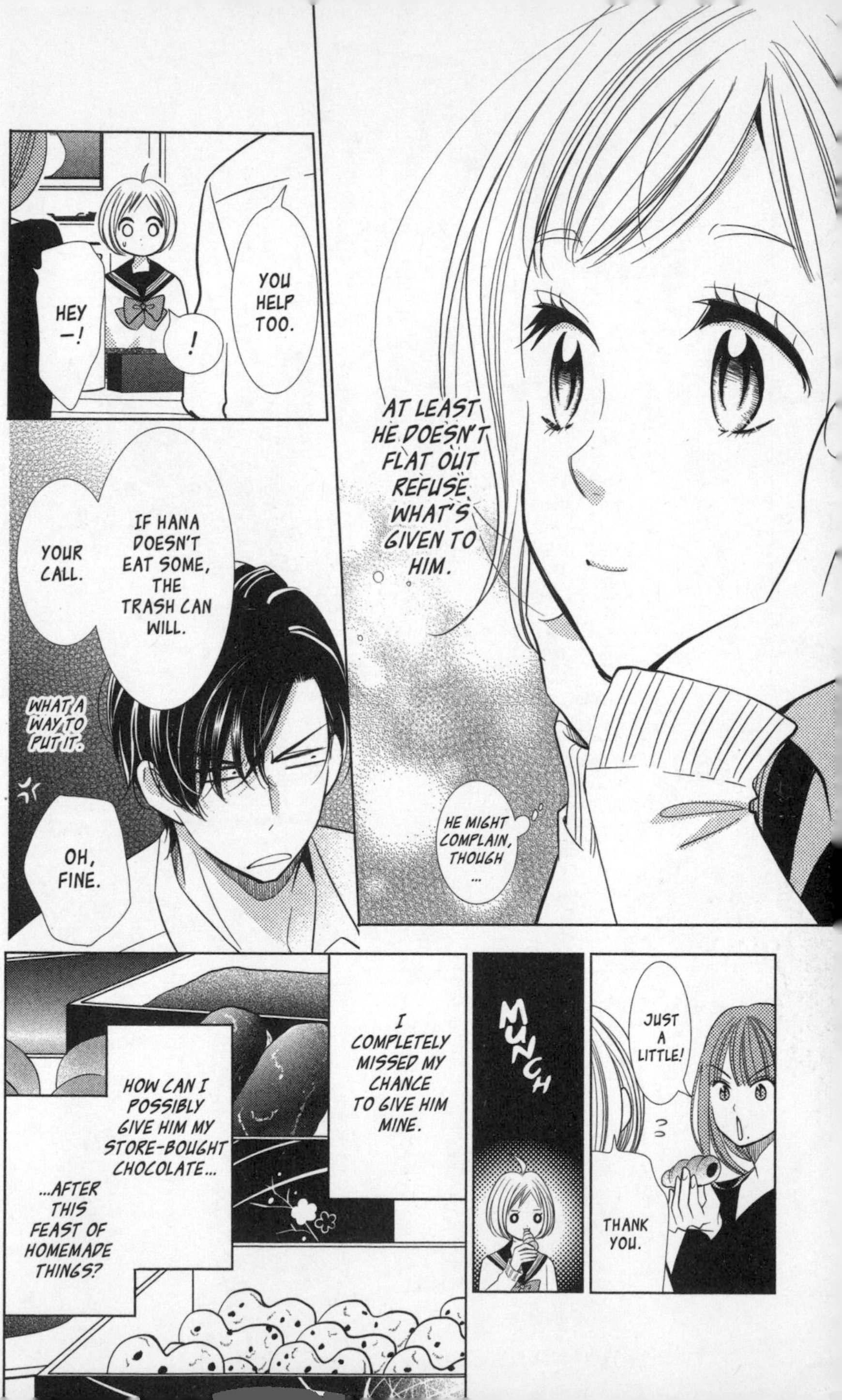
AT LEAST HE DOESN'T FLAT OUT REFUSE WHAT'S GIVEN TO HIM.
HE MIGHT COMPLAIN, THOUGH ...
YOU HELP TOO.
!
HEY —!
IF HANA DOESN'T EAT SOME, THE TRASH CAN WILL.
YOUR CALL.
WHAT A WAY TO PUT IT.
OH, FINE.
JUST A LITTLE!
THANK YOU.
MUNCH
I COMPLETELY MISSED MY CHANCE TO GIVE HIM MINE.
HOW CAN I POSSIBLY GIVE HIM MY STORE-BOUGHT CHOCOLATE...
...AFTER THIS FEAST OF HOMEMADE THINGS?

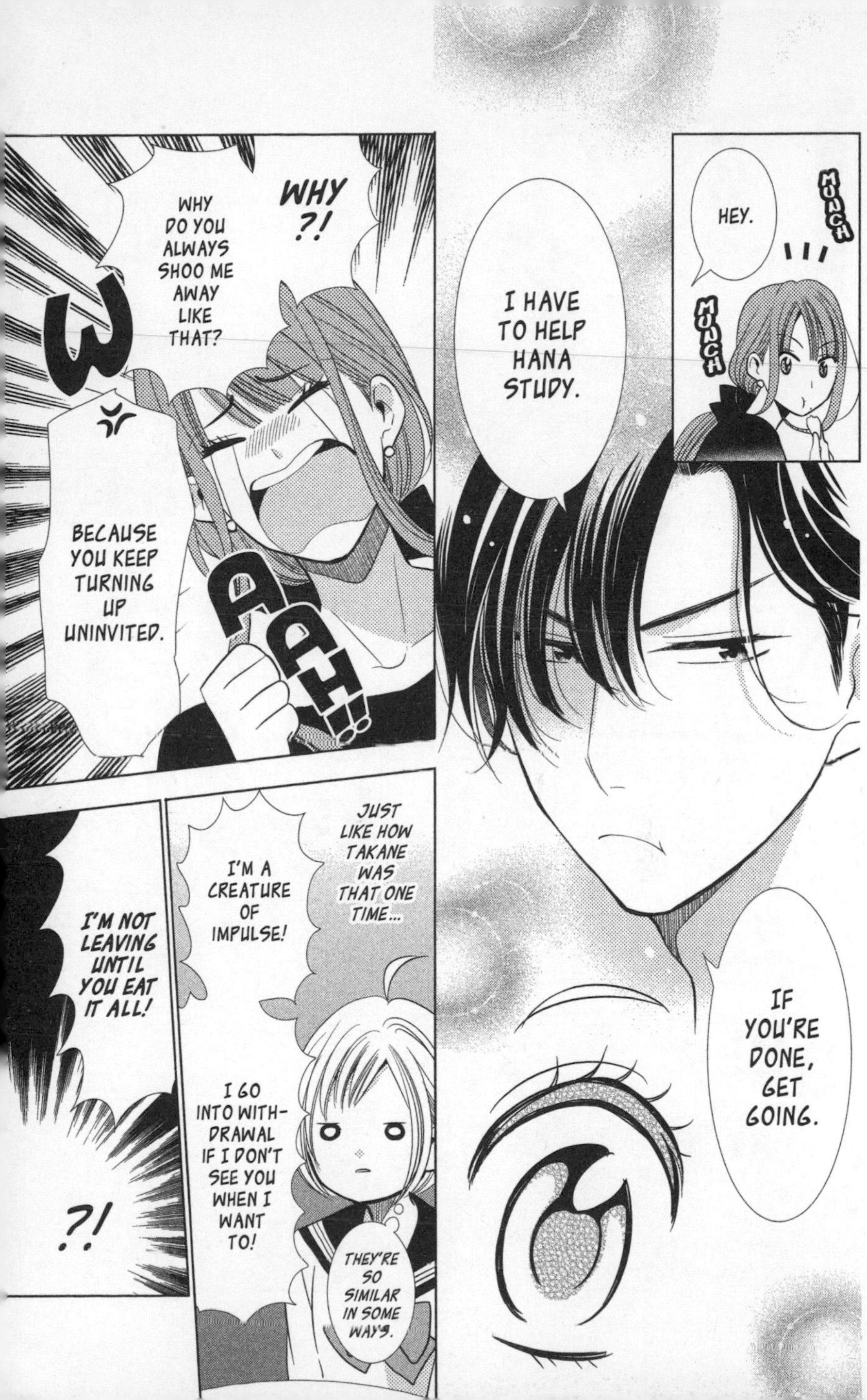
MUNCH
MUNCH
HEY.
I HAVE TO HELP HANA STUDY.
IF YOU'RE DONE, GET GOING.
WHY ?!
WHY DO YOU ALWAYS SHOO ME AWAY LIKE THAT?
AAH!!
BECAUSE YOU KEEP TURNING UP UNINVITED.
JUST LIKE HOW TAKANE WAS THAT ONE TIME...
I'M A CREATURE OF IMPULSE!
I GO INTO WITH-DRAWAL IF I DON'T SEE YOU WHEN I WANT TO!
THEY'RE SO SIMILAR IN SOME WAYS.
I'M NOT LEAVING UNTIL YOU EAT IT ALL!
?!

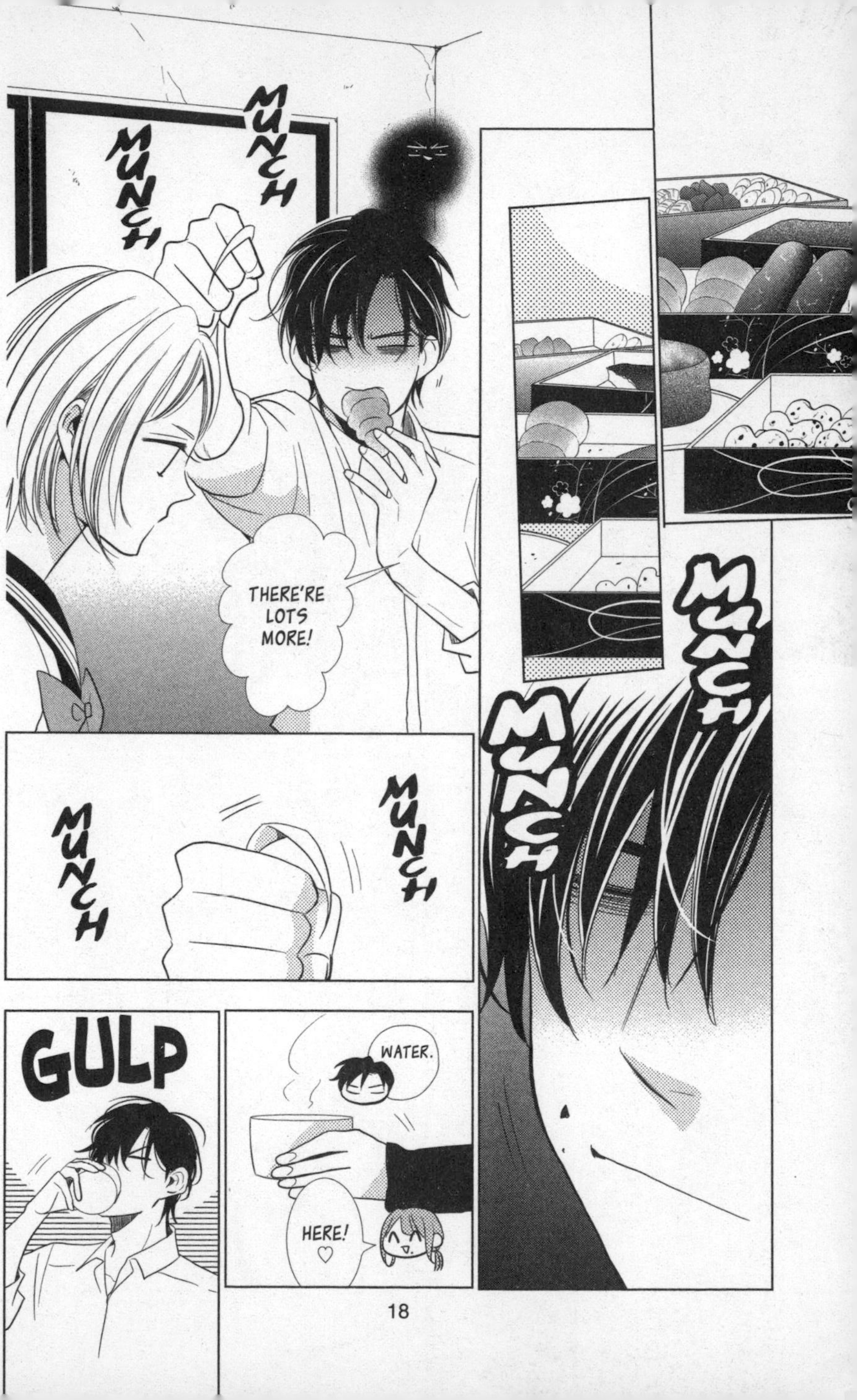
MUNCH
MUNCH
MUNCH
MUNCH
THERE'RE LOTS MORE!
MUNCH
MUNCH
WATER.
HERE! ♡
GULP

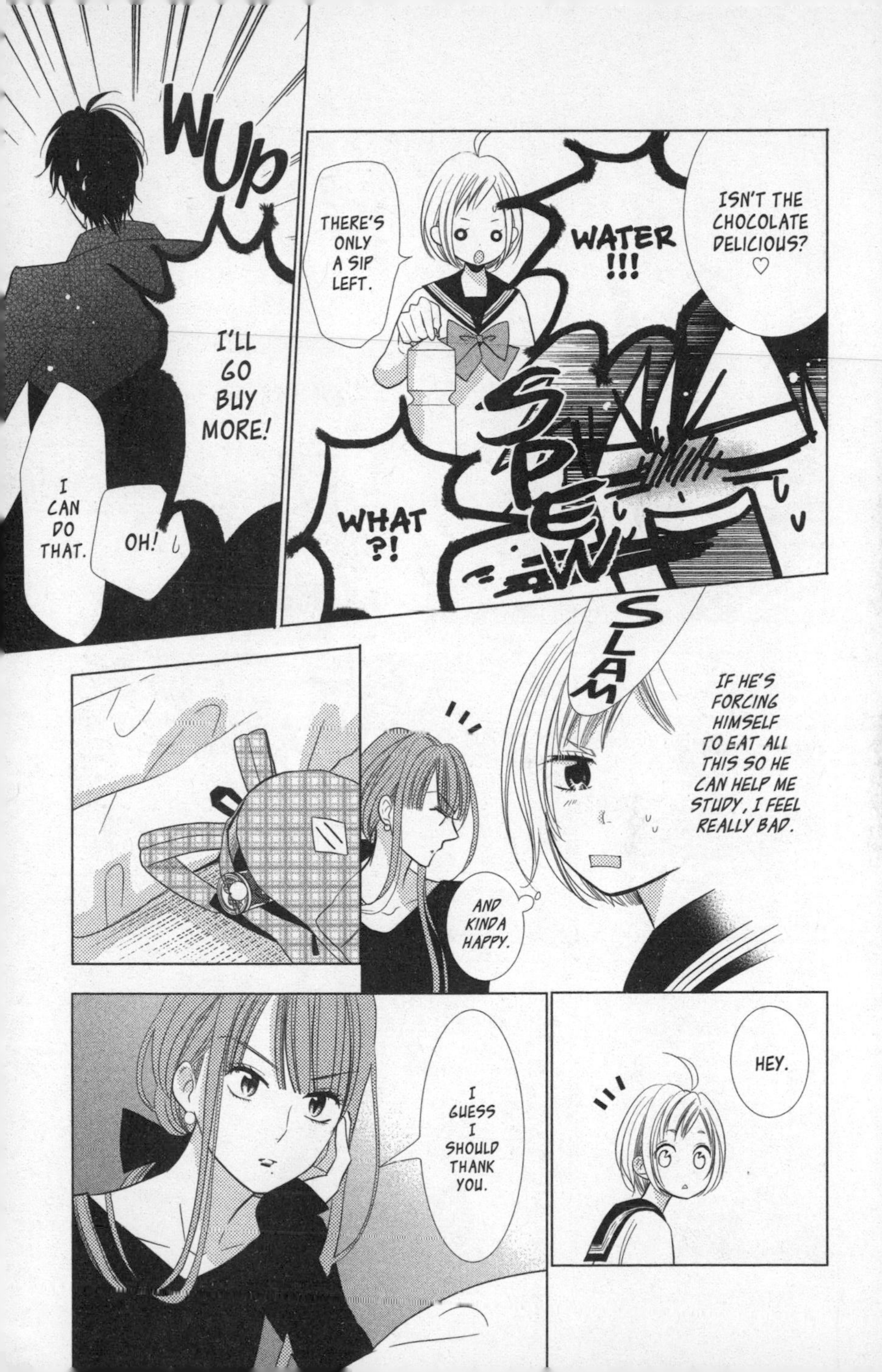
ISN'T THE CHOCOLATE DELICIOUS? ♡
WATER!!!
THERE'S ONLY A SIP LEFT.
SPEW
WHAT?!
WUP
I'LL GO BUY MORE!
OH!
I CAN DO THAT.
SLAM
IF HE'S FORCING HIMSELF TO EAT ALL THIS SO HE CAN HELP ME STUDY, I FEEL REALLY BAD.
AND KINDA HAPPY.
HEY.
I GUESS I SHOULD THANK YOU.

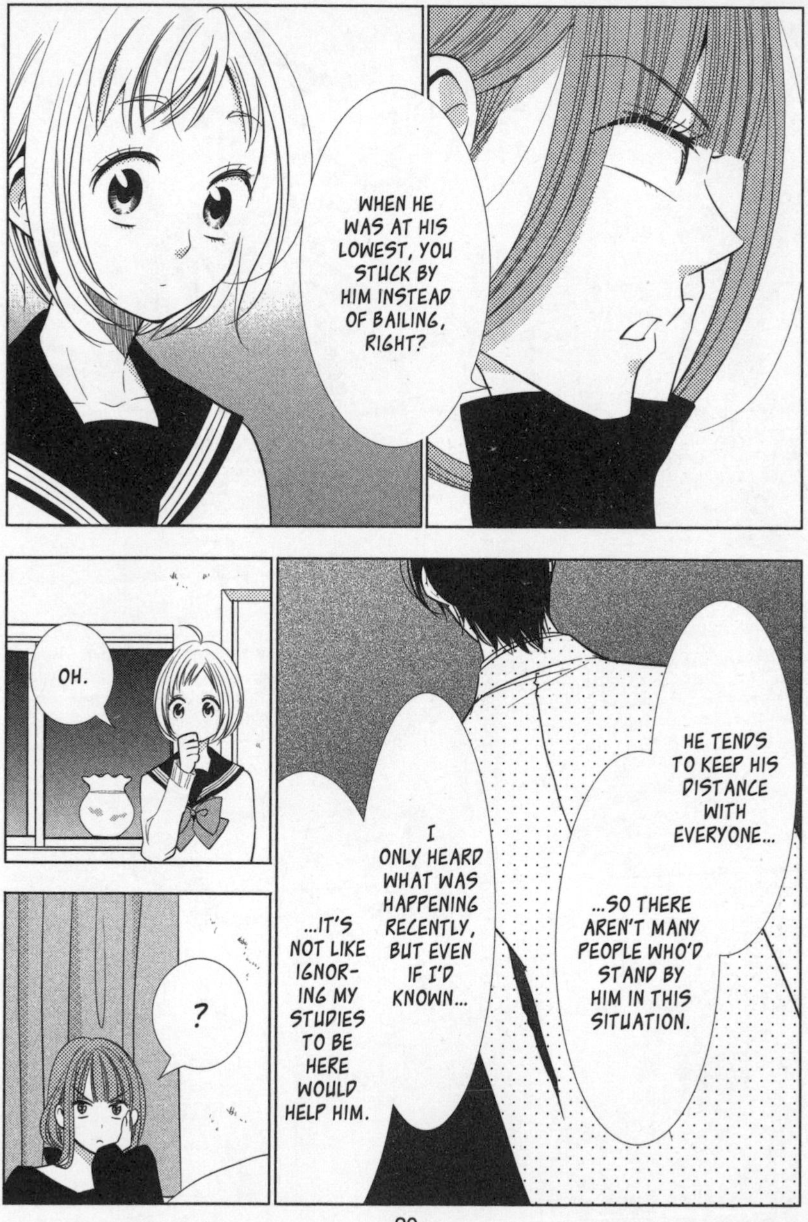
WHEN HE WAS AT HIS LOWEST, YOU STUCK BY HIM INSTEAD OF BAILING, RIGHT?
HE TENDS TO KEEP HIS DISTANCE WITH EVERYONE...
...SO THERE AREN'T MANY PEOPLE WHO'D STAND BY HIM IN THIS SITUATION.
I ONLY HEARD WHAT WAS HAPPENING RECENTLY, BUT EVEN IF I'D KNOWN...
...IT'S NOT LIKE IGNOR-ING MY STUDIES TO BE HERE WOULD HELP HIM.
OH.
?

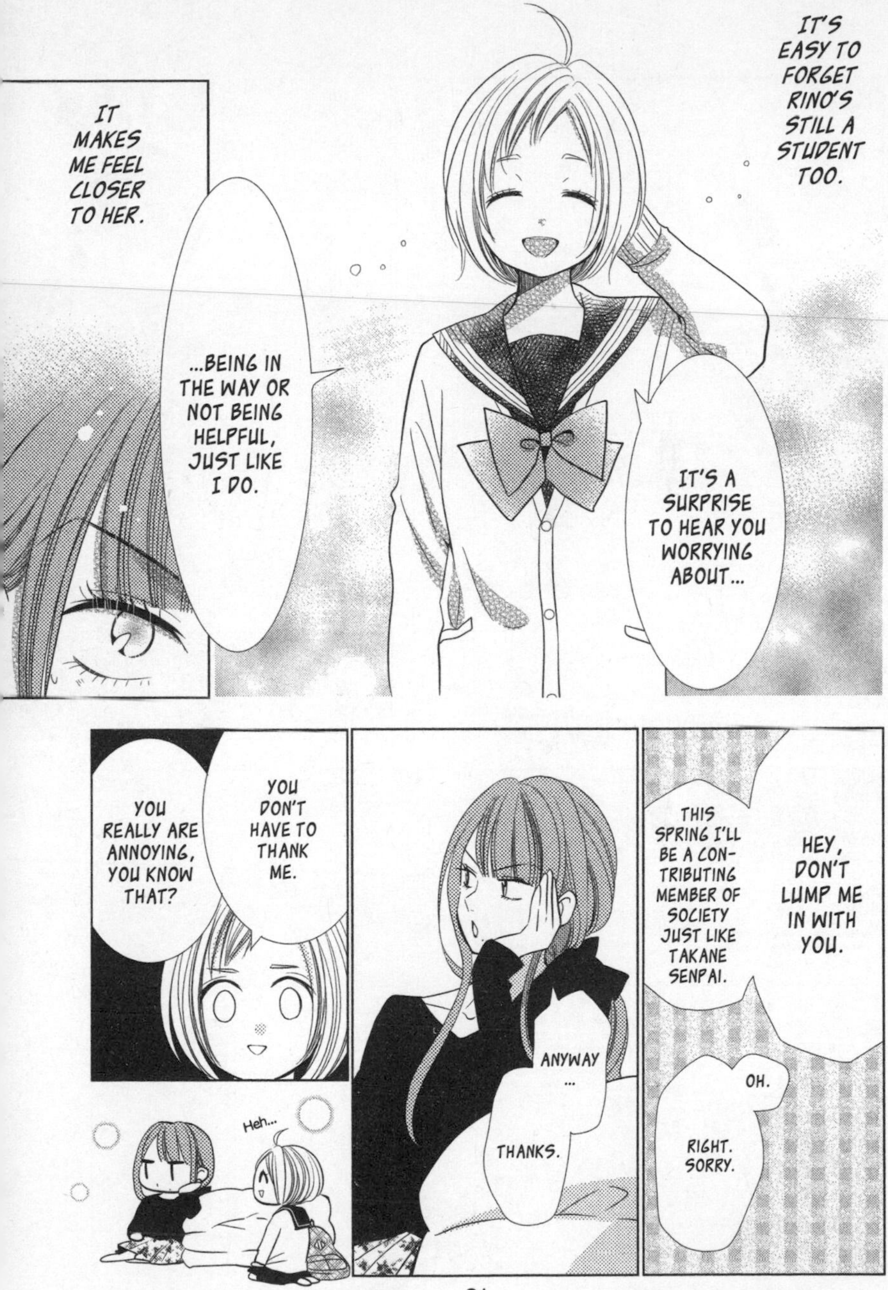
IT'S EASY TO FORGET RINO'S STILL A STUDENT TOO.
IT'S A SURPRISE TO HEAR YOU WORRYING ABOUT...
...BEING IN THE WAY OR NOT BEING HELPFUL, JUST LIKE I DO.
IT MAKES ME FEEL CLOSER TO HER.
HEY, DON'T LUMP ME IN WITH YOU.
THIS SPRING I'LL BE A CON-TRIBUTING MEMBER OF SOCIETY JUST LIKE TAKANE SENPAI.
OH.
RIGHT. SORRY.
ANYWAY...
THANKS.
YOU DON'T HAVE TO THANK ME.
YOU REALLY ARE ANNOYING, YOU KNOW THAT?
Heh...

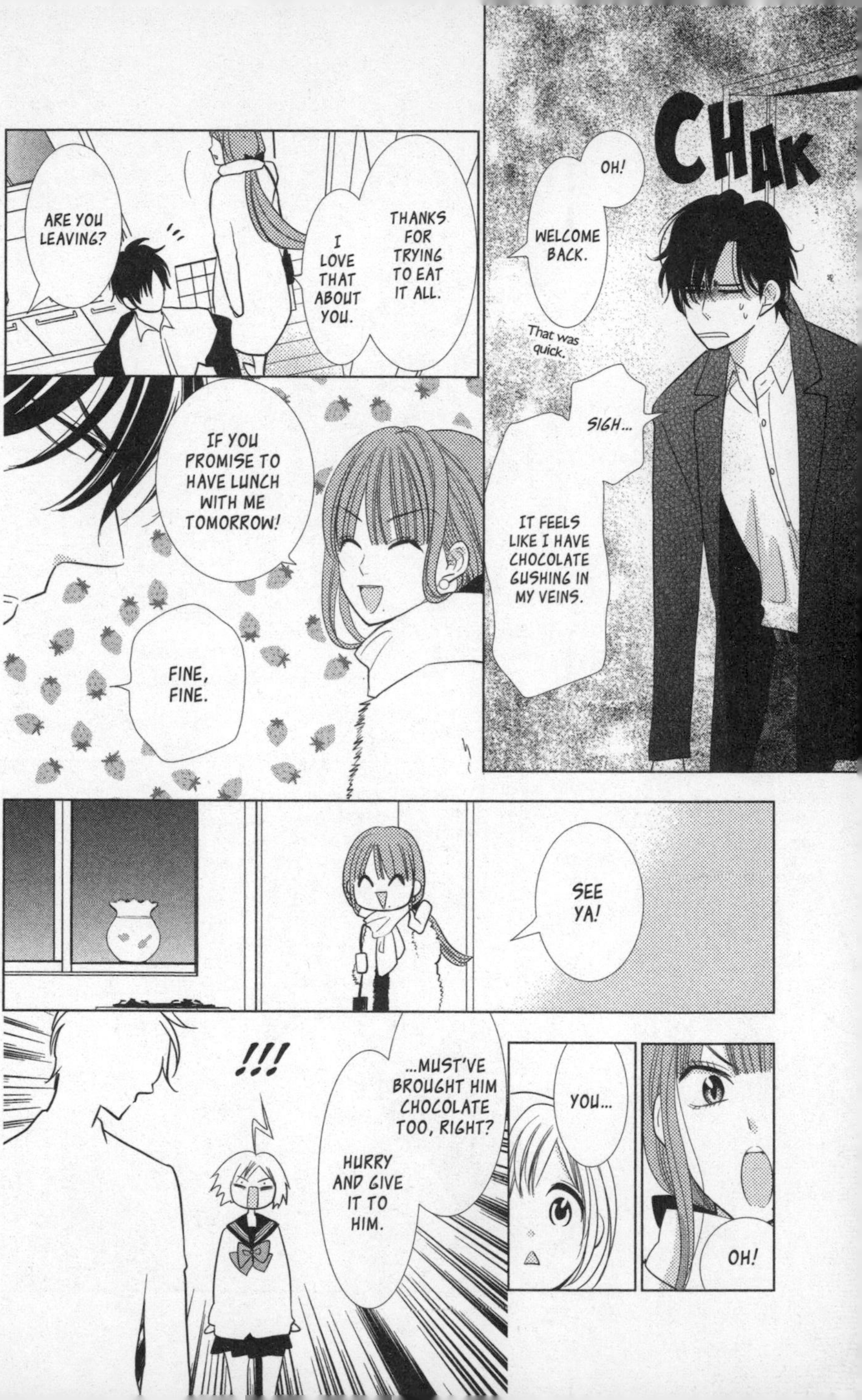
CHAK
OH!
WELCOME BACK.
That was quick.
SIGH...
IT FEELS LIKE I HAVE CHOCOLATE GUSHING IN MY VEINS.
THANKS FOR TRYING TO EAT IT ALL.
I LOVE THAT ABOUT YOU.
ARE YOU LEAVING?
IF YOU PROMISE TO HAVE LUNCH WITH ME TOMORROW!
FINE, FINE.
SEE YA!
OH!
YOU...
...MUST'VE BROUGHT HIM CHOCOLATE TOO, RIGHT?
HURRY AND GIVE IT TO HIM.
!!!

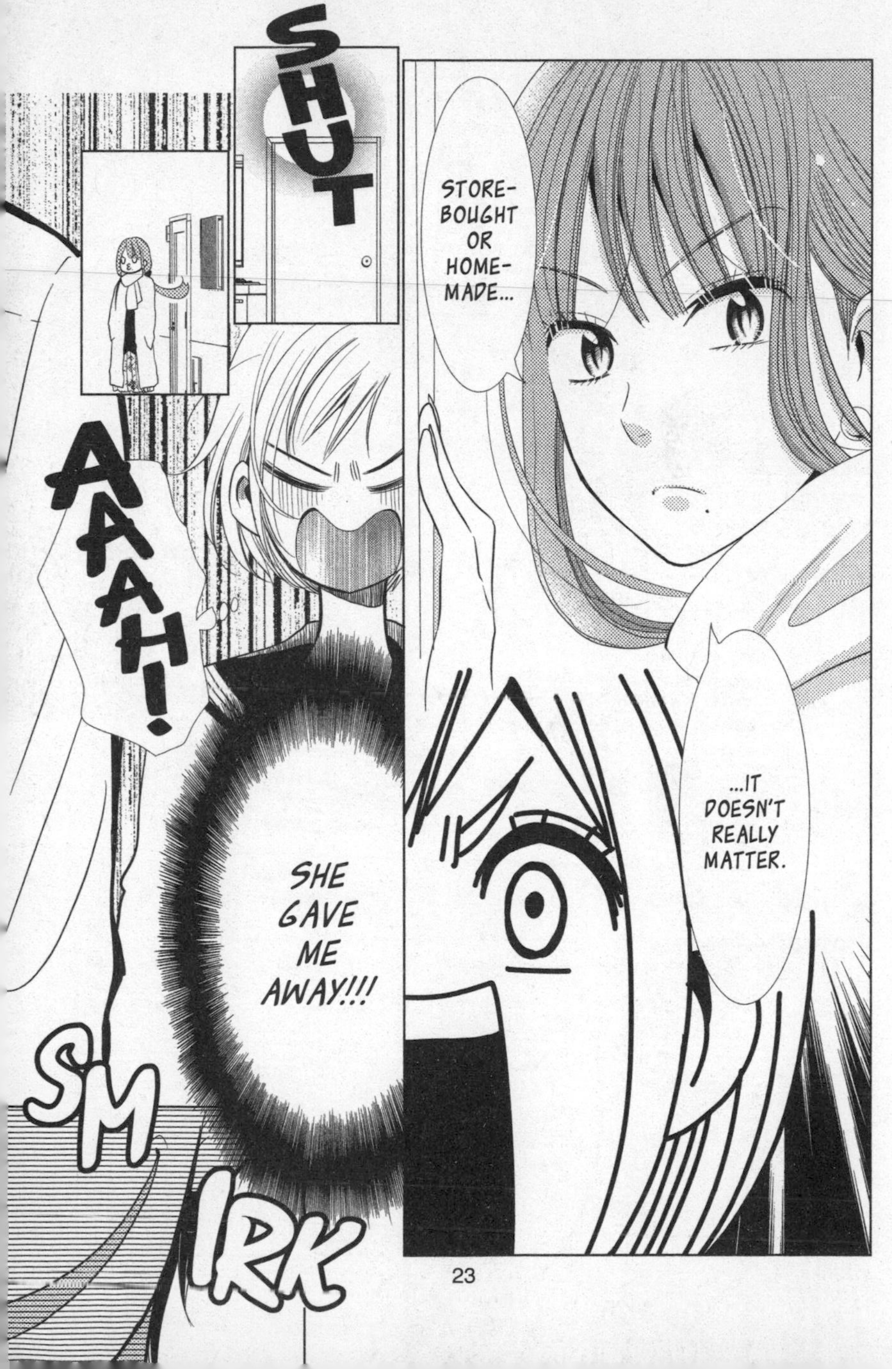
STORE-BOUGHT OR HOME-MADE...
...IT DOESN'T REALLY MATTER.
SHUT
AAAAH!
SHE GAVE ME AWAY!!!
SMIRK

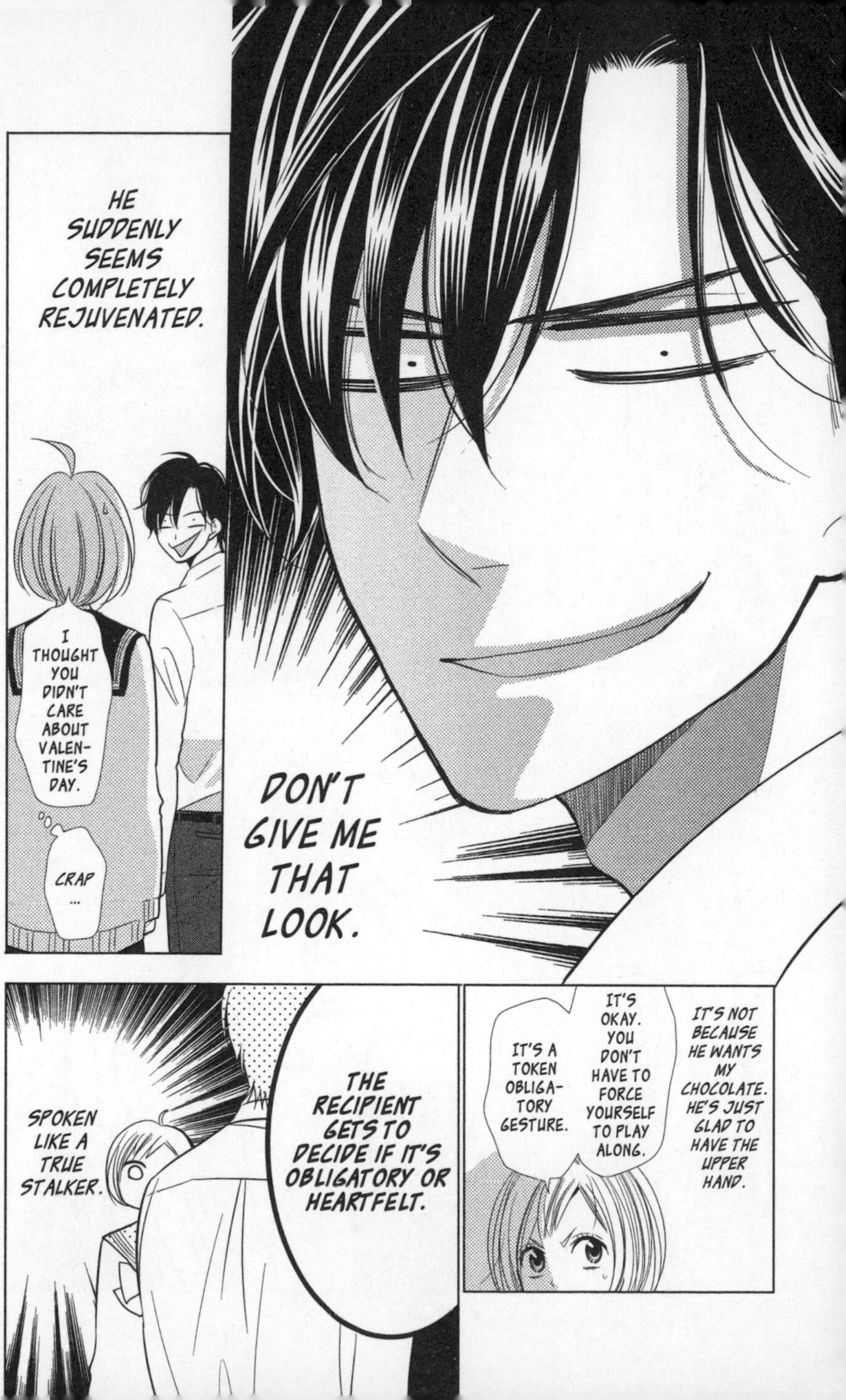
DON'T GIVE ME THAT LOOK.
HE SUDDENLY SEEMS COMPLETELY REJUVENATED.
I THOUGHT YOU DIDN'T CARE ABOUT VALEN-TINE'S DAY.
CRAP...
IT'S NOT BECAUSE HE WANTS MY CHOCOLATE. HE'S JUST GLAD TO HAVE THE UPPER HAND.
IT'S OKAY. YOU DON'T HAVE TO FORCE YOURSELF TO PLAY ALONG.
IT'S A TOKEN OBLIGA-TORY GESTURE.
THE RECIPIENT GETS TO DECIDE IF IT'S OBLIGATORY OR HEARTFELT.
SPOKEN LIKE A TRUE STALKER.

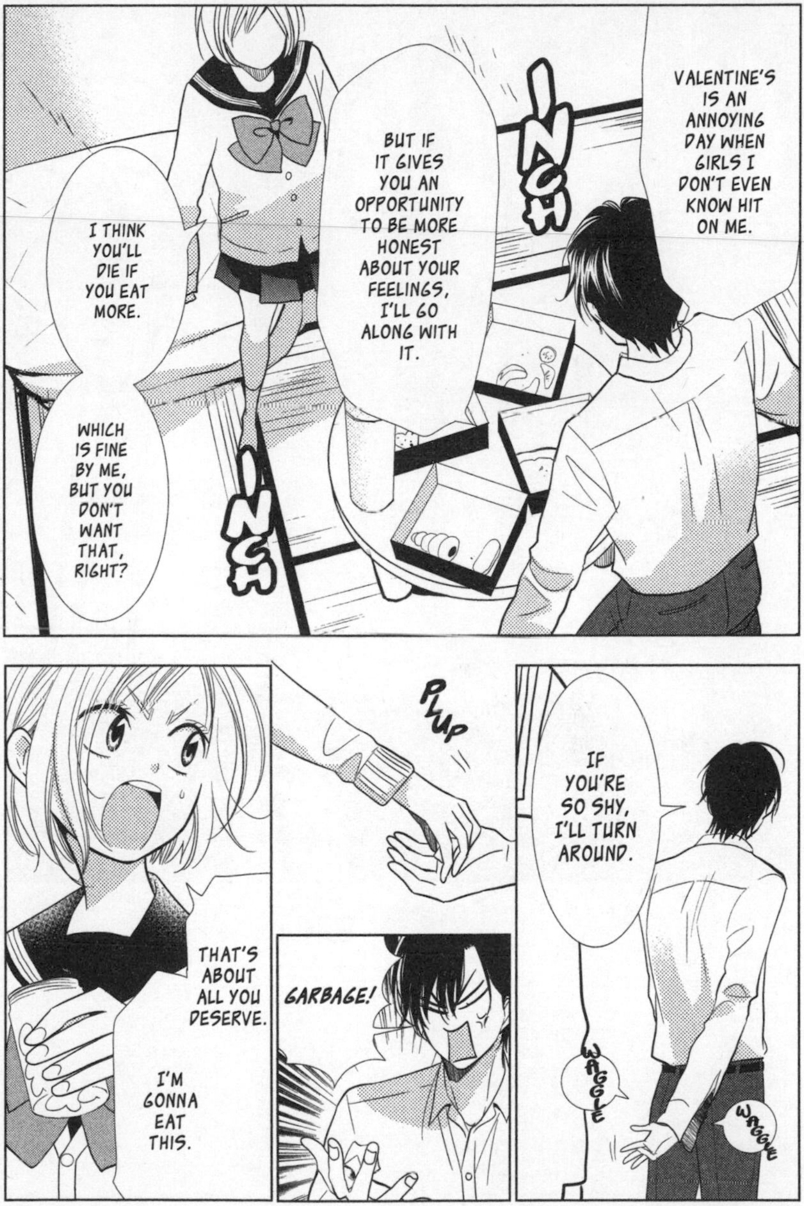
VALENTINE'S IS AN ANNOYING DAY WHEN GIRLS I DON'T EVEN KNOW HIT ON ME.
INCH
BUT IF IT GIVES YOU AN OPPORTUNITY TO BE MORE HONEST ABOUT YOUR FEELINGS, I'LL GO ALONG WITH IT.
I THINK YOU'LL DIE IF YOU EAT MORE.
WHICH IS FINE BY ME, BUT YOU DON'T WANT THAT, RIGHT?
INCH
IF YOU'RE SO SHY, I'LL TURN AROUND.
WAGGLE
WAGGLE
PLUP
GARBAGE!
THAT'S ABOUT ALL YOU DESERVE.
I'M GONNA EAT THIS.

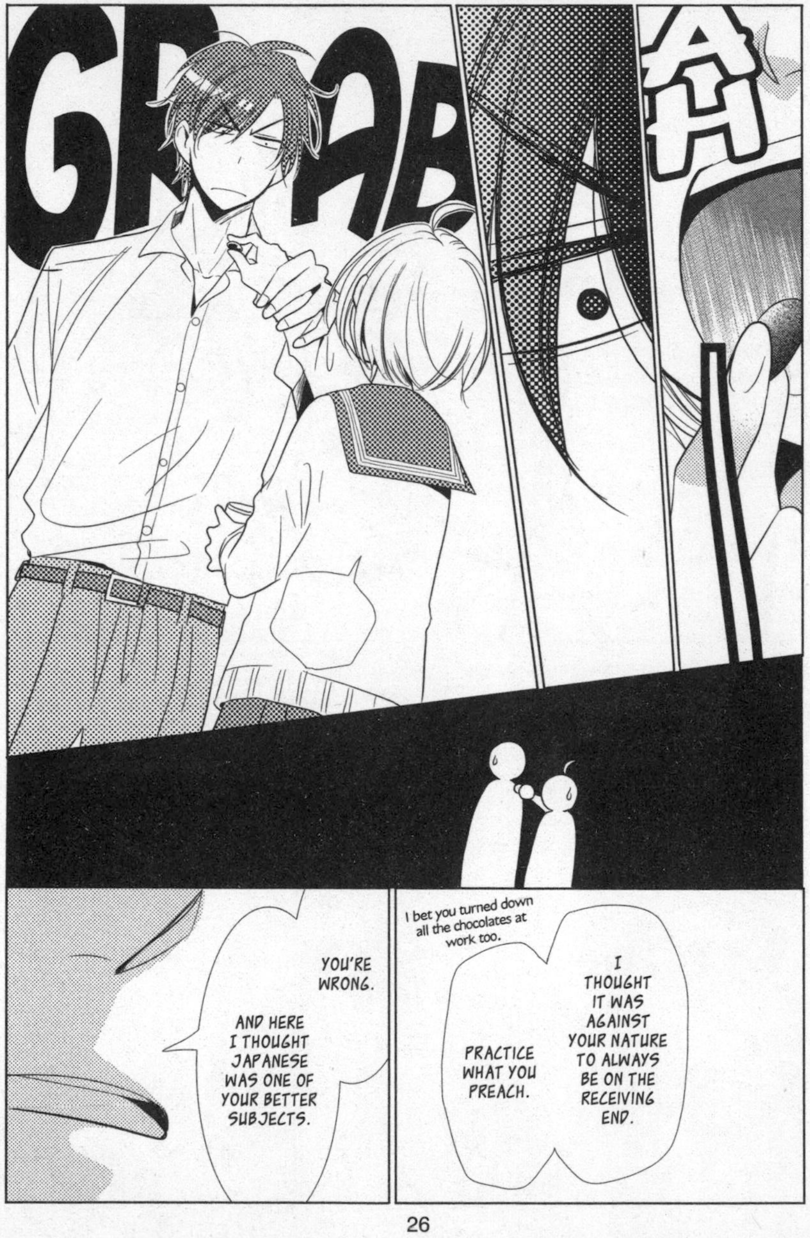
GRAB
I THOUGHT IT WAS AGAINST YOUR NATURE TO ALWAYS BE ON THE RECEIVING END.
PRACTICE WHAT YOU PREACH.
I bet you turned down all the chocolates at work too.
YOU'RE WRONG.
AND HERE I THOUGHT JAPANESE WAS ONE OF YOUR BETTER SUBJECTS.

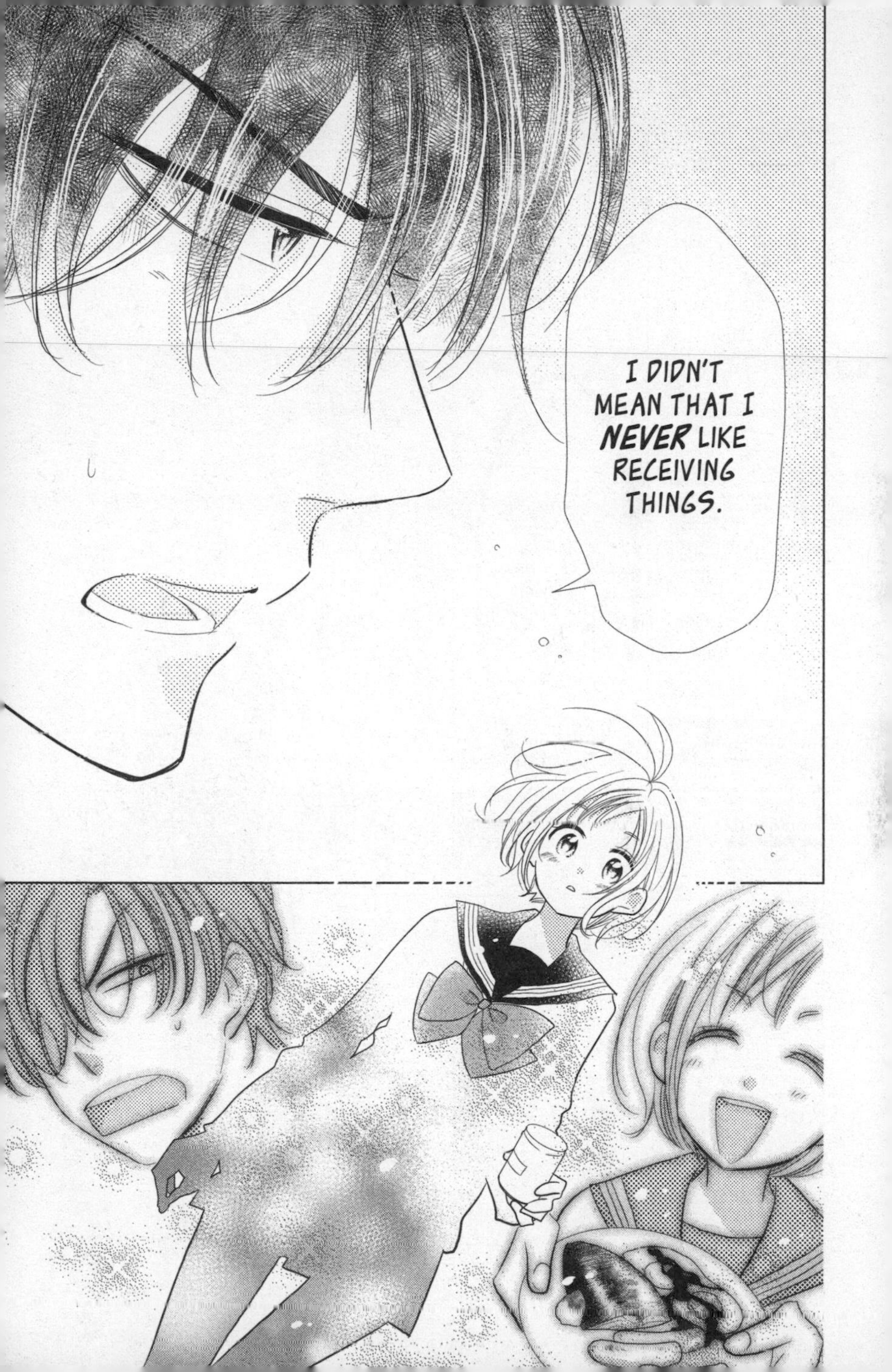
I DIDN'T MEAN THAT I NEVER LIKE RECEIVING THINGS.

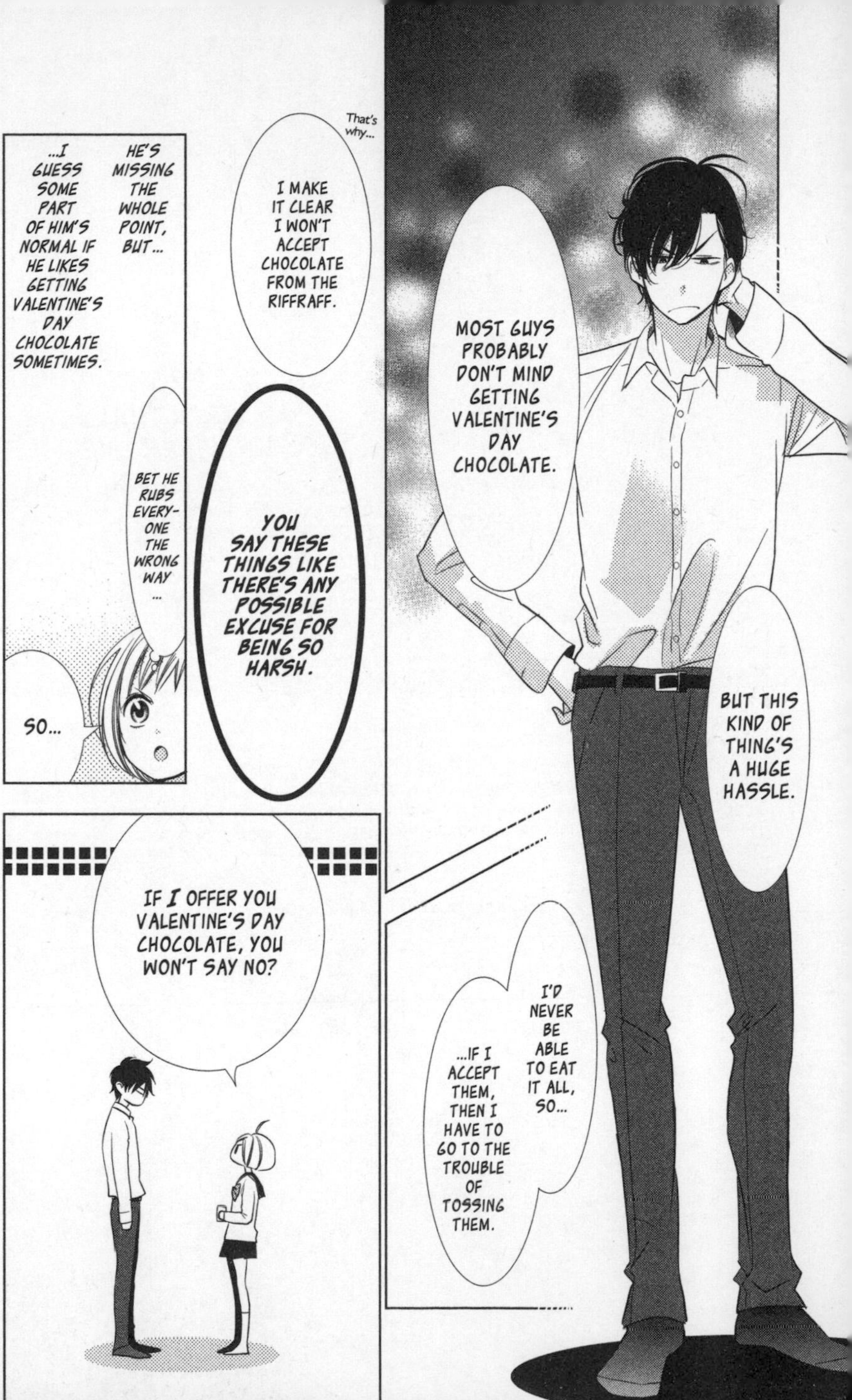
MOST GUYS PROBABLY DON'T MIND GETTING VALENTINE'S DAY CHOCOLATE.
BUT THIS KIND OF THING'S A HUGE HASSLE.
I'D NEVER BE ABLE TO EAT IT ALL, SO...
...IF I ACCEPT THEM, THEN I HAVE TO GO TO THE TROUBLE OF TOSSING THEM.
That's why...
I MAKE IT CLEAR I WON'T ACCEPT CHOCOLATE FROM THE RIFFRAFF.
YOU SAY THESE THINGS LIKE THERE'S ANY POSSIBLE EXCUSE FOR BEING SO HARSH.
HE'S MISSING THE WHOLE POINT, BUT...
...I GUESS SOME PART OF HIM'S NORMAL IF HE LIKES GETTING VALENTINE'S DAY CHOCOLATE SOMETIMES.
BET HE RUBS EVERY-ONE THE WRONG WAY ...
SO...
IF I OFFER YOU VALENTINE'S DAY CHOCOLATE, YOU WON'T SAY NO?

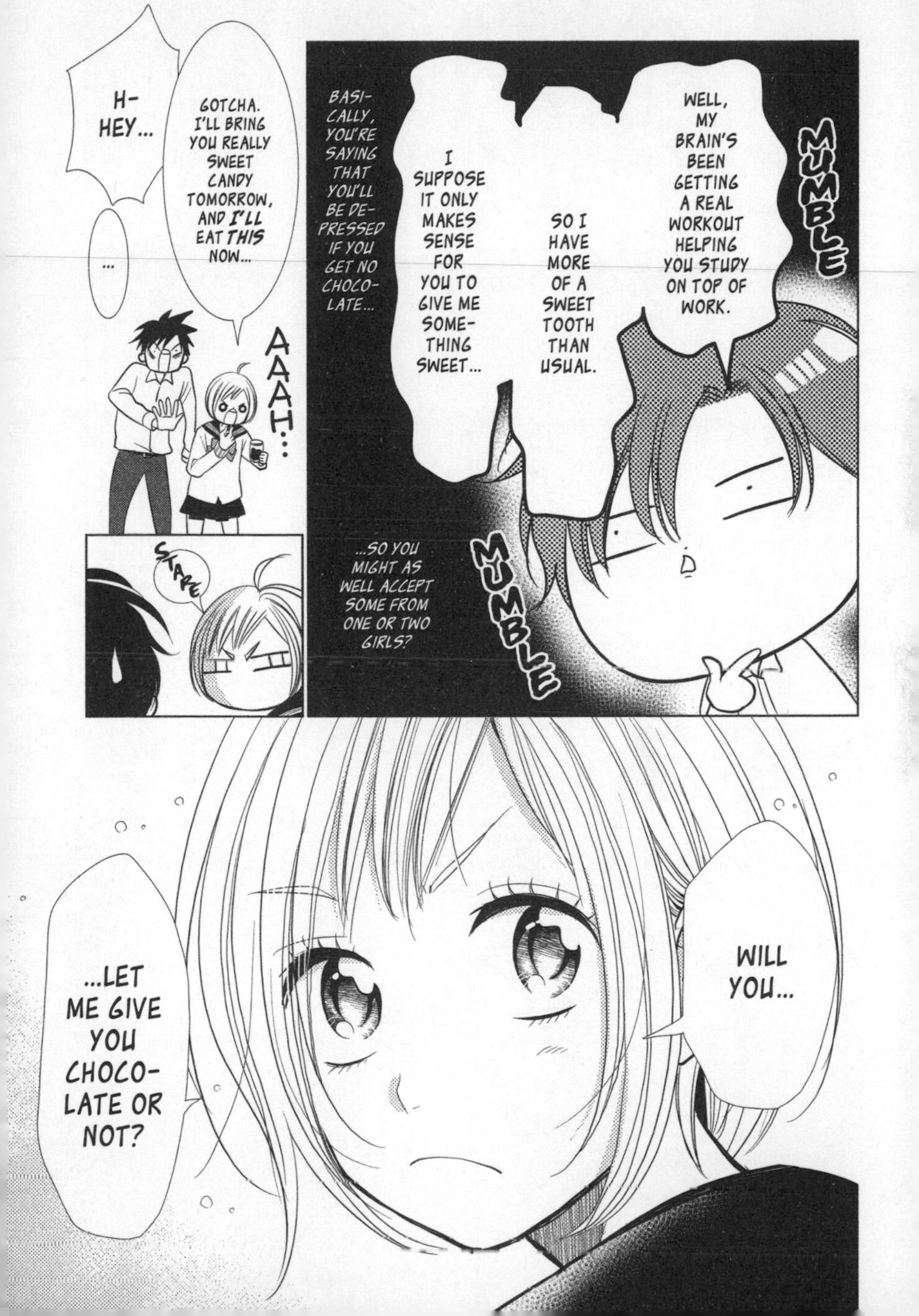
MUMBLE
WELL, MY BRAIN'S BEEN GETTING A REAL WORKOUT HELPING YOU STUDY ON TOP OF WORK.
SO I HAVE MORE OF A SWEET TOOTH THAN USUAL.
I SUPPOSE IT ONLY MAKES SENSE FOR YOU TO GIVE ME SOMETHING SWEET...
BASICALLY, YOU'RE SAYING THAT YOU'LL BE DEPRESSED IF YOU GET NO CHOCOLATE...
MUMBLE
...SO YOU MIGHT AS WELL ACCEPT SOME FROM ONE OR TWO GIRLS?
GOTCHA. I'LL BRING YOU REALLY SWEET CANDY TOMORROW, AND I'LL EAT THIS NOW...
H-HEY...
...
AAAH...
STARE
WILL YOU...
...LET ME GIVE YOU CHOCOLATE OR NOT?

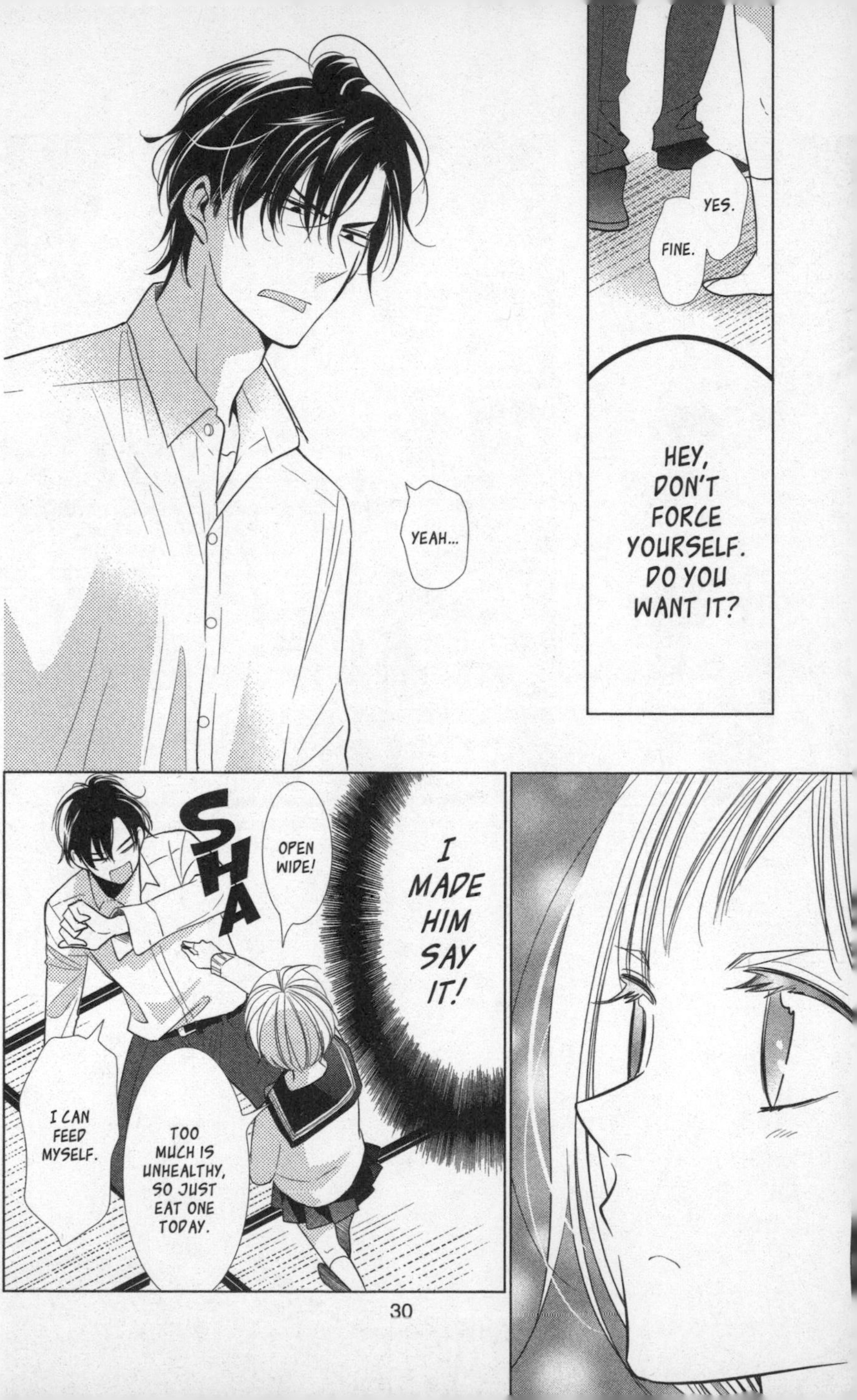
YES.
FINE.
HEY, DON'T FORCE YOURSELF. DO YOU WANT IT?
YEAH...
I MADE HIM SAY IT!
OPEN WIDE!
SHA
TOO MUCH IS UNHEALTHY, SO JUST EAT ONE TODAY.
I CAN FEED MYSELF.

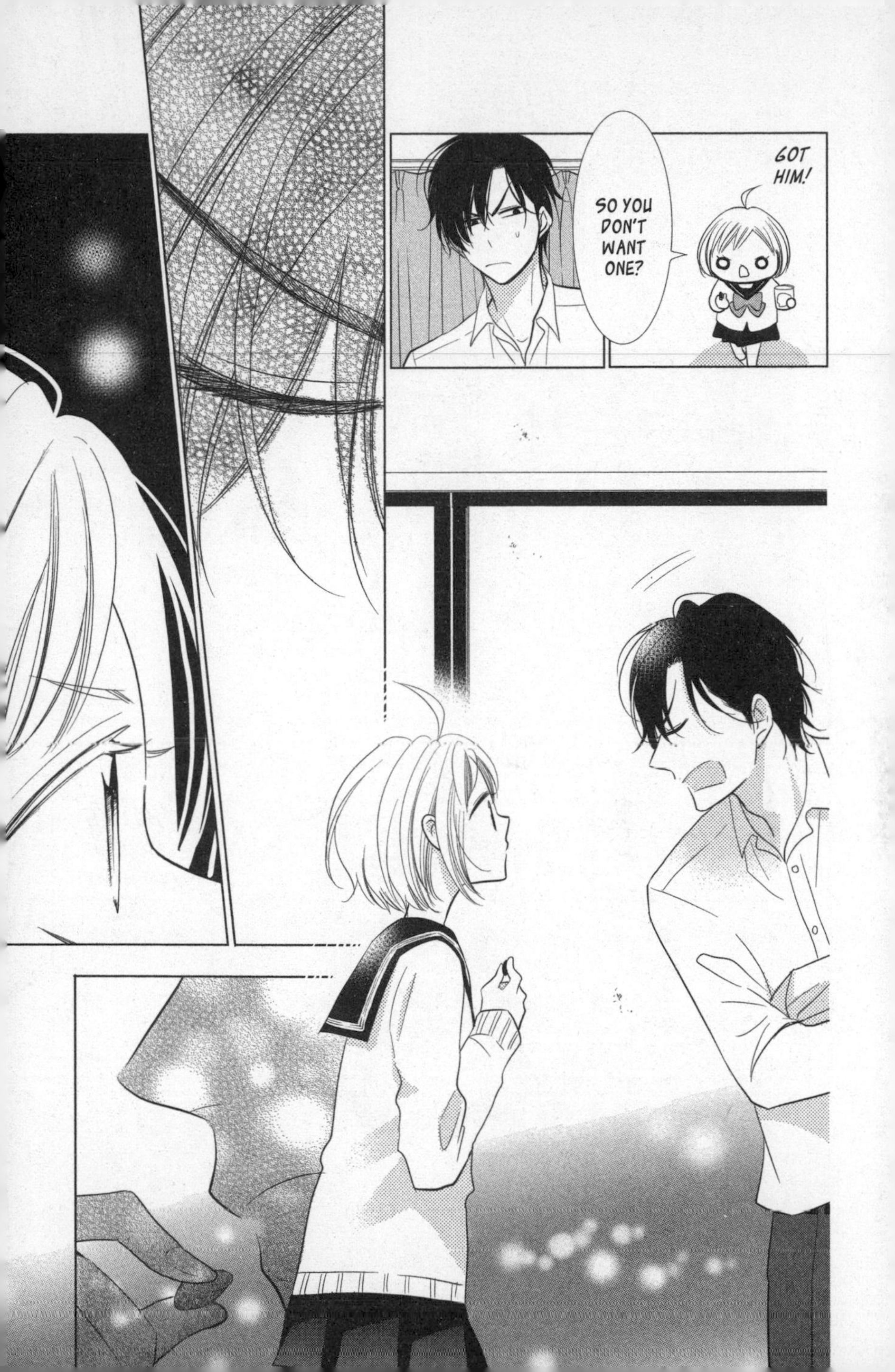
SO YOU DON'T WANT ONE?
GOT HIM!

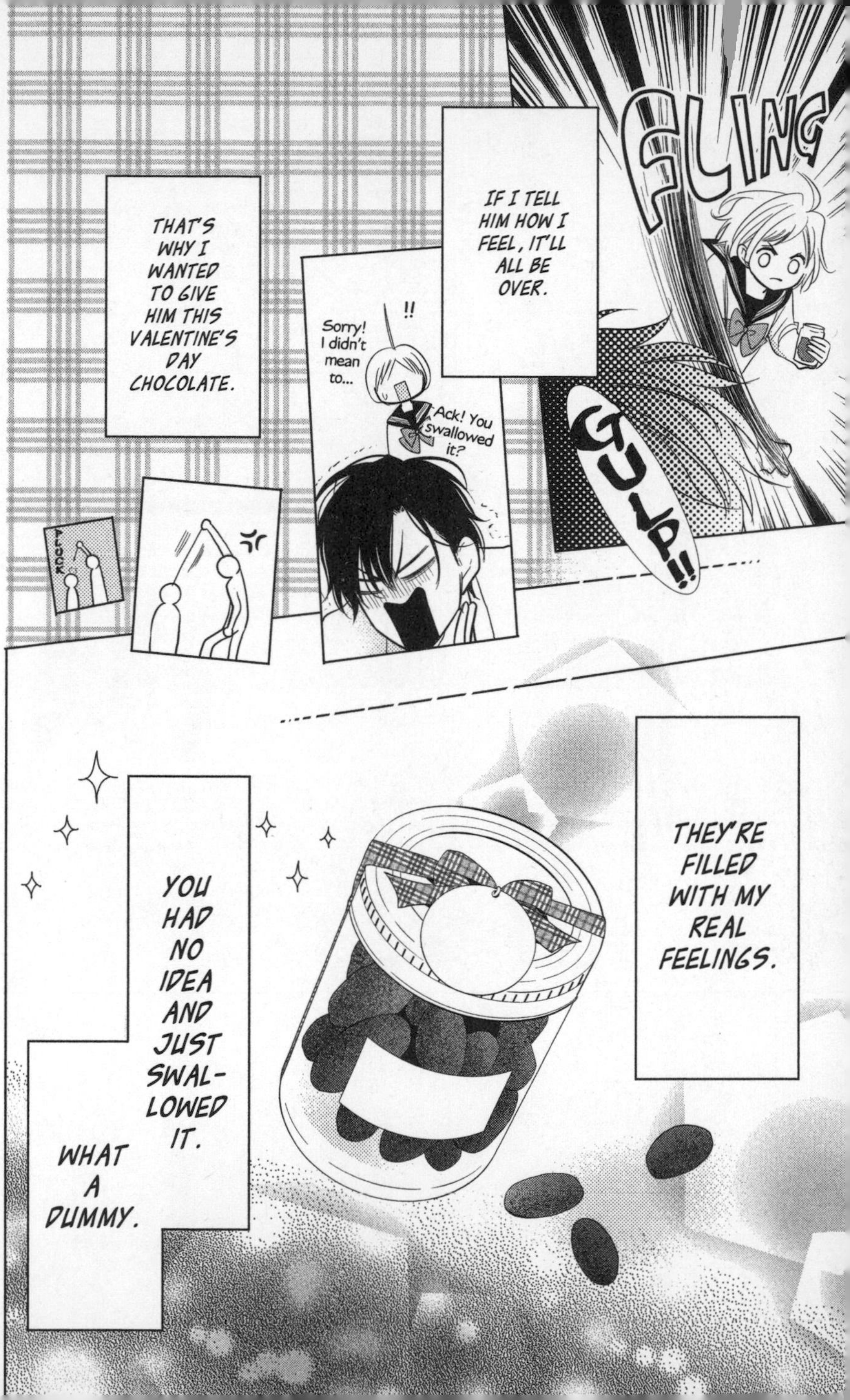
FLING
GULP!!
IF I TELL HIM HOW I FEEL, IT'LL ALL BE OVER.
!!
Ack! You swallowed it?
Sorry! I didn't mean to...
THAT'S WHY I WANTED TO GIVE HIM THIS VALENTINE'S DAY CHOCOLATE.
PLUCK
THEY'RE FILLED WITH MY REAL FEELINGS.
YOU HAD NO IDEA AND JUST SWAL-LOWED IT.
WHAT A DUMMY.

Chapter 41

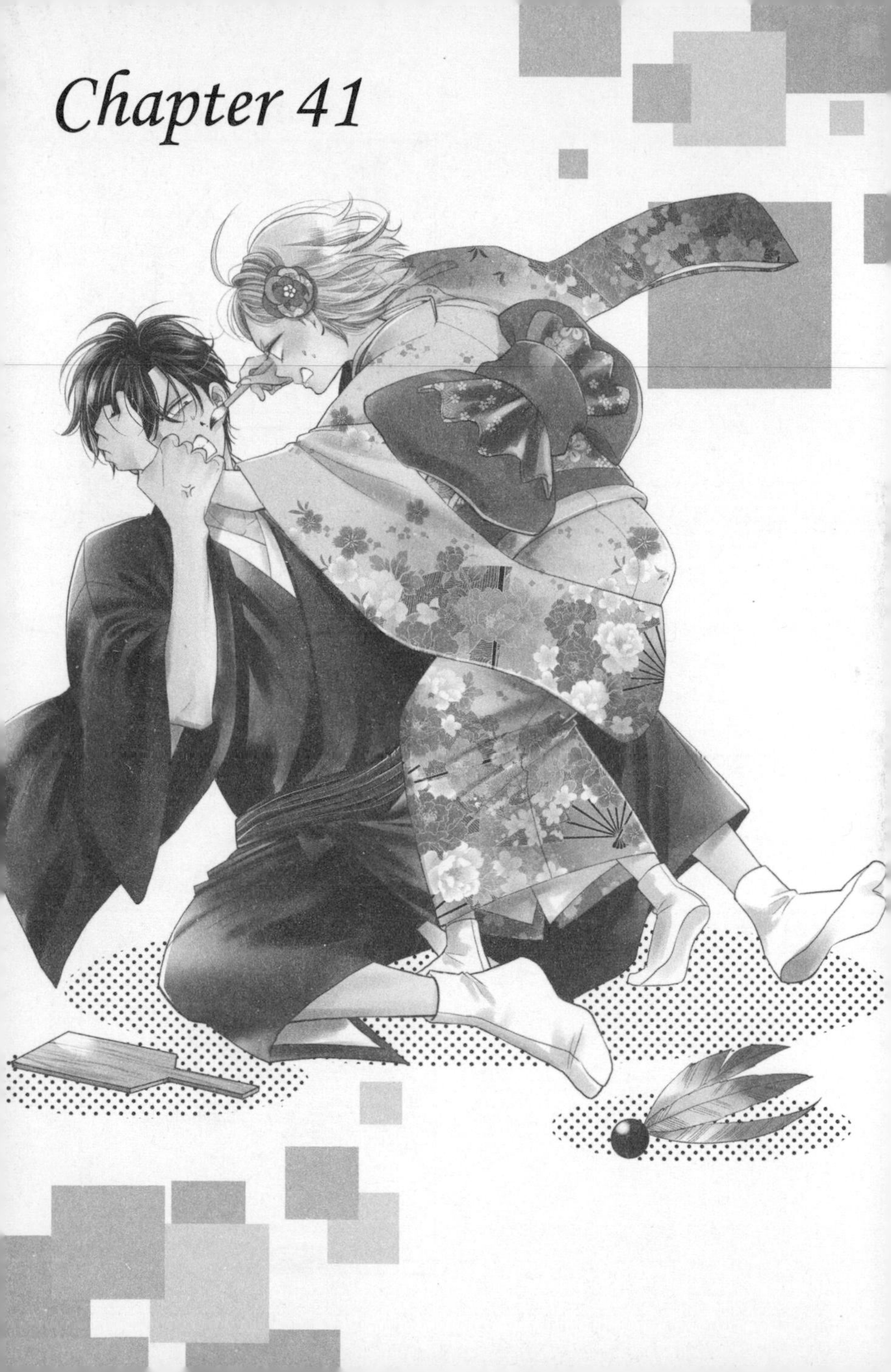

Later On

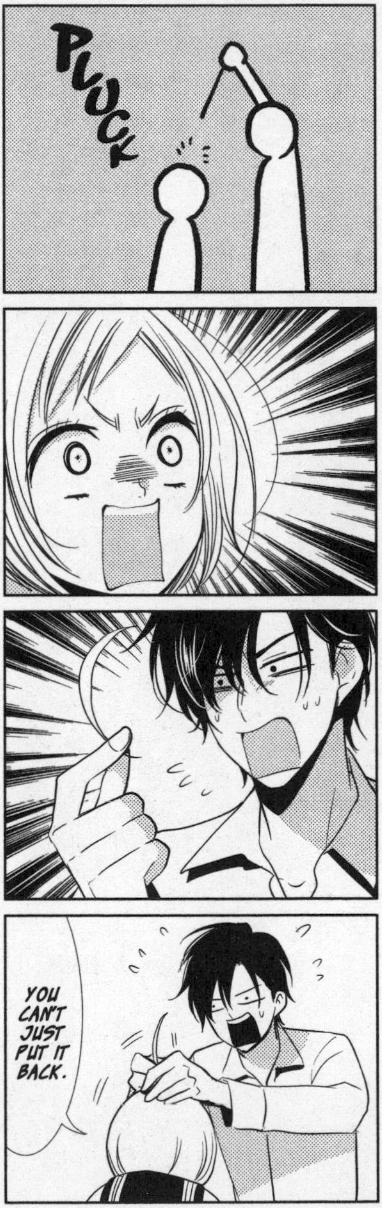
PLUCK
YOU CAN'T JUST PUT IT BACK.

•Q & A•

Q: Who is your favorite character in *Takane & Hana?*

A: I basically like all of my characters, but if I had to pick just one, it'd be Takane. He's very expressive, so he's fun to draw. And considering he's the male lead in a girls' manga, it's nice that there aren't too many things that are off-limits for him.

Q: How do you come up with Hana's snappy comebacks?

A: There's no one way. I just rack my brains until I come up with something. I need to think of things that'll rub Takane the wrong way without being abusive. My editor comes up with a lot of lines.

Q: Did you model the characters after anyone?

A: I draw on a lot of people I know rather than modeling a character on a specific individual.

Q: Will Hana's cowlick make a sudden comeback someday?

A: Actually, there's a backup cowlick growing underneath, so when her current cowlick falls out, the spare will pop up. But cowlicks move slowly, just like cows, so there's no guarantee it'll flip up right away.

Q: What was your childhood dream?

A: I wanted to be a dolphin trainer. I loved dolphins. They're so cute.

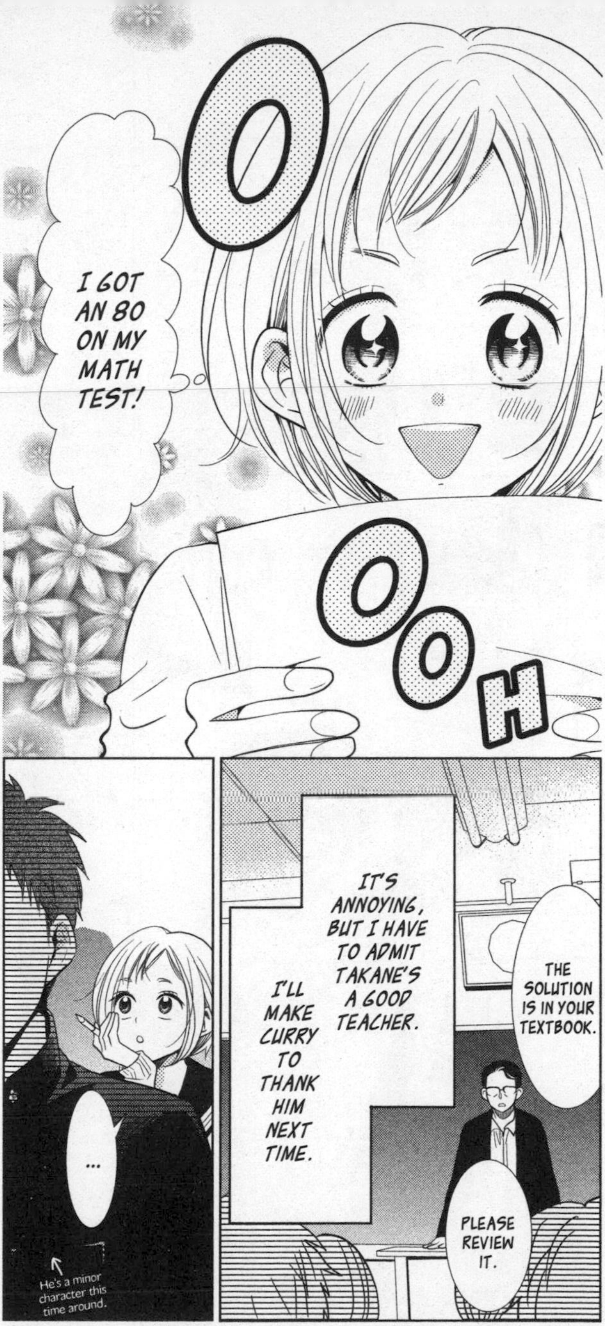
O
I GOT AN 80 ON MY MATH TEST!
OOOH
THE SOLUTION IS IN YOUR TEXTBOOK.
IT'S ANNOYING, BUT I HAVE TO ADMIT TAKANE'S A GOOD TEACHER.
I'LL MAKE CURRY TO THANK HIM NEXT TIME.
PLEASE REVIEW IT.
...
He's a minor character this time around.

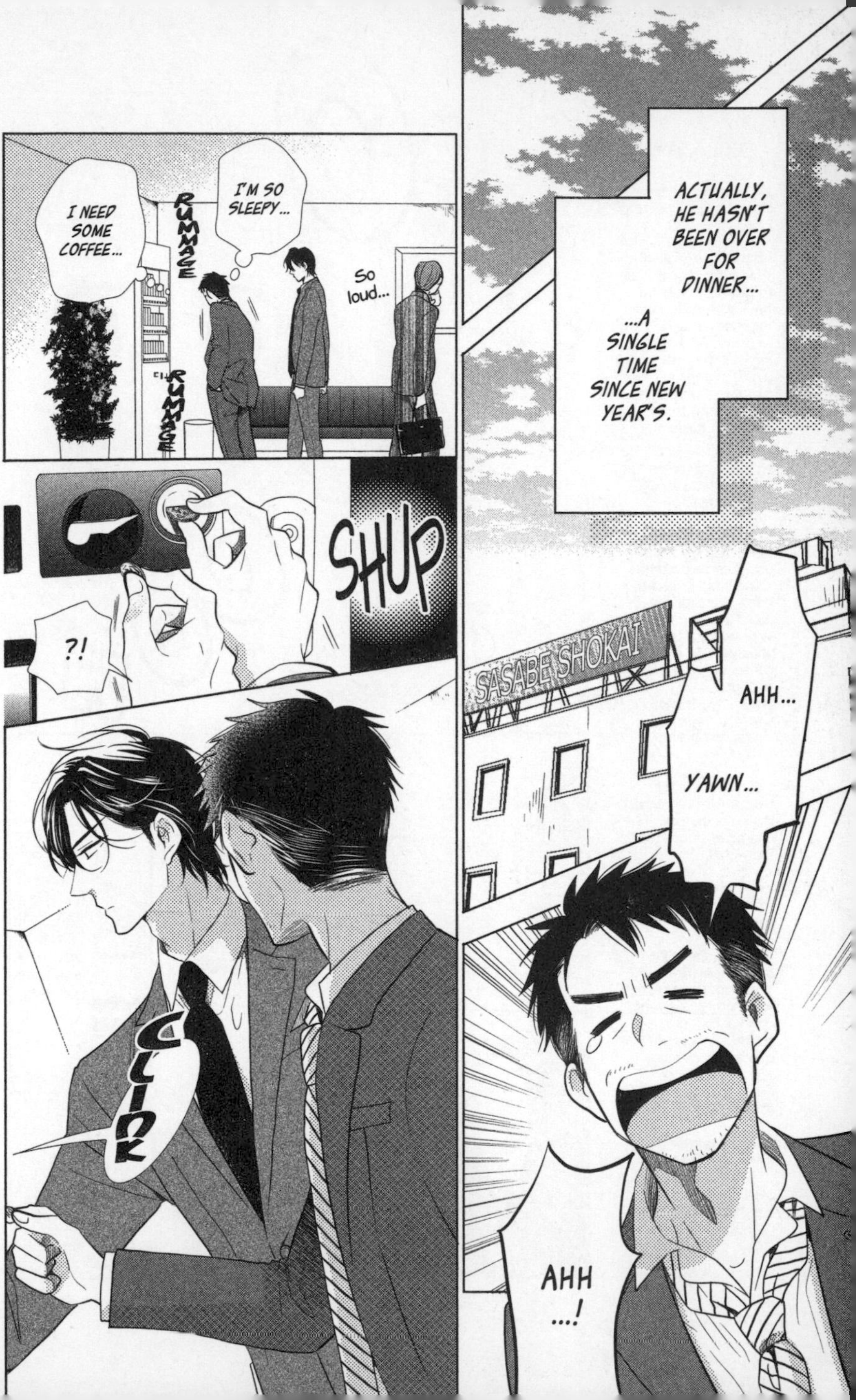
ACTUALLY, HE HASN'T BEEN OVER FOR DINNER...
...A SINGLE TIME SINCE NEW YEAR'S.
SASABE SHOKAI
AHH...
YAWN...
AHH ...!
So loud...
I'M SO SLEEPY...
RUMMAGE
RUMMAGE
I NEED SOME COFFEE...
SHUP
?!
CLINK

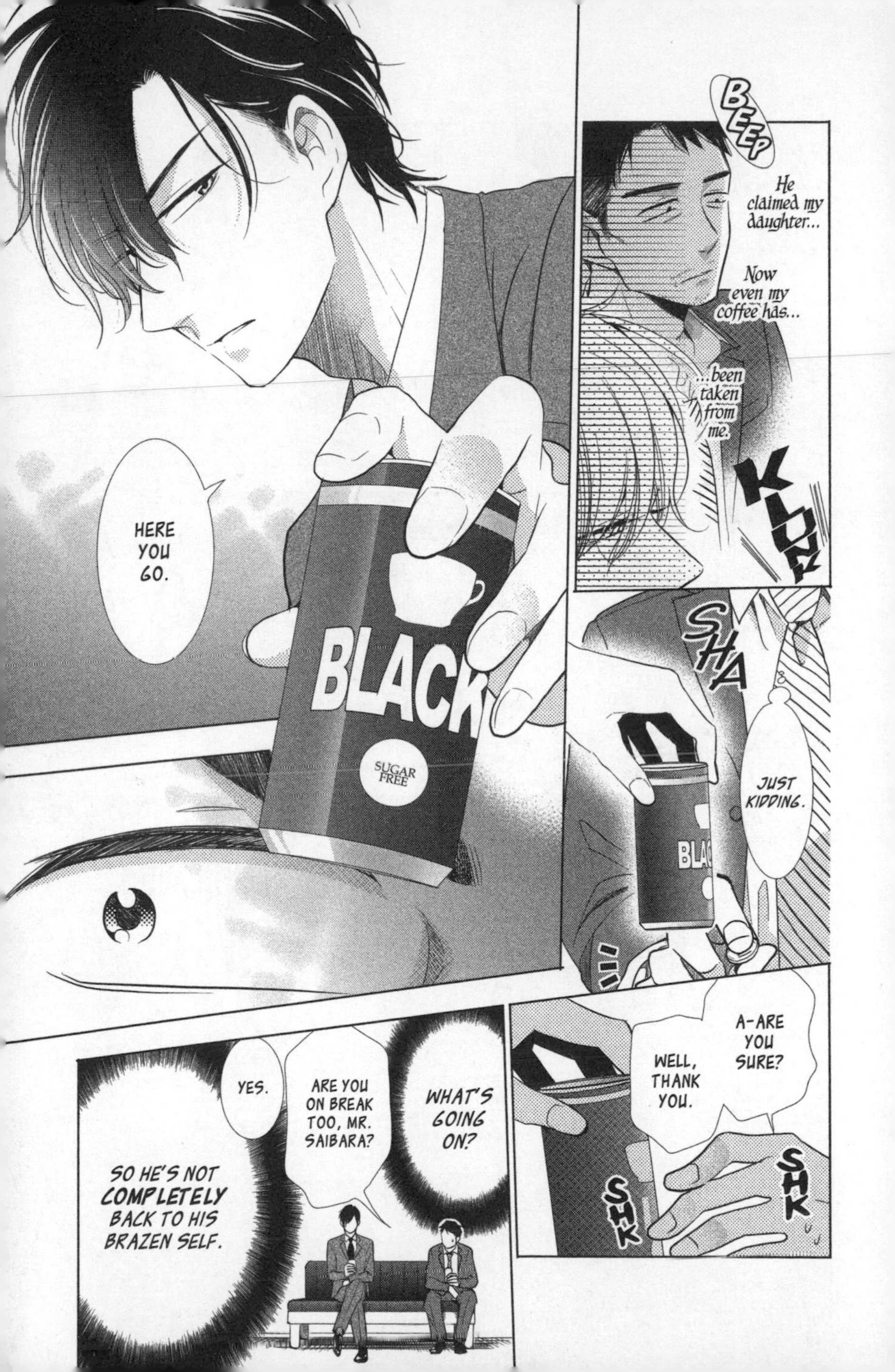
BEEP
He claimed my daughter...
Now even my coffee has...
...been taken from me.
KLUNK
SHA
JUST KIDDING.
HERE YOU GO.
BLACK
SUGAR FREE
A-ARE YOU SURE?
WELL, THANK YOU.
SHK
SHK
WHAT'S GOING ON?
ARE YOU ON BREAK TOO, MR. SAIBARA?
YES.
SO HE'S NOT COMPLETELY BACK TO HIS BRAZEN SELF.

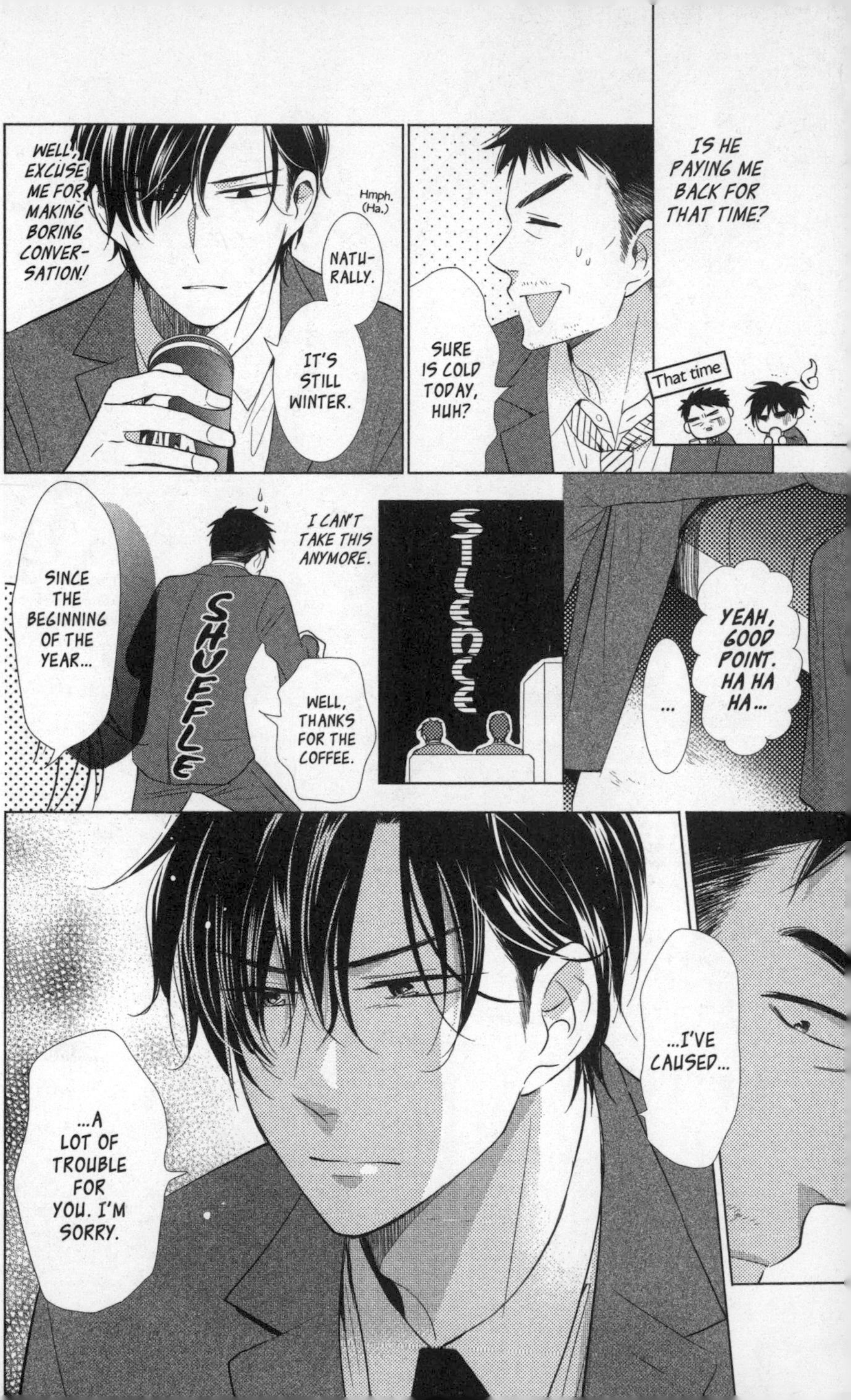
IS HE PAYING ME BACK FOR THAT TIME?
That time
SURE IS COLD TODAY, HUH?
Hmph. (Ha.)
NATU-RALLY.
IT'S STILL WINTER.
WELL, EXCUSE ME FOR MAKING BORING CONVER-SATION!
YEAH, GOOD POINT. HA HA HA...
...
SILENCE
I CAN'T TAKE THIS ANYMORE.
WELL, THANKS FOR THE COFFEE.
SHUFFLE
SINCE THE BEGINNING OF THE YEAR...
...I'VE CAUSED...
...A LOT OF TROUBLE FOR YOU. I'M SORRY.

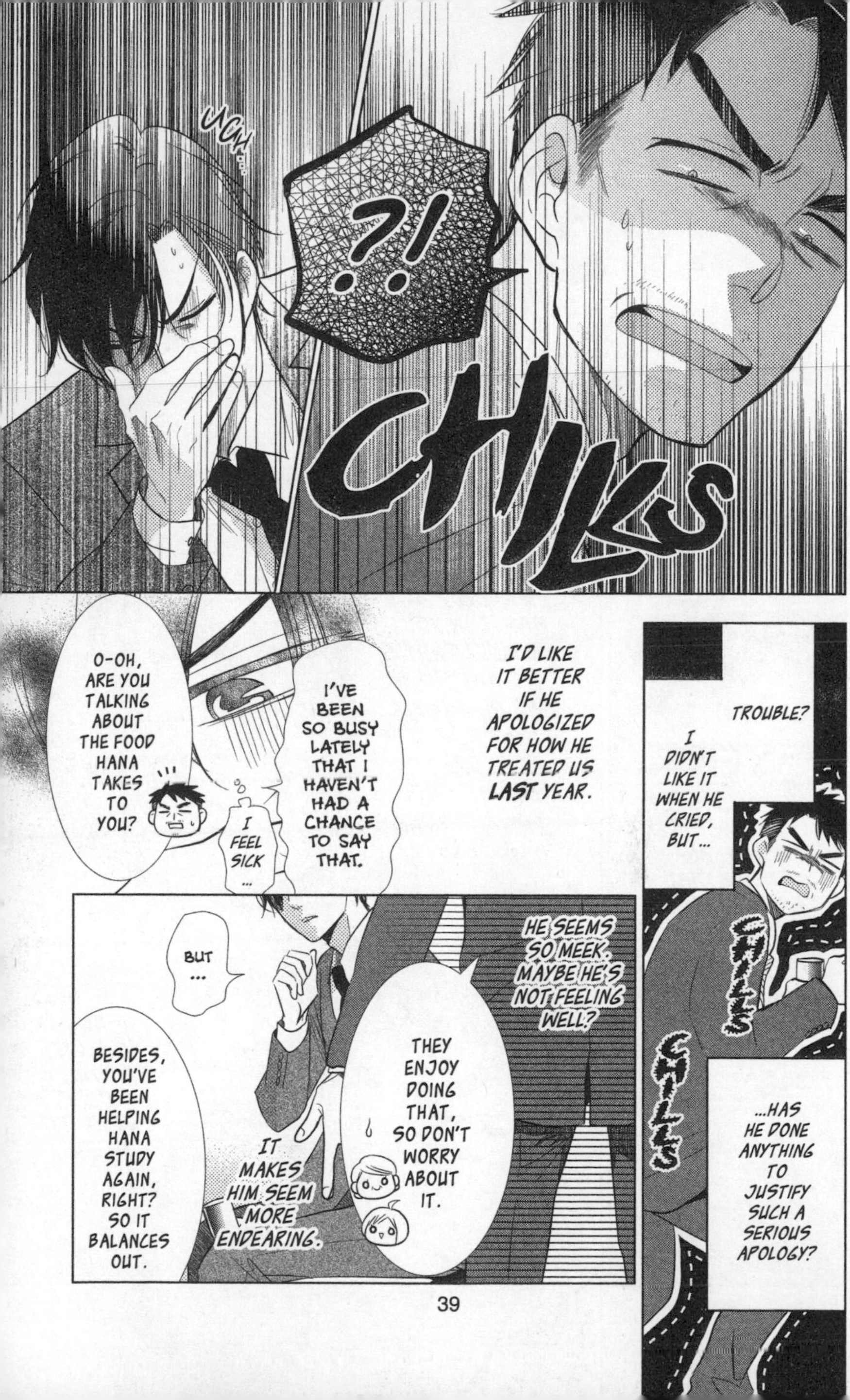
UGH...
?!
CHILLS
TROUBLE?
I DIDN'T LIKE IT WHEN HE CRIED, BUT...
CHILLS
CHILLS
...HAS HE DONE ANYTHING TO JUSTIFY SUCH A SERIOUS APOLOGY?
I'D LIKE IT BETTER IF HE APOLOGIZED FOR HOW HE TREATED US LAST YEAR.
I'VE BEEN SO BUSY LATELY THAT I HAVEN'T HAD A CHANCE TO SAY THAT.
I FEEL SICK...
O-OH, ARE YOU TALKING ABOUT THE FOOD HANA TAKES TO YOU?
HE SEEMS SO MEEK. MAYBE HE'S NOT FEELING WELL?
THEY ENJOY DOING THAT, SO DON'T WORRY ABOUT IT.
IT MAKES HIM SEEM MORE ENDEARING.
BUT...
BESIDES, YOU'VE BEEN HELPING HANA STUDY AGAIN, RIGHT? SO IT BALANCES OUT.

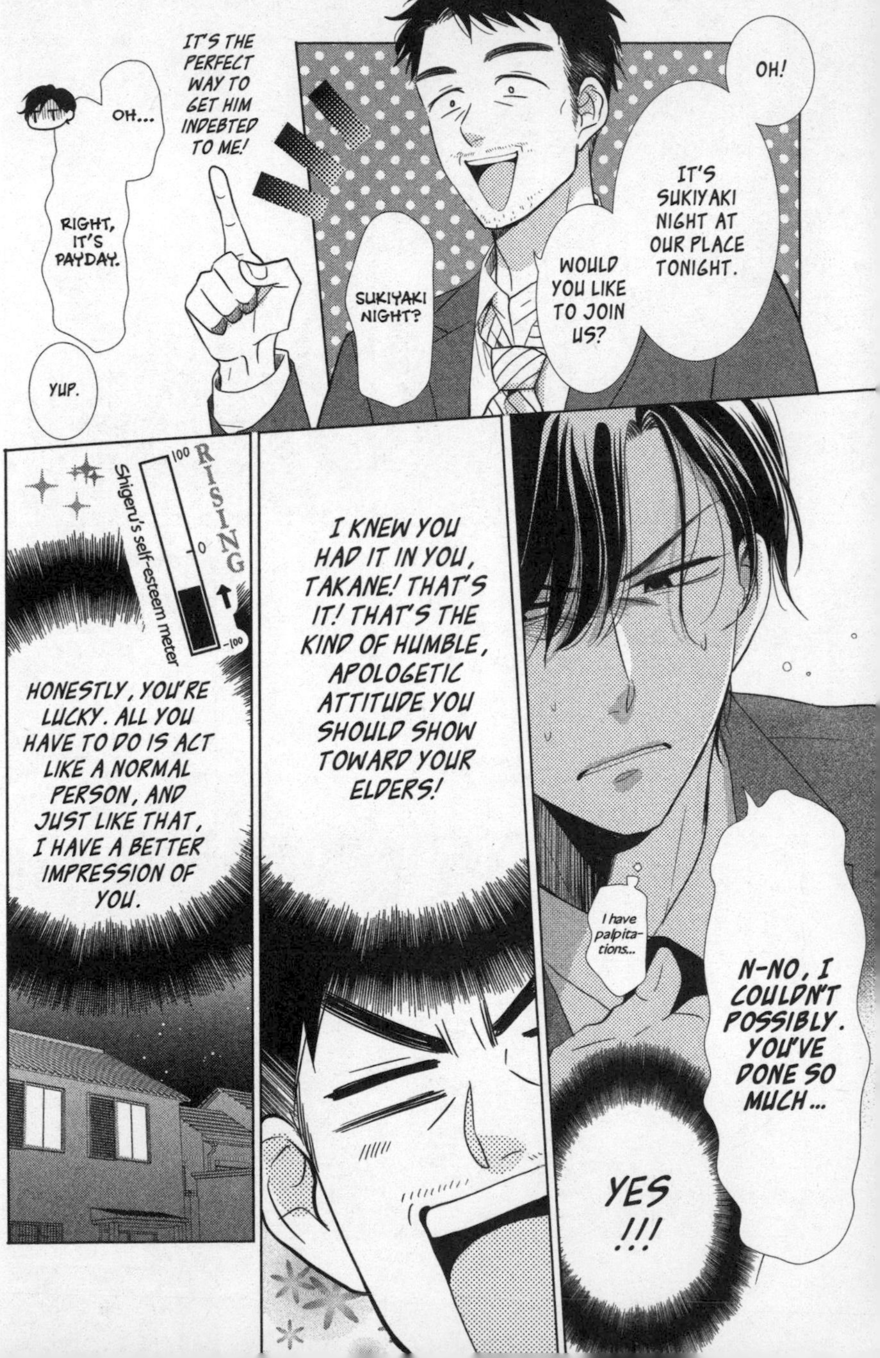
OH!
IT'S SUKIYAKI NIGHT AT OUR PLACE TONIGHT.
WOULD YOU LIKE TO JOIN US?
SUKIYAKI NIGHT?
IT'S THE PERFECT WAY TO GET HIM INDEBTED TO ME!
OH...
RIGHT, IT'S PAYDAY.
YUP.
N-NO, I COULDN'T POSSIBLY. YOU'VE DONE SO MUCH...
I have palpitations...
YES !!!
I KNEW YOU HAD IT IN YOU, TAKANE! THAT'S IT! THAT'S THE KIND OF HUMBLE, APOLOGETIC ATTITUDE YOU SHOULD SHOW TOWARD YOUR ELDERS!
RISING
100
0
-100
Shigeru's self-esteem meter
HONESTLY, YOU'RE LUCKY. ALL YOU HAVE TO DO IS ACT LIKE A NORMAL PERSON, AND JUST LIKE THAT, I HAVE A BETTER IMPRESSION OF YOU.

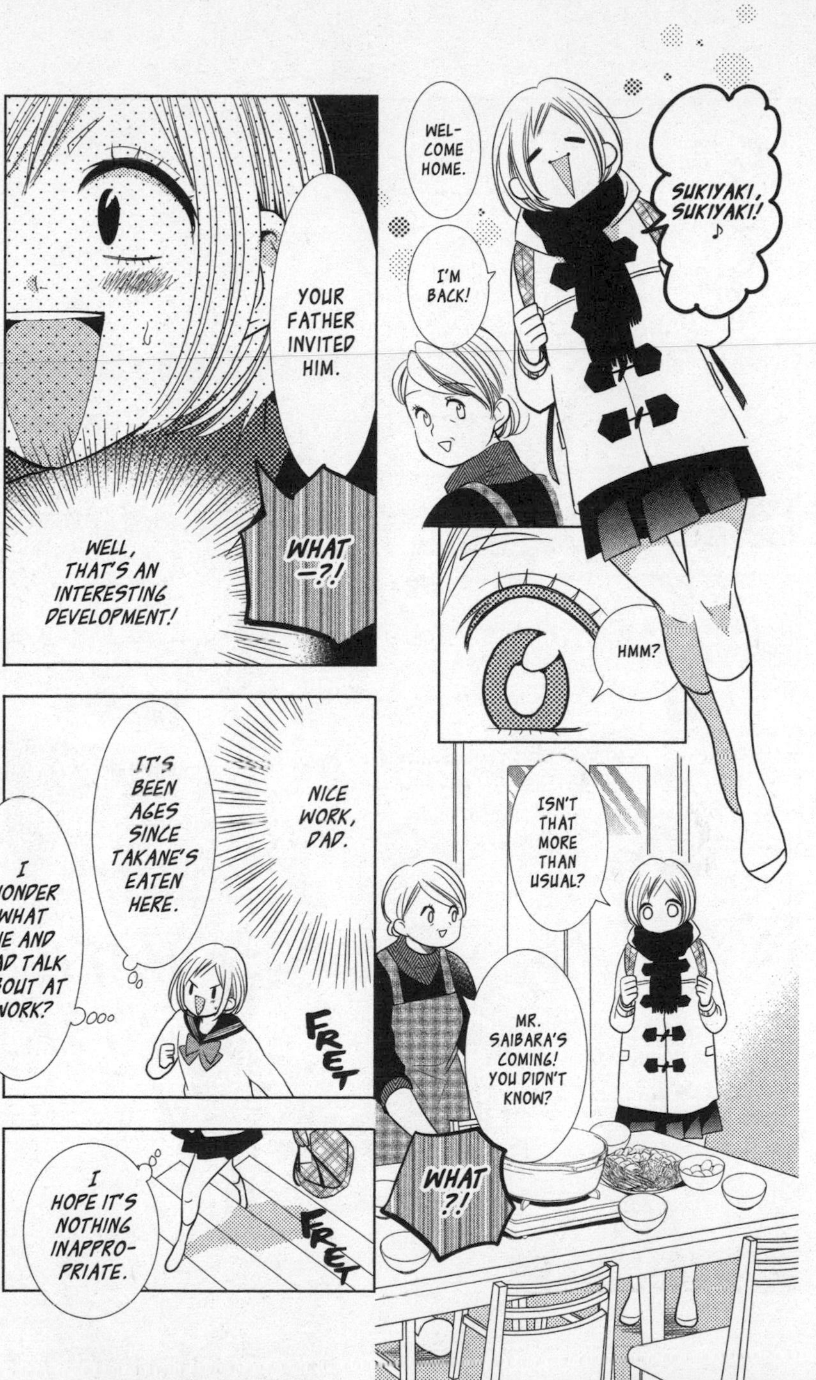
SUKIYAKI, SUKIYAKI! ♪
WEL-COME HOME.
I'M BACK!
HMM?
ISN'T THAT MORE THAN USUAL?
MR. SAIBARA'S COMING! YOU DIDN'T KNOW?
WHAT?!
YOUR FATHER INVITED HIM.
WHAT—?!
WELL, THAT'S AN INTERESTING DEVELOPMENT!
NICE WORK, DAD.
IT'S BEEN AGES SINCE TAKANE'S EATEN HERE.
I WONDER WHAT HE AND DAD TALK ABOUT AT WORK?
FRET
I HOPE IT'S NOTHING INAPPRO-PRIATE.
FRET

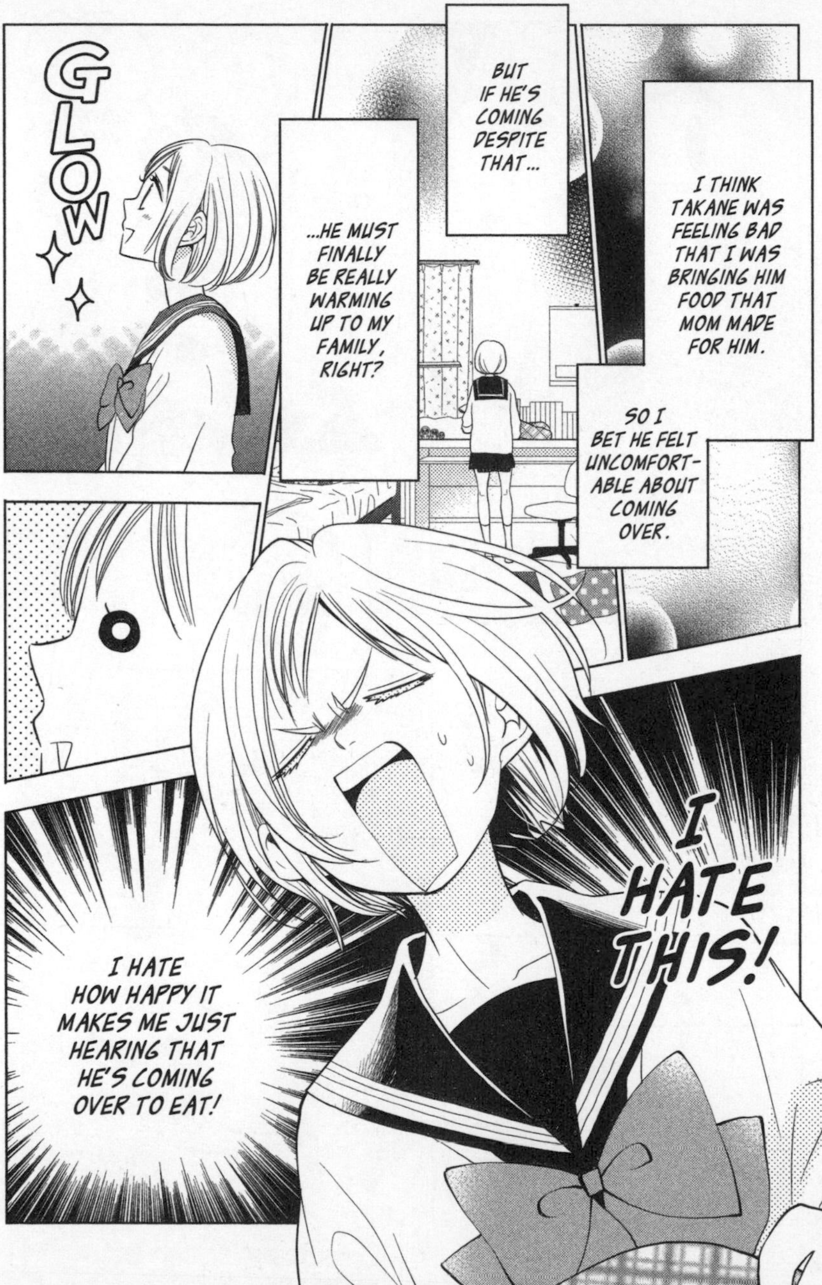
I THINK TAKANE WAS FEELING BAD THAT I WAS BRINGING HIM FOOD THAT MOM MADE FOR HIM.
SO I BET HE FELT UNCOMFORT-ABLE ABOUT COMING OVER.
BUT IF HE'S COMING DESPITE THAT...
...HE MUST FINALLY BE REALLY WARMING UP TO MY FAMILY, RIGHT?
GLOW
I HATE THIS!
I HATE HOW HAPPY IT MAKES ME JUST HEARING THAT HE'S COMING OVER TO EAT!

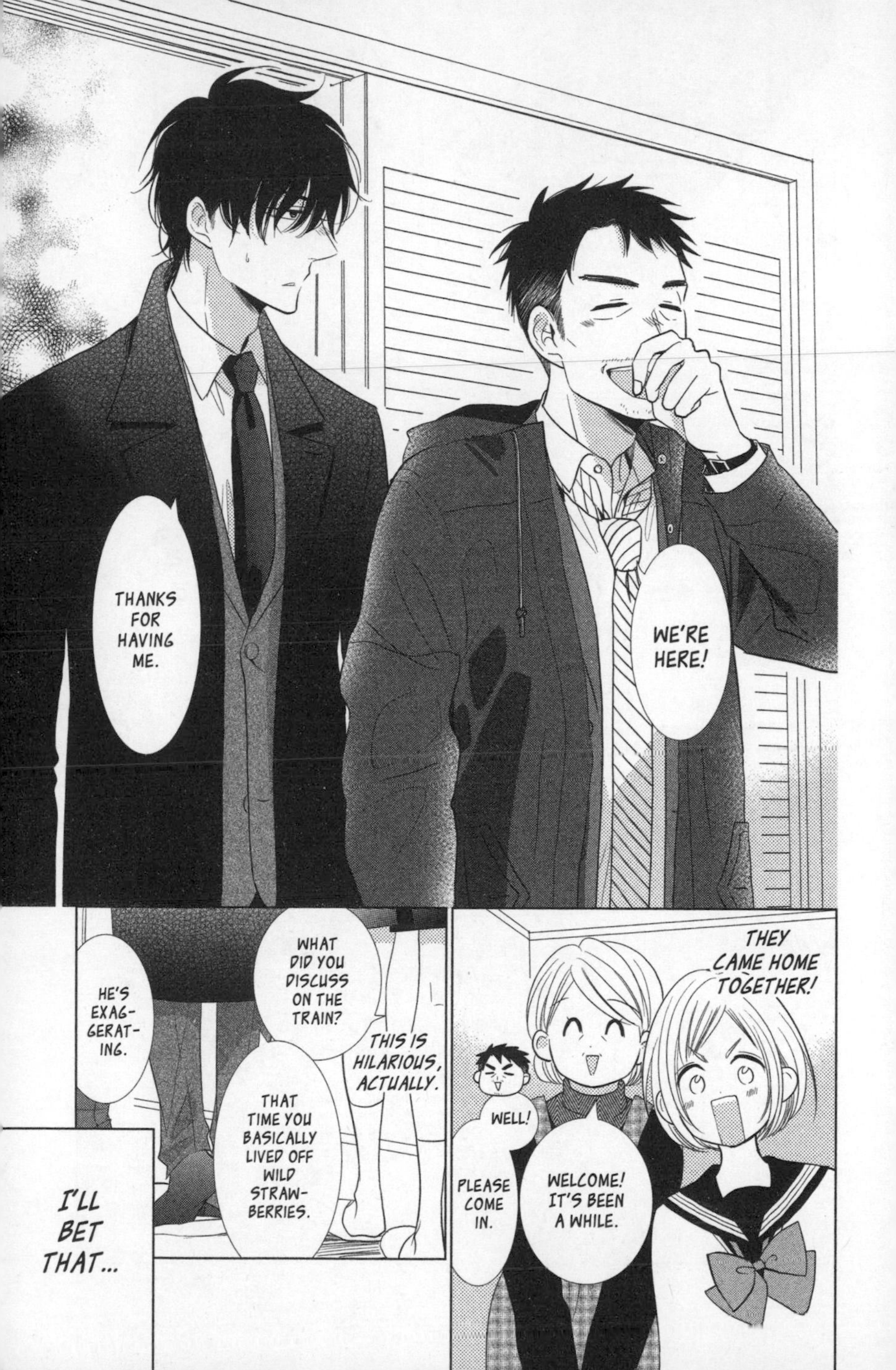
WE'RE HERE!
THANKS FOR HAVING ME.
THEY CAME HOME TOGETHER!
WELL!
WELCOME! IT'S BEEN A WHILE.
PLEASE COME IN.
WHAT DID YOU DISCUSS ON THE TRAIN?
THIS IS HILARIOUS, ACTUALLY.
HE'S EXAG-GERAT-ING.
THAT TIME YOU BASICALLY LIVED OFF WILD STRAW-BERRIES.
I'LL BET THAT...

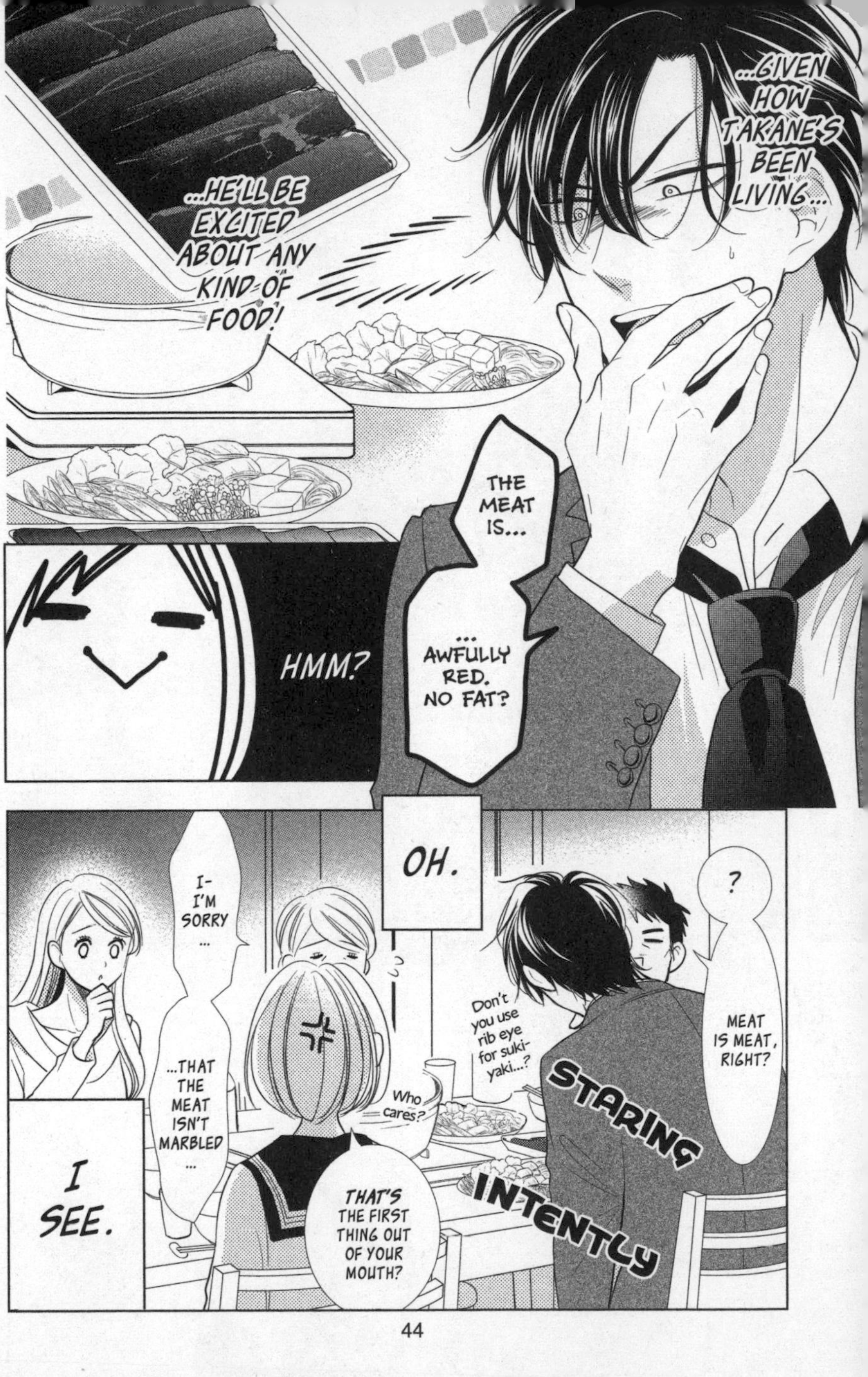
...GIVEN HOW TAKANE'S BEEN LIVING...
...HE'LL BE EXCITED ABOUT ANY KIND OF FOOD!
THE MEAT IS...
...AWFULLY RED. NO FAT?
HMM?
?
MEAT IS MEAT, RIGHT?
Don't you use rib eye for suki-yaki...?
STARING INTENTLY
OH.
Who cares?
THAT'S THE FIRST THING OUT OF YOUR MOUTH?
I- I'M SORRY...
...THAT THE MEAT ISN'T MARBLED...
I SEE.

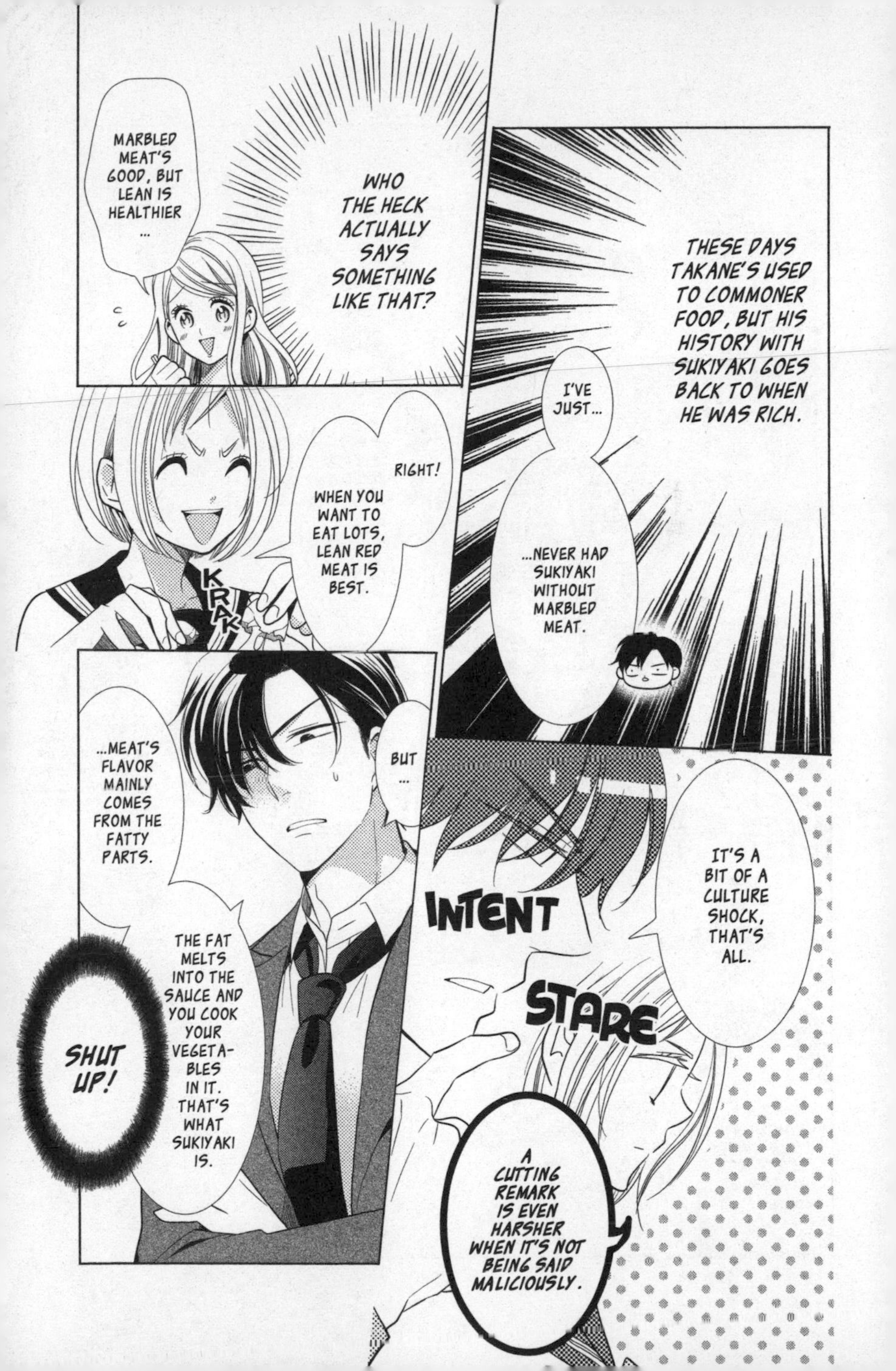
MARBLED MEAT'S GOOD, BUT LEAN IS HEALTHIER ...
WHO THE HECK ACTUALLY SAYS SOMETHING LIKE THAT?
RIGHT!
WHEN YOU WANT TO EAT LOTS, LEAN RED MEAT IS BEST.
KRAK
BUT ...
...MEAT'S FLAVOR MAINLY COMES FROM THE FATTY PARTS.
THE FAT MELTS INTO THE SAUCE AND YOU COOK YOUR VEGETA-BLES IN IT. THAT'S WHAT SUKIYAKI IS.
SHUT UP!
THESE DAYS TAKANE'S USED TO COMMONER FOOD, BUT HIS HISTORY WITH SUKIYAKI GOES BACK TO WHEN HE WAS RICH.
I'VE JUST...
...NEVER HAD SUKIYAKI WITHOUT MARBLED MEAT.
IT'S A BIT OF A CULTURE SHOCK, THAT'S ALL.
INTENT STARE
A CUTTING REMARK IS EVEN HARSHER WHEN IT'S NOT BEING SAID MALICIOUSLY.

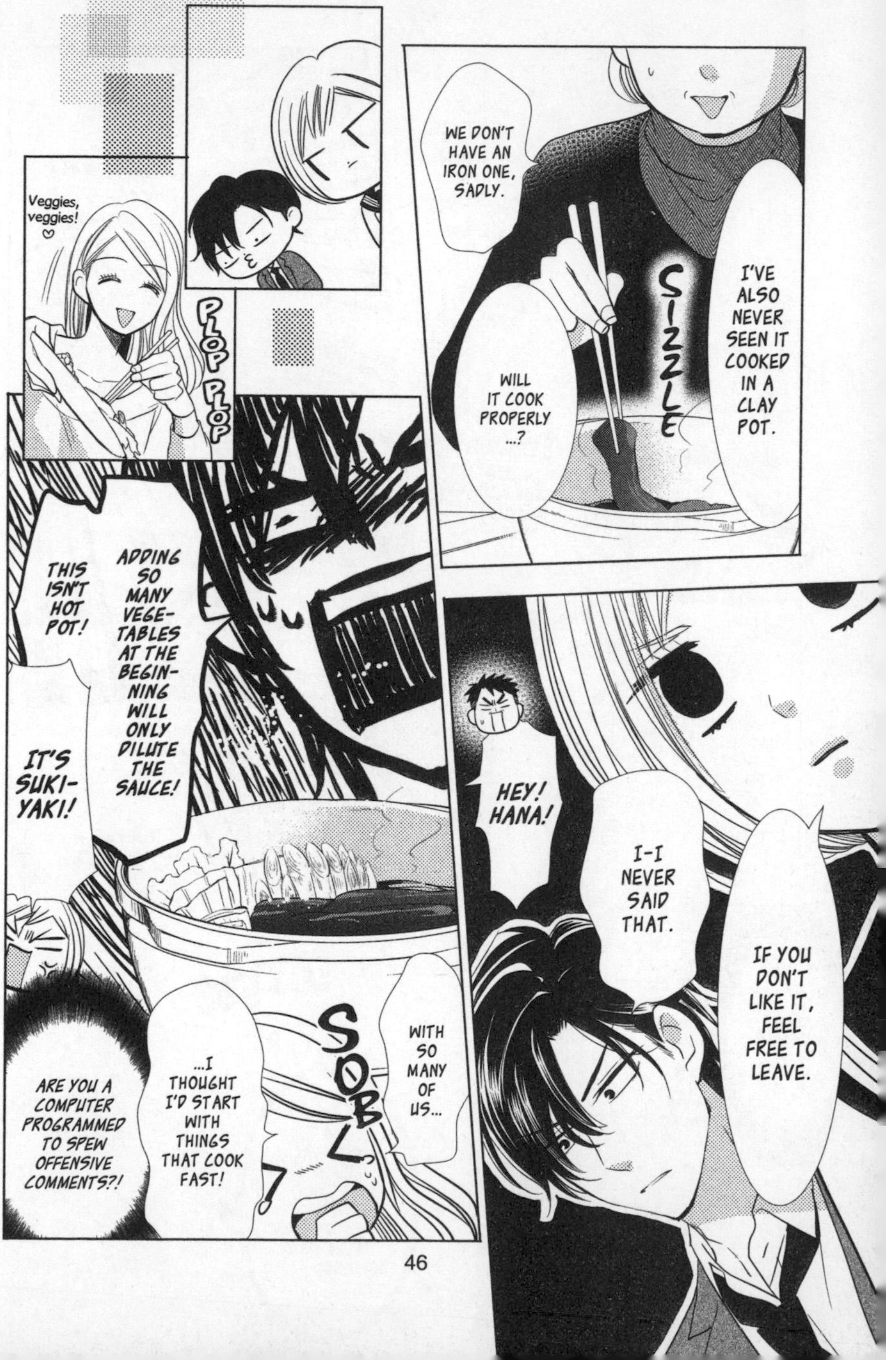

WE DON'T HAVE AN IRON ONE, SADLY.
I'VE ALSO NEVER SEEN IT COOKED IN A CLAY POT.
SIZZLE
WILL IT COOK PROPERLY ...?
Veggies, veggies! ♡
PLOP PLOP
IF YOU DON'T LIKE IT, FEEL FREE TO LEAVE.
I-I NEVER SAID THAT.
HEY! HANA!
THIS ISN'T HOT POT!
IT'S SUKI-YAKI!
ADDING SO MANY VEGE-TABLES AT THE BEGIN-NING WILL ONLY DILUTE THE SAUCE!
WITH SO MANY OF US...
...I THOUGHT I'D START WITH THINGS THAT COOK FAST!
SOB
ARE YOU A COMPUTER PROGRAMMED TO SPEW OFFENSIVE COMMENTS?!

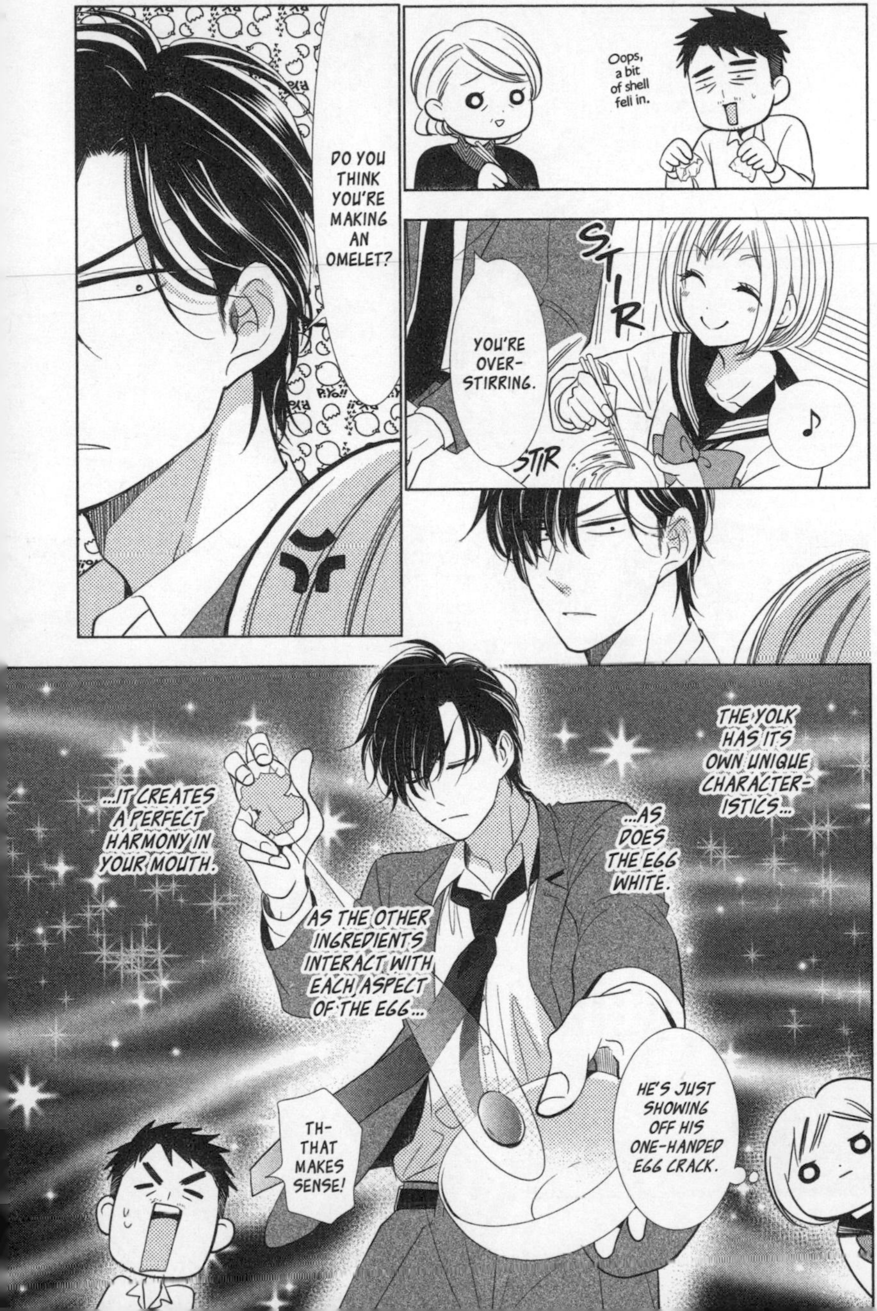
Oops, a bit of shell fell in.
STIR
YOU'RE OVER-STIRRING.
STIR
♪
DO YOU THINK YOU'RE MAKING AN OMELET?
THE YOLK HAS ITS OWN UNIQUE CHARACTER-ISTICS...
...AS DOES THE EGG WHITE.
AS THE OTHER INGREDIENTS INTERACT WITH EACH ASPECT OF THE EGG...
...IT CREATES A PERFECT HARMONY IN YOUR MOUTH.
HE'S JUST SHOWING OFF HIS ONE-HANDED EGG CRACK.
TH-THAT MAKES SENSE!

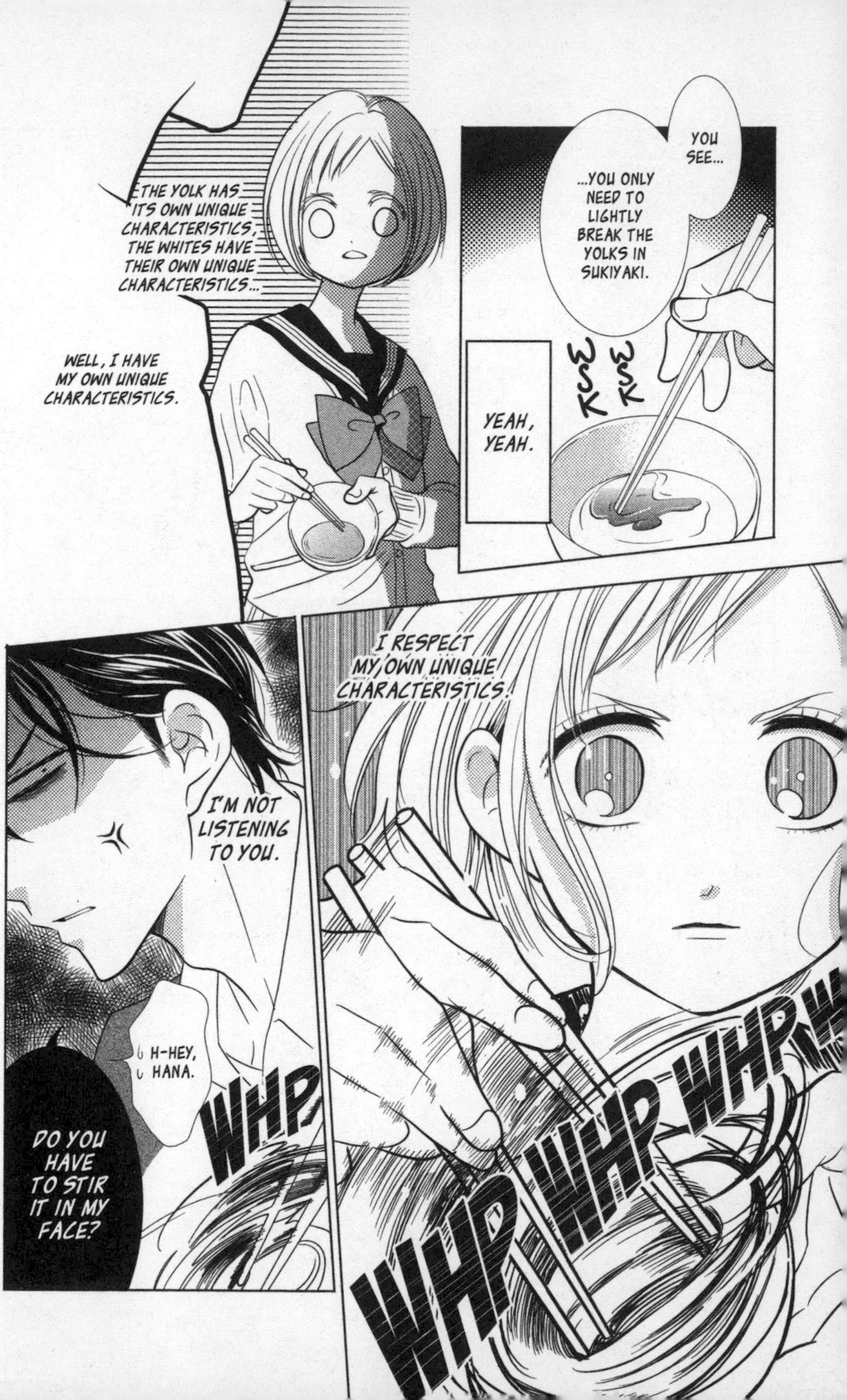
YOU SEE...
...YOU ONLY NEED TO LIGHTLY BREAK THE YOLKS IN SUKIYAKI.
WSK WSK
YEAH, YEAH.
THE YOLK HAS ITS OWN UNIQUE CHARACTERISTICS, THE WHITES HAVE THEIR OWN UNIQUE CHARACTERISTICS...
WELL, I HAVE MY OWN UNIQUE CHARACTERISTICS.
I RESPECT MY OWN UNIQUE CHARACTERISTICS.
WHP WHP WHP WHP
I'M NOT LISTENING TO YOU.
H-HEY, HANA.
DO YOU HAVE TO STIR IT IN MY FACE?
WHP

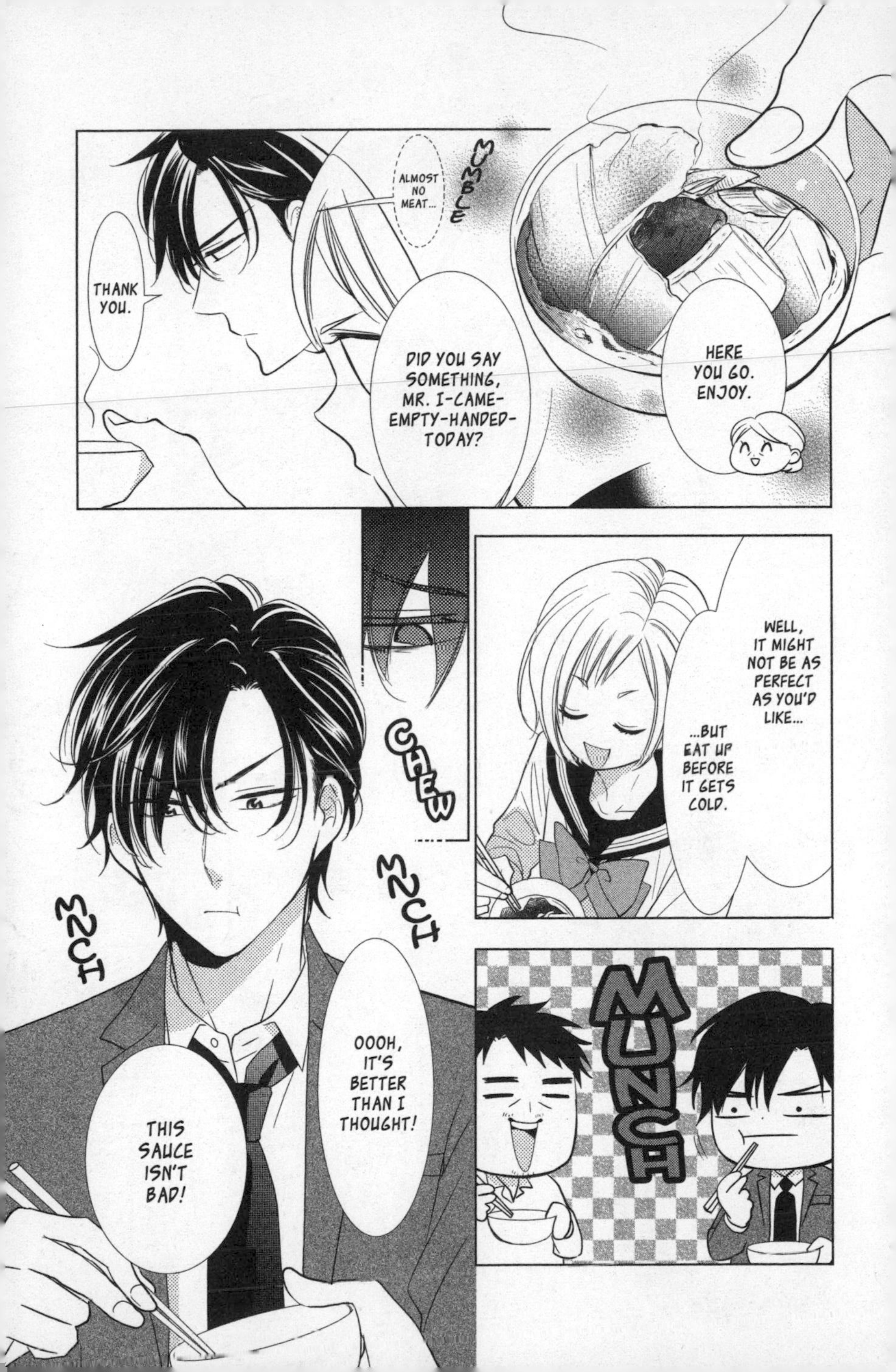
HERE YOU GO. ENJOY.
MUMBLE
ALMOST NO MEAT...
DID YOU SAY SOMETHING, MR. I-CAME-EMPTY-HANDED-TODAY?
THANK YOU.
WELL, IT MIGHT NOT BE AS PERFECT AS YOU'D LIKE...
...BUT EAT UP BEFORE IT GETS COLD.
MUNCH
CHEW
MUNCH
MUNCH
OOOH, IT'S BETTER THAN I THOUGHT!
THIS SAUCE ISN'T BAD!

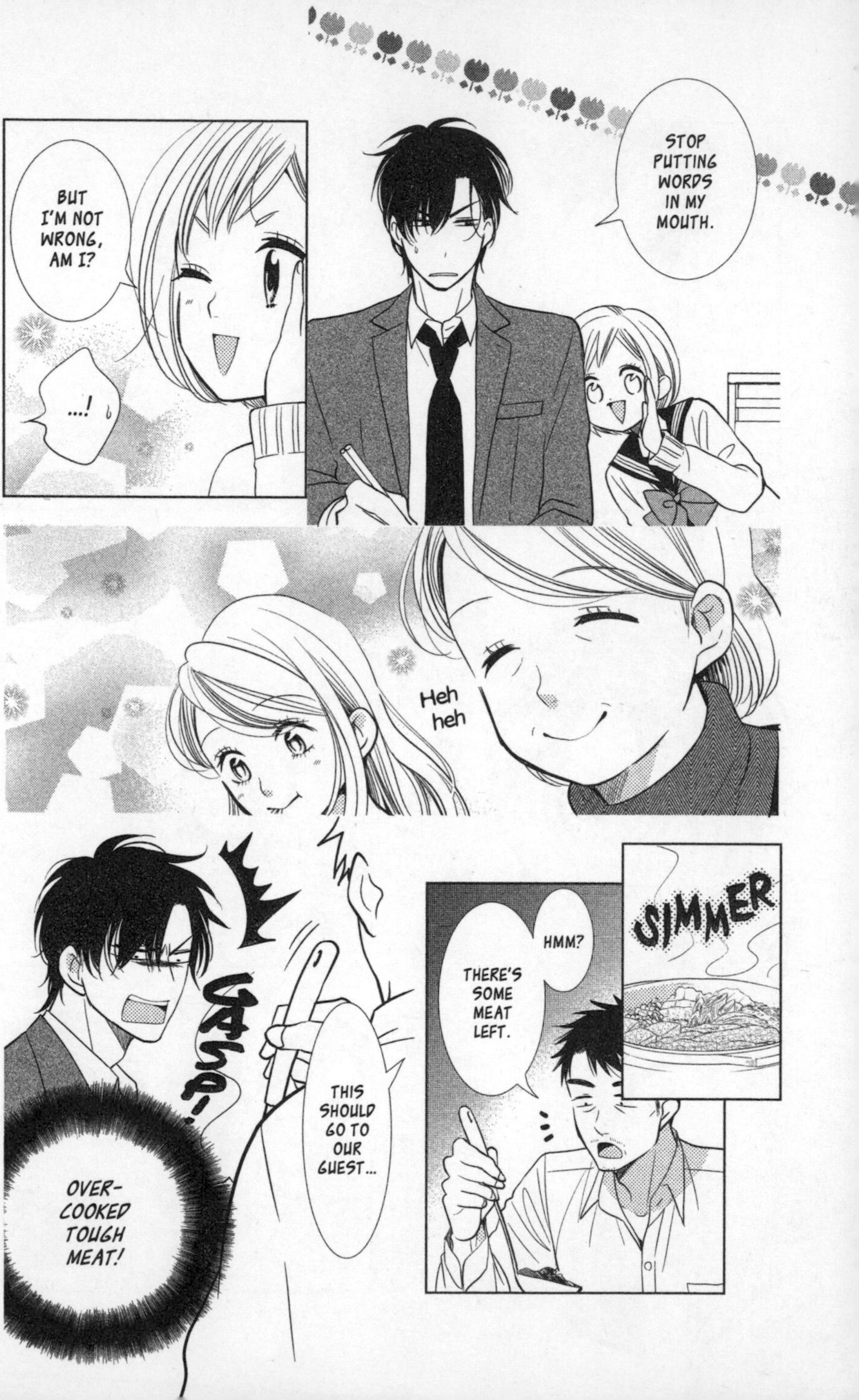
STOP PUTTING WORDS IN MY MOUTH.
BUT I'M NOT WRONG, AM I?
...!
Heh heh
SIMMER
HMM?
THERE'S SOME MEAT LEFT.
GASP!
THIS SHOULD GO TO OUR GUEST...
OVER-COOKED TOUGH MEAT!

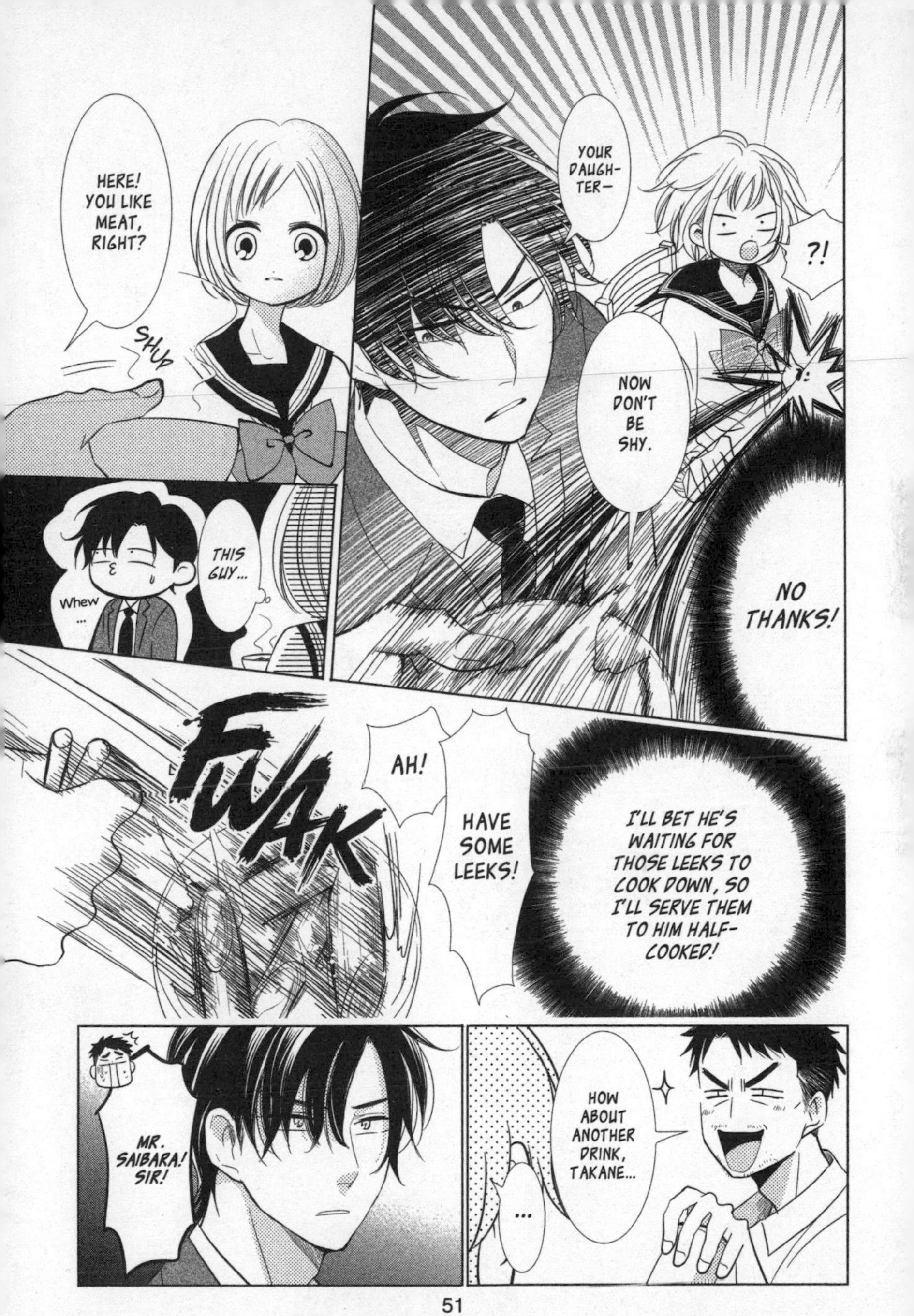
YOUR DAUGHTER—
?!
NOW DON'T BE SHY.
NO THANKS!
HERE! YOU LIKE MEAT, RIGHT?
SHUP
THIS GUY...
Whew ...
I'LL BET HE'S WAITING FOR THOSE LEEKS TO COOK DOWN, SO I'LL SERVE THEM TO HIM HALF-COOKED!
AH!
HAVE SOME LEEKS!
FWAK
HOW ABOUT ANOTHER DRINK, TAKANE...
...
MR. SAIBARA! SIR!

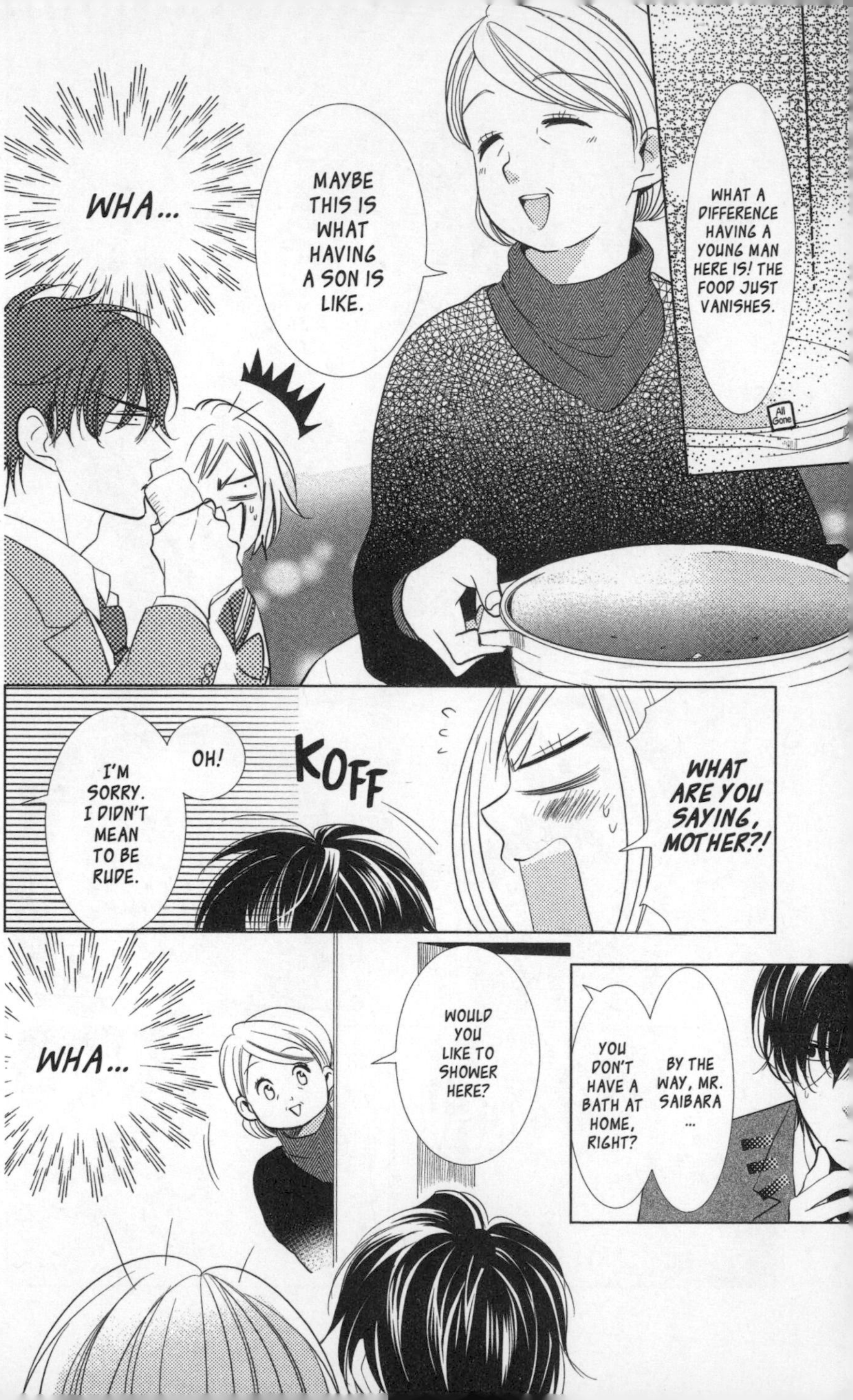
WHAT A DIFFERENCE HAVING A YOUNG MAN HERE IS! THE FOOD JUST VANISHES.
All Gone
MAYBE THIS IS WHAT HAVING A SON IS LIKE.
WHA...
WHAT ARE YOU SAYING, MOTHER?!
KOFF
OH!
I'M SORRY. I DIDN'T MEAN TO BE RUDE.
BY THE WAY, MR. SAIBARA ...
YOU DON'T HAVE A BATH AT HOME, RIGHT?
WOULD YOU LIKE TO SHOWER HERE?
WHA...

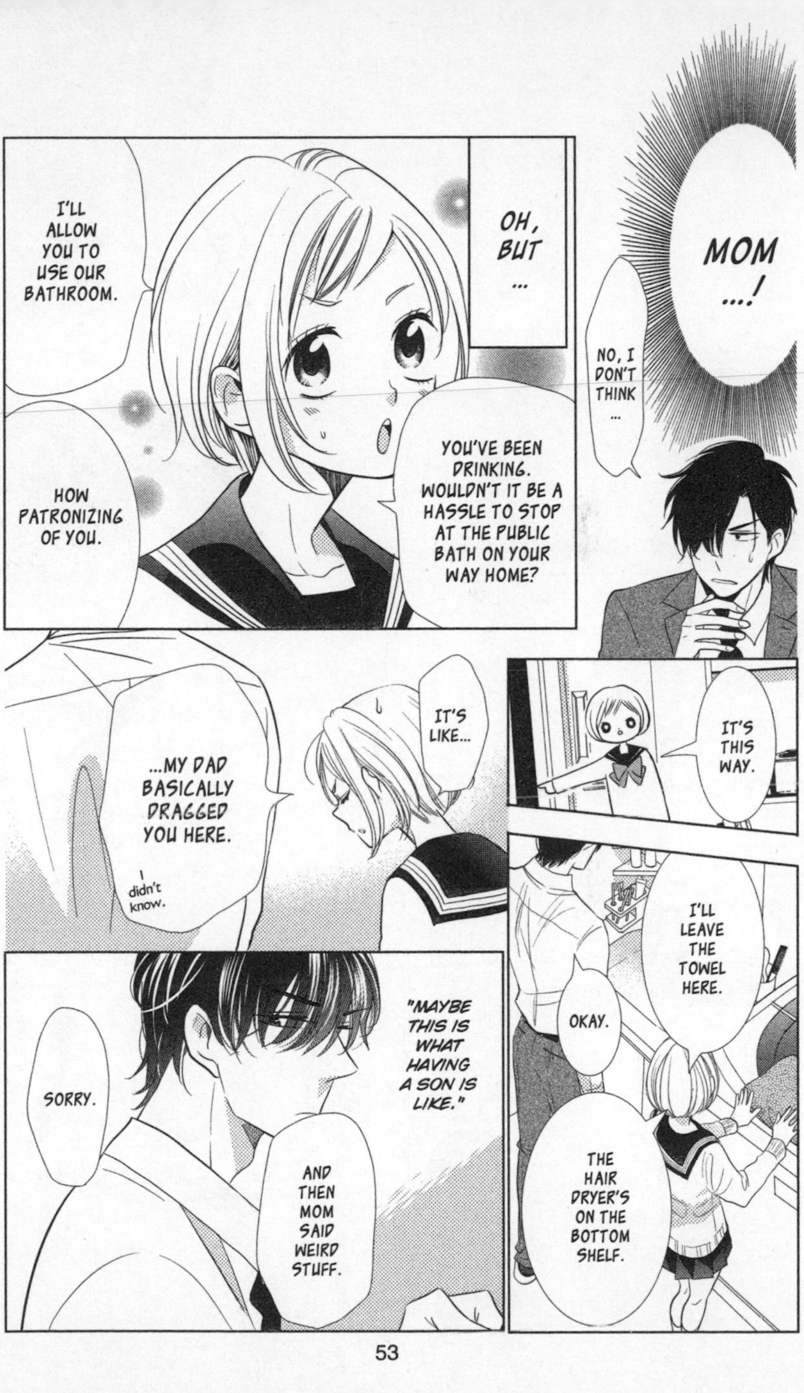
MOM ...!
NO, I DON'T THINK ...
OH, BUT ...
YOU'VE BEEN DRINKING. WOULDN'T IT BE A HASSLE TO STOP AT THE PUBLIC BATH ON YOUR WAY HOME?
I'LL ALLOW YOU TO USE OUR BATHROOM.
HOW PATRONIZING OF YOU.
IT'S THIS WAY.
I'LL LEAVE THE TOWEL HERE.
OKAY.
THE HAIR DRYER'S ON THE BOTTOM SHELF.
IT'S LIKE...
...MY DAD BASICALLY DRAGGED YOU HERE.
I didn't know.
"MAYBE THIS IS WHAT HAVING A SON IS LIKE."
AND THEN MOM SAID WEIRD STUFF.
SORRY.

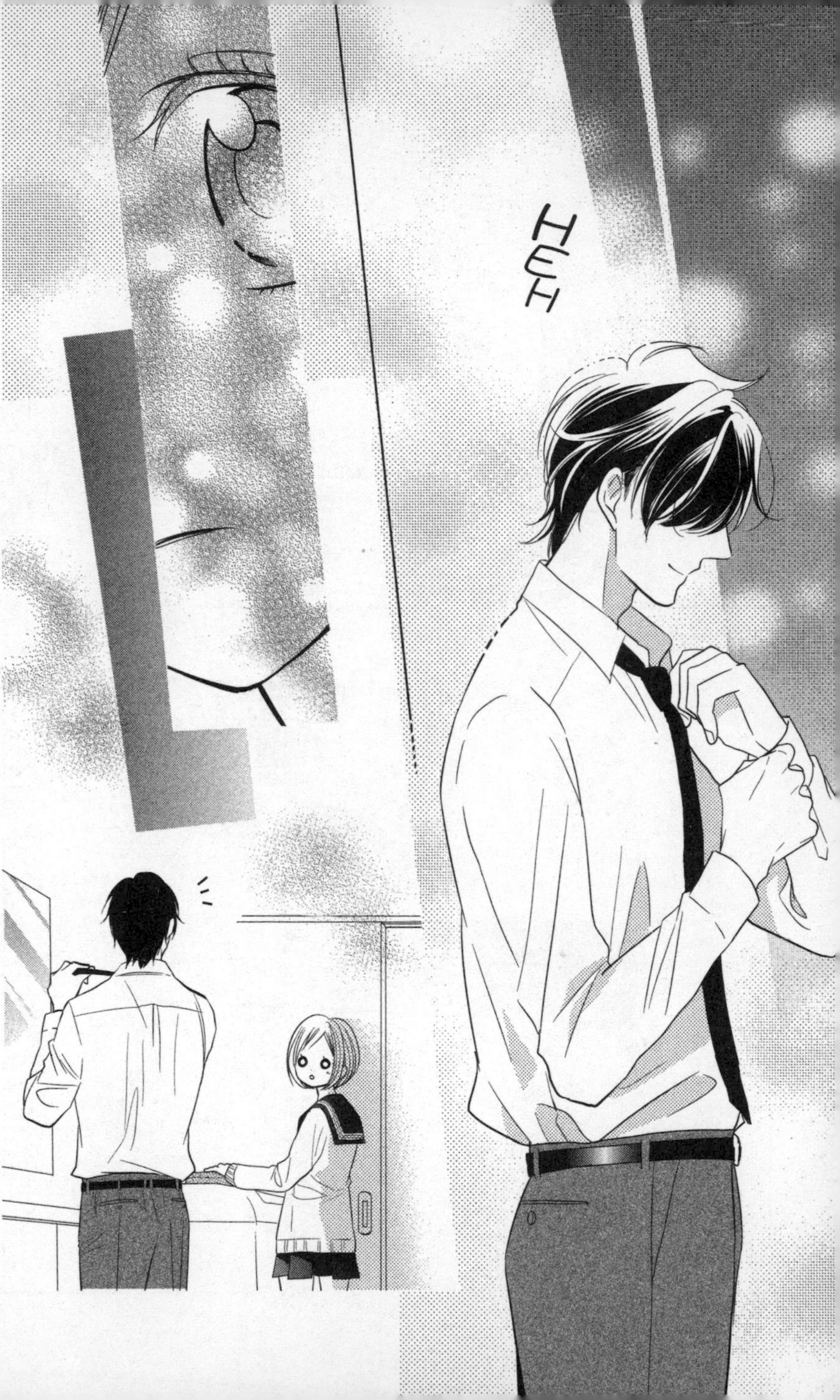
HEH

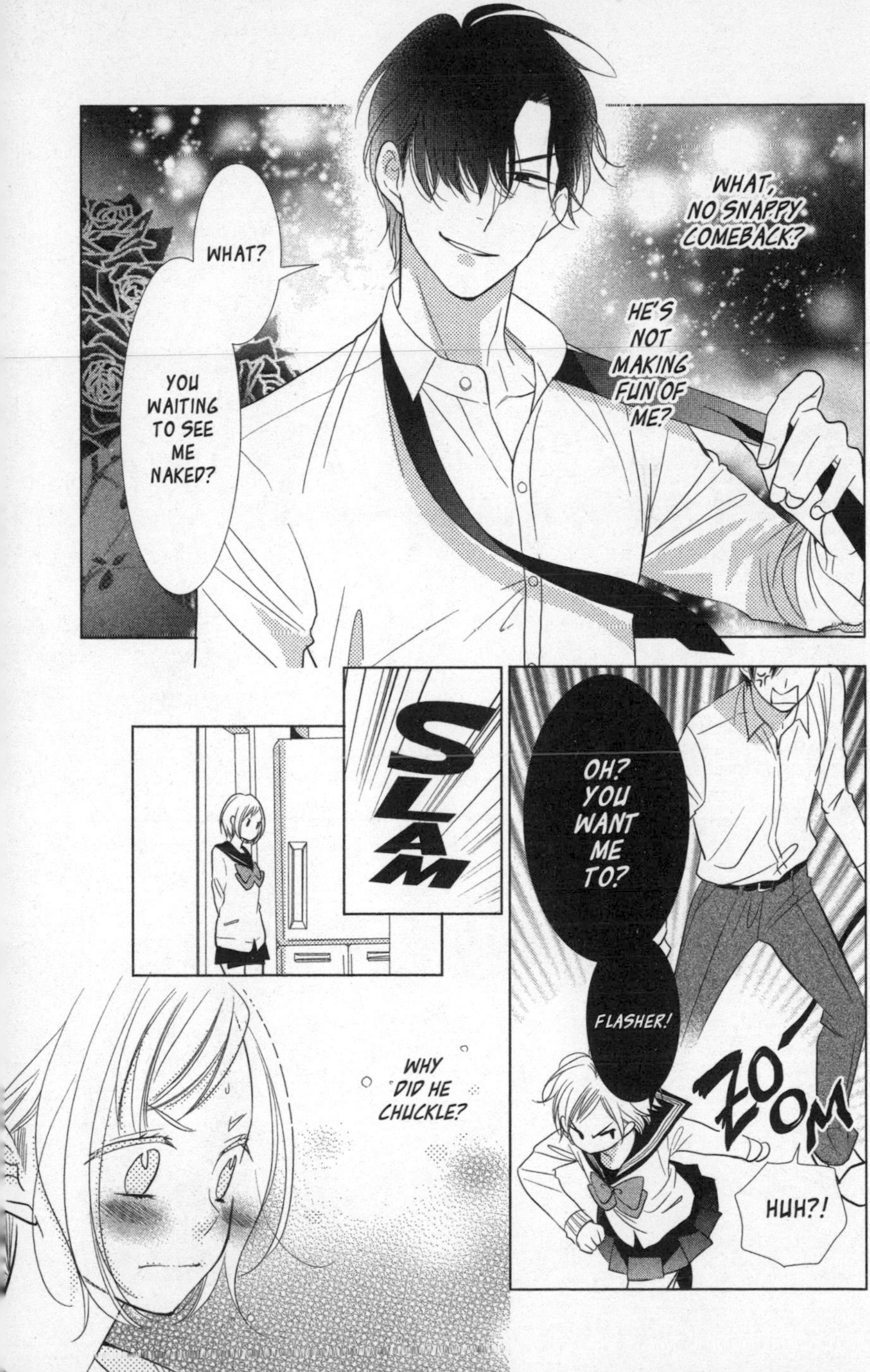
WHAT, NO SNAPPY COMEBACK?
HE'S NOT MAKING FUN OF ME?
WHAT?
YOU WAITING TO SEE ME NAKED?
OH? YOU WANT ME TO?
FLASHER!
ZOOM
HUH?!
SLAM
WHY DID HE CHUCKLE?

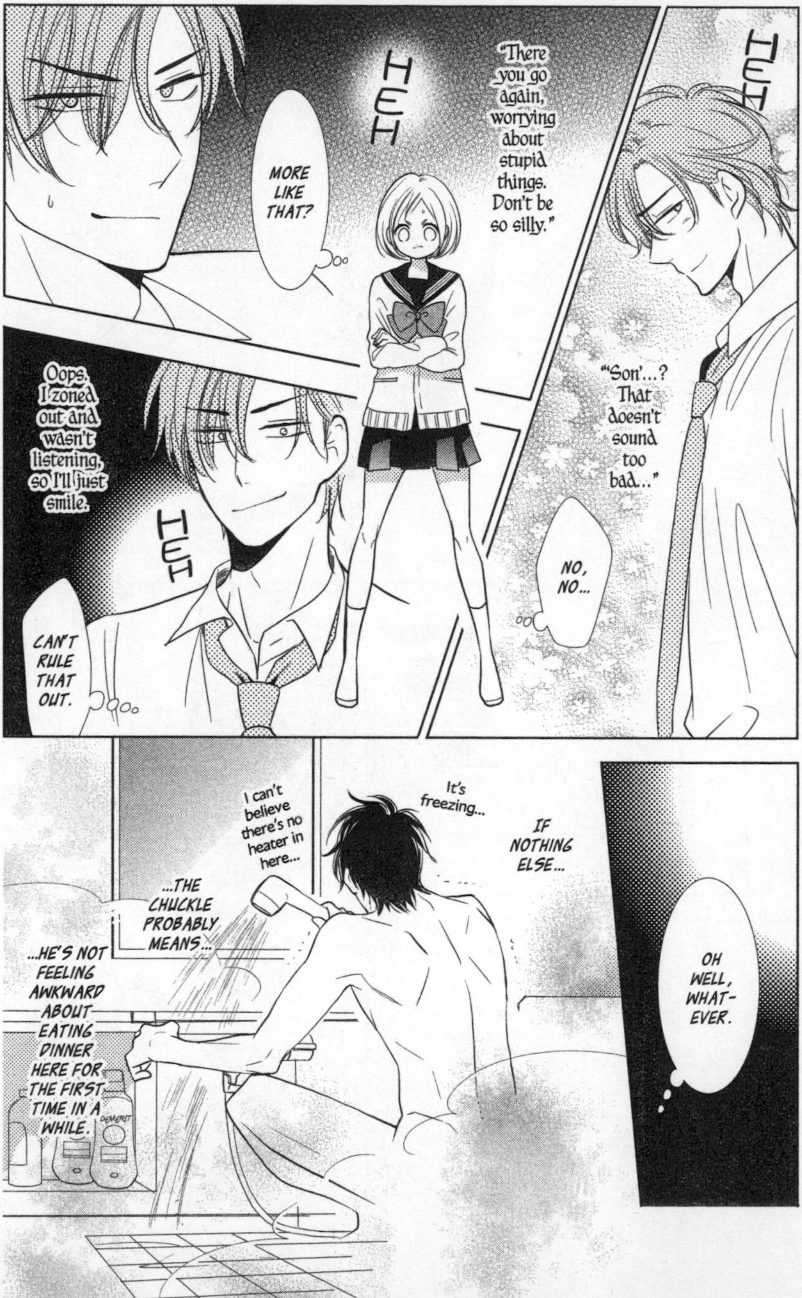
HEH
"Son'...? That doesn't sound too bad..."
NO, NO...
"There you go again, worrying about stupid things. Don't be so silly."
HEH
MORE LIKE THAT?
Oops. I zoned out and wasn't listening, so I'll just smile.
HEH
CAN'T RULE THAT OUT.
OH WELL, WHAT-EVER.
It's freezing...
I can't believe there's no heater in here...
IF NOTHING ELSE...
...THE CHUCKLE PROBABLY MEANS...
...HE'S NOT FEELING AWKWARD ABOUT EATING DINNER HERE FOR THE FIRST TIME IN A WHILE.
DEMERIT

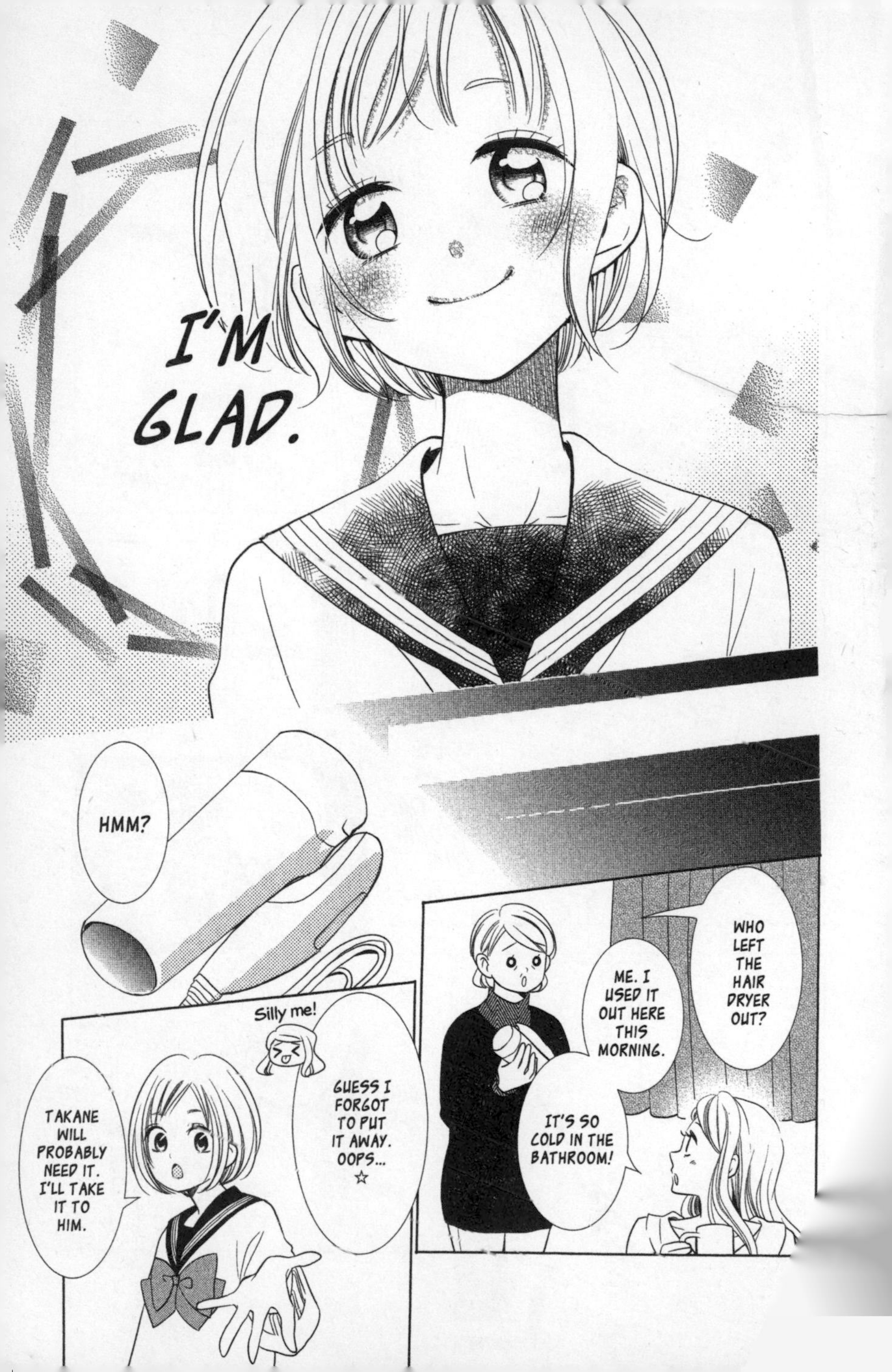
I'M GLAD.
WHO LEFT THE HAIR DRYER OUT?
ME. I USED IT OUT HERE THIS MORNING.
IT'S SO COLD IN THE BATHROOM!
HMM?
Silly me!
GUESS I FORGOT TO PUT IT AWAY. OOPS... ☆
TAKANE WILL PROBABLY NEED IT. I'LL TAKE IT TO HIM.

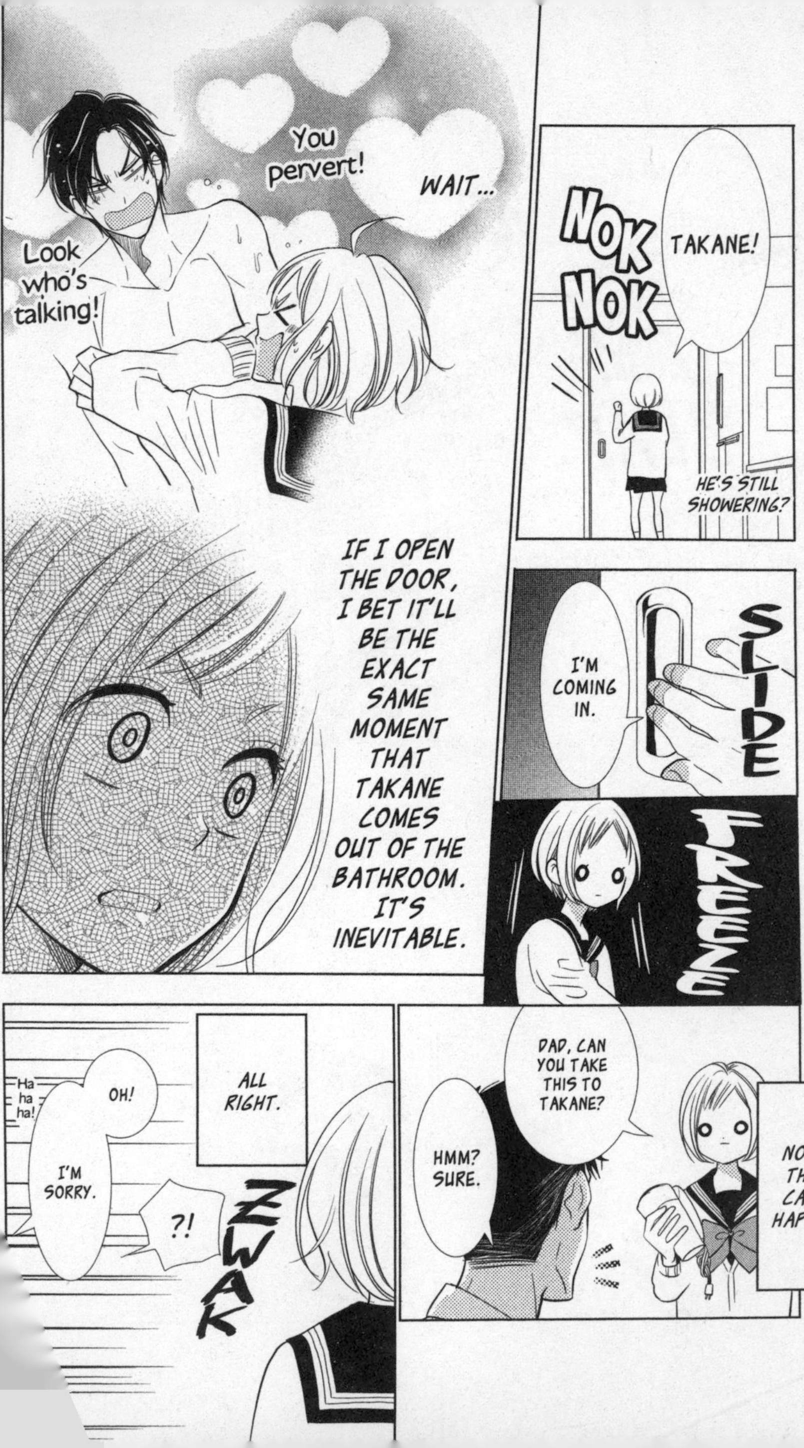
TAKANE!
NOK NOK
HE'S STILL SHOWERING?
I'M COMING IN.
SLIDE
FREEZE
WAIT...
You pervert!
Look who's talking!
IF I OPEN THE DOOR, I BET IT'LL BE THE EXACT SAME MOMENT THAT TAKANE COMES OUT OF THE BATHROOM. IT'S INEVITABLE.
NOPE, THAT CAN'T HAPPEN.
DAD, CAN YOU TAKE THIS TO TAKANE?
HMM? SURE.
ALL RIGHT.
OH!
Ha ha ha!
I'M SORRY.
?!
ZWAK

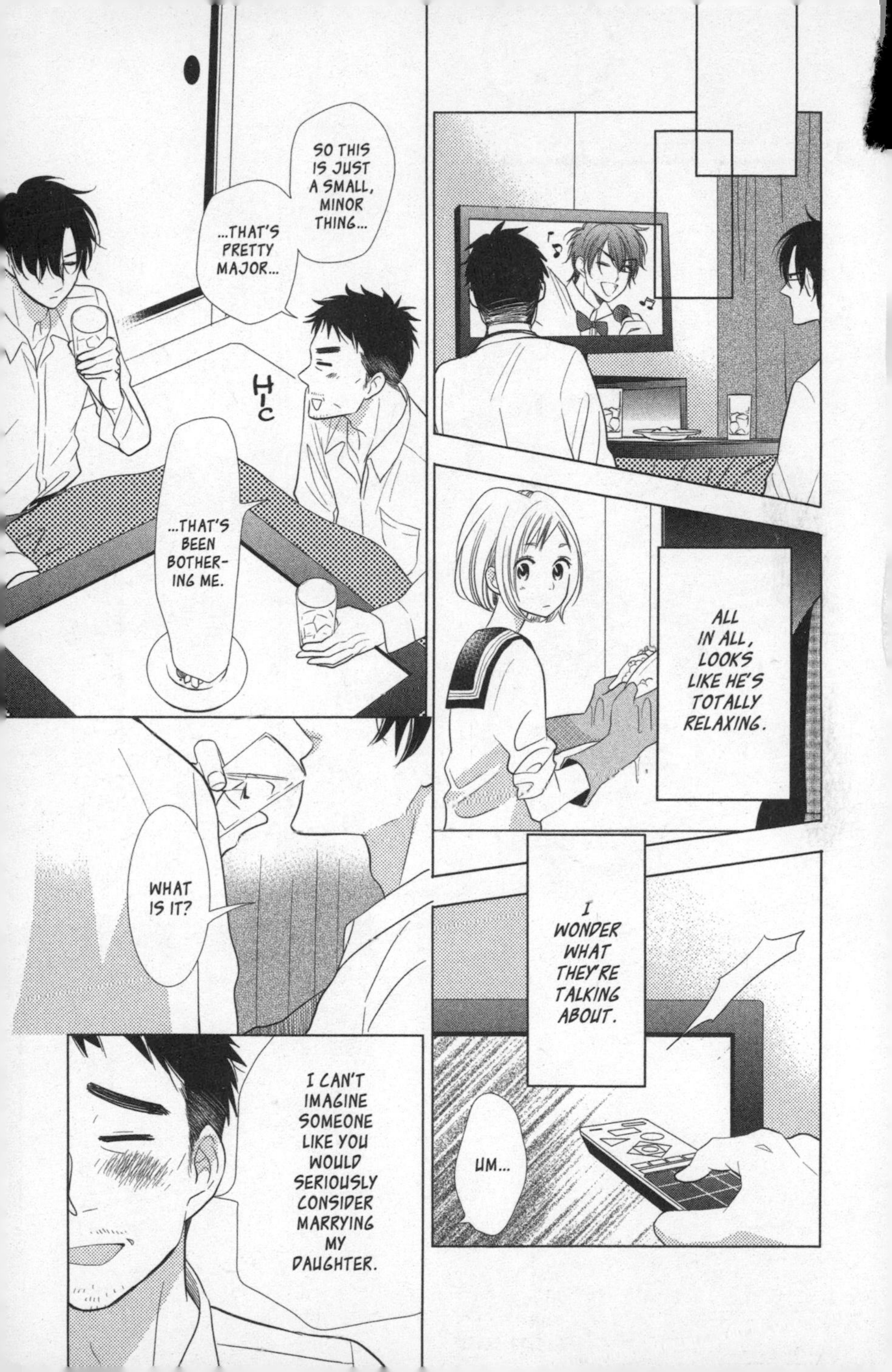
ALL IN ALL, LOOKS LIKE HE'S TOTALLY RELAXING.
SO THIS IS JUST A SMALL, MINOR THING...
...THAT'S PRETTY MAJOR...
HIC
...THAT'S BEEN BOTHERING ME.
I WONDER WHAT THEY'RE TALKING ABOUT.
UM...
WHAT IS IT?
I CAN'T IMAGINE SOMEONE LIKE YOU WOULD SERIOUSLY CONSIDER MARRYING MY DAUGHTER.

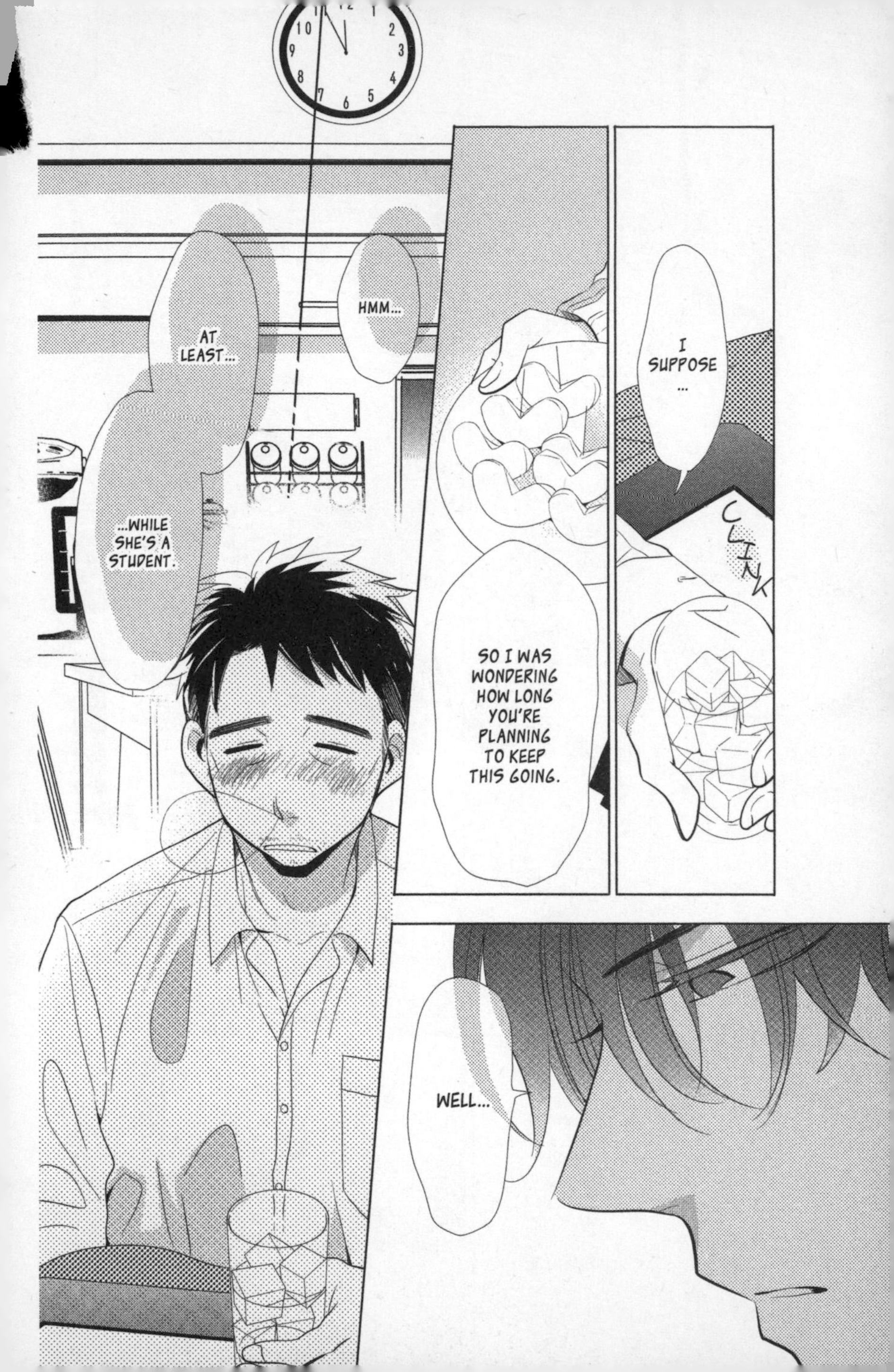

I SUPPOSE ...
CLINK
SO I WAS WONDERING HOW LONG YOU'RE PLANNING TO KEEP THIS GOING.
WELL...
HMM...
AT LEAST...
...WHILE SHE'S A STUDENT.

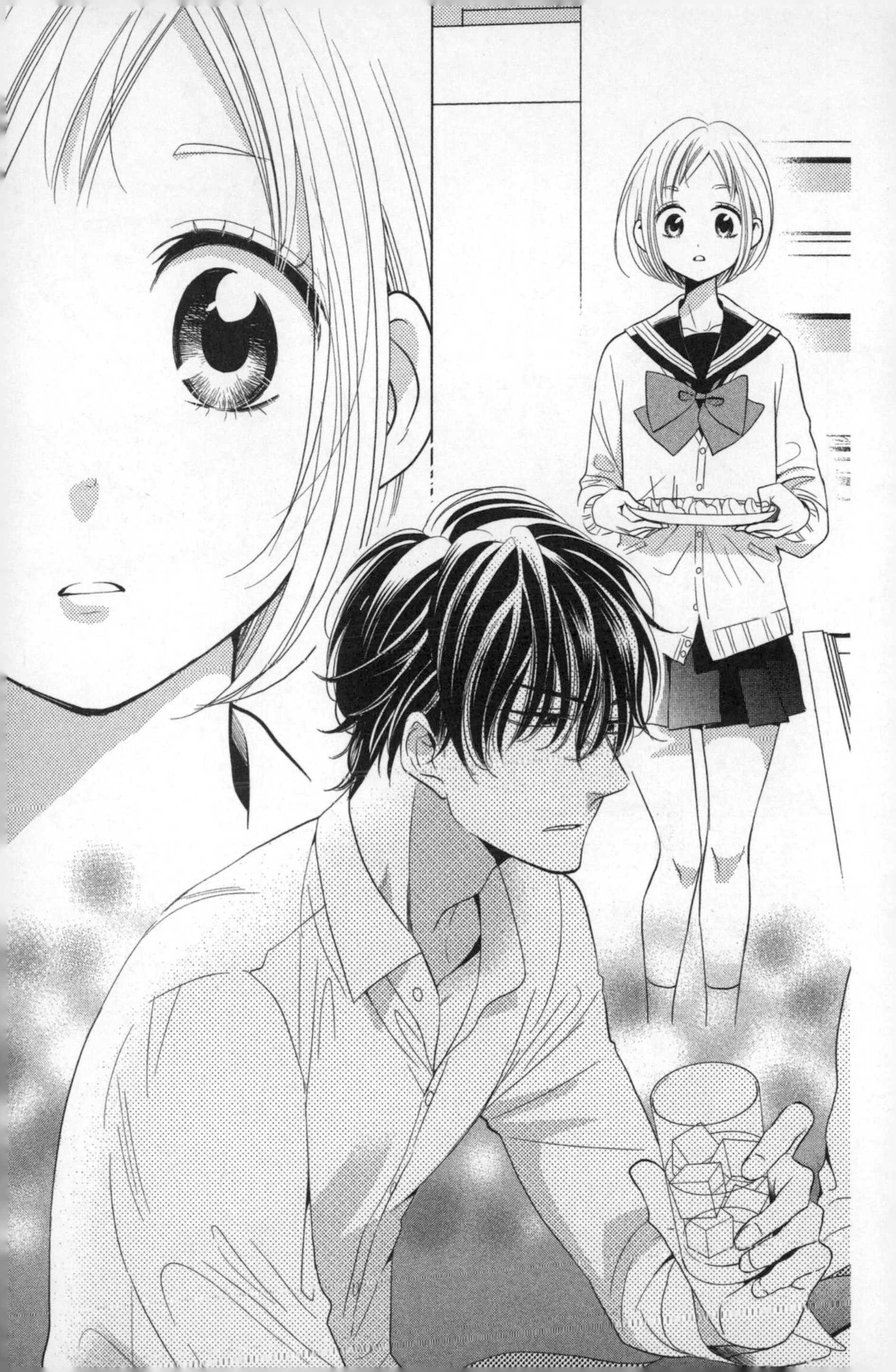

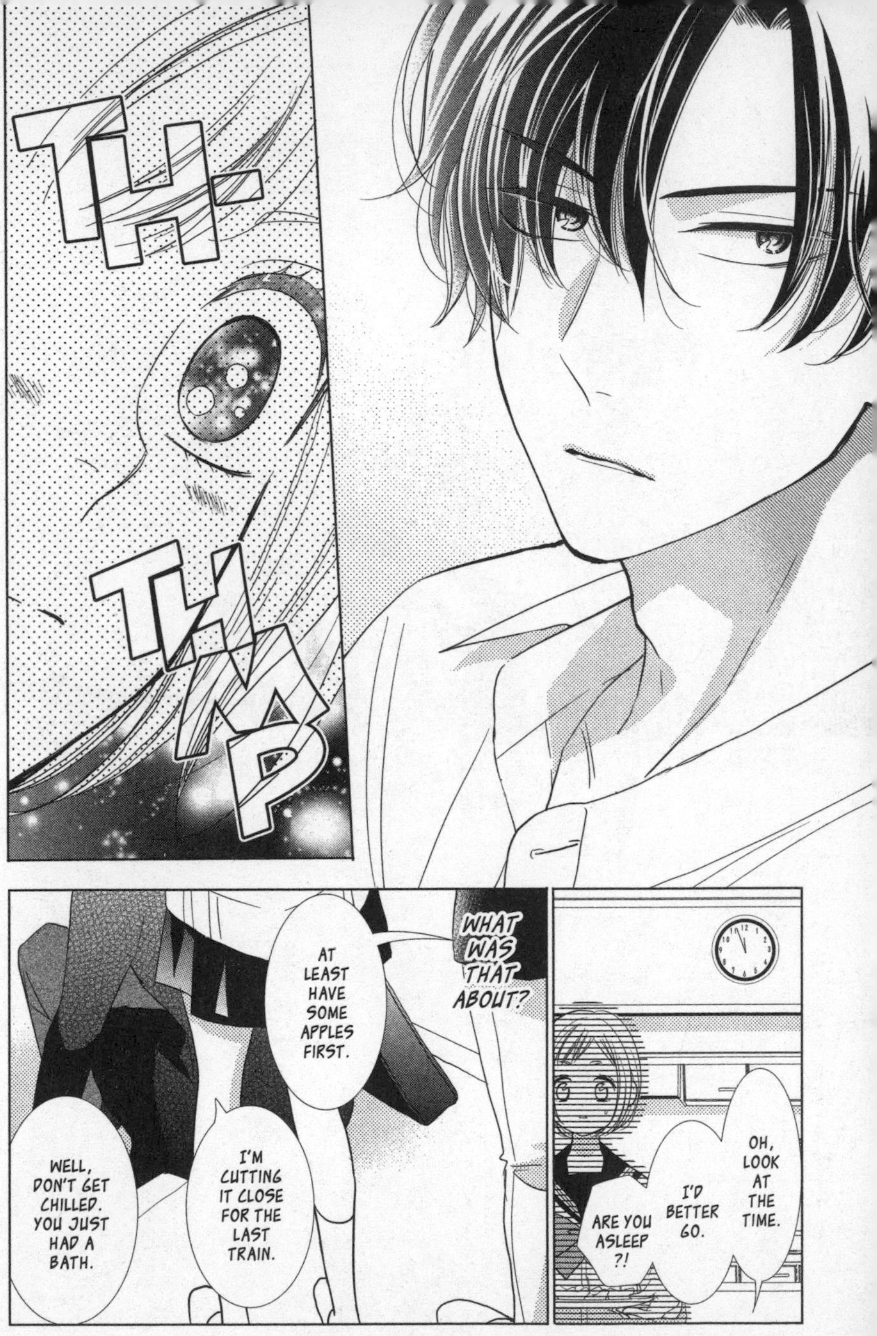
TH-
THUMP
OH, LOOK AT THE TIME.
I'D BETTER GO.
ARE YOU ASLEEP?!
WHAT WAS THAT ABOUT?
AT LEAST HAVE SOME APPLES FIRST.
I'M CUTTING IT CLOSE FOR THE LAST TRAIN.
WELL, DON'T GET CHILLED. YOU JUST HAD A BATH.

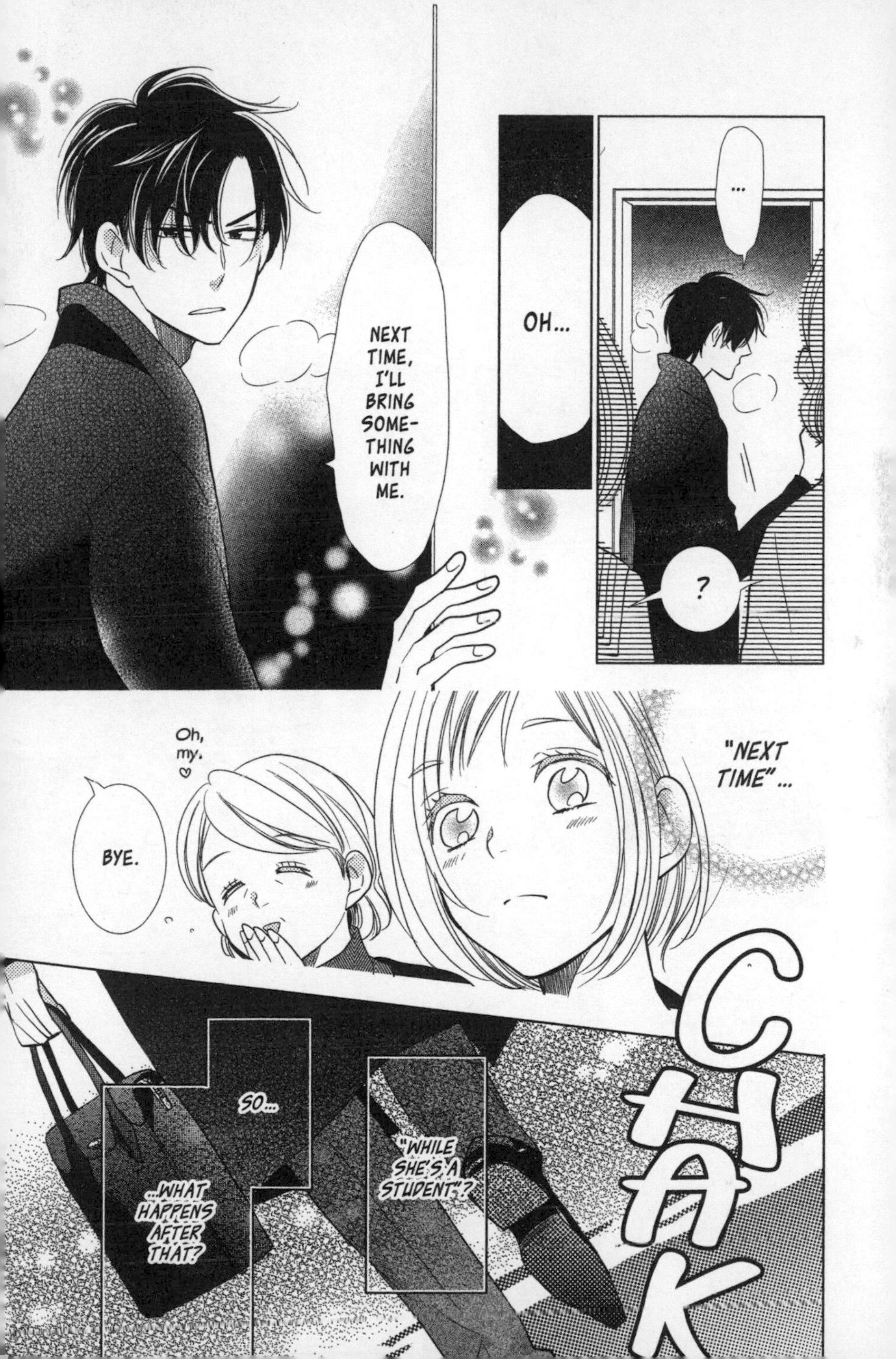
...
?
OH...
NEXT TIME, I'LL BRING SOMETHING WITH ME.
"NEXT TIME"...
Oh, my. ♡
BYE.
CHAK
"WHILE SHE'S A STUDENT"?
SO...
...WHAT HAPPENS AFTER THAT?

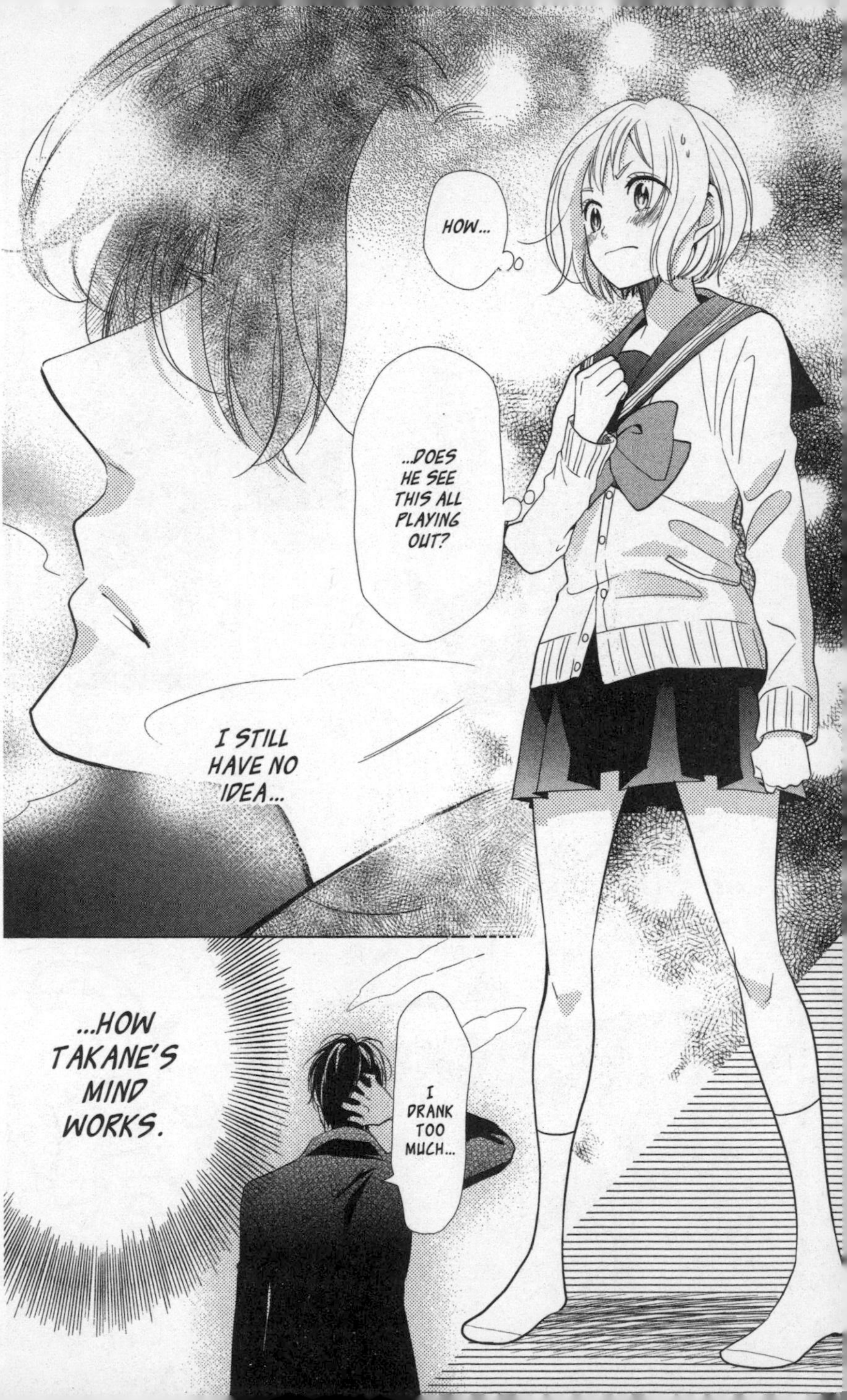
HOW...
...DOES HE SEE THIS ALL PLAYING OUT?
I STILL HAVE NO IDEA...
...HOW TAKANE'S MIND WORKS.
I DRANK TOO MUCH...

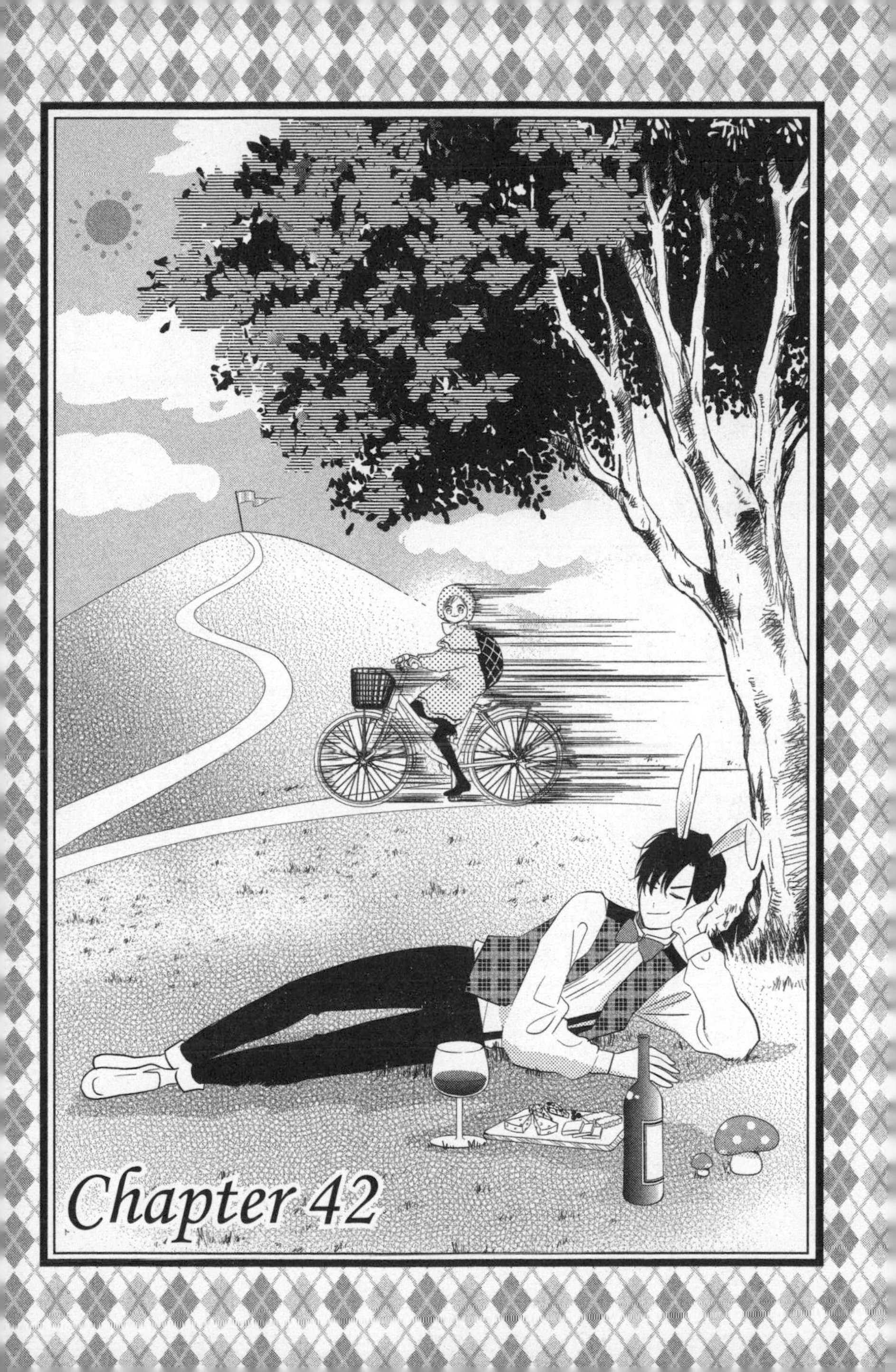
Chapter 42

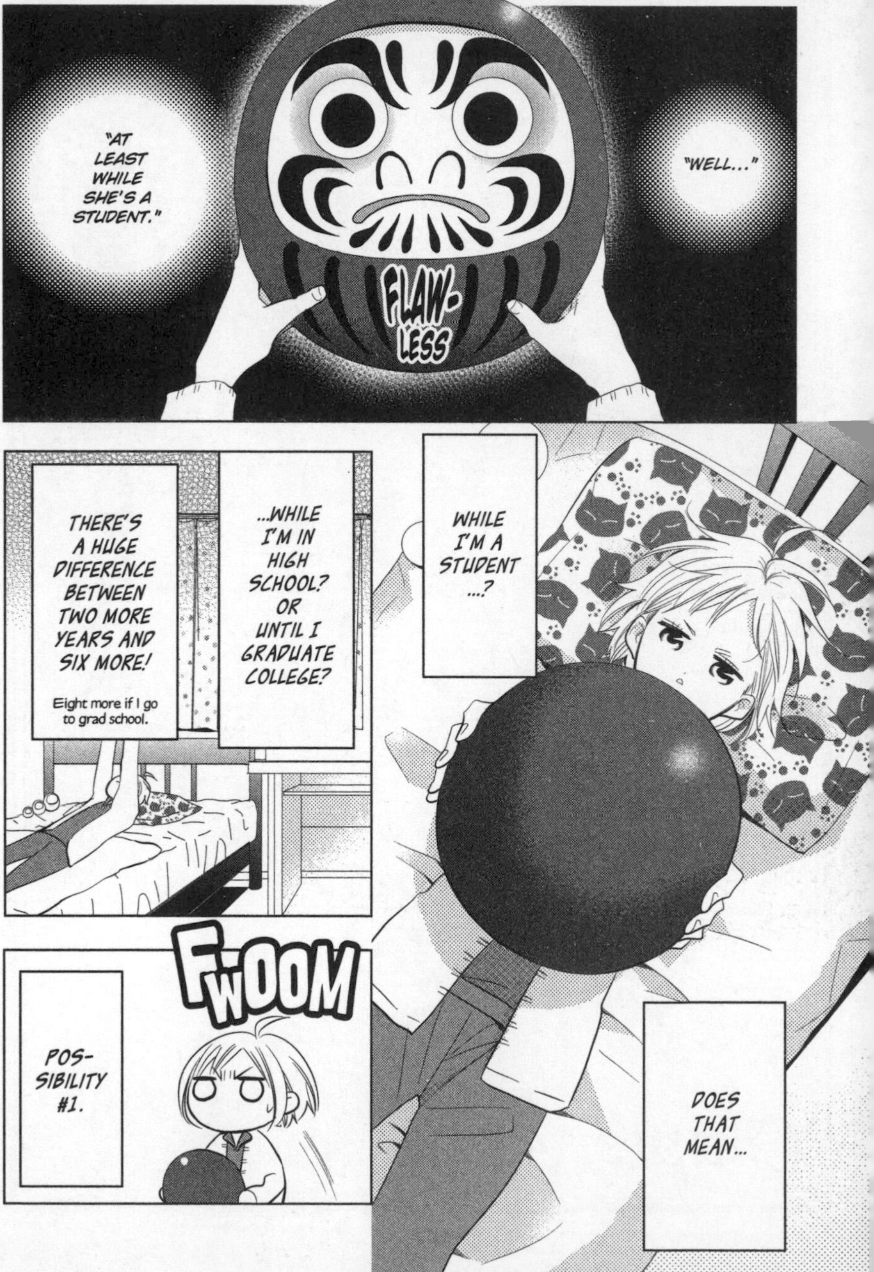
"WELL..."
"AT LEAST WHILE SHE'S A STUDENT."
FLAW-LESS
WHILE I'M A STUDENT ...?
DOES THAT MEAN...
...WHILE I'M IN HIGH SCHOOL? OR UNTIL I GRADUATE COLLEGE?
THERE'S A HUGE DIFFERENCE BETWEEN TWO MORE YEARS AND SIX MORE!
Eight more if I go to grad school.
FWOOM
POS-SIBILITY #1.

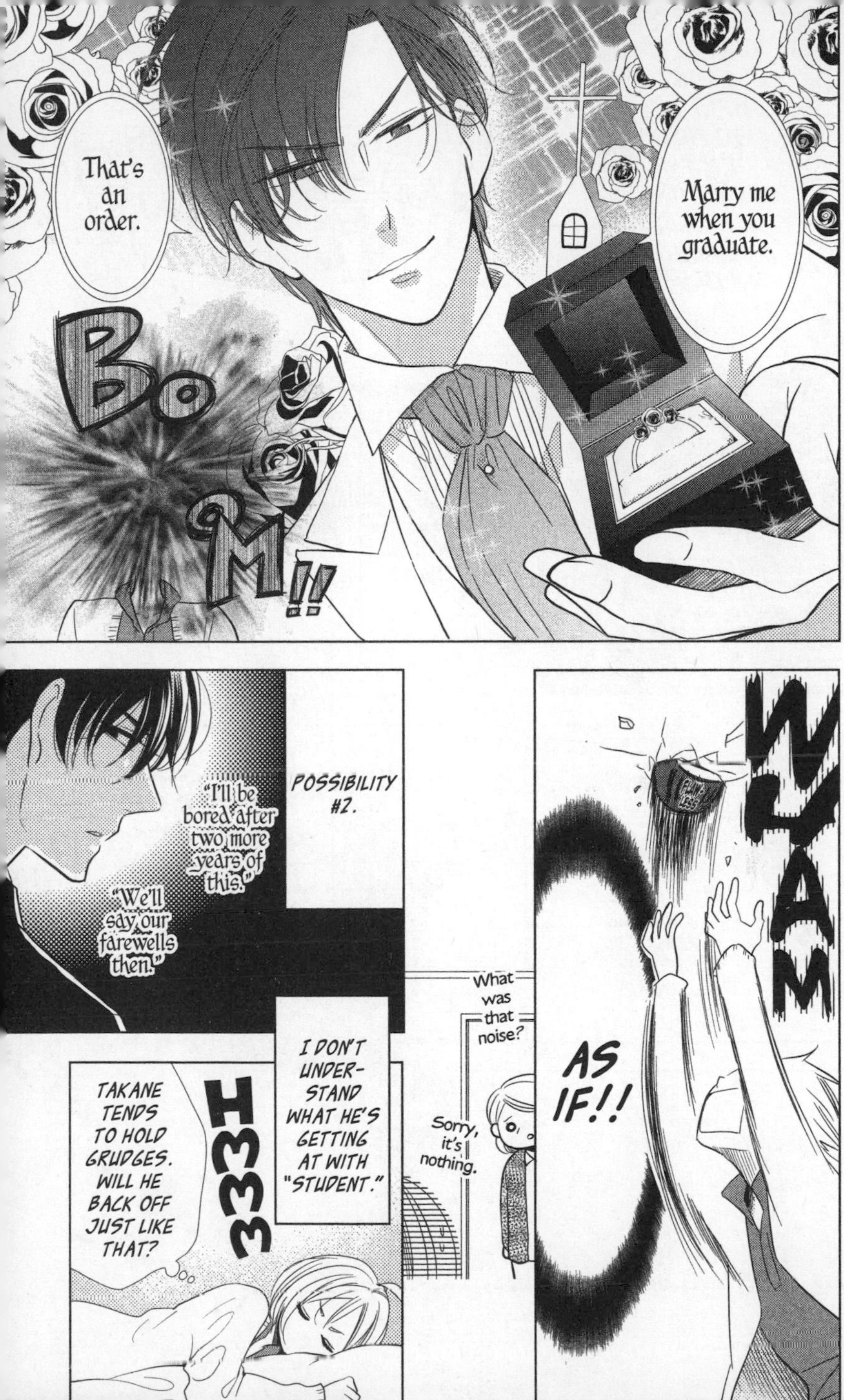
Marry me when you graduate.
That's an order.
BOOM!!
WHAM
AS IF!!
What was that noise?
Sorry, it's nothing.
POSSIBILITY #2.
"I'll be bored after two more years of this."
"We'll say our farewells then."
I DON'T UNDER-STAND WHAT HE'S GETTING AT WITH "STUDENT."
HMMM
TAKANE TENDS TO HOLD GRUDGES. WILL HE BACK OFF JUST LIKE THAT?

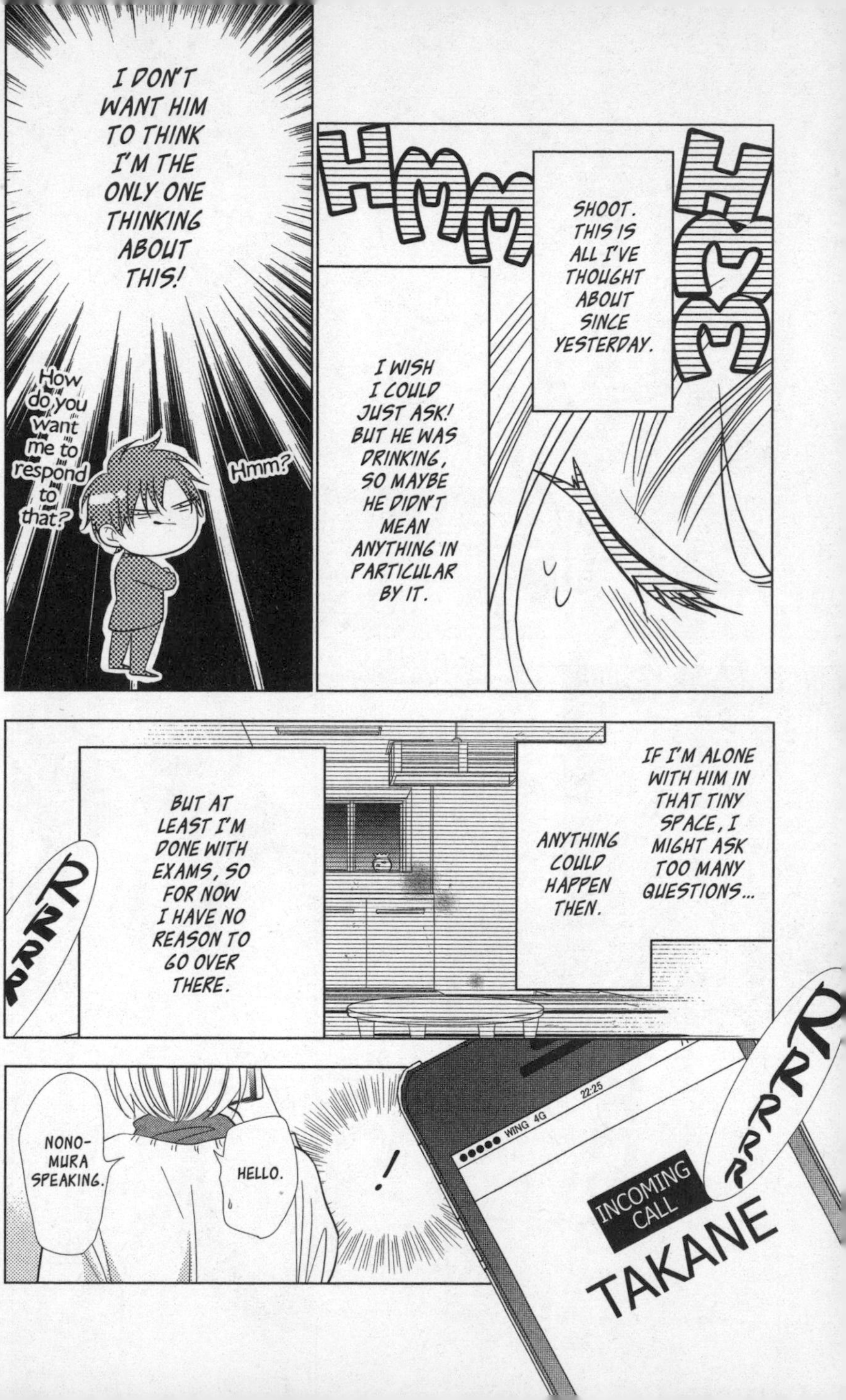
HMMM
HMMM
SHOOT. THIS IS ALL I'VE THOUGHT ABOUT SINCE YESTERDAY.
I WISH I COULD JUST ASK! BUT HE WAS DRINKING, SO MAYBE HE DIDN'T MEAN ANYTHING IN PARTICULAR BY IT.
I DON'T WANT HIM TO THINK I'M THE ONLY ONE THINKING ABOUT THIS!
Hmm?
How do you want me to respond to that?
IF I'M ALONE WITH HIM IN THAT TINY SPACE, I MIGHT ASK TOO MANY QUESTIONS...
ANYTHING COULD HAPPEN THEN.
BUT AT LEAST I'M DONE WITH EXAMS, SO FOR NOW I HAVE NO REASON TO GO OVER THERE.
RRRR
RRRRR
WING 4G
22:25
INCOMING CALL
TAKANE
!
HELLO.
NONO-MURA SPEAKING.

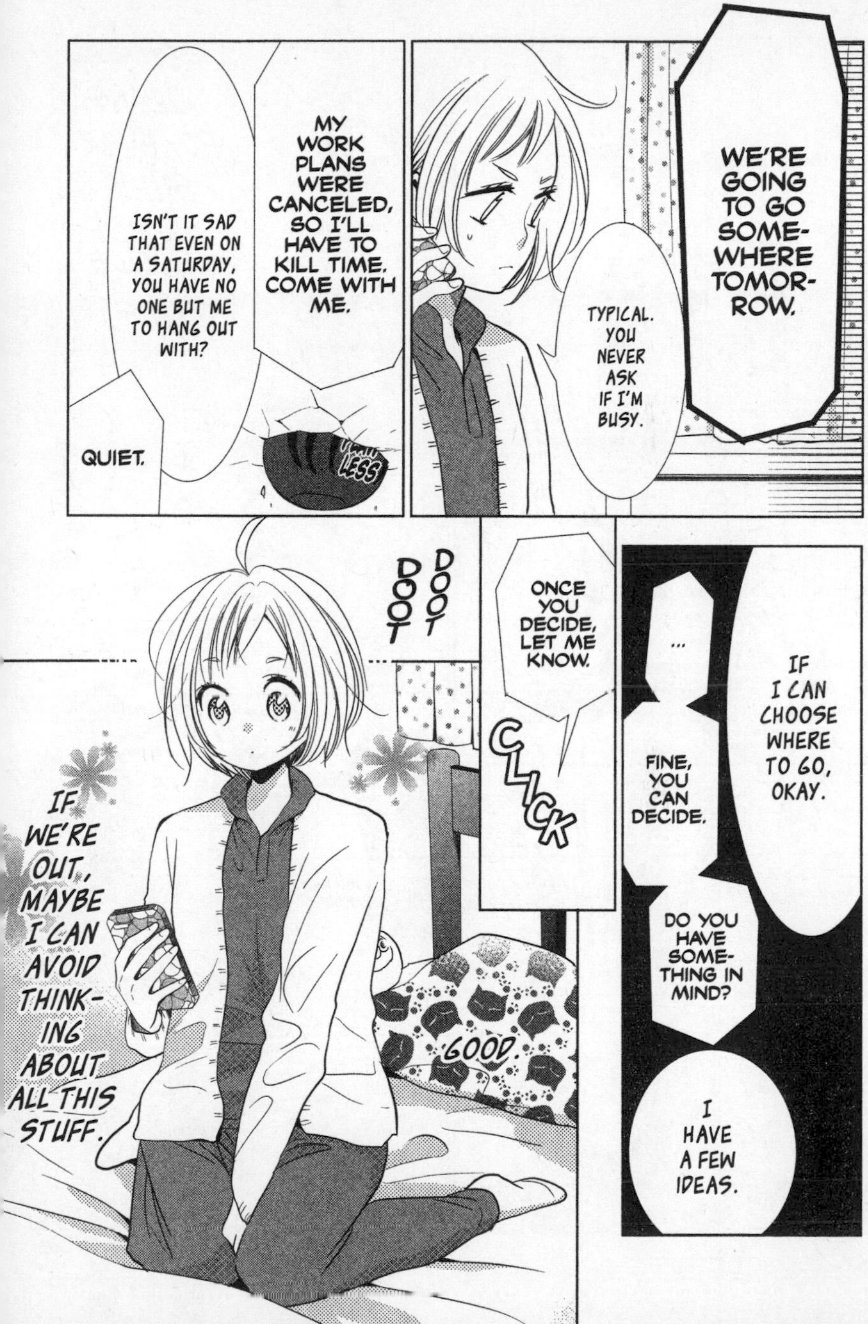
WE'RE GOING TO GO SOME-WHERE TOMOR-ROW.
TYPICAL. YOU NEVER ASK IF I'M BUSY.
MY WORK PLANS WERE CANCELED, SO I'LL HAVE TO KILL TIME. COME WITH ME.
ISN'T IT SAD THAT EVEN ON A SATURDAY, YOU HAVE NO ONE BUT ME TO HANG OUT WITH?
QUIET.
IF I CAN CHOOSE WHERE TO GO, OKAY.
...
FINE, YOU CAN DECIDE.
DO YOU HAVE SOME-THING IN MIND?
I HAVE A FEW IDEAS.
ONCE YOU DECIDE, LET ME KNOW.
CLICK
DOOT DOOT
GOOD.
IF WE'RE OUT, MAYBE I CAN AVOID THINK-ING ABOUT ALL THIS STUFF.

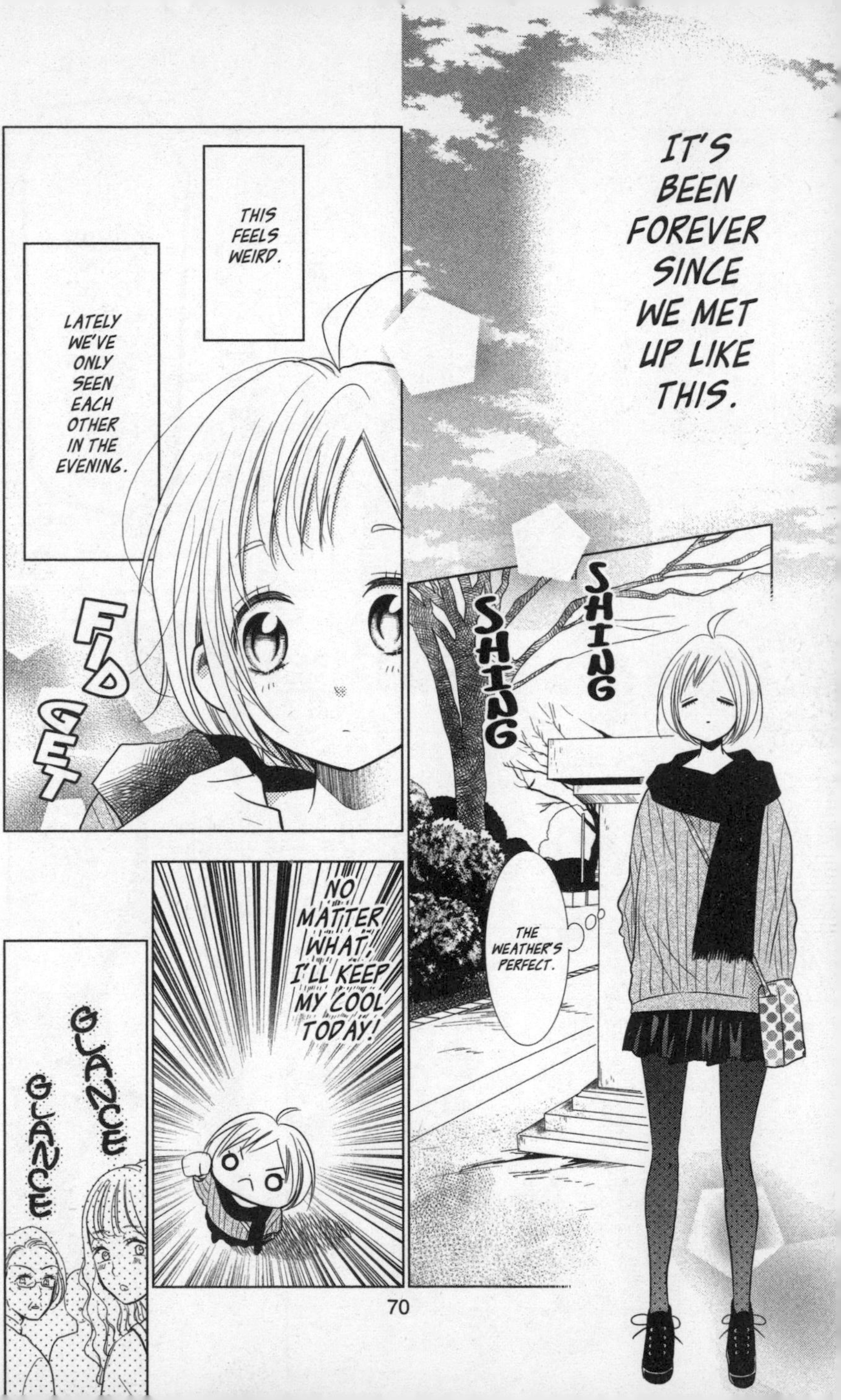
IT'S BEEN FOREVER SINCE WE MET UP LIKE THIS.
SHING SHING
THE WEATHER'S PERFECT.
THIS FEELS WEIRD.
LATELY WE'VE ONLY SEEN EACH OTHER IN THE EVENING.
FIDGET
NO MATTER WHAT, I'LL KEEP MY COOL TODAY!
GLANCE GLANCE

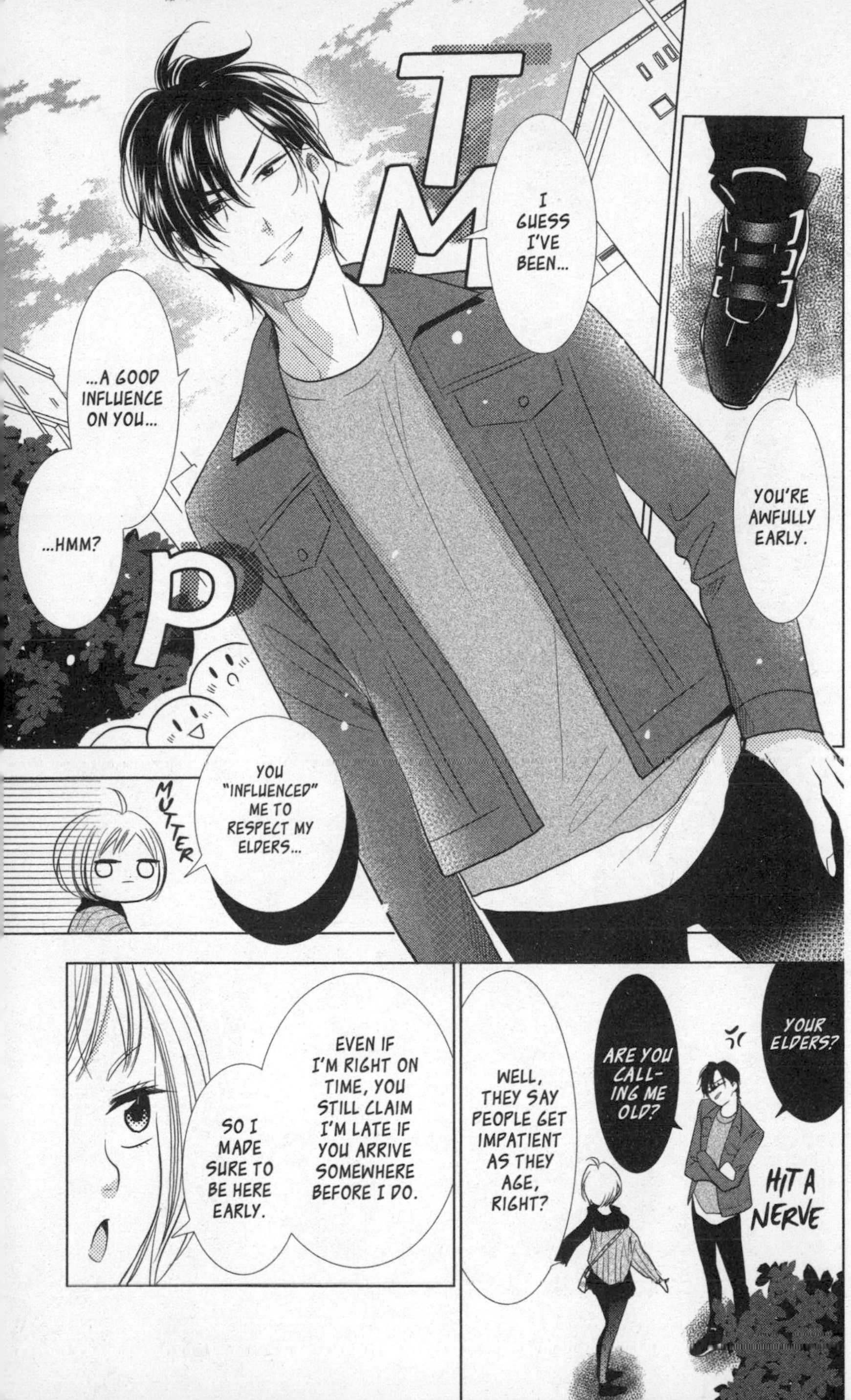
YOU'RE AWFULLY EARLY.
I GUESS I'VE BEEN...
...A GOOD INFLUENCE ON YOU...
...HMM?
TMP
YOU "INFLUENCED" ME TO RESPECT MY ELDERS...
MUTTER
YOUR ELDERS?
ARE YOU CALLING ME OLD?
HIT A NERVE
WELL, THEY SAY PEOPLE GET IMPATIENT AS THEY AGE, RIGHT?
EVEN IF I'M RIGHT ON TIME, YOU STILL CLAIM I'M LATE IF YOU ARRIVE SOMEWHERE BEFORE I DO.
SO I MADE SURE TO BE HERE EARLY.

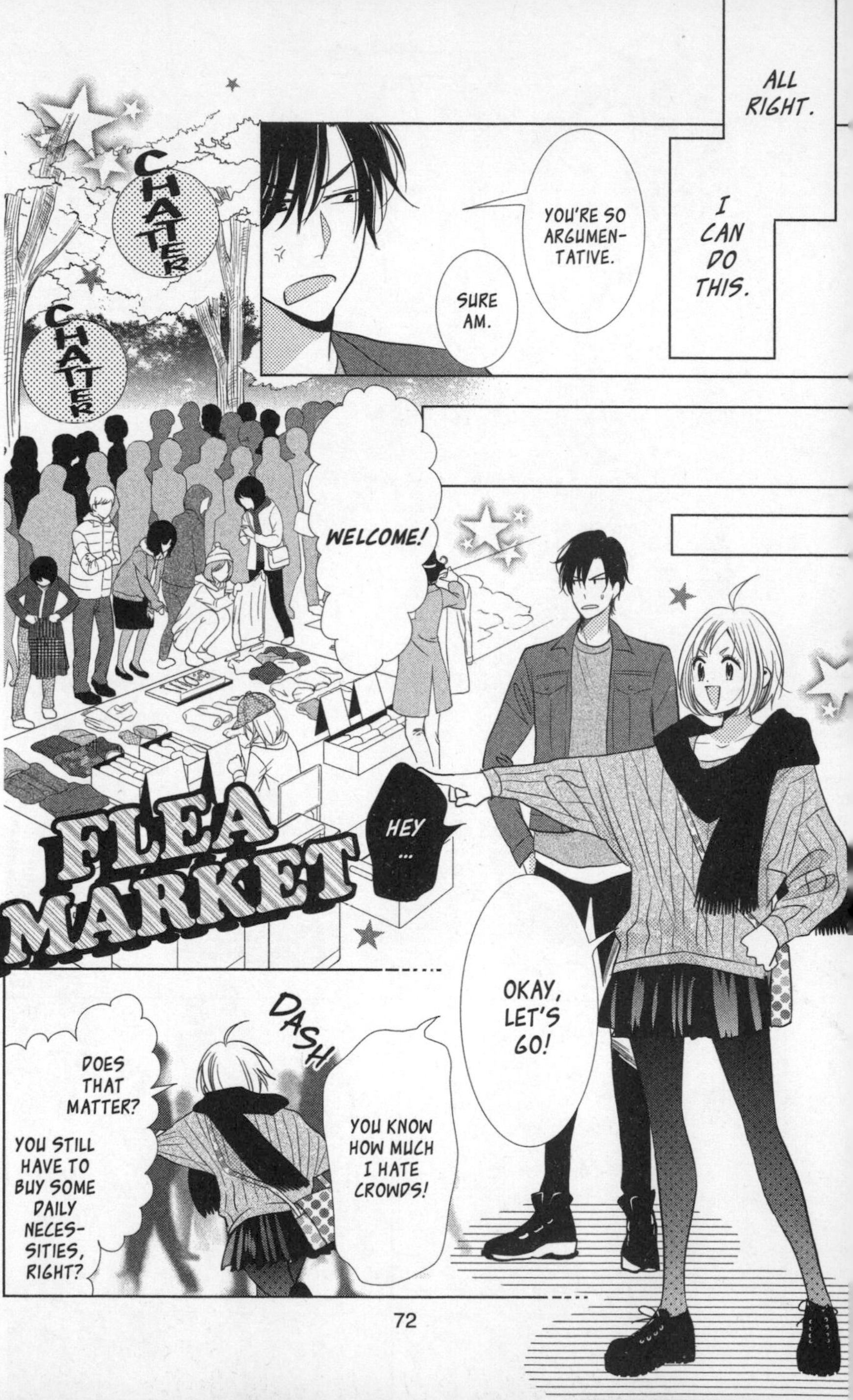
ALL RIGHT.
I CAN DO THIS.
YOU'RE SO ARGUMENTATIVE.
SURE AM.
CHATTER
CHATTER
WELCOME!
HEY...
OKAY, LET'S GO!
FLEA MARKET
DASH
YOU KNOW HOW MUCH I HATE CROWDS!
DOES THAT MATTER?
YOU STILL HAVE TO BUY SOME DAILY NECESSITIES, RIGHT?

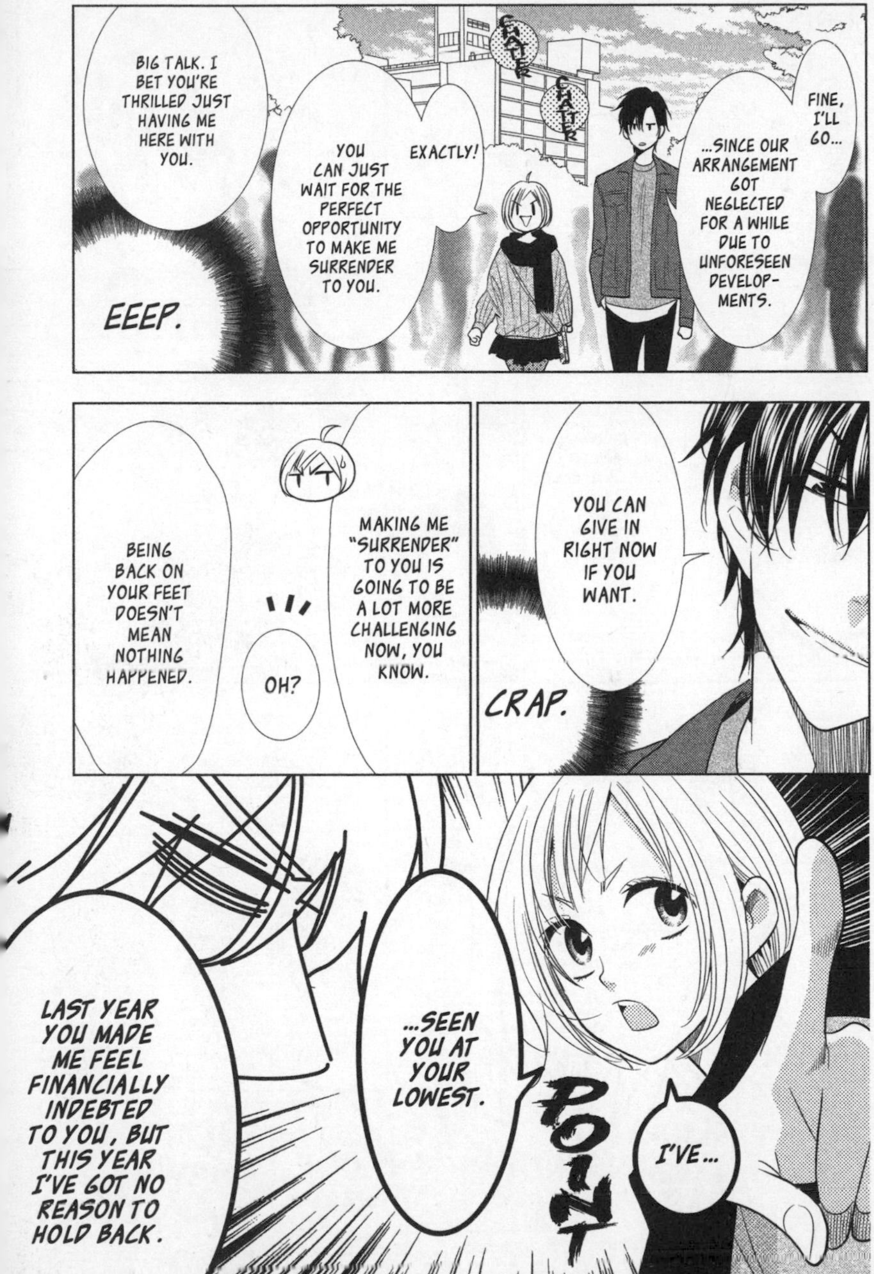
FINE, I'LL GO...
...SINCE OUR ARRANGEMENT GOT NEGLECTED FOR A WHILE DUE TO UNFORESEEN DEVELOPMENTS.
CHATTER
CHATTER
EXACTLY!
YOU CAN JUST WAIT FOR THE PERFECT OPPORTUNITY TO MAKE ME SURRENDER TO YOU.
BIG TALK. I BET YOU'RE THRILLED JUST HAVING ME HERE WITH YOU.
EEEP.
YOU CAN GIVE IN RIGHT NOW IF YOU WANT.
CRAP.
MAKING ME "SURRENDER" TO YOU IS GOING TO BE A LOT MORE CHALLENGING NOW, YOU KNOW.
OH?
BEING BACK ON YOUR FEET DOESN'T MEAN NOTHING HAPPENED.
I'VE...
POINT
...SEEN YOU AT YOUR LOWEST.
LAST YEAR YOU MADE ME FEEL FINANCIALLY INDEBTED TO YOU, BUT THIS YEAR I'VE GOT NO REASON TO HOLD BACK.

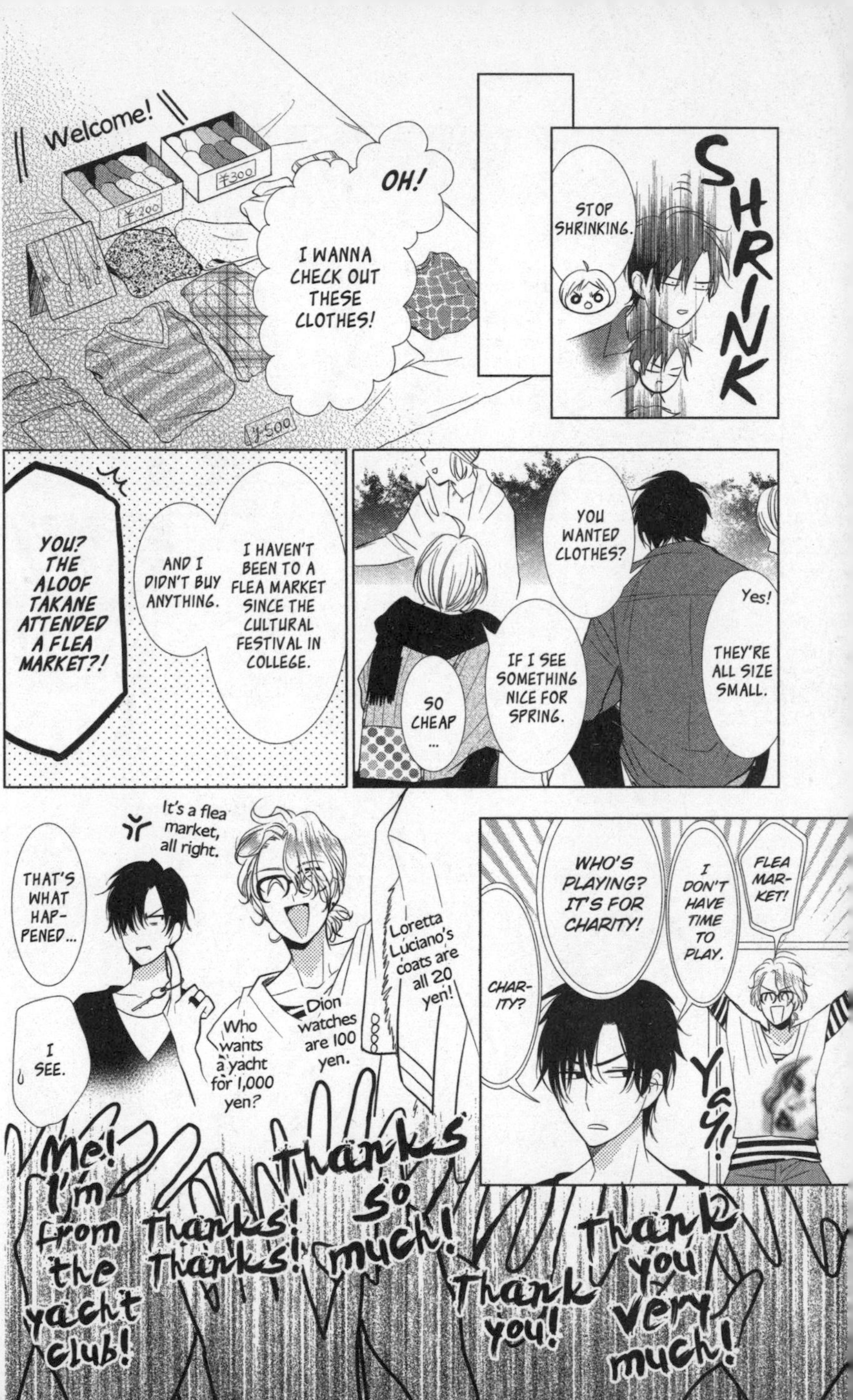
SHRINK
STOP SHRINKING.
Welcome!
OH!
I WANNA CHECK OUT THESE CLOTHES!
¥300
¥200
¥500
YOU WANTED CLOTHES?
Yes!
THEY'RE ALL SIZE SMALL.
IF I SEE SOMETHING NICE FOR SPRING.
SO CHEAP ...
I HAVEN'T BEEN TO A FLEA MARKET SINCE THE CULTURAL FESTIVAL IN COLLEGE.
AND I DIDN'T BUY ANYTHING.
YOU? THE ALOOF TAKANE ATTENDED A FLEA MARKET?!
FLEA MAR-KET!
I DON'T HAVE TIME TO PLAY.
WHO'S PLAYING? IT'S FOR CHARITY!
CHAR-ITY?
YES!
It's a flea market, all right.
THAT'S WHAT HAP-PENED...
Loretta Luciano's coats are all 20 yen!
Dion watches are 100 yen.
Who wants a yacht for 1,000 yen?
I SEE.
Thank you very much!
Thank you!
Thanks so much!
Thanks! Thanks!
Me! I'm from the yacht club!

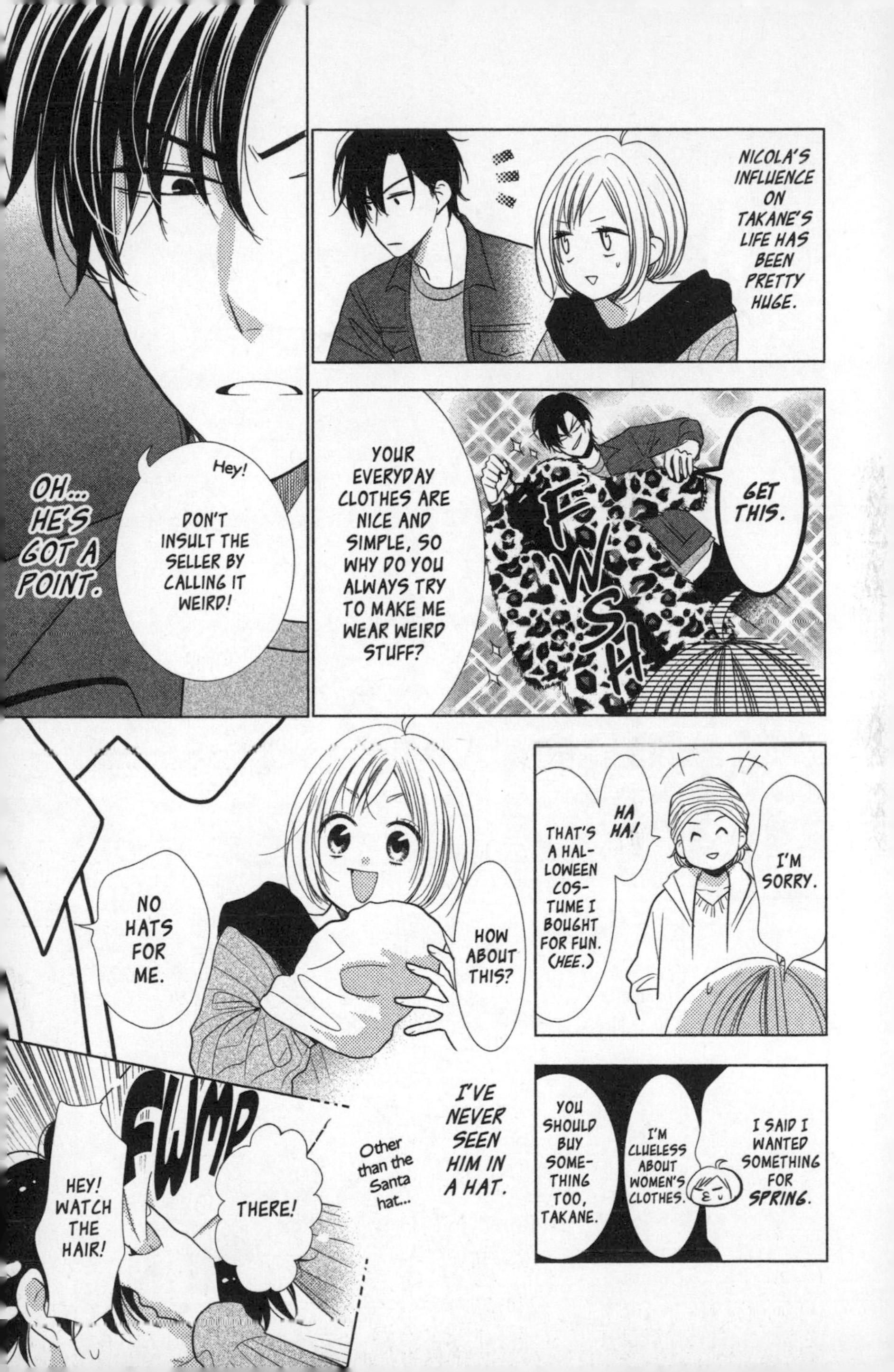
NICOLA'S INFLUENCE ON TAKANE'S LIFE HAS BEEN PRETTY HUGE.
GET THIS.
FWSH
YOUR EVERYDAY CLOTHES ARE NICE AND SIMPLE, SO WHY DO YOU ALWAYS TRY TO MAKE ME WEAR WEIRD STUFF?
Hey!
DON'T INSULT THE SELLER BY CALLING IT WEIRD!
OH... HE'S GOT A POINT.
I'M SORRY.
HA HA!
THAT'S A HALLOWEEN COS-TUME I BOUGHT FOR FUN. (HEE.)
I SAID I WANTED SOMETHING FOR SPRING.
I'M CLUELESS ABOUT WOMEN'S CLOTHES.
YOU SHOULD BUY SOME-THING TOO, TAKANE.
HOW ABOUT THIS?
NO HATS FOR ME.
I'VE NEVER SEEN HIM IN A HAT.
Other than the Santa hat...
THERE!
FWUMP
HEY! WATCH THE HAIR!

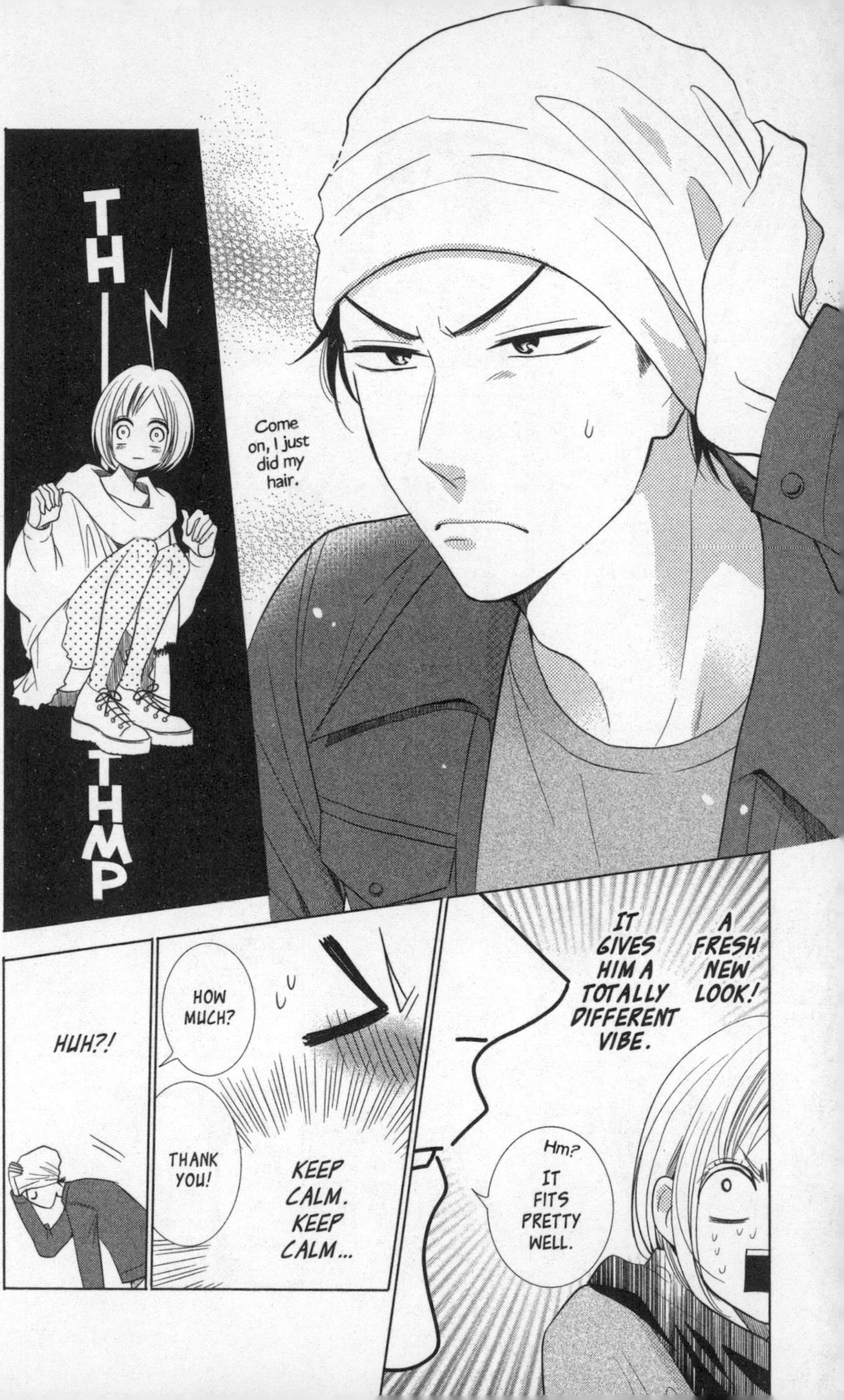
Come on, I just did my hair.
THI—THMP
A FRESH NEW LOOK!
IT GIVES HIM A TOTALLY DIFFERENT VIBE.
Hm? IT FITS PRETTY WELL.
HOW MUCH?
THANK YOU!
KEEP CALM. KEEP CALM...
HUH?!

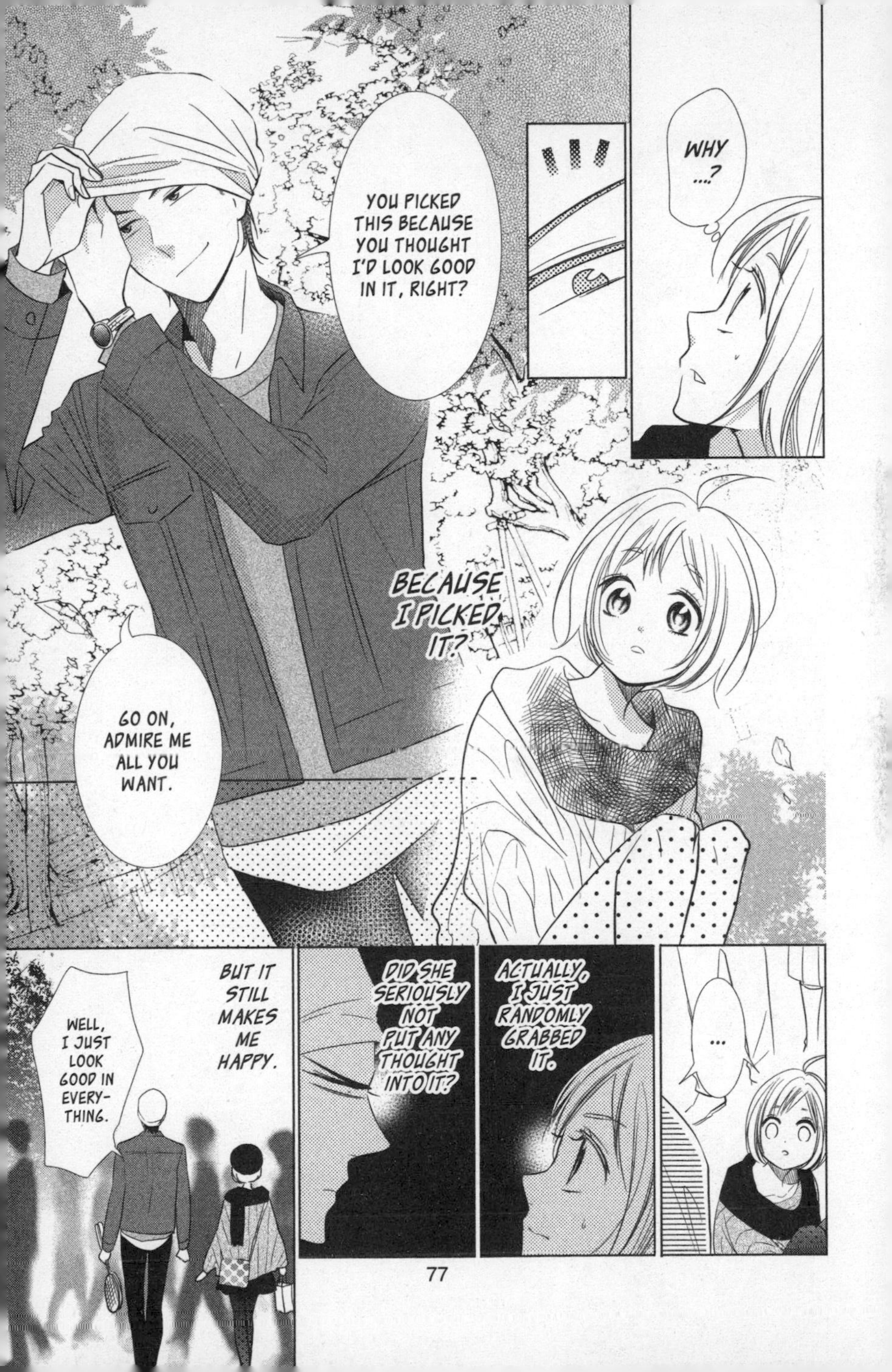
WHY ...?
!!!
YOU PICKED THIS BECAUSE YOU THOUGHT I'D LOOK GOOD IN IT, RIGHT?
BECAUSE I PICKED IT?
GO ON, ADMIRE ME ALL YOU WANT.
...
ACTUALLY, I JUST RANDOMLY GRABBED IT.
DID SHE SERIOUSLY NOT PUT ANY THOUGHT INTO IT?
BUT IT STILL MAKES ME HAPPY.
WELL, I JUST LOOK GOOD IN EVERY-THING.

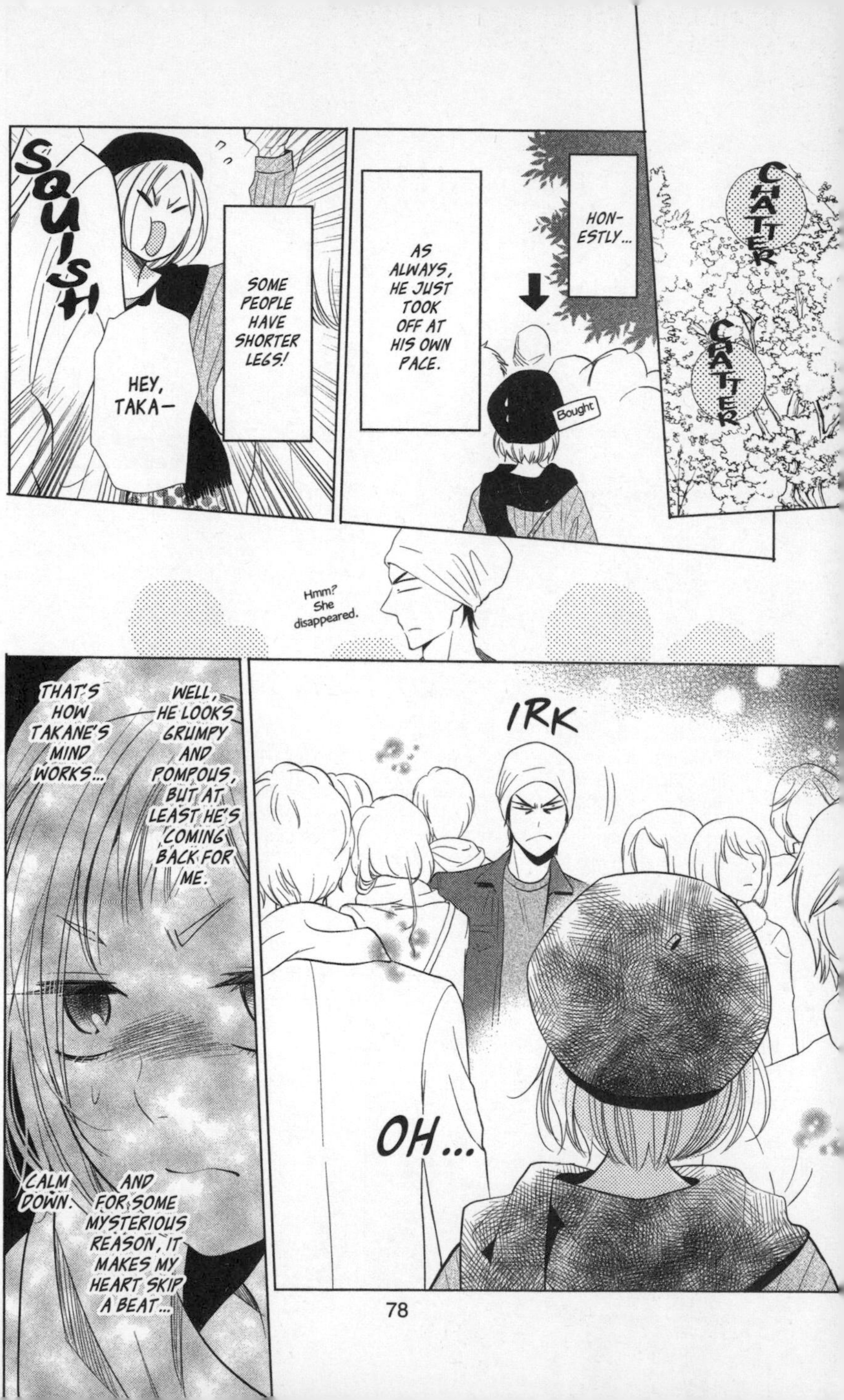
CHATTER
CHATTER
HON-ESTLY...
AS ALWAYS, HE JUST TOOK OFF AT HIS OWN PACE.
Bought
SOME PEOPLE HAVE SHORTER LEGS!
HEY, TAKA—
SQUISH
Hmm? She disappeared.
IRK
OH...
WELL, HE LOOKS GRUMPY AND POMPOUS, BUT AT LEAST HE'S COMING BACK FOR ME.
THAT'S HOW TAKANE'S MIND WORKS...
AND FOR SOME MYSTERIOUS REASON, IT MAKES MY HEART SKIP A BEAT...
CALM DOWN.

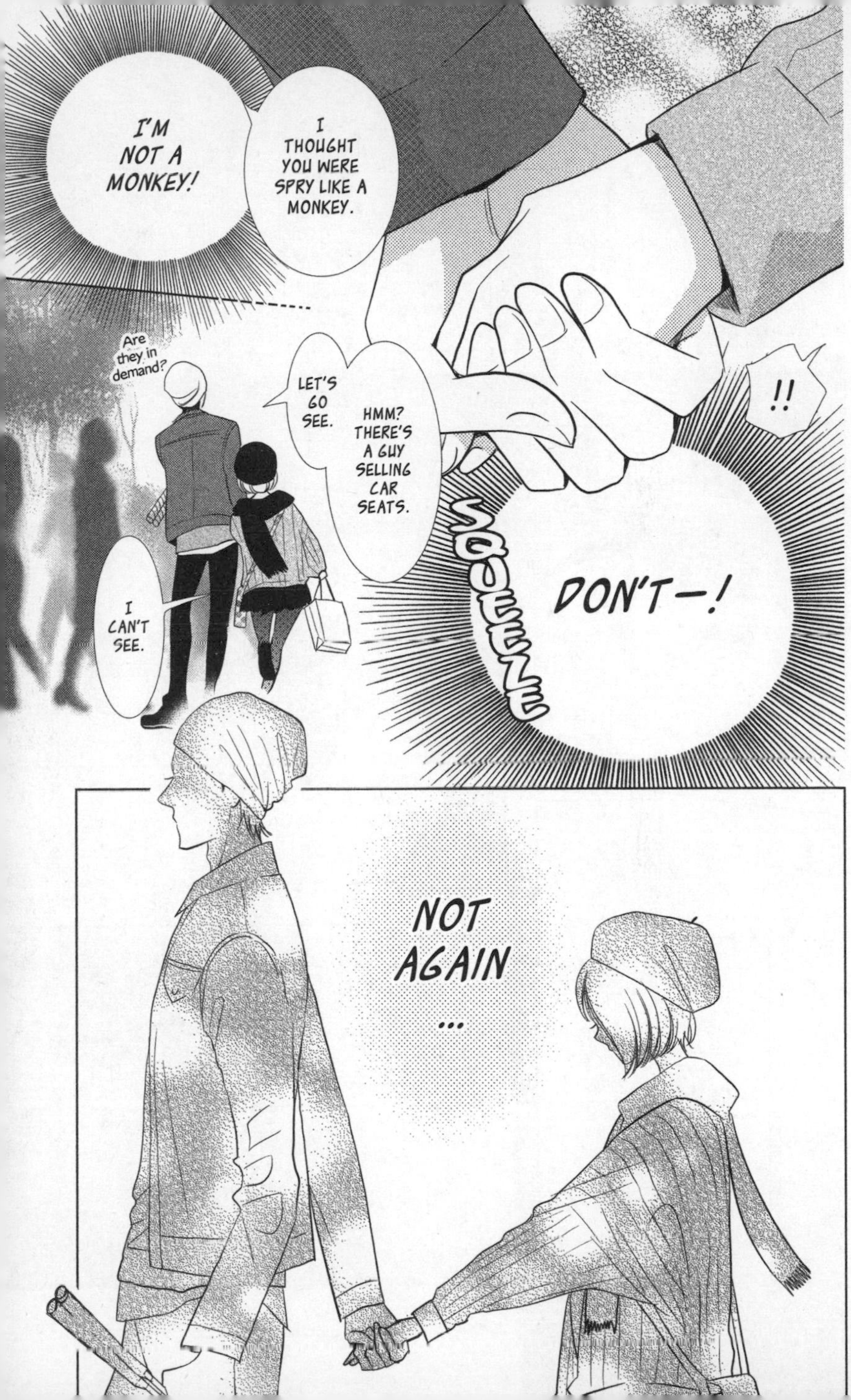
I THOUGHT YOU WERE SPRY LIKE A MONKEY.
I'M NOT A MONKEY!
!!
SQUEEZE
DON'T—!
HMM? THERE'S A GUY SELLING CAR SEATS.
LET'S GO SEE.
Are they in demand?
I CAN'T SEE.
NOT AGAIN ...

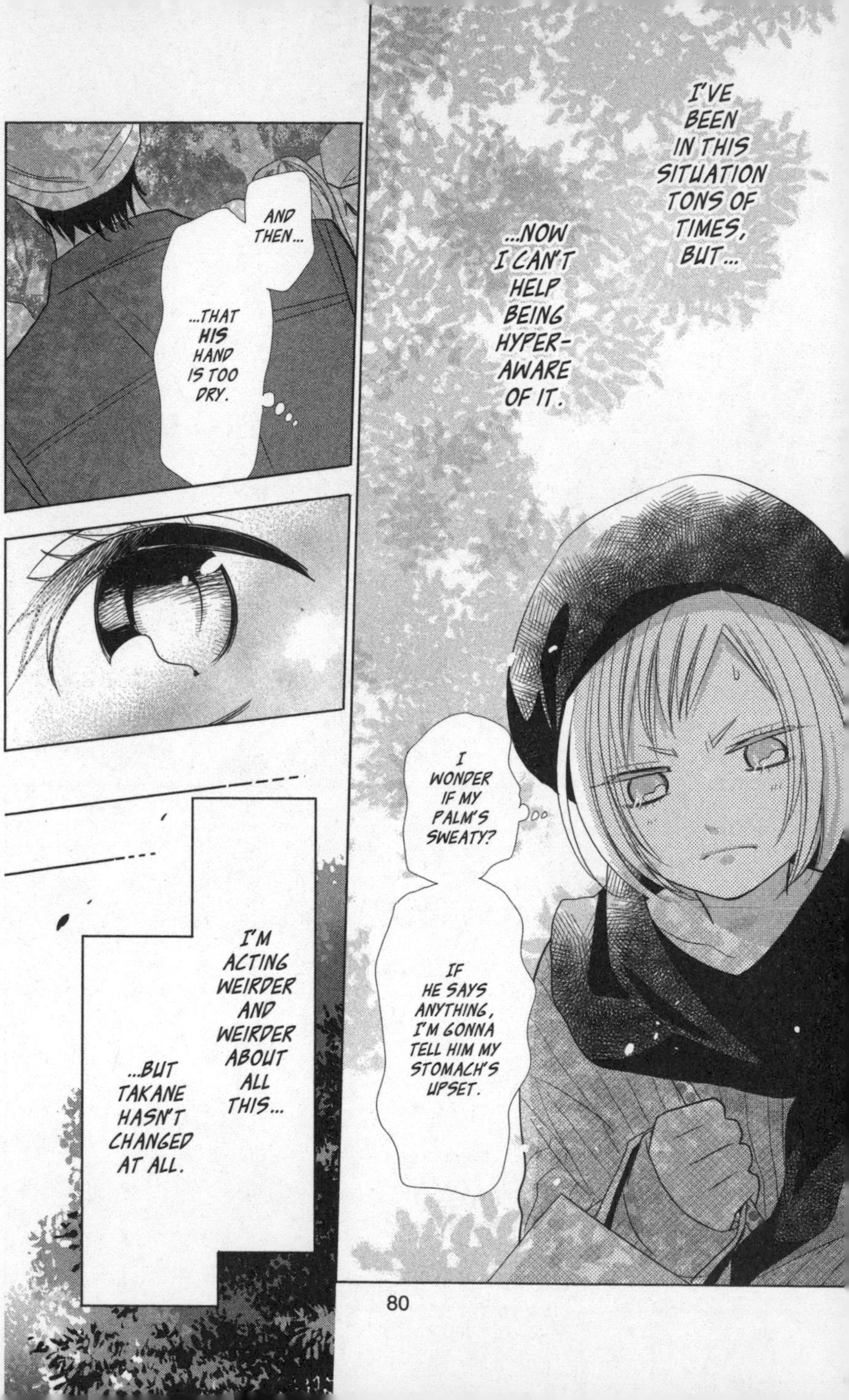
I'VE BEEN IN THIS SITUATION TONS OF TIMES, BUT...
...NOW I CAN'T HELP BEING HYPER-AWARE OF IT.
I WONDER IF MY PALM'S SWEATY?
IF HE SAYS ANYTHING, I'M GONNA TELL HIM MY STOMACH'S UPSET.
AND THEN...
...THAT HIS HAND IS TOO DRY.
I'M ACTING WEIRDER AND WEIRDER ABOUT ALL THIS...
...BUT TAKANE HASN'T CHANGED AT ALL.

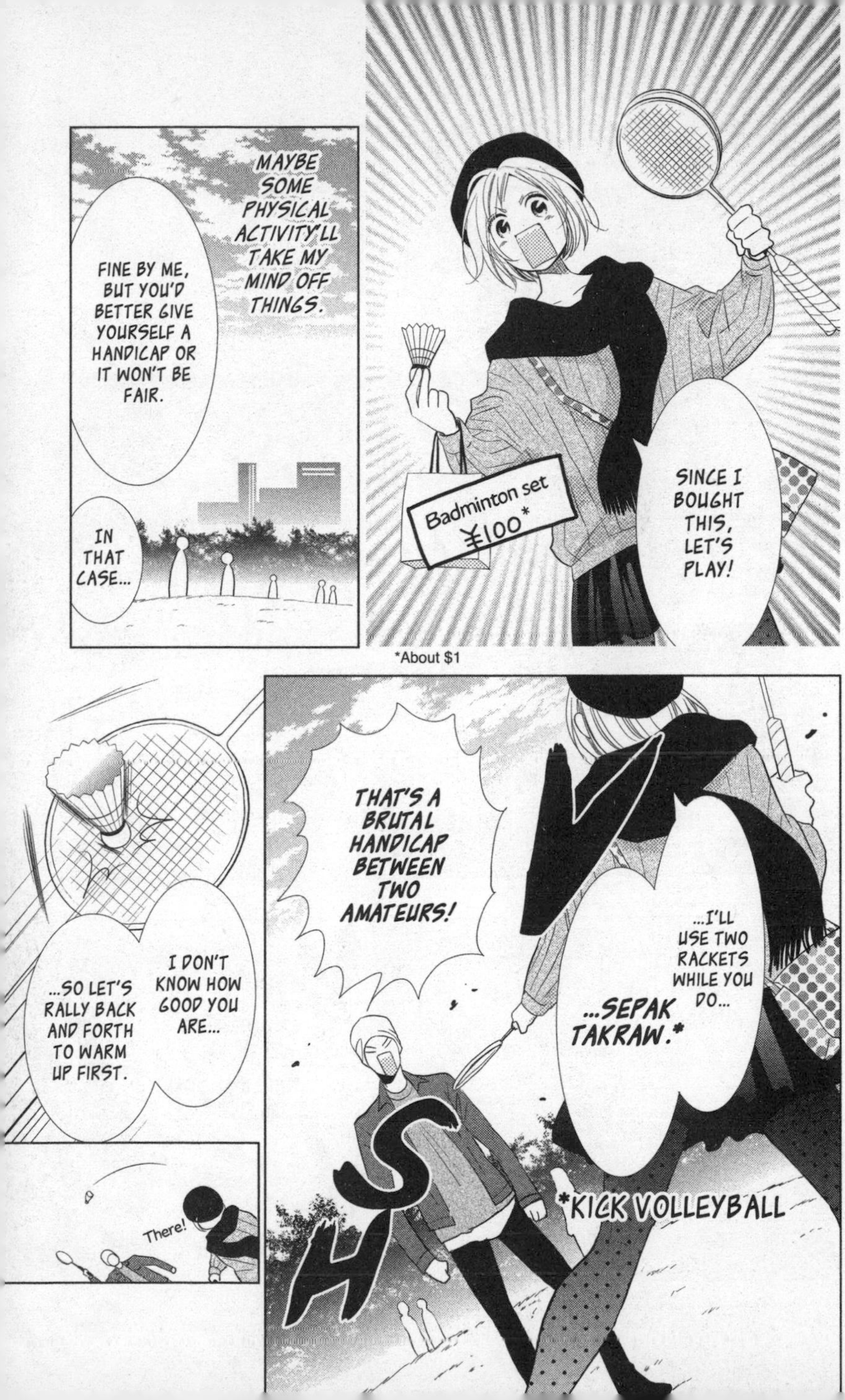
Badminton set ¥100*
SINCE I BOUGHT THIS, LET'S PLAY!
MAYBE SOME PHYSICAL ACTIVITY'LL TAKE MY MIND OFF THINGS.
FINE BY ME, BUT YOU'D BETTER GIVE YOURSELF A HANDICAP OR IT WON'T BE FAIR.
IN THAT CASE...
*About $1
...I'LL USE TWO RACKETS WHILE YOU DO...
...SEPAK TAKRAW.*
THAT'S A BRUTAL HANDICAP BETWEEN TWO AMATEURS!
*KICK VOLLEYBALL
I DON'T KNOW HOW GOOD YOU ARE...
...SO LET'S RALLY BACK AND FORTH TO WARM UP FIRST.
There!

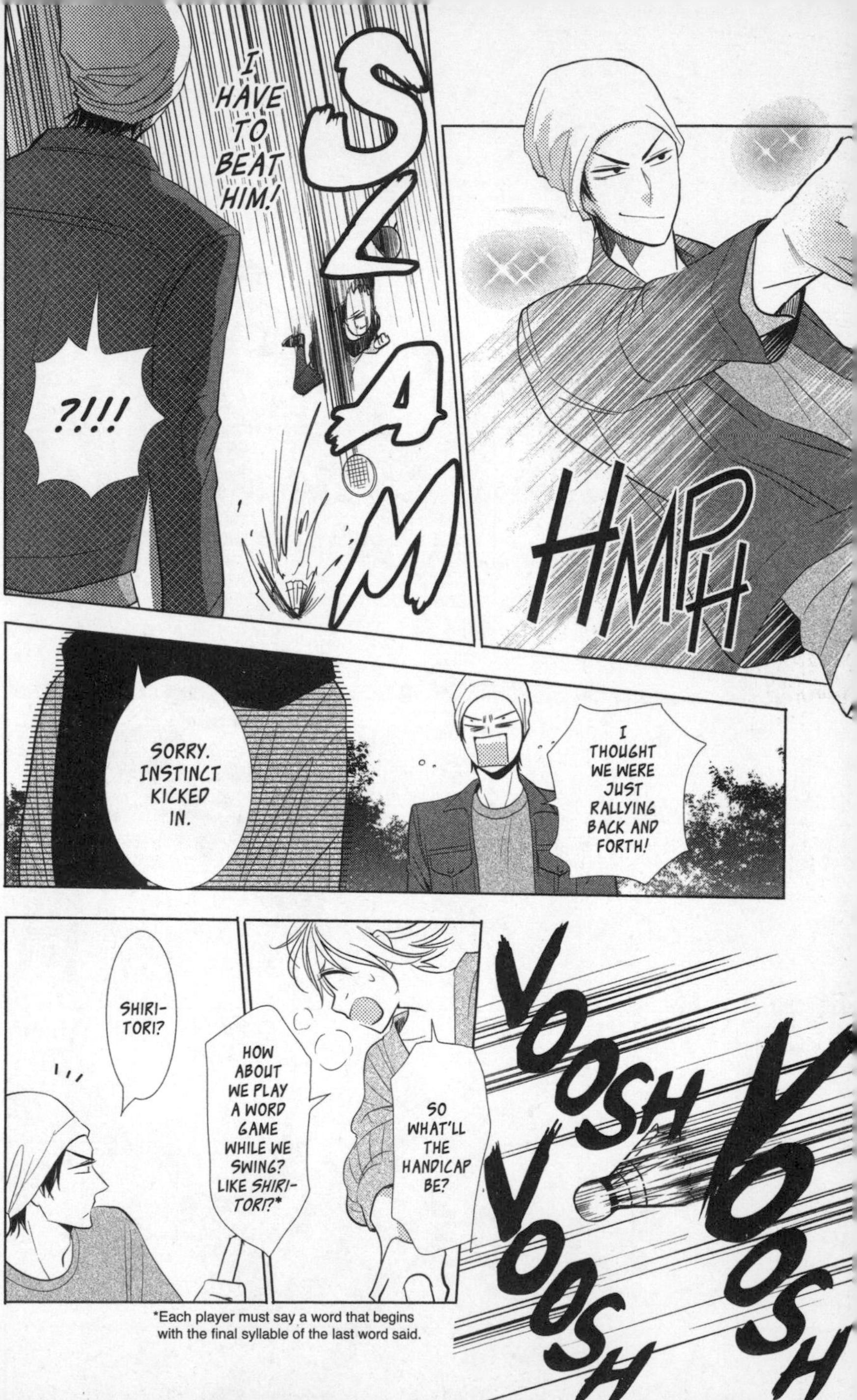
HMPH
I HAVE TO BEAT HIM!
SLAM
?!!!
I THOUGHT WE WERE JUST RALLYING BACK AND FORTH!
SORRY. INSTINCT KICKED IN.
VOOSH VOOSH
VOOSH VOOSH
SO WHAT'LL THE HANDICAP BE?
HOW ABOUT WE PLAY A WORD GAME WHILE WE SWING? LIKE *SHIRITORI*?*
SHIRITORI?

*Each player must say a word that begins with the final syllable of the last word said.

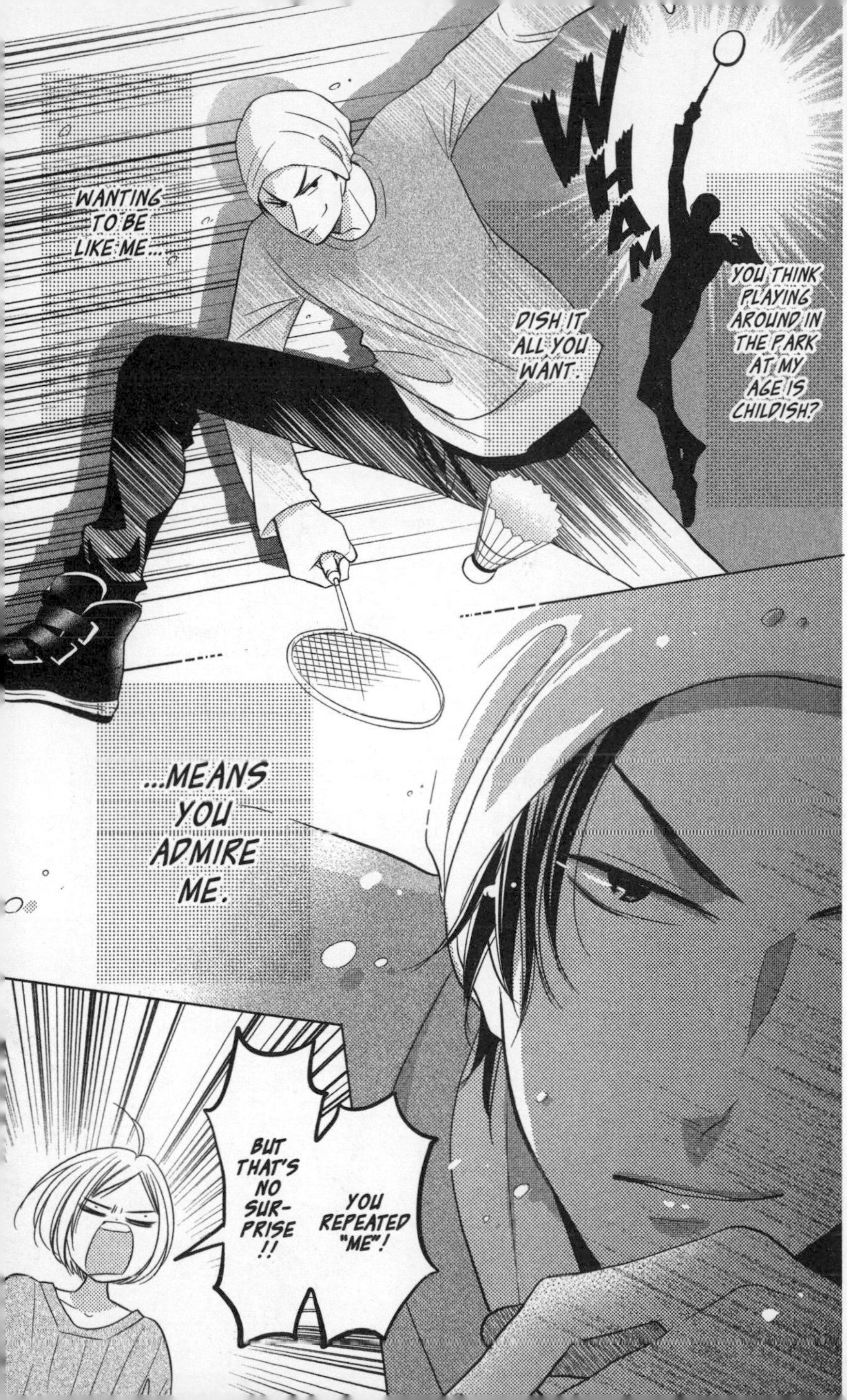
YOU THINK PLAYING AROUND IN THE PARK AT MY AGE IS CHILDISH?
WHAM
DISH IT ALL YOU WANT.
WANTING TO BE LIKE ME...
...MEANS YOU ADMIRE ME.
BUT THAT'S NO SURPRISE!! YOU REPEATED "ME"!

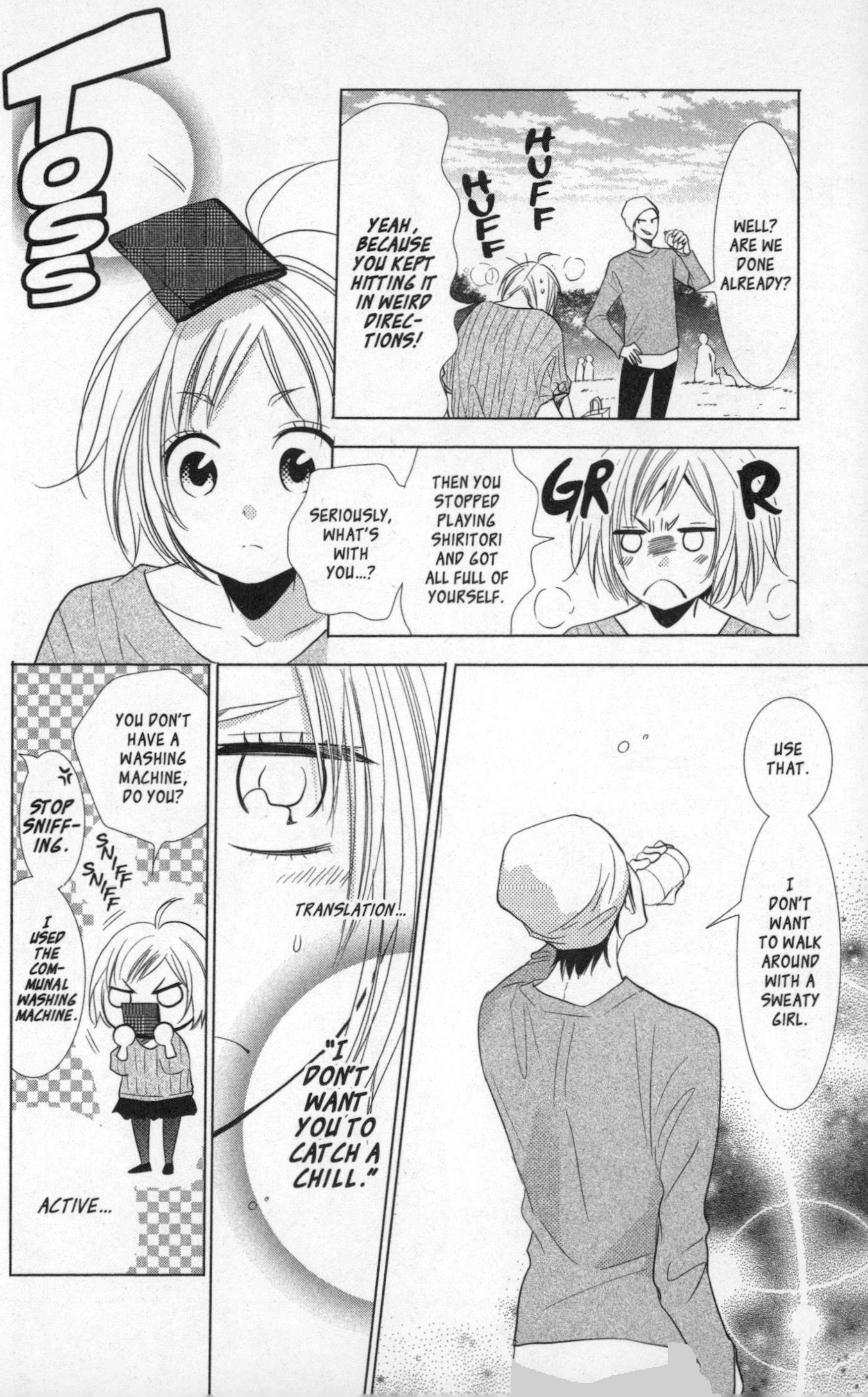
WELL? ARE WE DONE ALREADY?
HUFF
HUFF
YEAH, BECAUSE YOU KEPT HITTING IT IN WEIRD DIREC-TIONS!
GR R
THEN YOU STOPPED PLAYING SHIRITORI AND GOT ALL FULL OF YOURSELF.
SERIOUSLY, WHAT'S WITH YOU...?
TOSS
USE THAT.
I DON'T WANT TO WALK AROUND WITH A SWEATY GIRL.
TRANSLATION...
"I DON'T WANT YOU TO CATCH A CHILL."
YOU DON'T HAVE A WASHING MACHINE, DO YOU?
STOP SNIFF-ING.
SNIFF
SNIFF
I USED THE COM-MUNAL WASHING MACHINE.
ACTIVE...

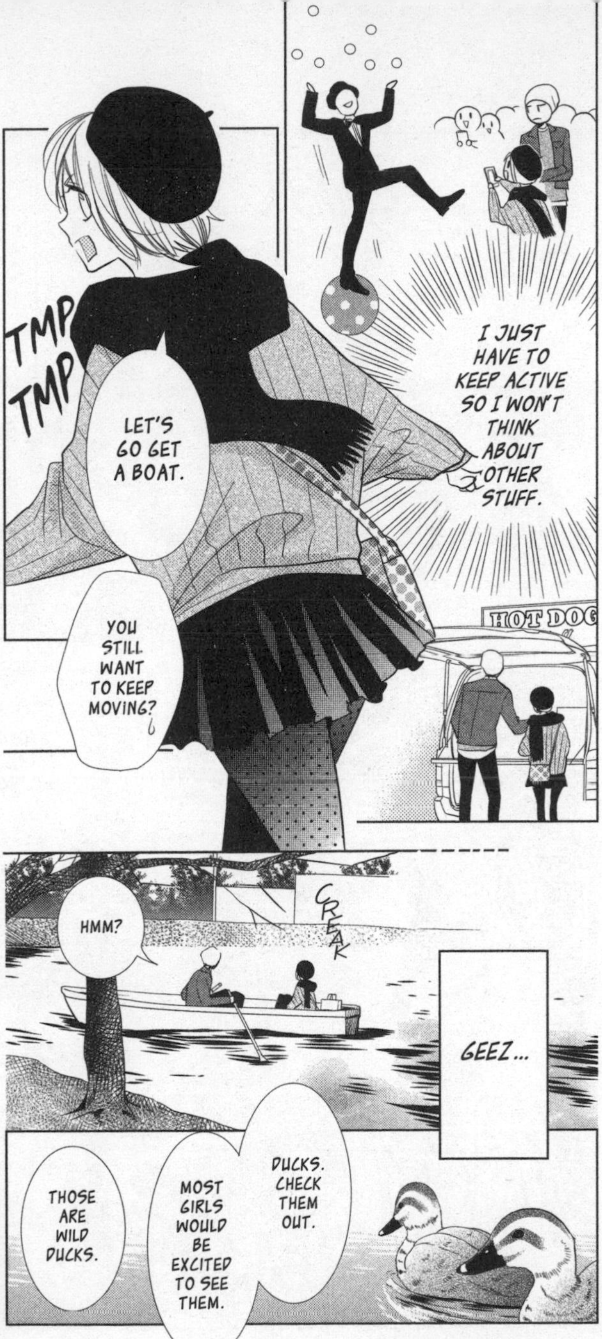
I JUST HAVE TO KEEP ACTIVE SO I WON'T THINK ABOUT OTHER STUFF.
HOT DOG
TMP TMP
LET'S GO GET A BOAT.
YOU STILL WANT TO KEEP MOVING?
CREAK
HMM?
GEEZ...
DUCKS. CHECK THEM OUT.
MOST GIRLS WOULD BE EXCITED TO SEE THEM.
THOSE ARE WILD DUCKS.

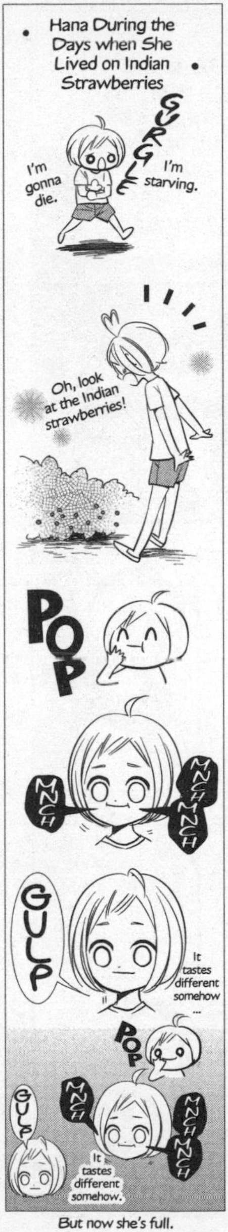
Hana During the Days when She Lived on Indian Strawberries
GURGLE
I'm starving.
I'm gonna die.
Oh, look at the Indian strawberries!
POP
MNCH
MNCHMNCH
GULP
It tastes different somehow ...
POP
MNCH
MNCHMNCH
GULP
It tastes different somehow.

But now she's full.

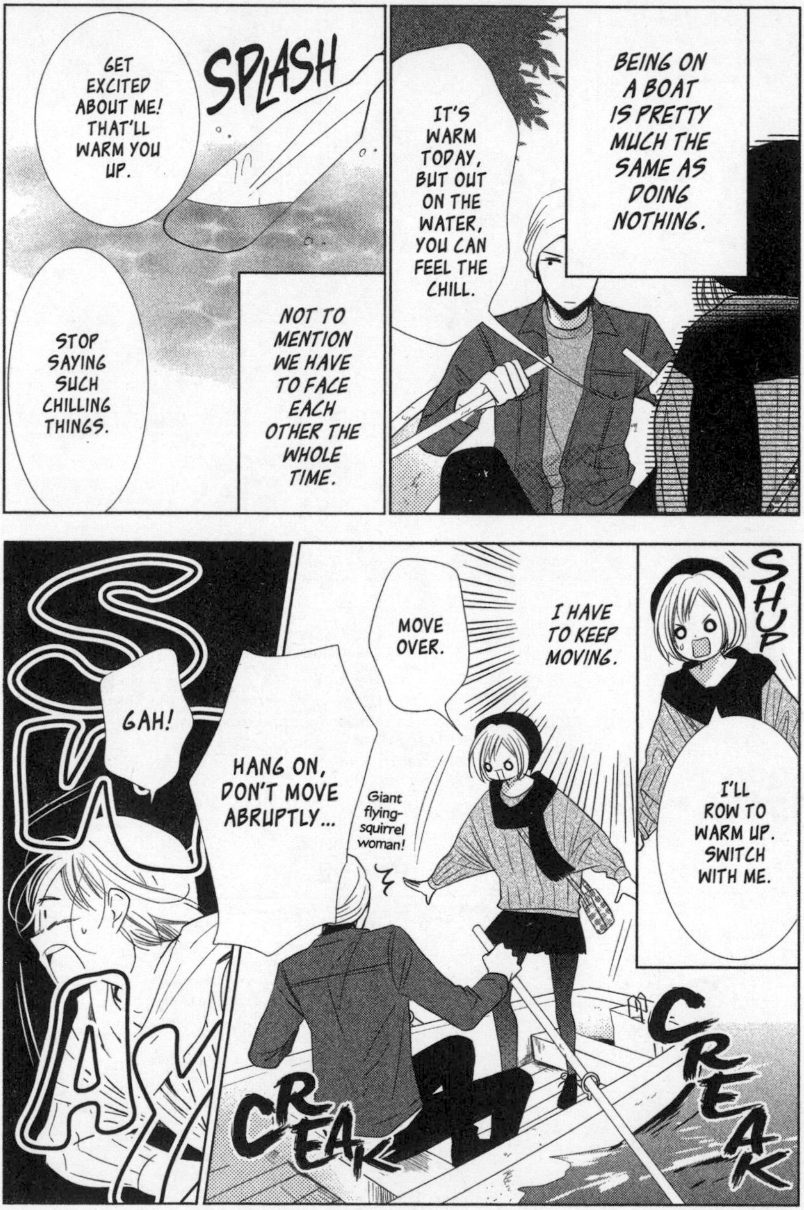
BEING ON A BOAT IS PRETTY MUCH THE SAME AS DOING NOTHING.
IT'S WARM TODAY, BUT OUT ON THE WATER, YOU CAN FEEL THE CHILL.
SPLASH
GET EXCITED ABOUT ME! THAT'LL WARM YOU UP.
NOT TO MENTION WE HAVE TO FACE EACH OTHER THE WHOLE TIME.
STOP SAYING SUCH CHILLING THINGS.
SHUP
I'LL ROW TO WARM UP. SWITCH WITH ME.
I HAVE TO KEEP MOVING.
MOVE OVER.
Giant flying-squirrel woman!
HANG ON, DON'T MOVE ABRUPTLY...
CREAK
CREAK
GAH!

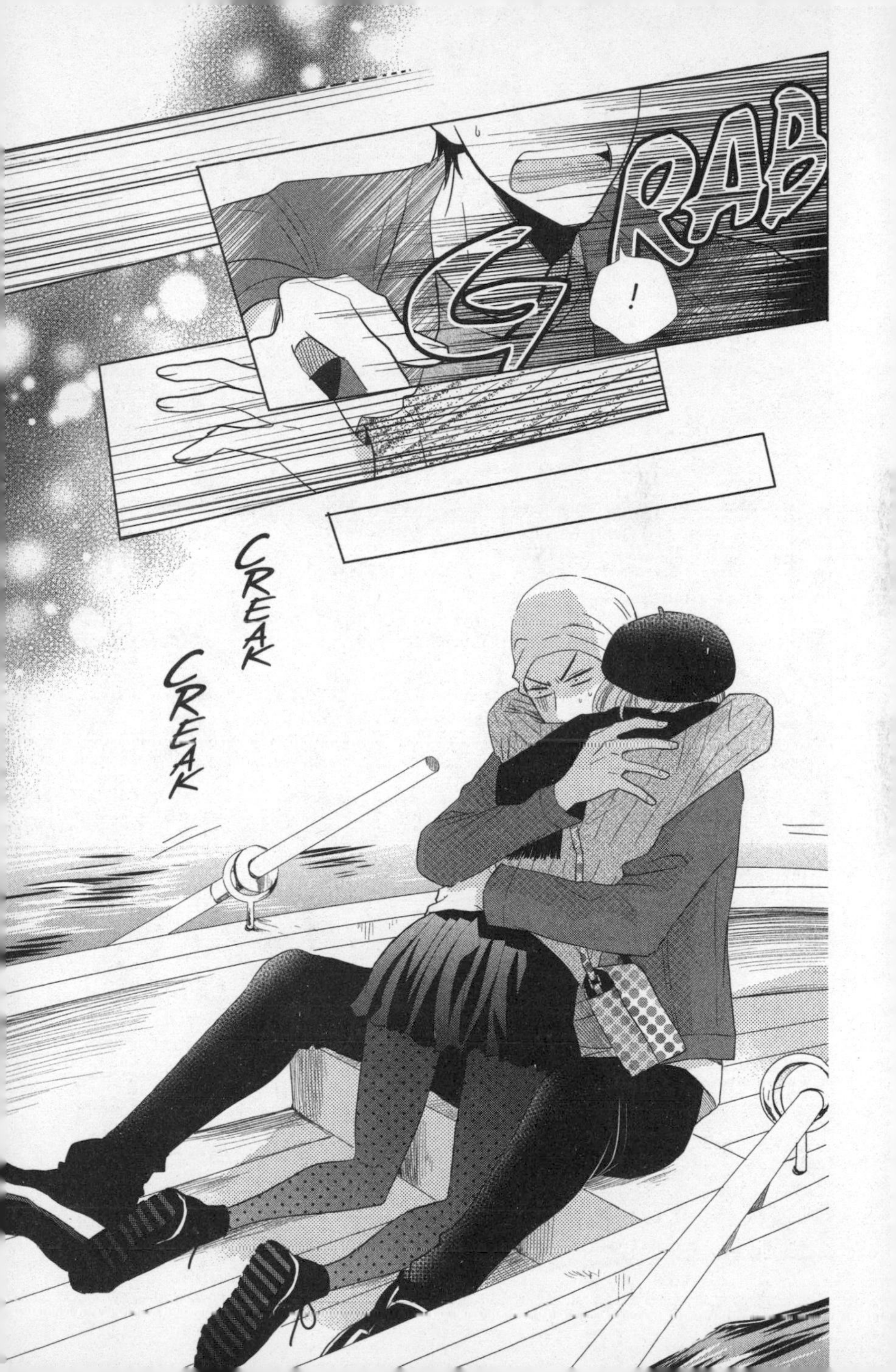
GRAB
!
CREAK
CREAK

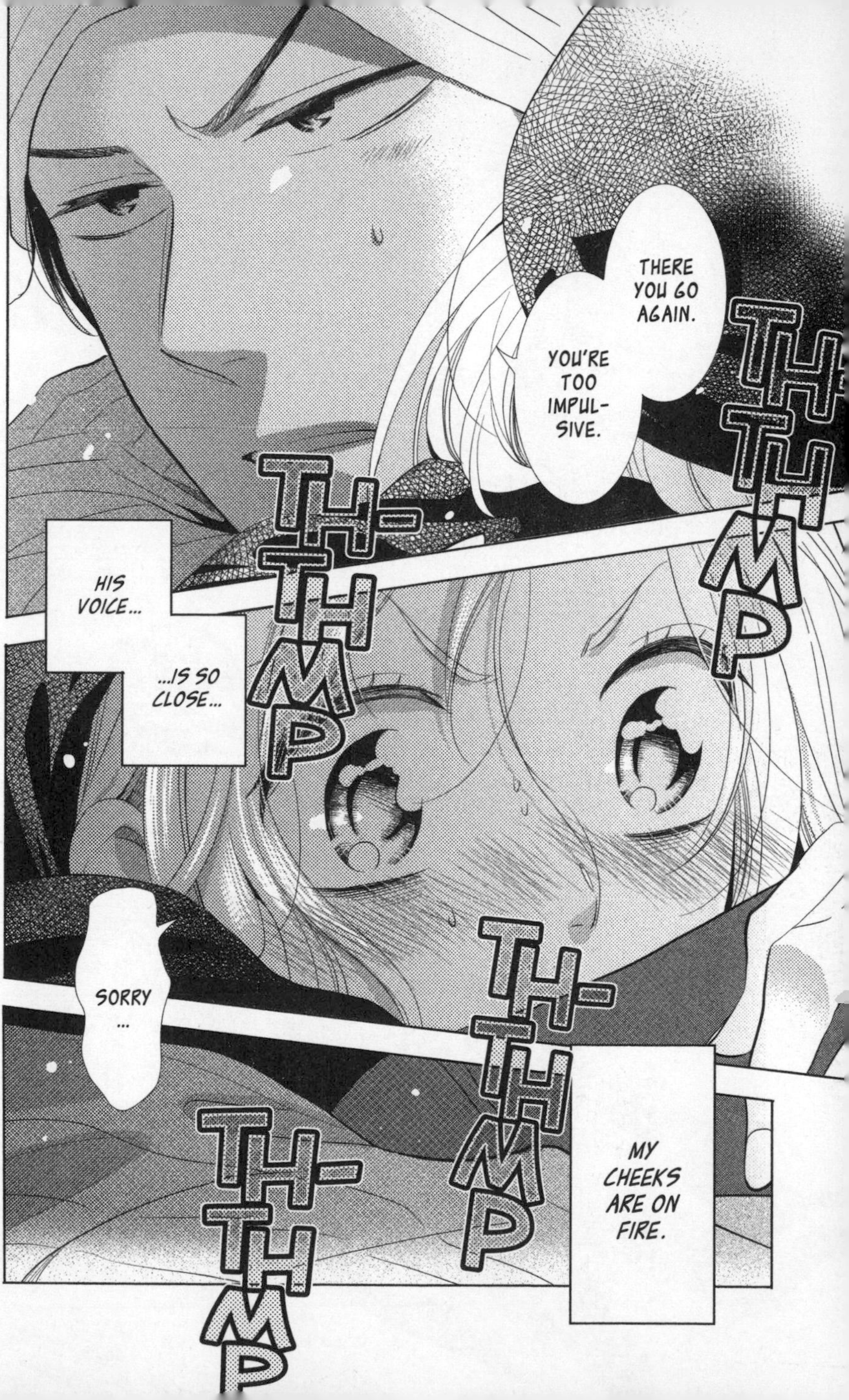

THERE YOU GO AGAIN.
YOU'RE TOO IMPUL-SIVE.
TH-THUMP
TH-THUMP
HIS VOICE...
...IS SO CLOSE...
TH-THUMP
MY CHEEKS ARE ON FIRE.
SORRY...
TH-THUMP

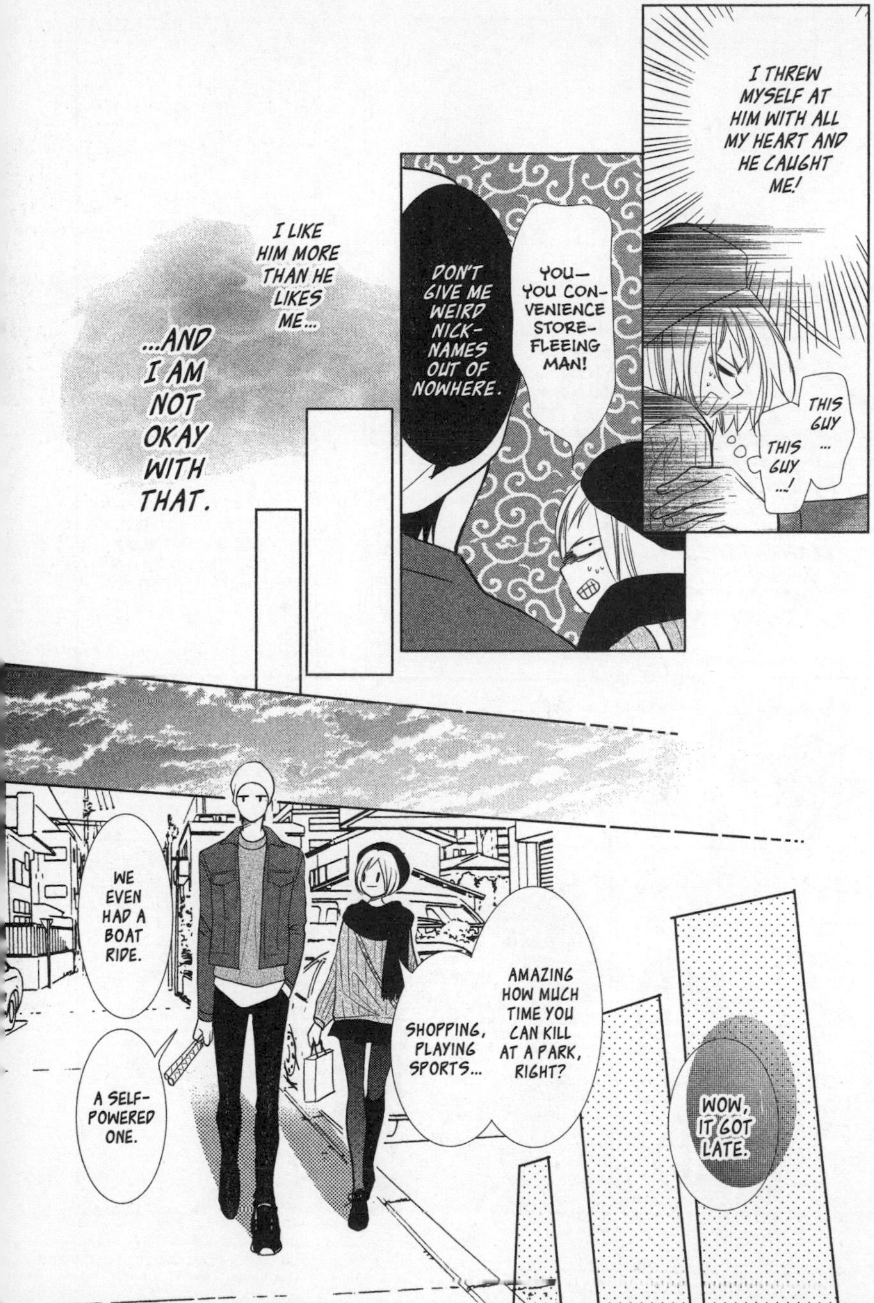
I THREW MYSELF AT HIM WITH ALL MY HEART AND HE CAUGHT ME!
THIS GUY ...
THIS GUY ...!
YOU— YOU CON-VENIENCE STORE-FLEEING MAN!
DON'T GIVE ME WEIRD NICK-NAMES OUT OF NOWHERE.
I LIKE HIM MORE THAN HE LIKES ME...
...AND I AM NOT OKAY WITH THAT.
WOW, IT GOT LATE.
AMAZING HOW MUCH TIME YOU CAN KILL AT A PARK, RIGHT?
SHOPPING, PLAYING SPORTS...
WE EVEN HAD A BOAT RIDE.
A SELF-POWERED ONE.

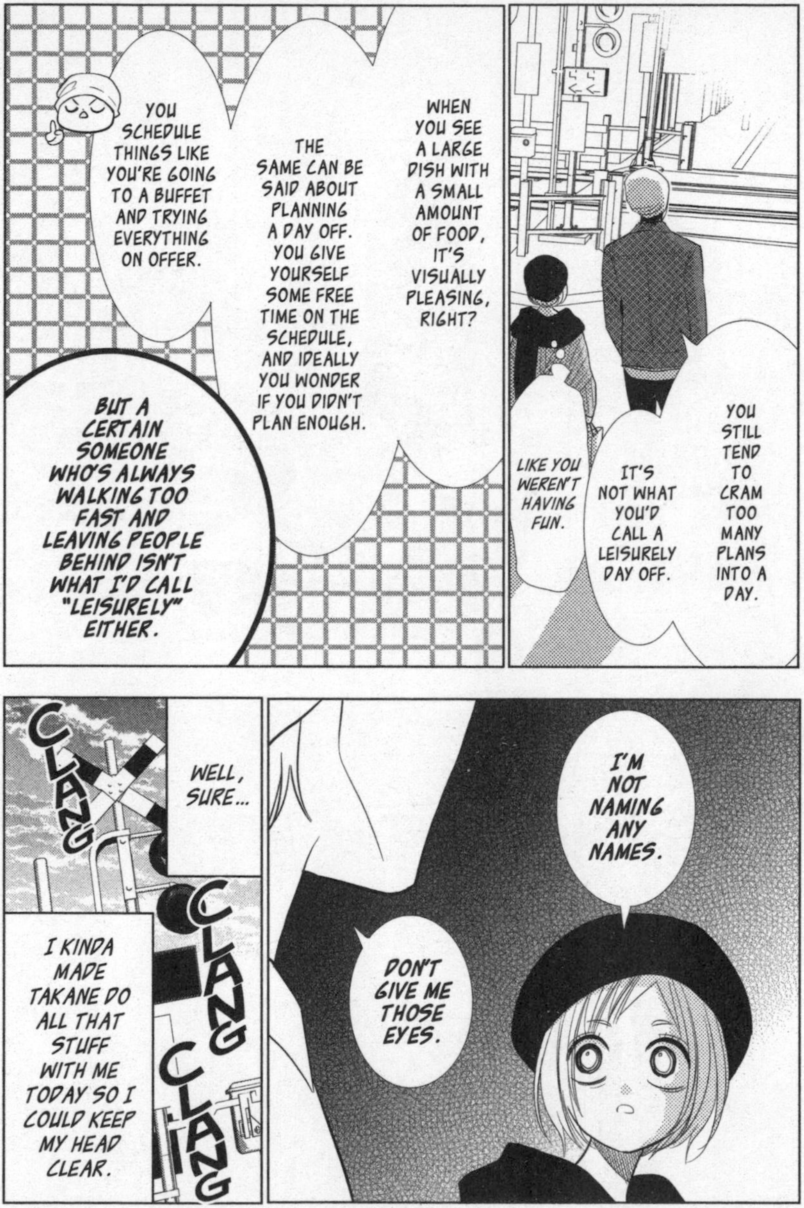

YOU STILL TEND TO CRAM TOO MANY PLANS INTO A DAY.
IT'S NOT WHAT YOU'D CALL A LEISURELY DAY OFF.
LIKE YOU WEREN'T HAVING FUN.
WHEN YOU SEE A LARGE DISH WITH A SMALL AMOUNT OF FOOD, IT'S VISUALLY PLEASING, RIGHT?
THE SAME CAN BE SAID ABOUT PLANNING A DAY OFF. YOU GIVE YOURSELF SOME FREE TIME ON THE SCHEDULE, AND IDEALLY YOU WONDER IF YOU DIDN'T PLAN ENOUGH.
YOU SCHEDULE THINGS LIKE YOU'RE GOING TO A BUFFET AND TRYING EVERYTHING ON OFFER.
BUT A CERTAIN SOMEONE WHO'S ALWAYS WALKING TOO FAST AND LEAVING PEOPLE BEHIND ISN'T WHAT I'D CALL "LEISURELY" EITHER.
I'M NOT NAMING ANY NAMES.
DON'T GIVE ME THOSE EYES.
CLANG
WELL, SURE...
CLANG
CLANG
I KINDA MADE TAKANE DO ALL THAT STUFF WITH ME TODAY SO I COULD KEEP MY HEAD CLEAR.

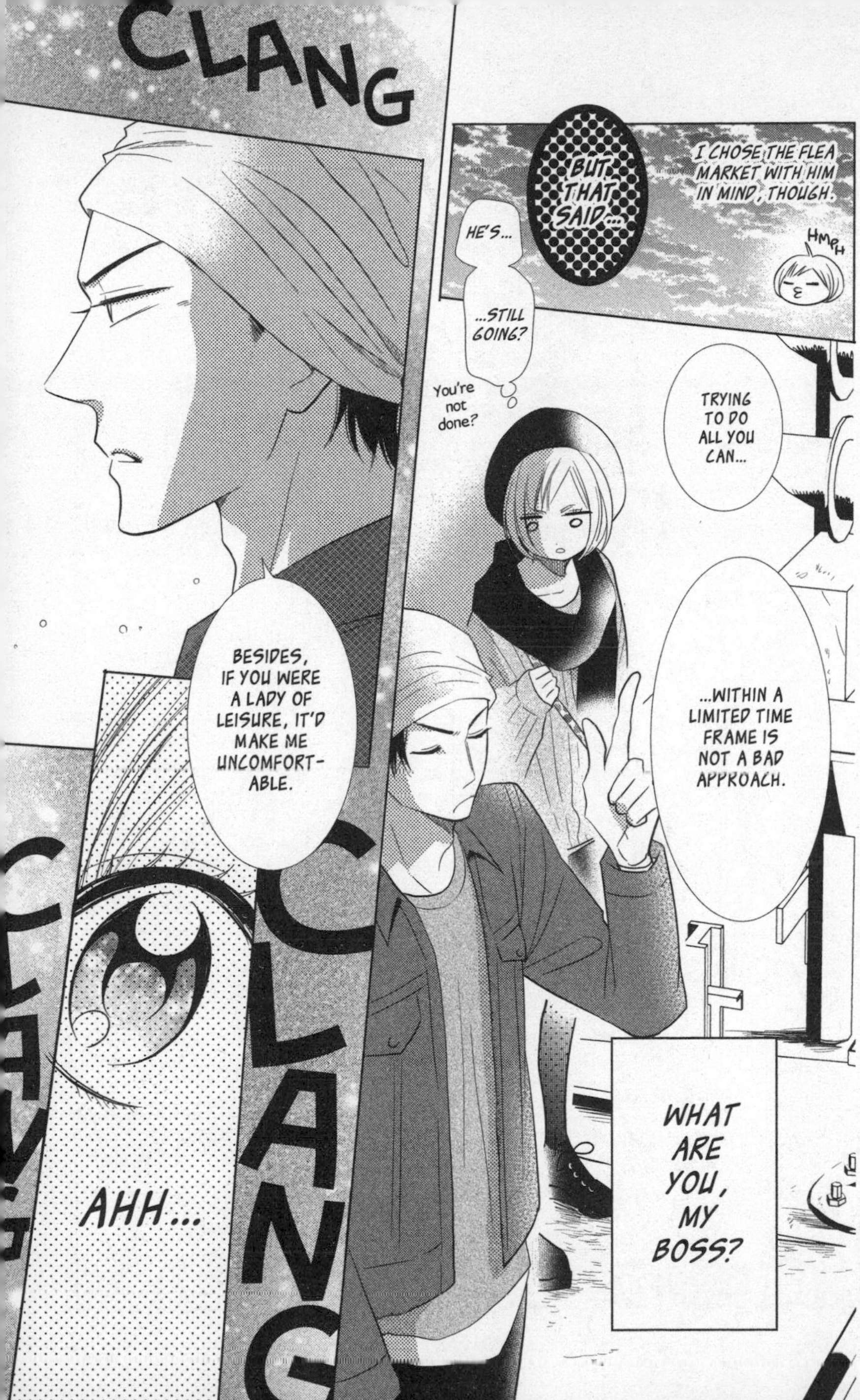
I CHOSE THE FLEA MARKET WITH HIM IN MIND, THOUGH.
HMPH
BUT THAT SAID...
HE'S...
...STILL GOING?
You're not done?
TRYING TO DO ALL YOU CAN...
...WITHIN A LIMITED TIME FRAME IS NOT A BAD APPROACH.
WHAT ARE YOU, MY BOSS?
CLANG
BESIDES, IF YOU WERE A LADY OF LEISURE, IT'D MAKE ME UNCOMFORTABLE.
CLANG
AHH...

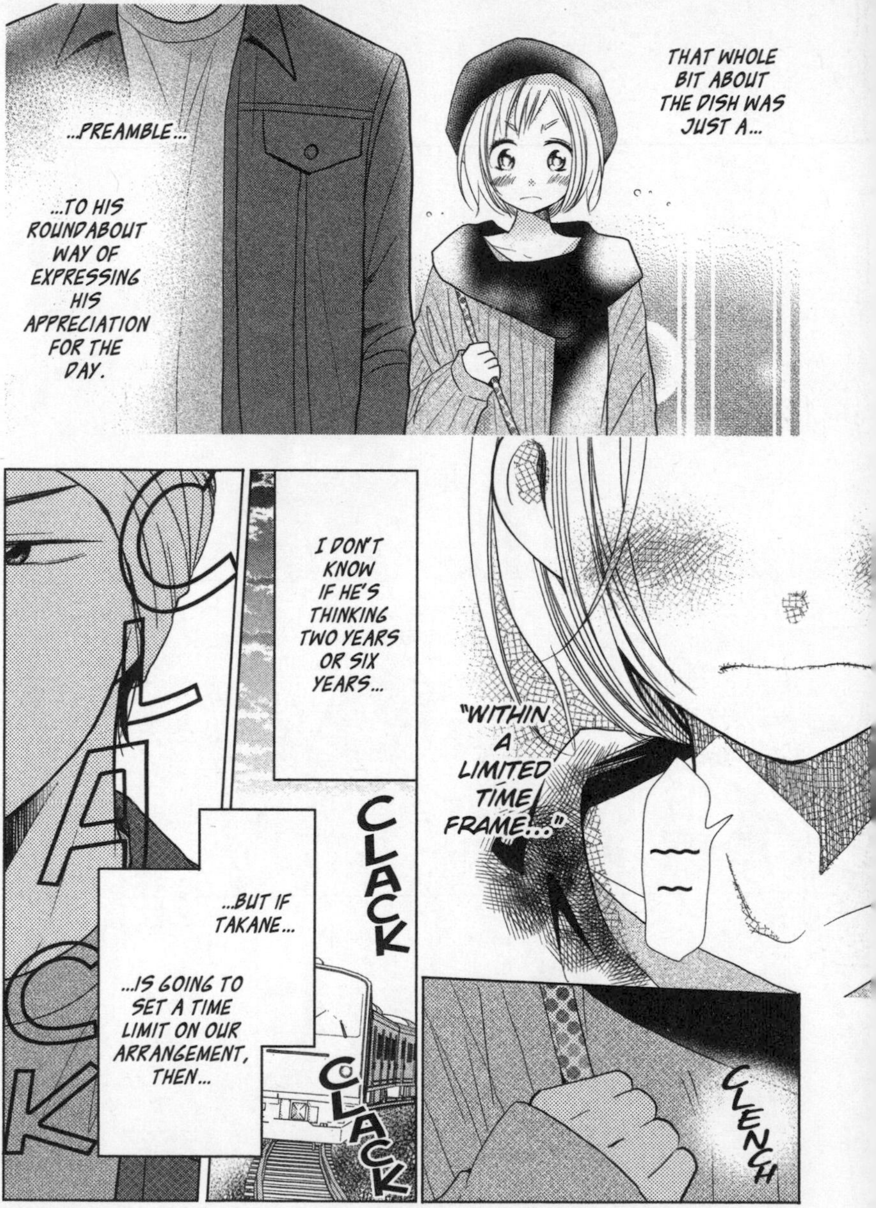
THAT WHOLE BIT ABOUT THE DISH WAS JUST A...
...PREAMBLE...
...TO HIS ROUNDABOUT WAY OF EXPRESSING HIS APPRECIATION FOR THE DAY.
"WITHIN A LIMITED TIME FRAME..."
CLENCH
I DON'T KNOW IF HE'S THINKING TWO YEARS OR SIX YEARS...
CLACK
...BUT IF TAKANE...
...IS GOING TO SET A TIME LIMIT ON OUR ARRANGEMENT, THEN...
CLACK
CLACK
CLACK

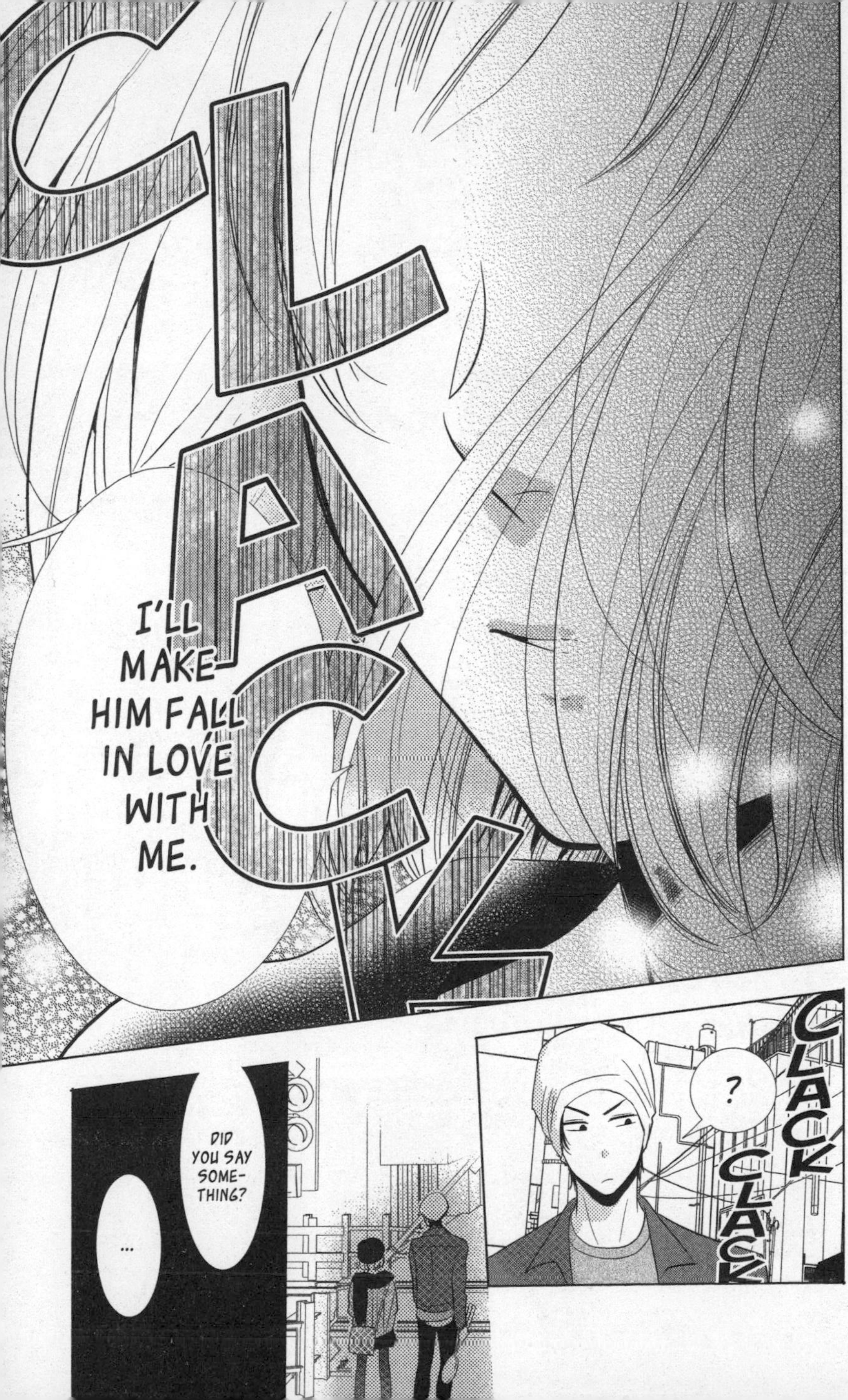
CLACK
I'LL MAKE HIM FALL IN LOVE WITH ME.
CLACK
CLACK
?
DID YOU SAY SOME-THING?
...

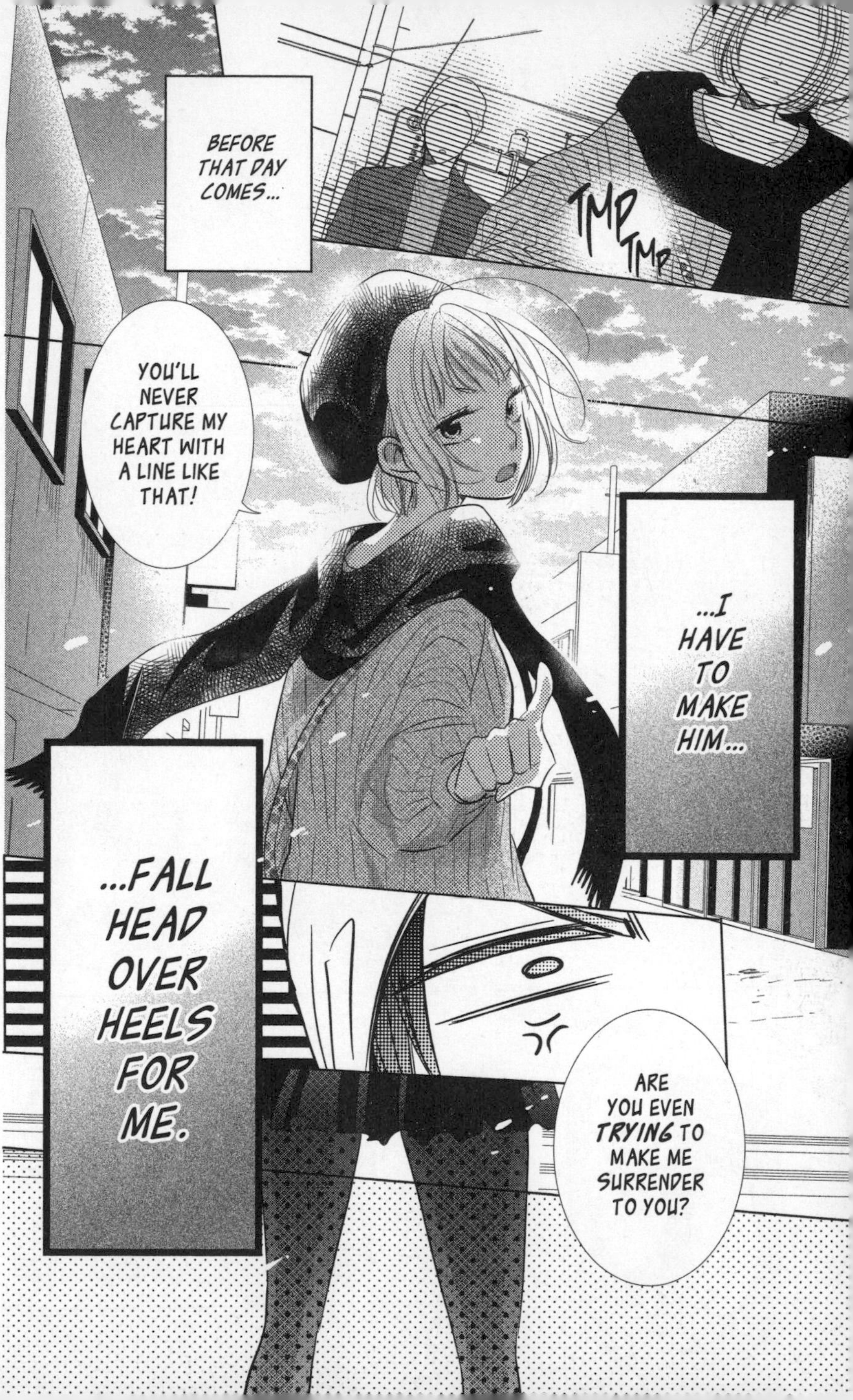
TMP TMP
BEFORE THAT DAY COMES...
ARE YOU EVEN TRYING TO MAKE ME SURRENDER TO YOU?
YOU'LL NEVER CAPTURE MY HEART WITH A LINE LIKE THAT!
...I HAVE TO MAKE HIM...
...FALL HEAD OVER HEELS FOR ME.

Chapter 43

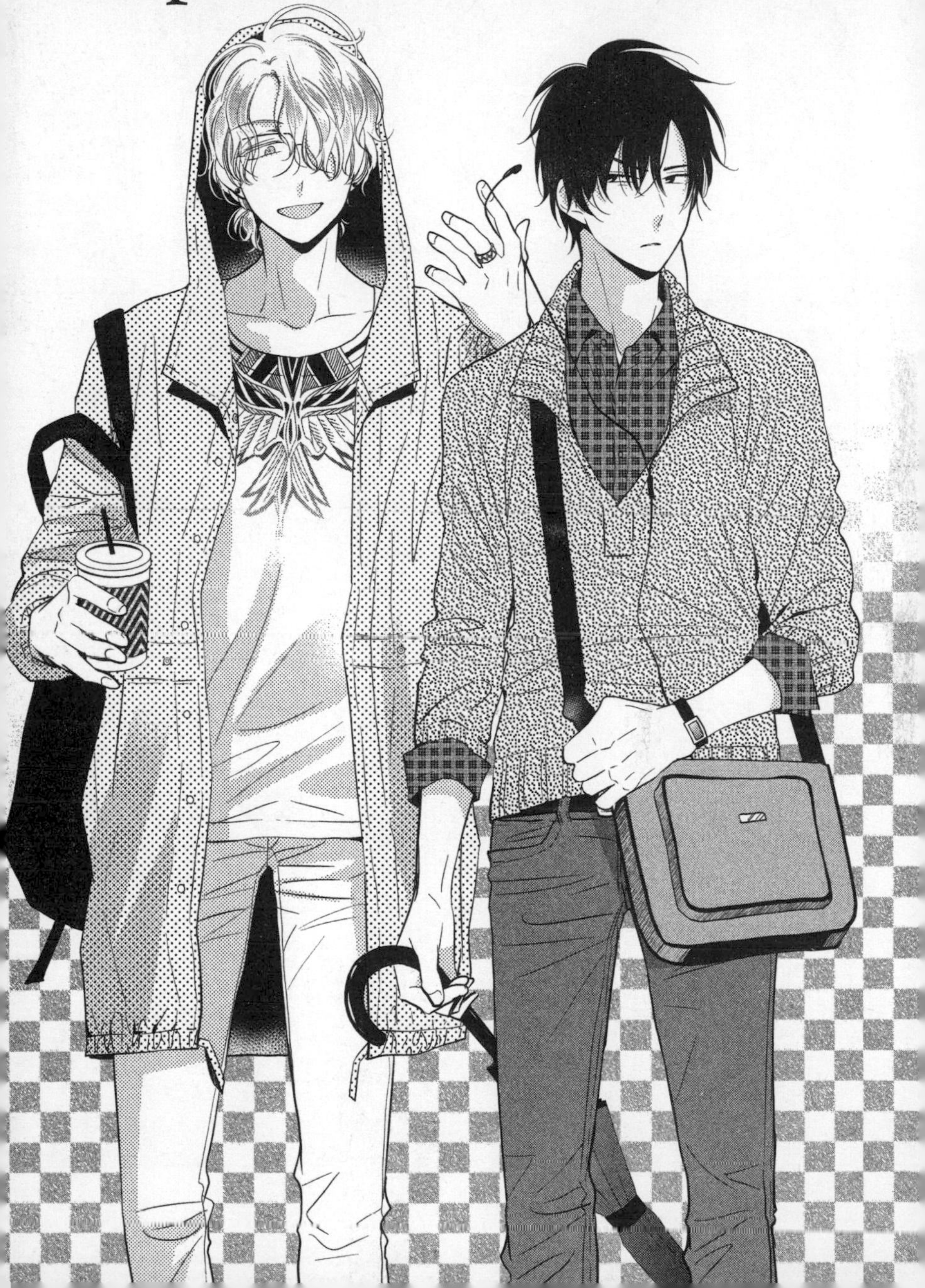

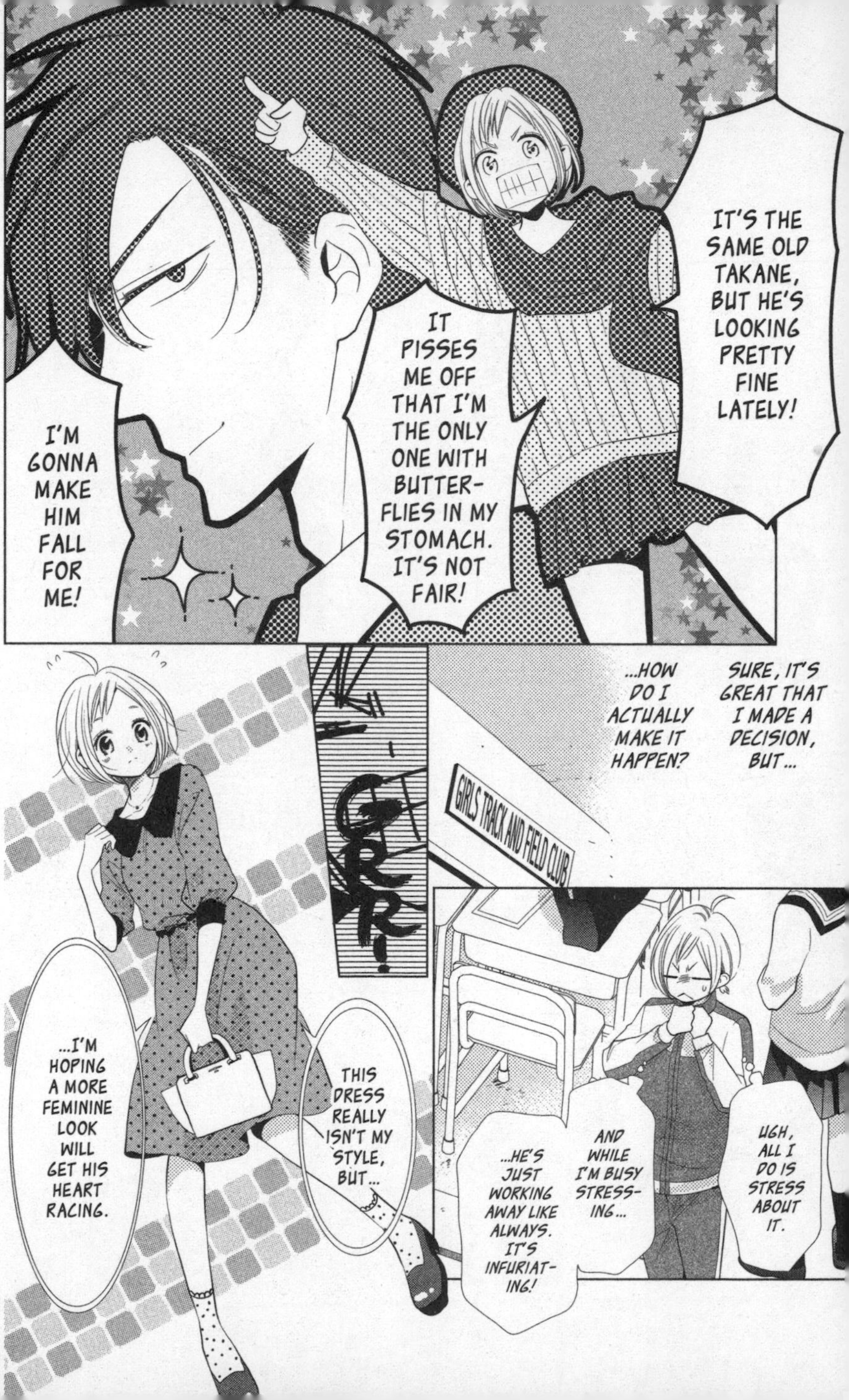
IT'S THE SAME OLD TAKANE, BUT HE'S LOOKING PRETTY FINE LATELY!
IT PISSES ME OFF THAT I'M THE ONLY ONE WITH BUTTER-FLIES IN MY STOMACH. IT'S NOT FAIR!
I'M GONNA MAKE HIM FALL FOR ME!
SURE, IT'S GREAT THAT I MADE A DECISION, BUT...
...HOW DO I ACTUALLY MAKE IT HAPPEN?
GIRLS TRACK AND FIELD CLUB
UGH, ALL I DO IS STRESS ABOUT IT.
AND WHILE I'M BUSY STRESS-ING...
...HE'S JUST WORKING AWAY LIKE ALWAYS. IT'S INFURIAT-ING!
GRR!
THIS DRESS REALLY ISN'T MY STYLE, BUT...
...I'M HOPING A MORE FEMININE LOOK WILL GET HIS HEART RACING.

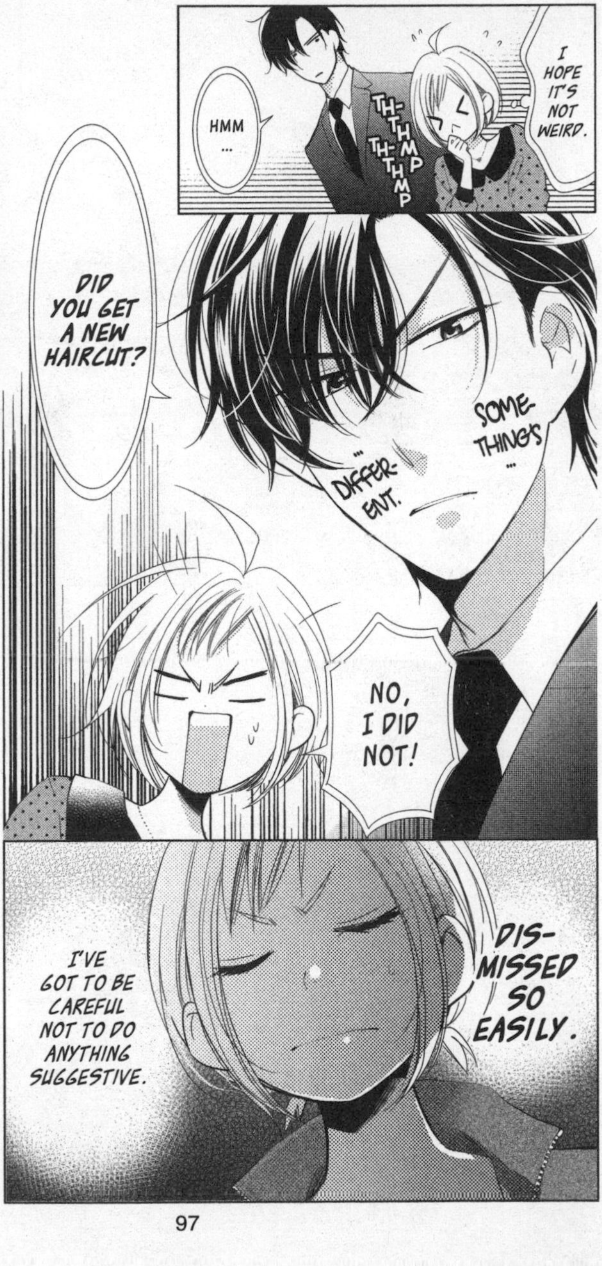
I HOPE IT'S NOT WEIRD.
TH-THMP TH-THMP
HMM ...
SOME-THING'S ...
... DIFFER-ENT.
DID YOU GET A NEW HAIRCUT?
NO, I DID NOT!
DIS-MISSED SO EASILY.
I'VE GOT TO BE CAREFUL NOT TO DO ANYTHING SUGGESTIVE.

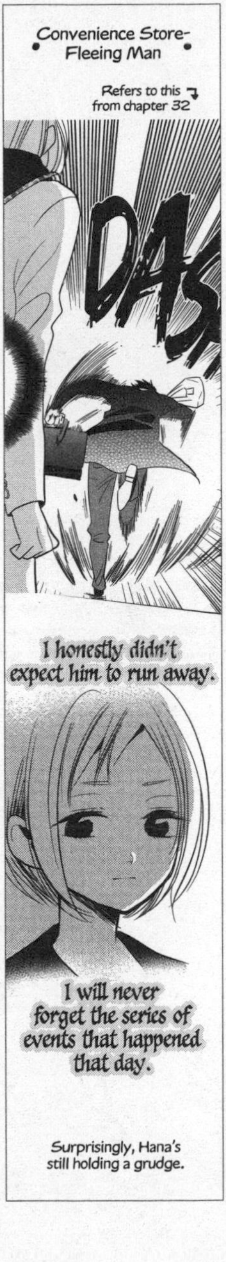
Convenience Store-Fleeing Man
Refers to this from chapter 32
DAS
I honestly didn't expect him to run away.
I will never forget the series of events that happened that day.
Surprisingly, Hana's still holding a grudge.

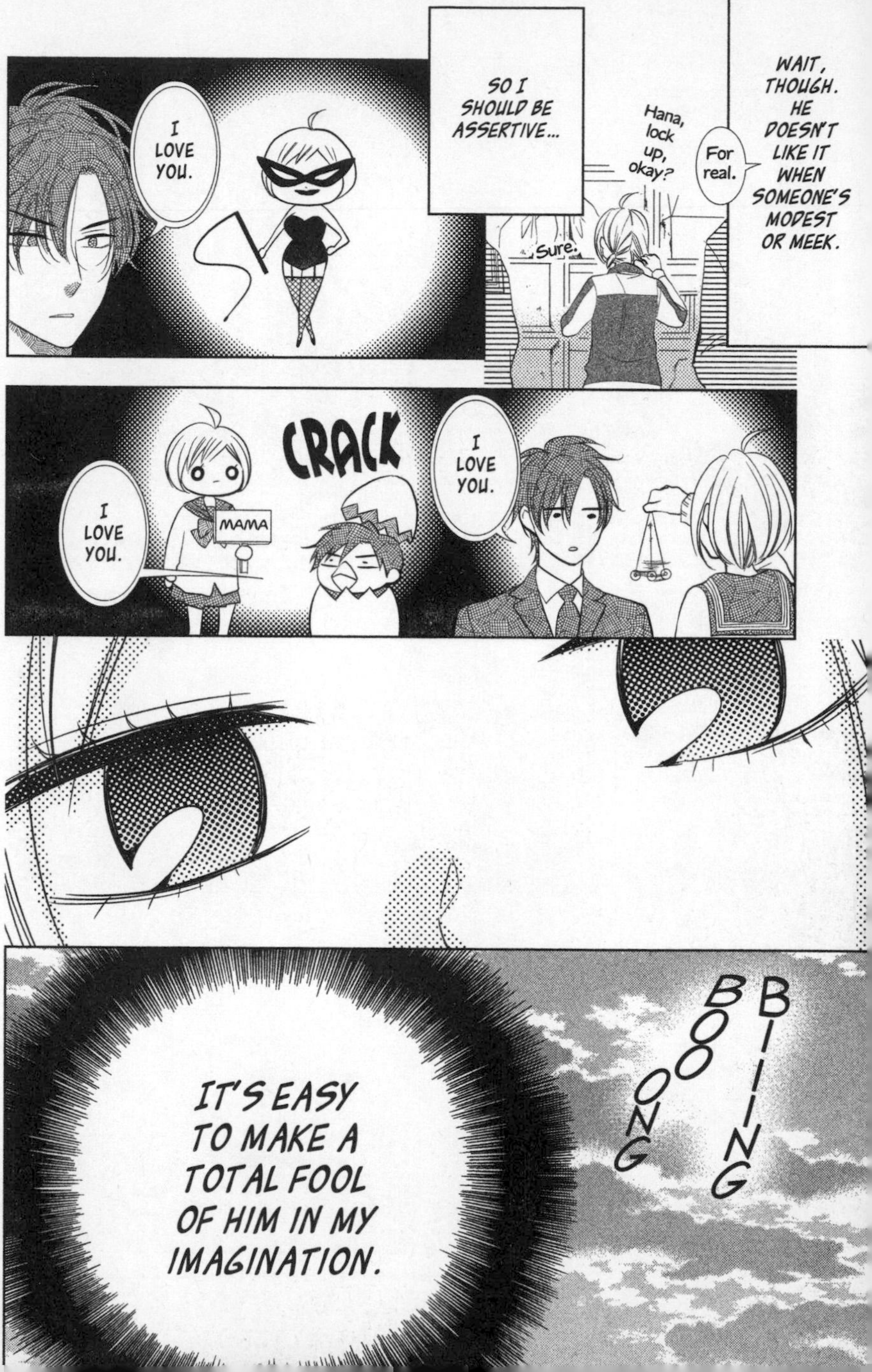
WAIT, THOUGH. HE DOESN'T LIKE IT WHEN SOMEONE'S MODEST OR MEEK.
For real.
Hana, lock up, okay?
Sure.
SO I SHOULD BE ASSERTIVE...
I LOVE YOU.
I LOVE YOU.
CRACK
MAMA
I LOVE YOU.
BIIING
BOOONG
IT'S EASY TO MAKE A TOTAL FOOL OF HIM IN MY IMAGINATION.

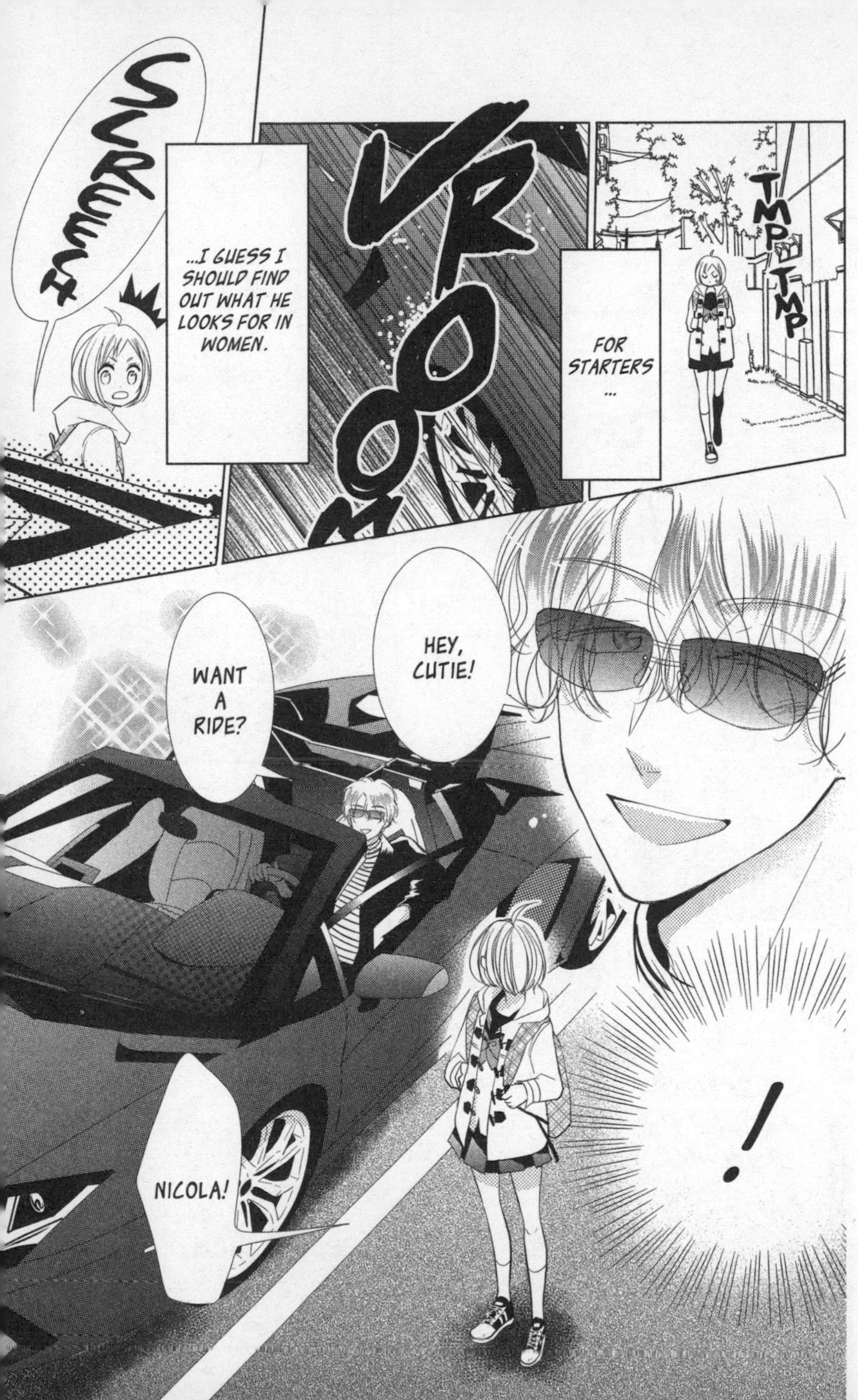
TMP TMP
FOR STARTERS ...
VROOM
...I GUESS I SHOULD FIND OUT WHAT HE LOOKS FOR IN WOMEN.
SCREECH
HEY, CUTIE!
WANT A RIDE?
!
NICOLA!

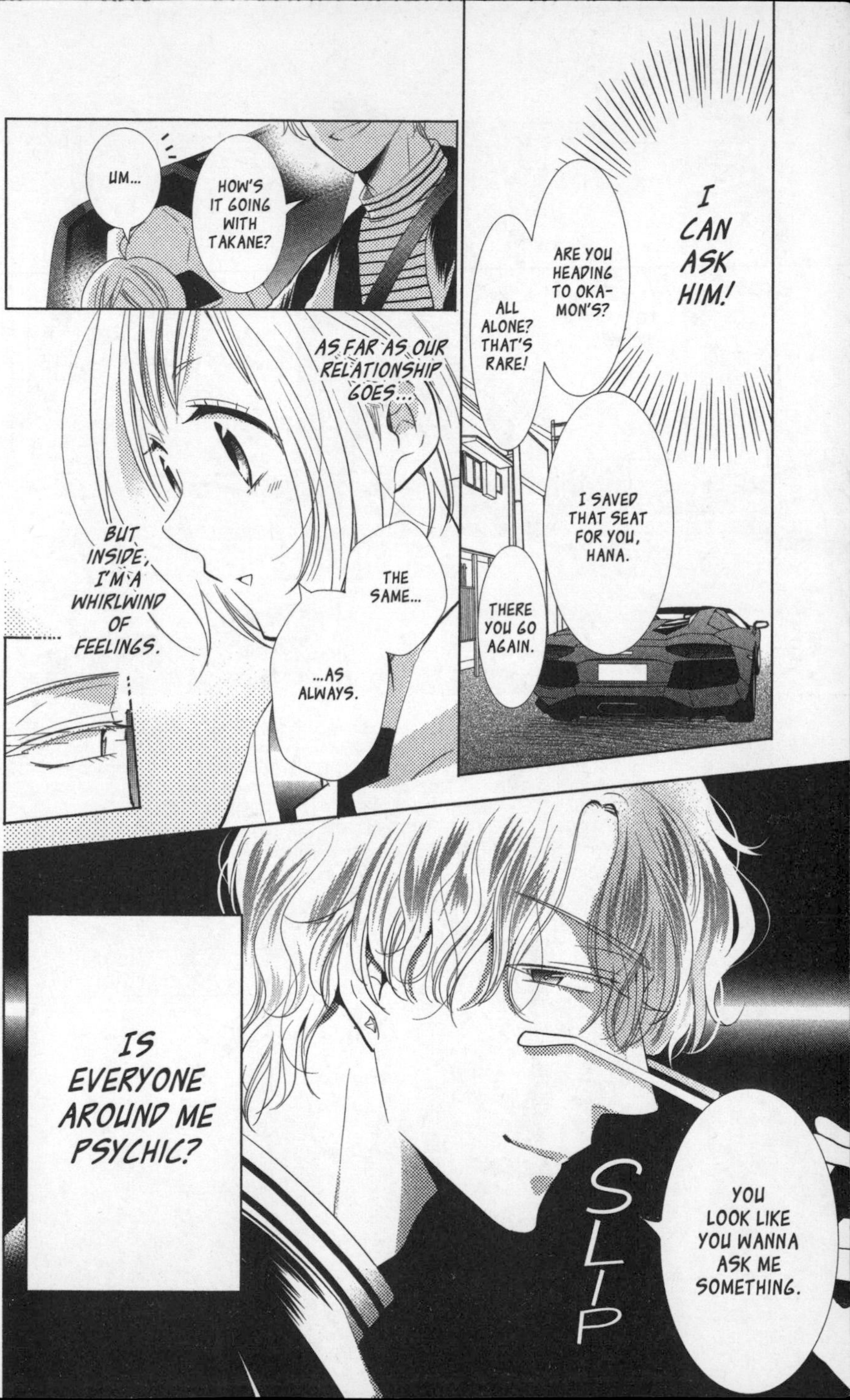
I CAN ASK HIM!
ARE YOU HEADING TO OKA-MON'S?
ALL ALONE? THAT'S RARE!
I SAVED THAT SEAT FOR YOU, HANA.
THERE YOU GO AGAIN.
HOW'S IT GOING WITH TAKANE?
UM...
AS FAR AS OUR RELATIONSHIP GOES...
THE SAME...
...AS ALWAYS.
BUT INSIDE, I'M A WHIRLWIND OF FEELINGS.
YOU LOOK LIKE YOU WANNA ASK ME SOMETHING.
SLIP
IS EVERYONE AROUND ME PSYCHIC?

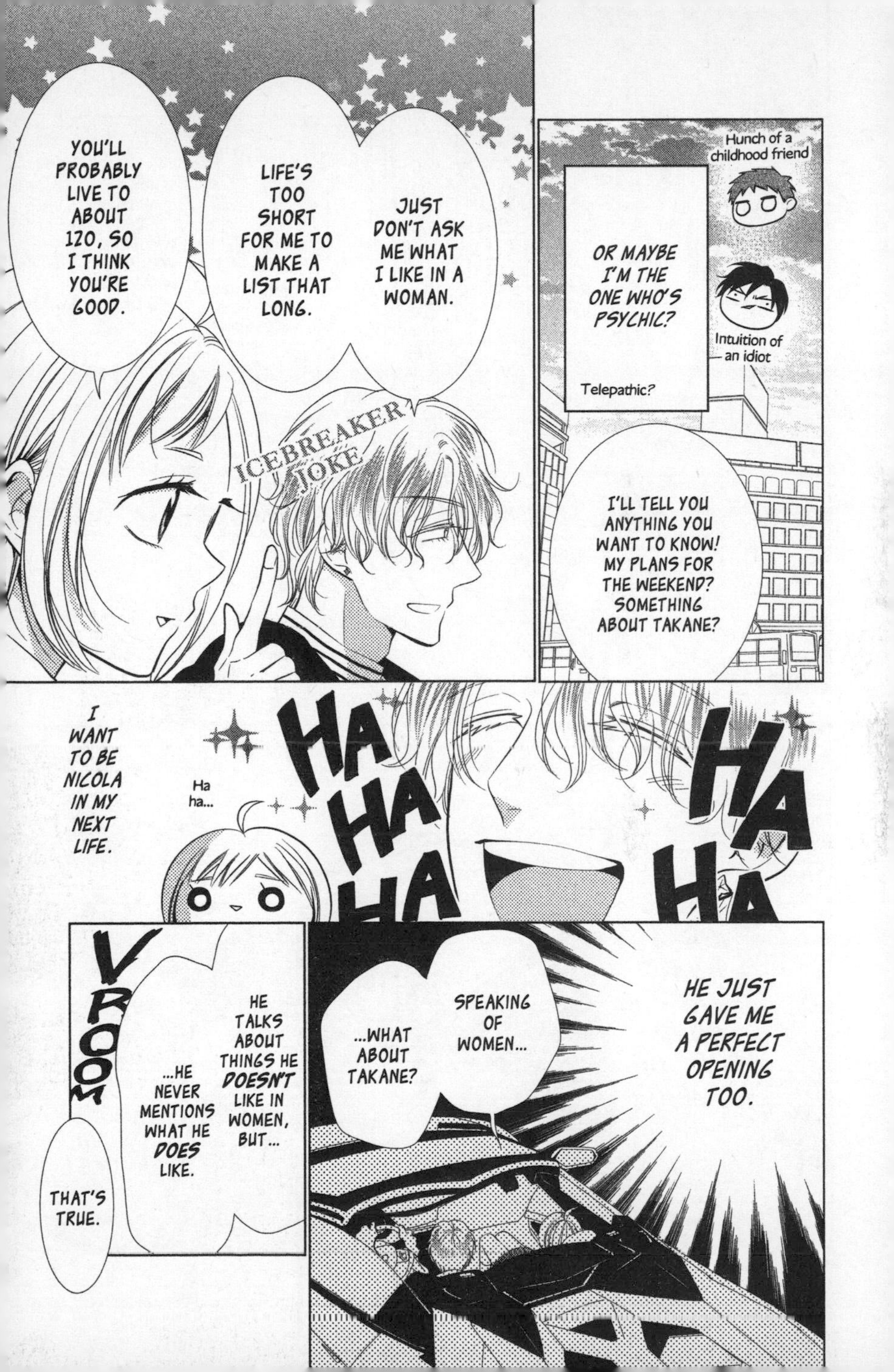
Hunch of a childhood friend
OR MAYBE I'M THE ONE WHO'S PSYCHIC?
Intuition of an idiot
Telepathic?
I'LL TELL YOU ANYTHING YOU WANT TO KNOW! MY PLANS FOR THE WEEKEND? SOMETHING ABOUT TAKANE?
JUST DON'T ASK ME WHAT I LIKE IN A WOMAN.
LIFE'S TOO SHORT FOR ME TO MAKE A LIST THAT LONG.
YOU'LL PROBABLY LIVE TO ABOUT 120, SO I THINK YOU'RE GOOD.
ICEBREAKER JOKE
HA HA
HA HA HA
Ha ha...
I WANT TO BE NICOLA IN MY NEXT LIFE.
HE JUST GAVE ME A PERFECT OPENING TOO.
SPEAKING OF WOMEN...
...WHAT ABOUT TAKANE?
HE TALKS ABOUT THINGS HE *DOESN'T* LIKE IN WOMEN, BUT...
...HE NEVER MENTIONS WHAT HE *DOES* LIKE.
VROOM
THAT'S TRUE.

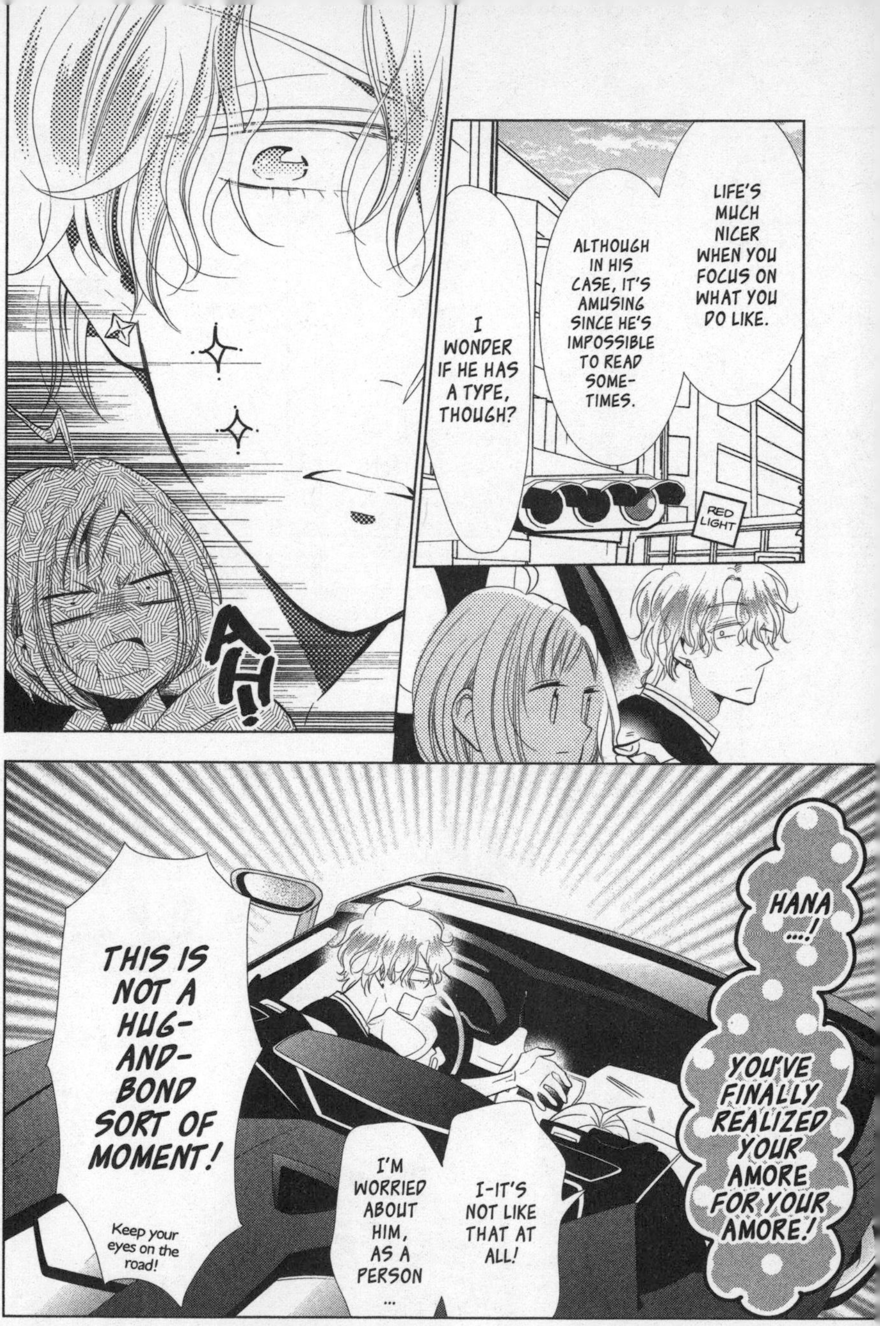
LIFE'S MUCH NICER WHEN YOU FOCUS ON WHAT YOU DO LIKE.
ALTHOUGH IN HIS CASE, IT'S AMUSING SINCE HE'S IMPOSSIBLE TO READ SOME-TIMES.
I WONDER IF HE HAS A TYPE, THOUGH?
RED LIGHT
AH!
HANA ...!
YOU'VE FINALLY REALIZED YOUR AMORE FOR YOUR AMORE!
I-IT'S NOT LIKE THAT AT ALL!
I'M WORRIED ABOUT HIM, AS A PERSON ...
THIS IS NOT A HUG-AND-BOND SORT OF MOMENT!
Keep your eyes on the road!

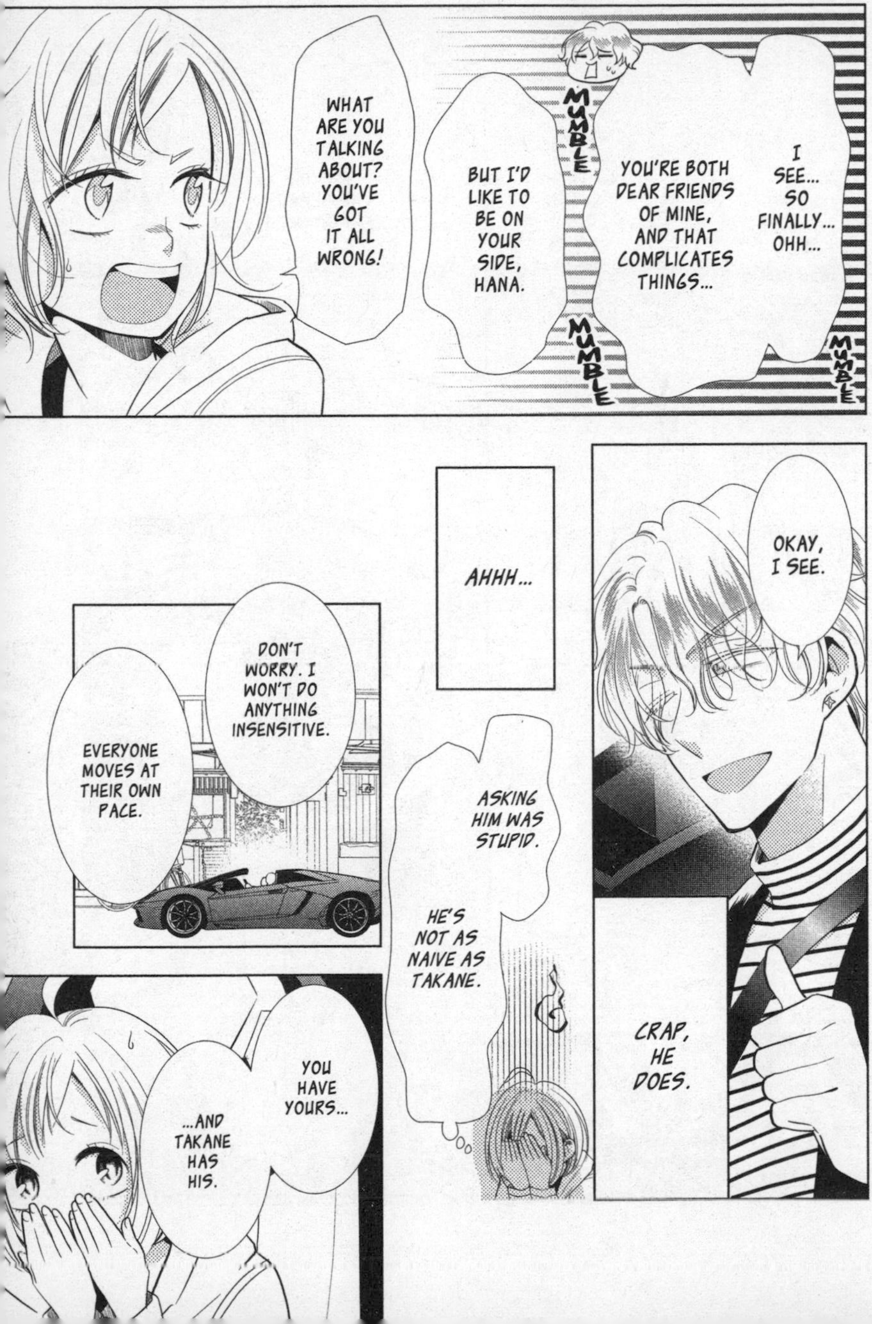
I SEE... SO FINALLY... OHH...
MUMBLE
YOU'RE BOTH DEAR FRIENDS OF MINE, AND THAT COMPLICATES THINGS...
MUMBLE
MUMBLE
BUT I'D LIKE TO BE ON YOUR SIDE, HANA.
WHAT ARE YOU TALKING ABOUT? YOU'VE GOT IT ALL WRONG!
OKAY, I SEE.
AHHH...
DON'T WORRY. I WON'T DO ANYTHING INSENSITIVE.
EVERYONE MOVES AT THEIR OWN PACE.
ASKING HIM WAS STUPID.
HE'S NOT AS NAIVE AS TAKANE.
CRAP, HE DOES.
YOU HAVE YOURS...
...AND TAKANE HAS HIS.

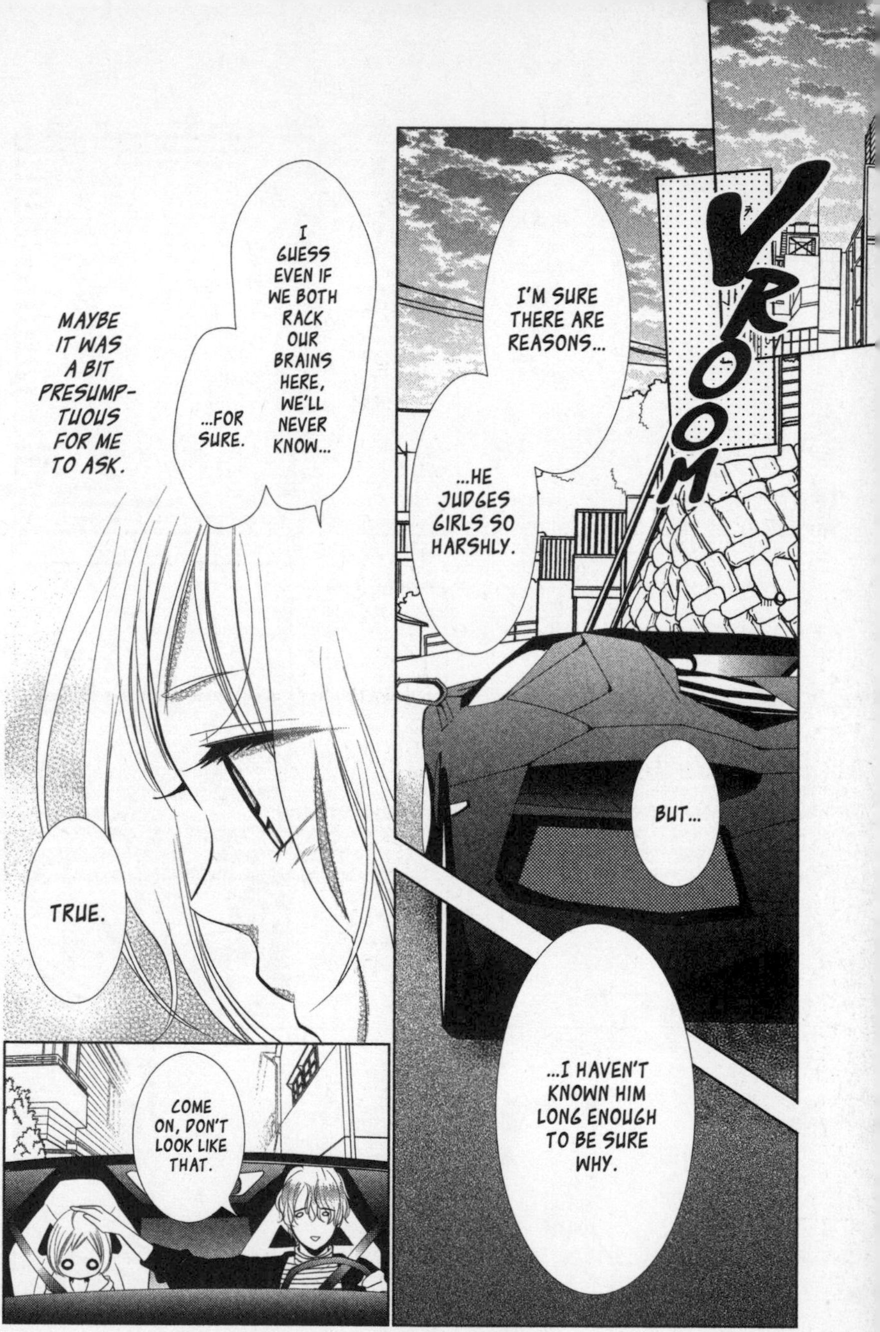
VROOM
I'M SURE THERE ARE REASONS...
...HE JUDGES GIRLS SO HARSHLY.
BUT...
...I HAVEN'T KNOWN HIM LONG ENOUGH TO BE SURE WHY.
I GUESS EVEN IF WE BOTH RACK OUR BRAINS HERE, WE'LL NEVER KNOW...
...FOR SURE.
MAYBE IT WAS A BIT PRESUMPTUOUS FOR ME TO ASK.
TRUE.
COME ON, DON'T LOOK LIKE THAT.

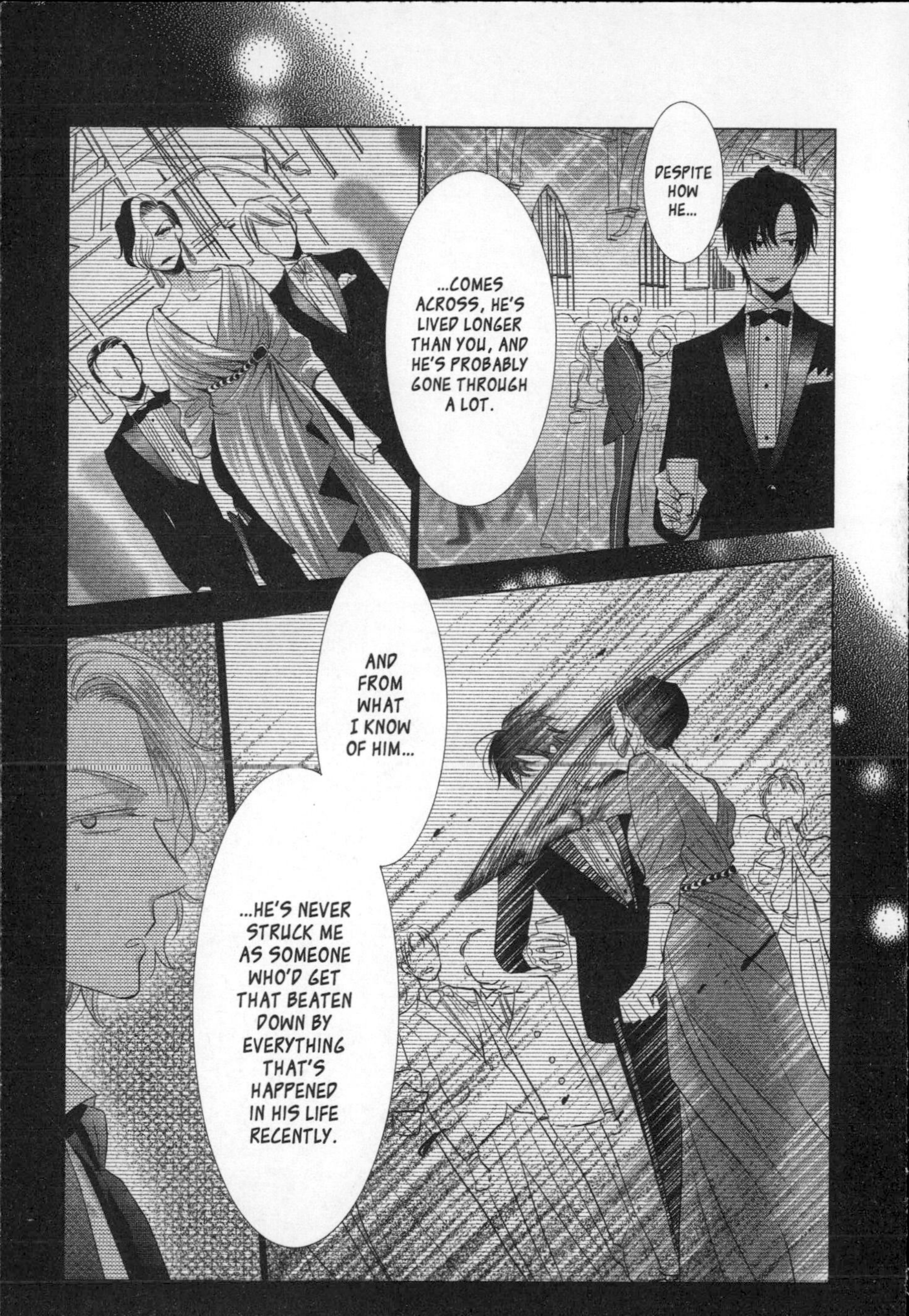
DESPITE HOW HE...
...COMES ACROSS, HE'S LIVED LONGER THAN YOU, AND HE'S PROBABLY GONE THROUGH A LOT.
AND FROM WHAT I KNOW OF HIM...
...HE'S NEVER STRUCK ME AS SOMEONE WHO'D GET THAT BEATEN DOWN BY EVERYTHING THAT'S HAPPENED IN HIS LIFE RECENTLY.

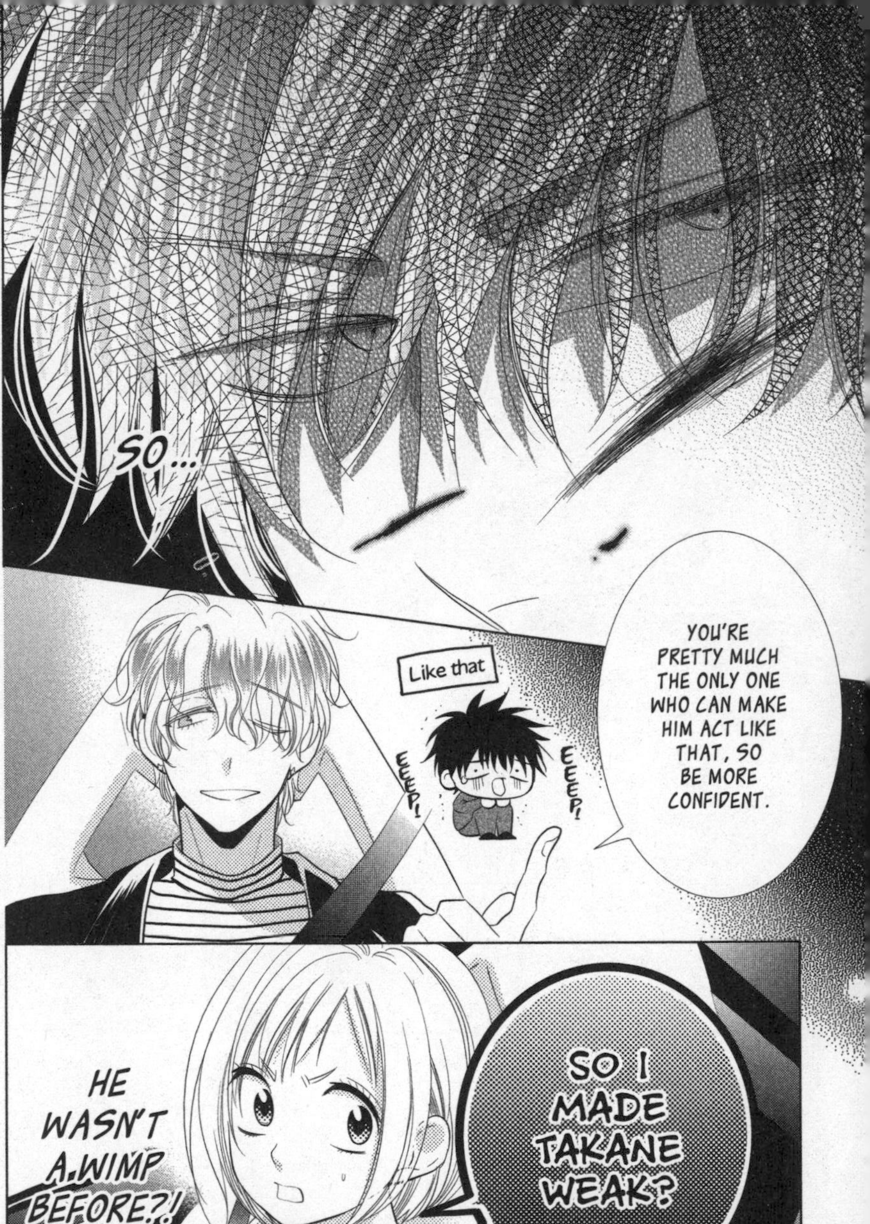
SO...
YOU'RE PRETTY MUCH THE ONLY ONE WHO CAN MAKE HIM ACT LIKE THAT, SO BE MORE CONFIDENT.
EEEP!
EEEP!
Like that
SO I MADE TAKANE WEAK?
HE WASN'T A WIMP BEFORE?!

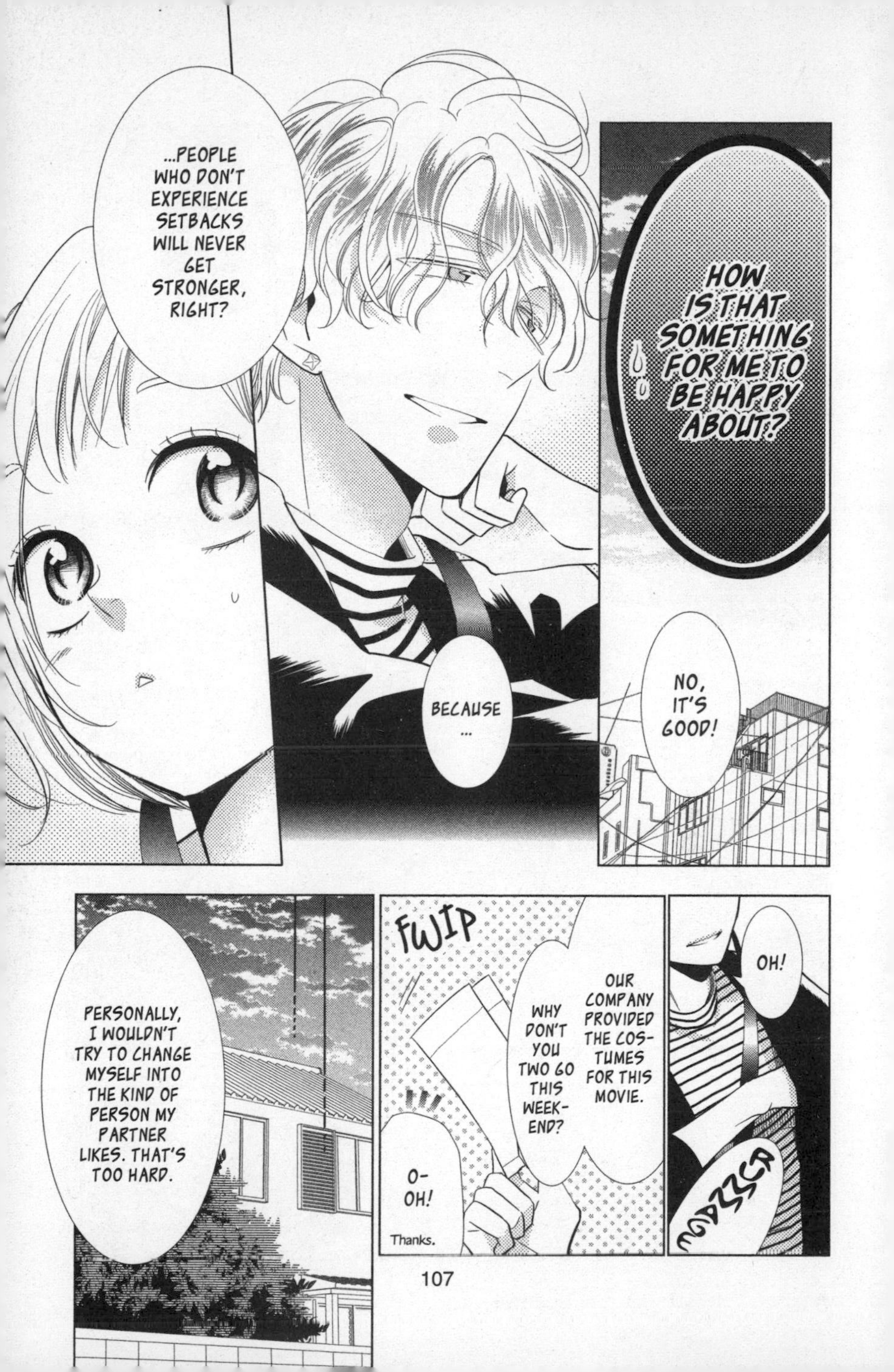

HOW IS THAT SOMETHING FOR ME TO BE HAPPY ABOUT?
NO, IT'S GOOD!
BECAUSE ...
...PEOPLE WHO DON'T EXPERIENCE SETBACKS WILL NEVER GET STRONGER, RIGHT?
OH!
MGDZZSCR
FWIP
OUR COMPANY PROVIDED THE COS-TUMES FOR THIS MOVIE.
WHY DON'T YOU TWO GO THIS WEEK-END?
O-OH!
Thanks.
PERSONALLY, I WOULDN'T TRY TO CHANGE MYSELF INTO THE KIND OF PERSON MY PARTNER LIKES. THAT'S TOO HARD.

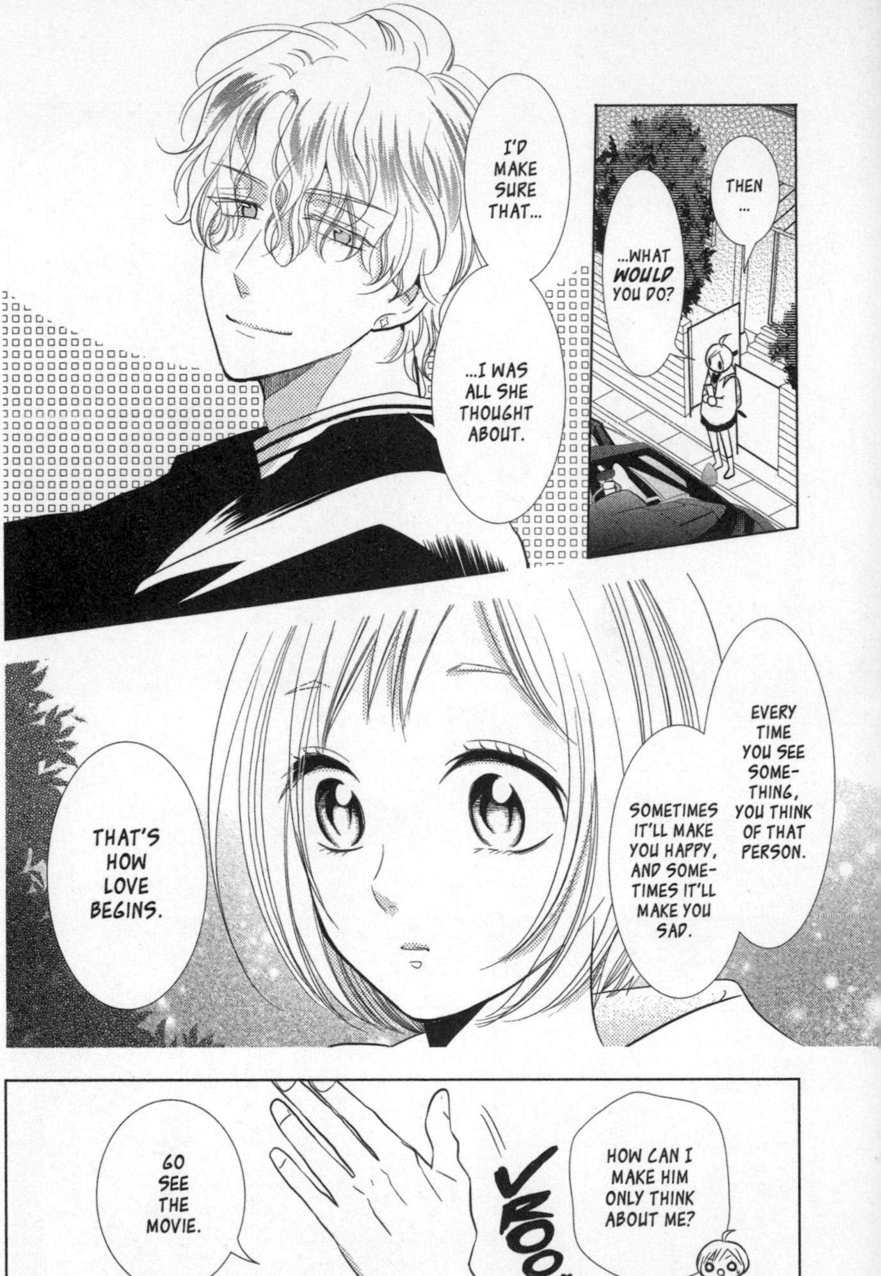
THEN ...
...WHAT WOULD YOU DO?
I'D MAKE SURE THAT...
...I WAS ALL SHE THOUGHT ABOUT.
EVERY TIME YOU SEE SOME-THING, YOU THINK OF THAT PERSON.
SOMETIMES IT'LL MAKE YOU HAPPY, AND SOME-TIMES IT'LL MAKE YOU SAD.
THAT'S HOW LOVE BEGINS.
HOW CAN I MAKE HIM ONLY THINK ABOUT ME?
VROOM
GO SEE THE MOVIE.

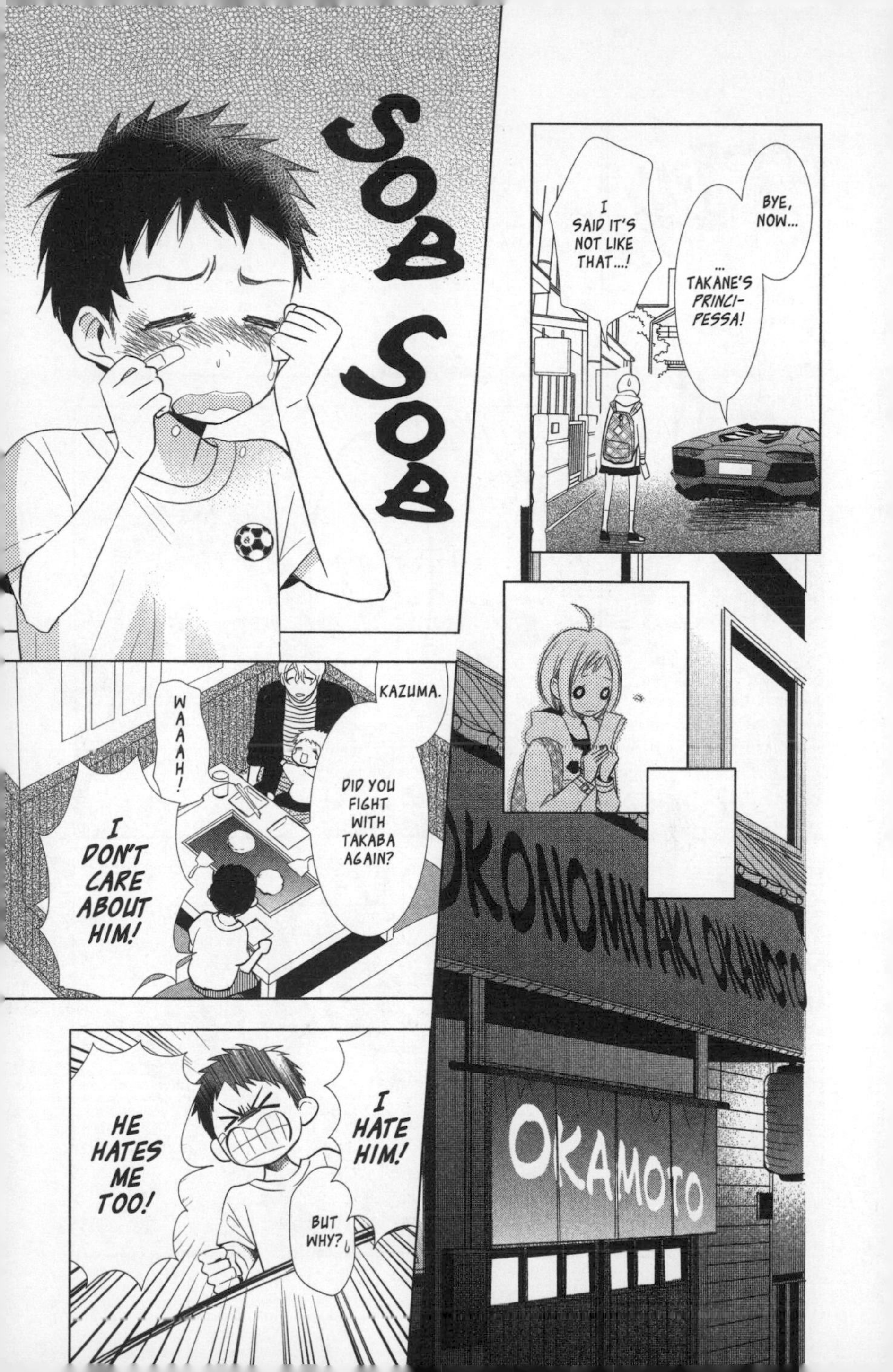
BYE, NOW... ... TAKANE'S PRINCIPESSA!
I SAID IT'S NOT LIKE THAT...!
SOB SOB SOB
OKONOMIYAKI OKAMOTO
OKAMOTO
KAZUMA.
DID YOU FIGHT WITH TAKABA AGAIN?
WAAAAH!
I DON'T CARE ABOUT HIM!
I HATE HIM!
BUT WHY?
HE HATES ME TOO!

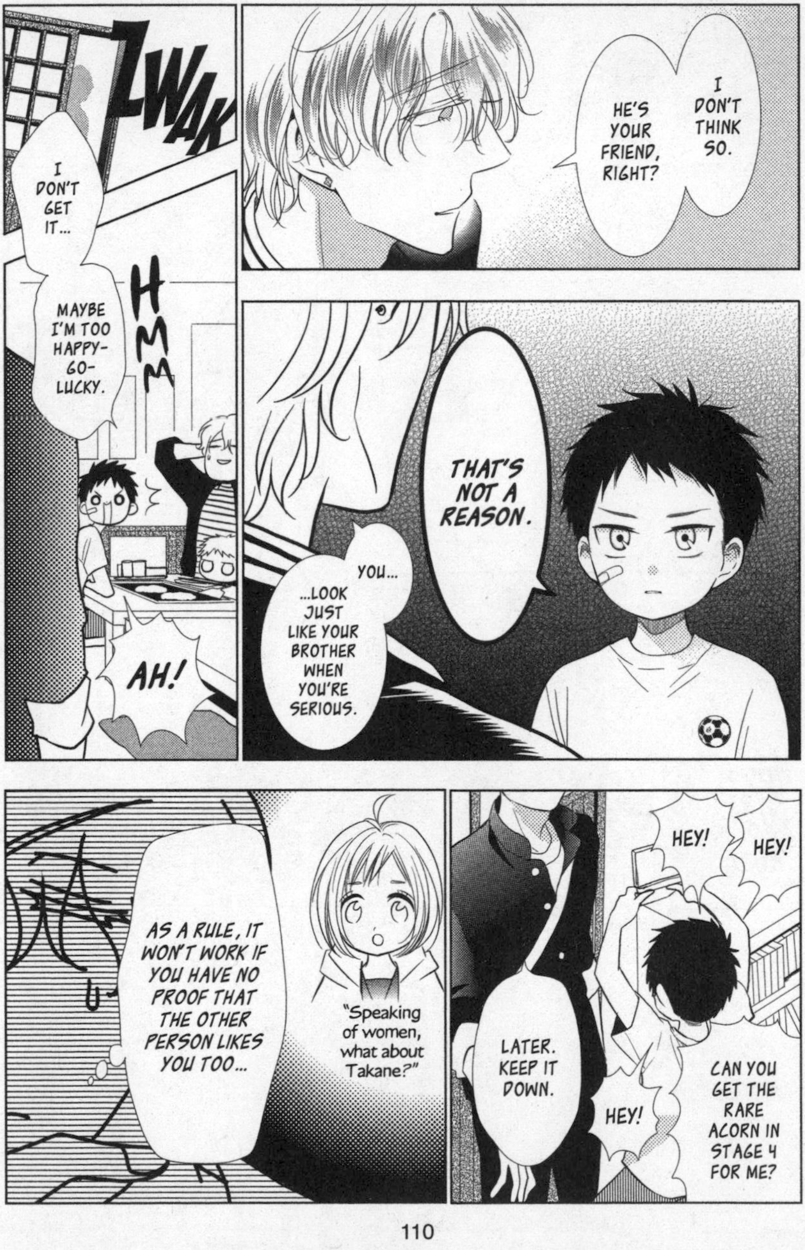
I DON'T THINK SO.
HE'S YOUR FRIEND, RIGHT?
THAT'S NOT A REASON.
YOU...
...LOOK JUST LIKE YOUR BROTHER WHEN YOU'RE SERIOUS.
ZWAK
I DON'T GET IT...
HMM
MAYBE I'M TOO HAPPY-GO-LUCKY.
AH!
HEY!
HEY!
CAN YOU GET THE RARE ACORN IN STAGE 4 FOR ME?
HEY!
LATER. KEEP IT DOWN.
"Speaking of women, what about Takane?"
AS A RULE, IT WON'T WORK IF YOU HAVE NO PROOF THAT THE OTHER PERSON LIKES YOU TOO...

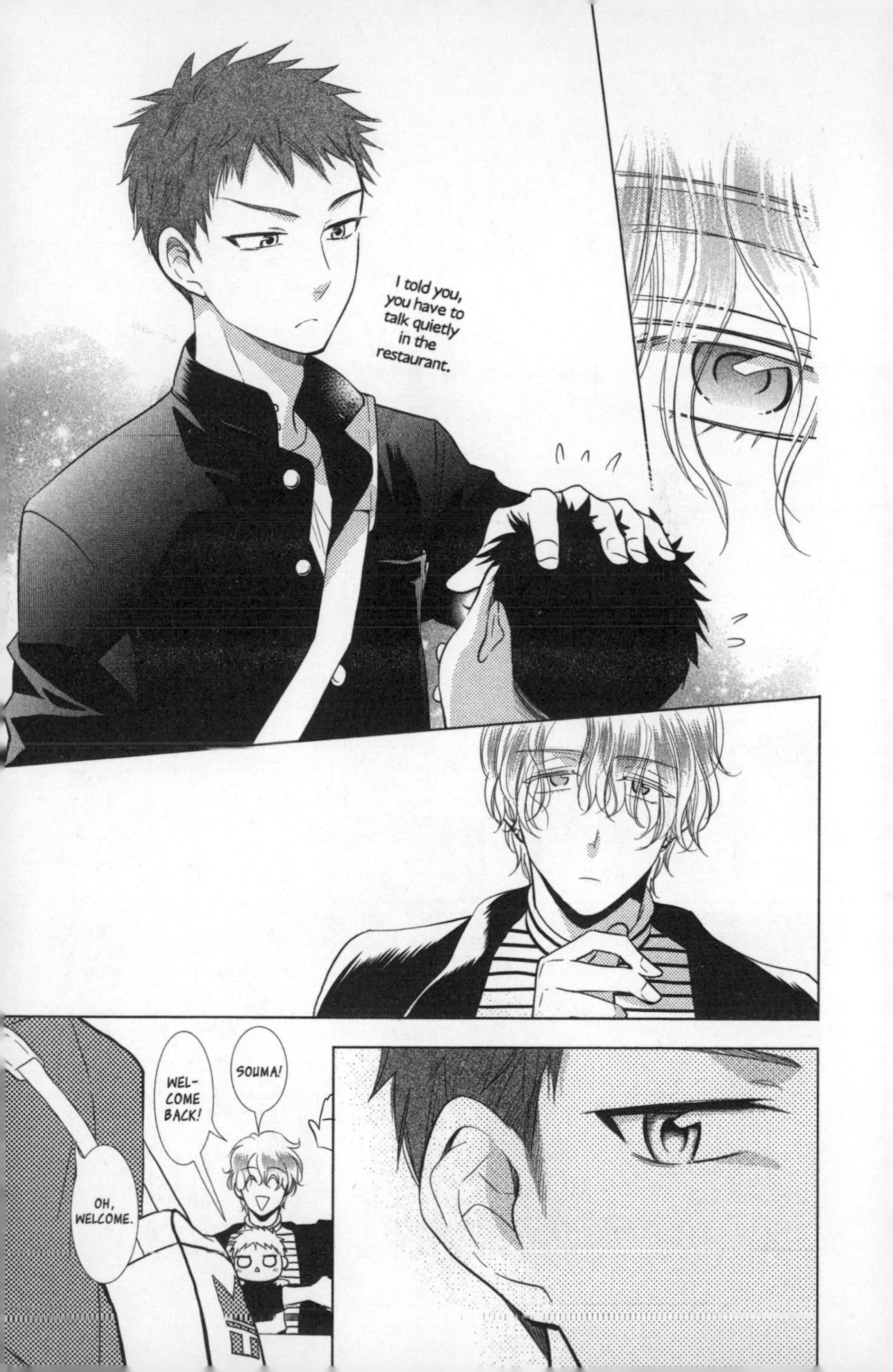
I told you, you have to talk quietly in the restaurant.
SOUMA!
WEL-COME BACK!
OH, WELCOME.

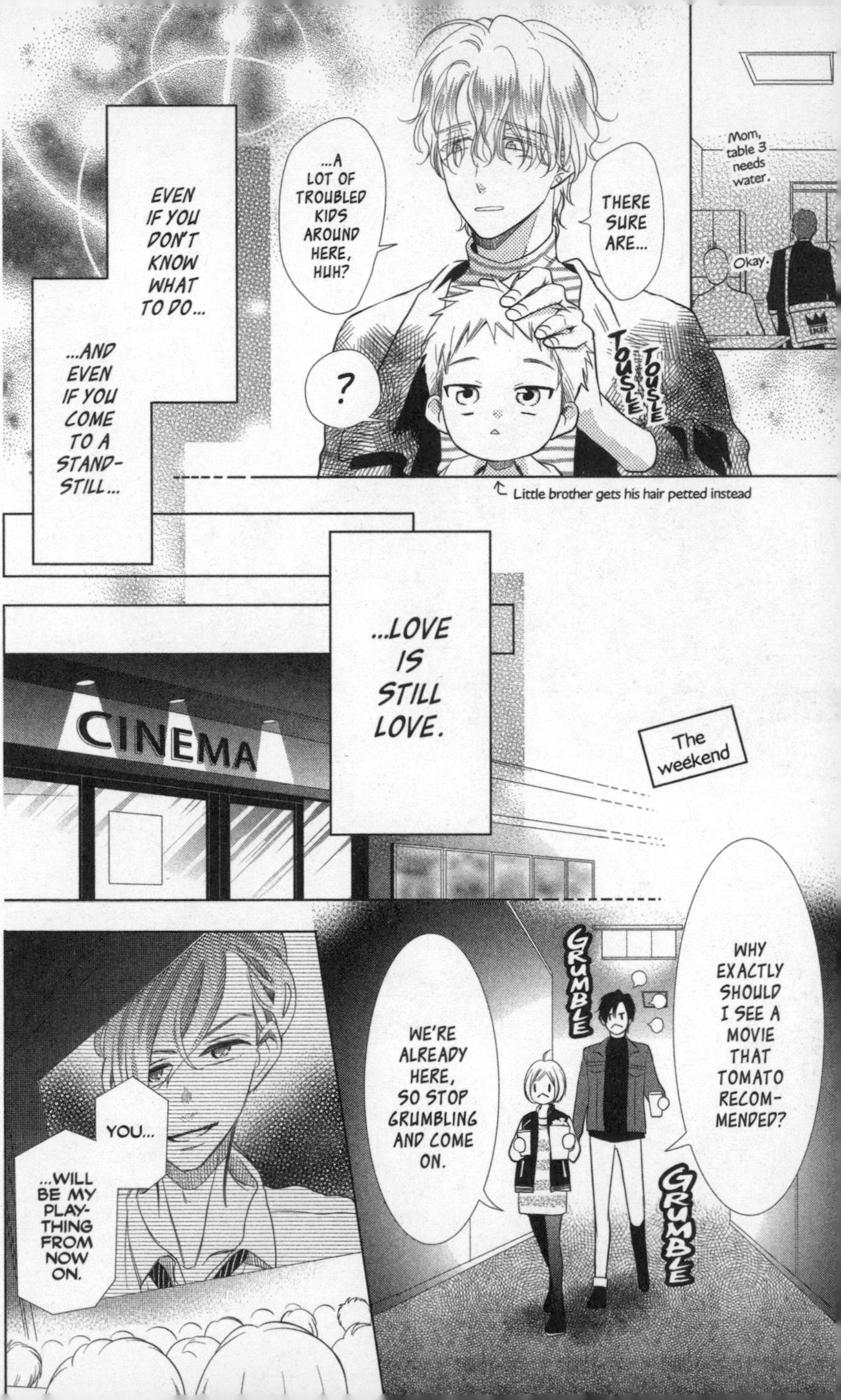
Mom, table 3 needs water.
Okay.
THERE SURE ARE...
...A LOT OF TROUBLED KIDS AROUND HERE, HUH?
TOUSLE TOUSLE
?
EVEN IF YOU DON'T KNOW WHAT TO DO...
...AND EVEN IF YOU COME TO A STAND-STILL...
Little brother gets his hair petted instead
The weekend
...LOVE IS STILL LOVE.
CINEMA
WHY EXACTLY SHOULD I SEE A MOVIE THAT TOMATO RECOM-MENDED?
GRUMBLE
GRUMBLE
WE'RE ALREADY HERE, SO STOP GRUMBLING AND COME ON.
YOU...
...WILL BE MY PLAY-THING FROM NOW ON.

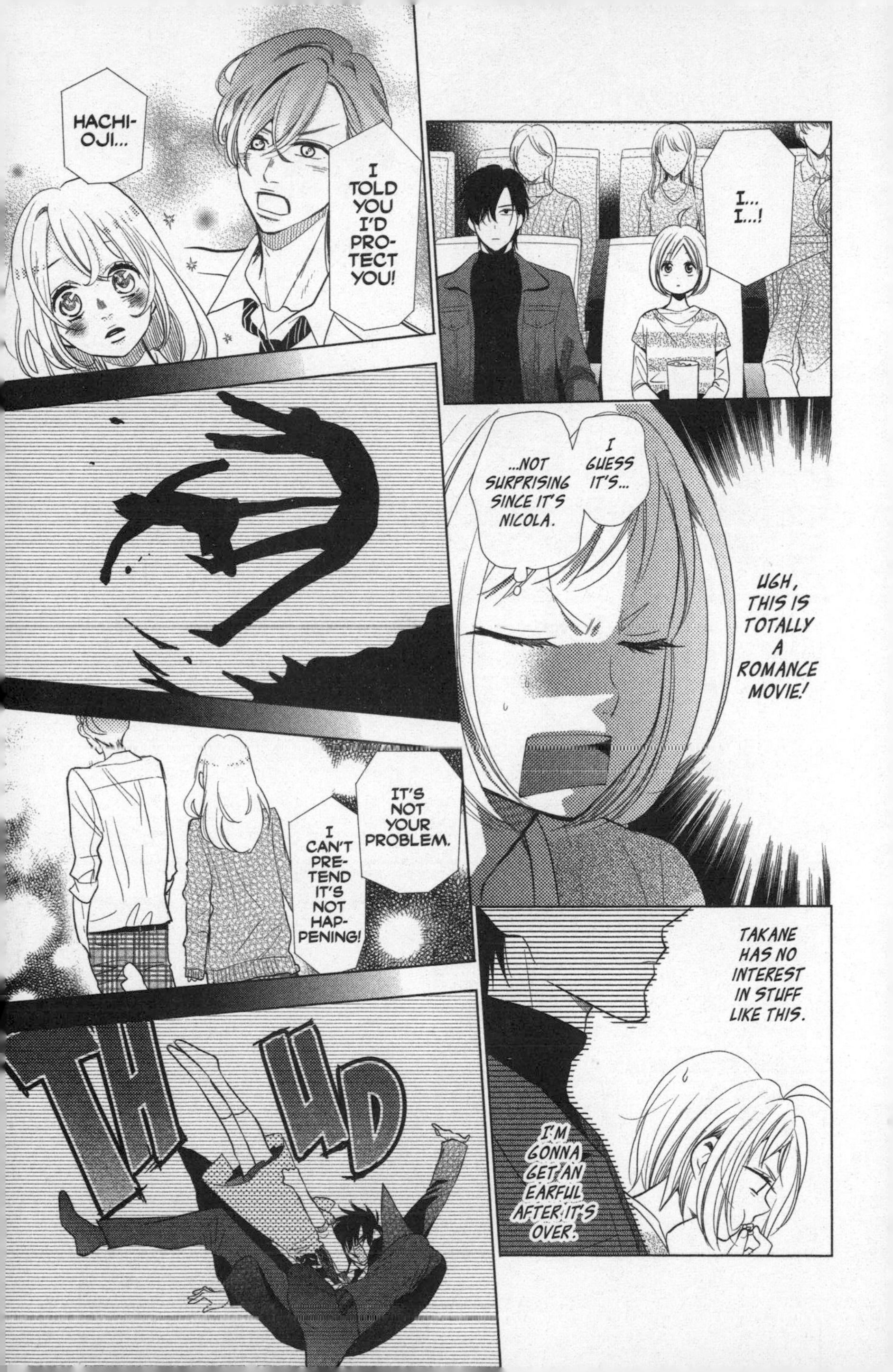
HACHI-OJI...
I TOLD YOU I'D PROTECT YOU!
I... I...!
I GUESS IT'S...
...NOT SURPRISING SINCE IT'S NICOLA.
UGH, THIS IS TOTALLY A ROMANCE MOVIE!
IT'S NOT YOUR PROBLEM.
I CAN'T PRETEND IT'S NOT HAPPENING!
TAKANE HAS NO INTEREST IN STUFF LIKE THIS.
I'M GONNA GET AN EARFUL AFTER IT'S OVER.
THUD

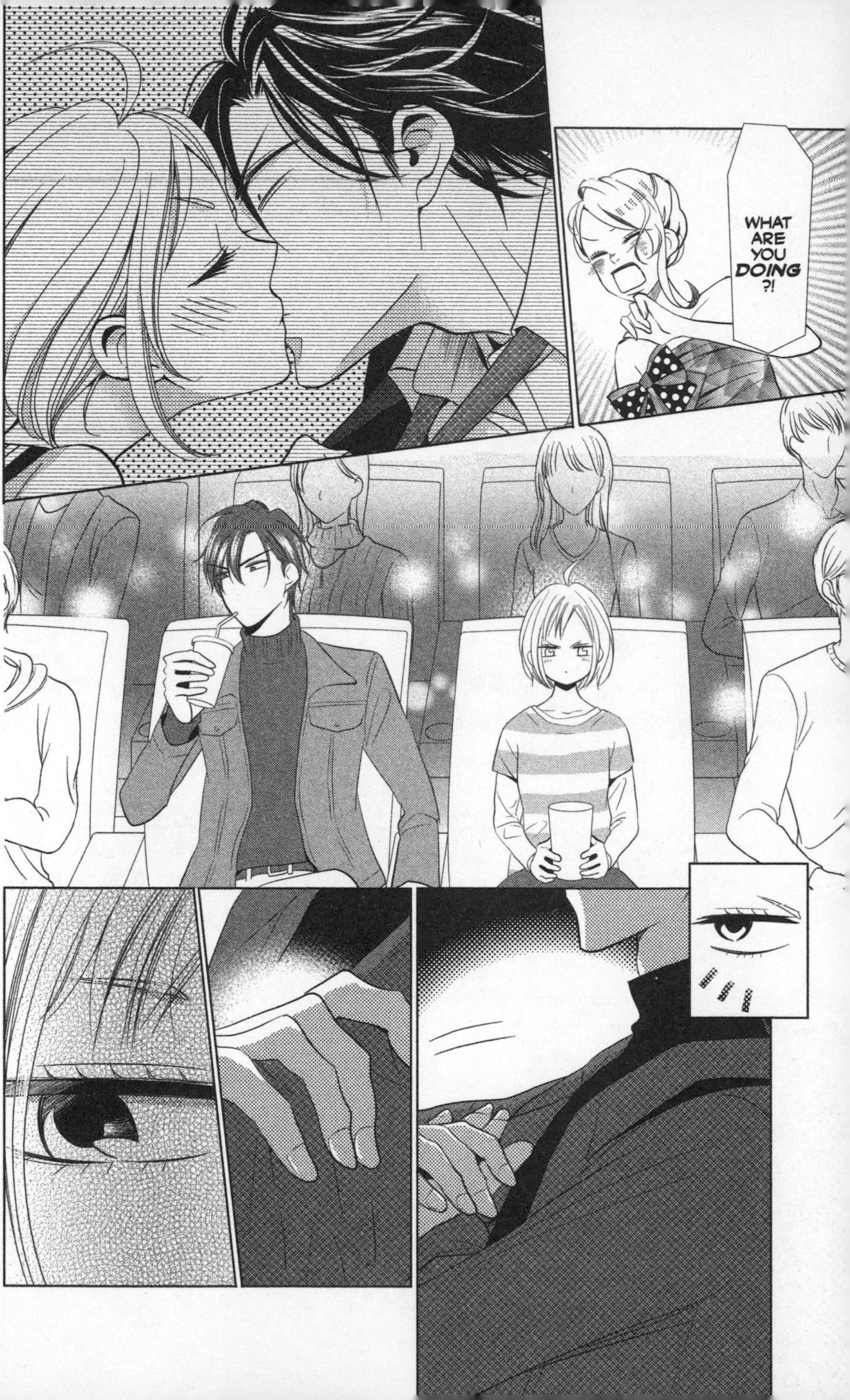
WHAT ARE YOU DOING?!

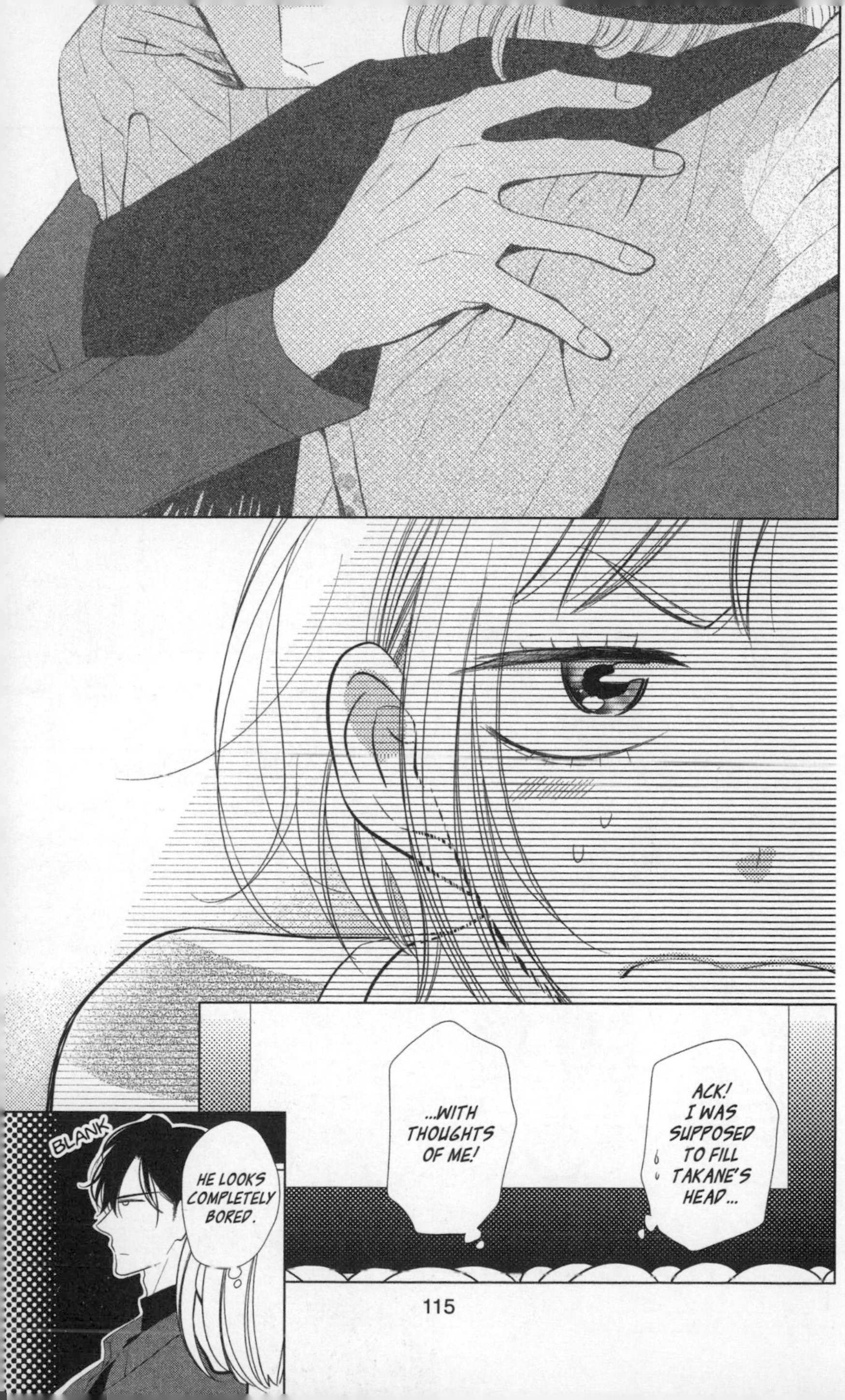
ACK! I WAS SUPPOSED TO FILL TAKANE'S HEAD...
...WITH THOUGHTS OF ME!
BLANK
HE LOOKS COMPLETELY BORED.

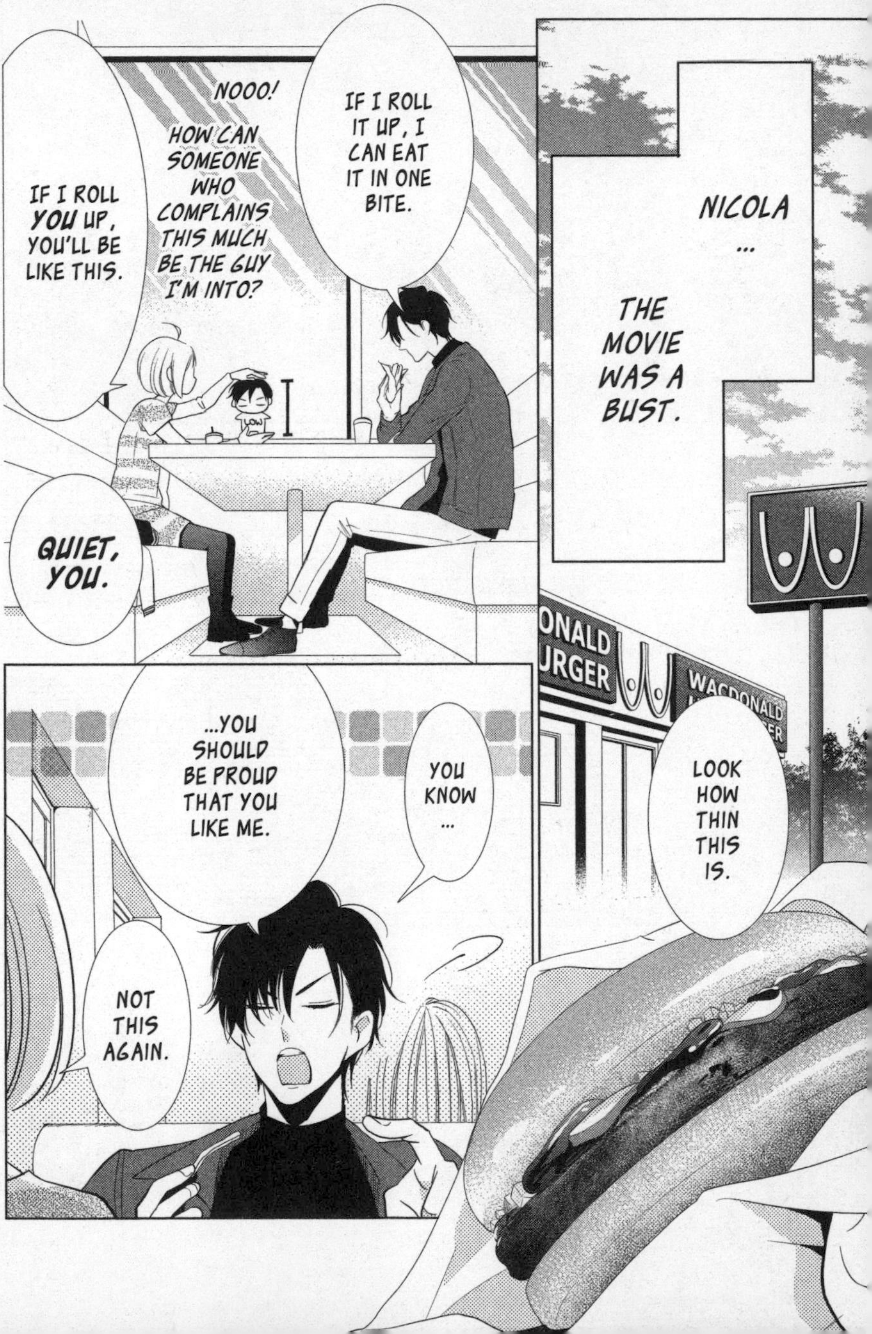
NICOLA ...
THE MOVIE WAS A BUST.
WACDONALD
LOOK HOW THIN THIS IS.
IF I ROLL IT UP, I CAN EAT IT IN ONE BITE.
NOOO! HOW CAN SOMEONE WHO COMPLAINS THIS MUCH BE THE GUY I'M INTO?
IF I ROLL **YOU** UP, YOU'LL BE LIKE THIS.
QUIET, YOU.
YOU KNOW ...
...YOU SHOULD BE PROUD THAT YOU LIKE ME.
NOT THIS AGAIN.

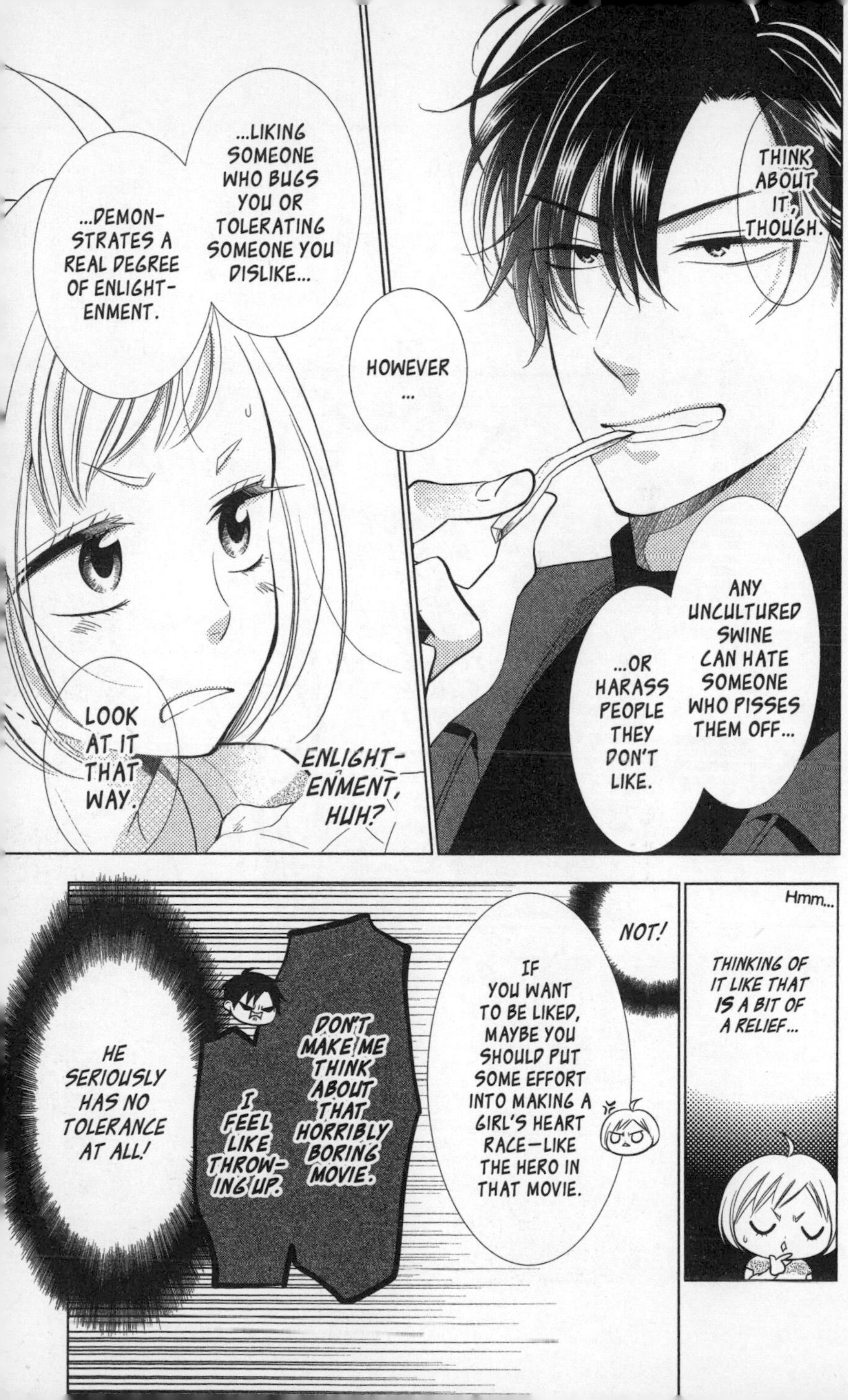
THINK ABOUT IT, THOUGH.
ANY UNCULTURED SWINE CAN HATE SOMEONE WHO PISSES THEM OFF...
...OR HARASS PEOPLE THEY DON'T LIKE.
HOWEVER...
...LIKING SOMEONE WHO BUGS YOU OR TOLERATING SOMEONE YOU DISLIKE...
...DEMONSTRATES A REAL DEGREE OF ENLIGHTENMENT.
ENLIGHTENMENT, HUH?
LOOK AT IT THAT WAY.
Hmm...
THINKING OF IT LIKE THAT IS A BIT OF A RELIEF...
NOT!
IF YOU WANT TO BE LIKED, MAYBE YOU SHOULD PUT SOME EFFORT INTO MAKING A GIRL'S HEART RACE—LIKE THE HERO IN THAT MOVIE.
DON'T MAKE ME THINK ABOUT THAT HORRIBLY BORING MOVIE.
I FEEL LIKE THROWING UP.
HE SERIOUSLY HAS NO TOLERANCE AT ALL!

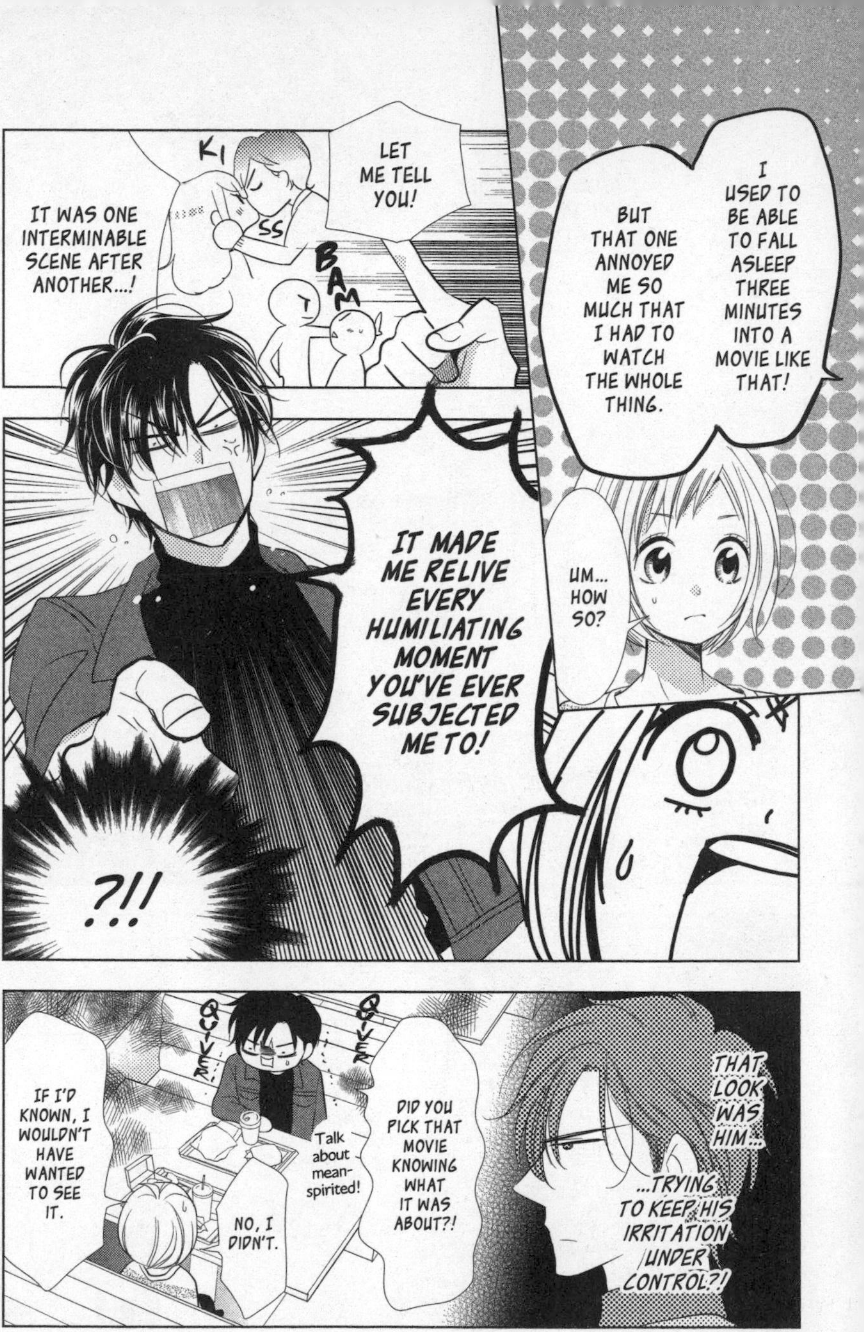
I USED TO BE ABLE TO FALL ASLEEP THREE MINUTES INTO A MOVIE LIKE THAT!
BUT THAT ONE ANNOYED ME SO MUCH THAT I HAD TO WATCH THE WHOLE THING.
UM... HOW SO?
LET ME TELL YOU!
IT WAS ONE INTERMINABLE SCENE AFTER ANOTHER...!
KI
SS
BAM
IT MADE ME RELIVE EVERY HUMILIATING MOMENT YOU'VE EVER SUBJECTED ME TO!
?!!
THAT LOOK WAS HIM...
...TRYING TO KEEP HIS IRRITATION UNDER CONTROL?!
QUIVER
QUIVER
DID YOU PICK THAT MOVIE KNOWING WHAT IT WAS ABOUT?!
Talk about mean-spirited!
NO, I DIDN'T.
IF I'D KNOWN, I WOULDN'T HAVE WANTED TO SEE IT.

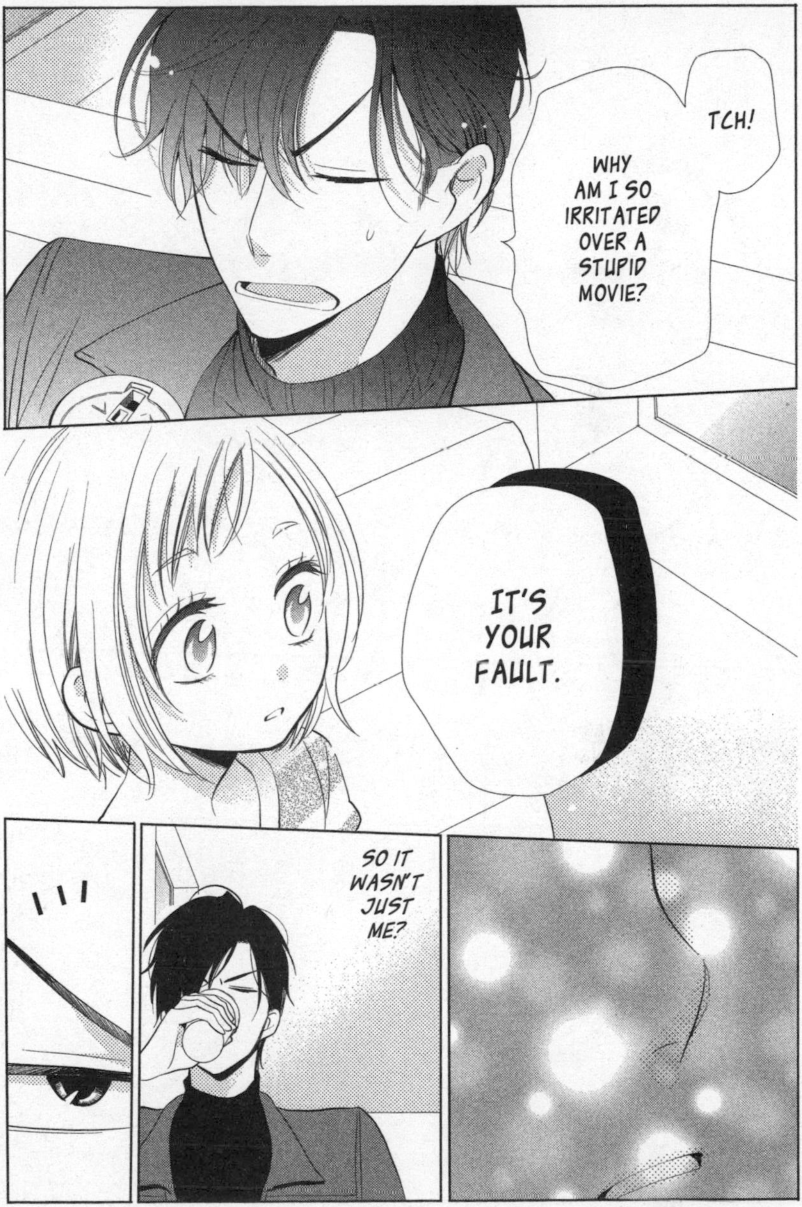
TCH!
WHY AM I SO IRRITATED OVER A STUPID MOVIE?
IT'S YOUR FAULT.
SO IT WASN'T JUST ME?
///

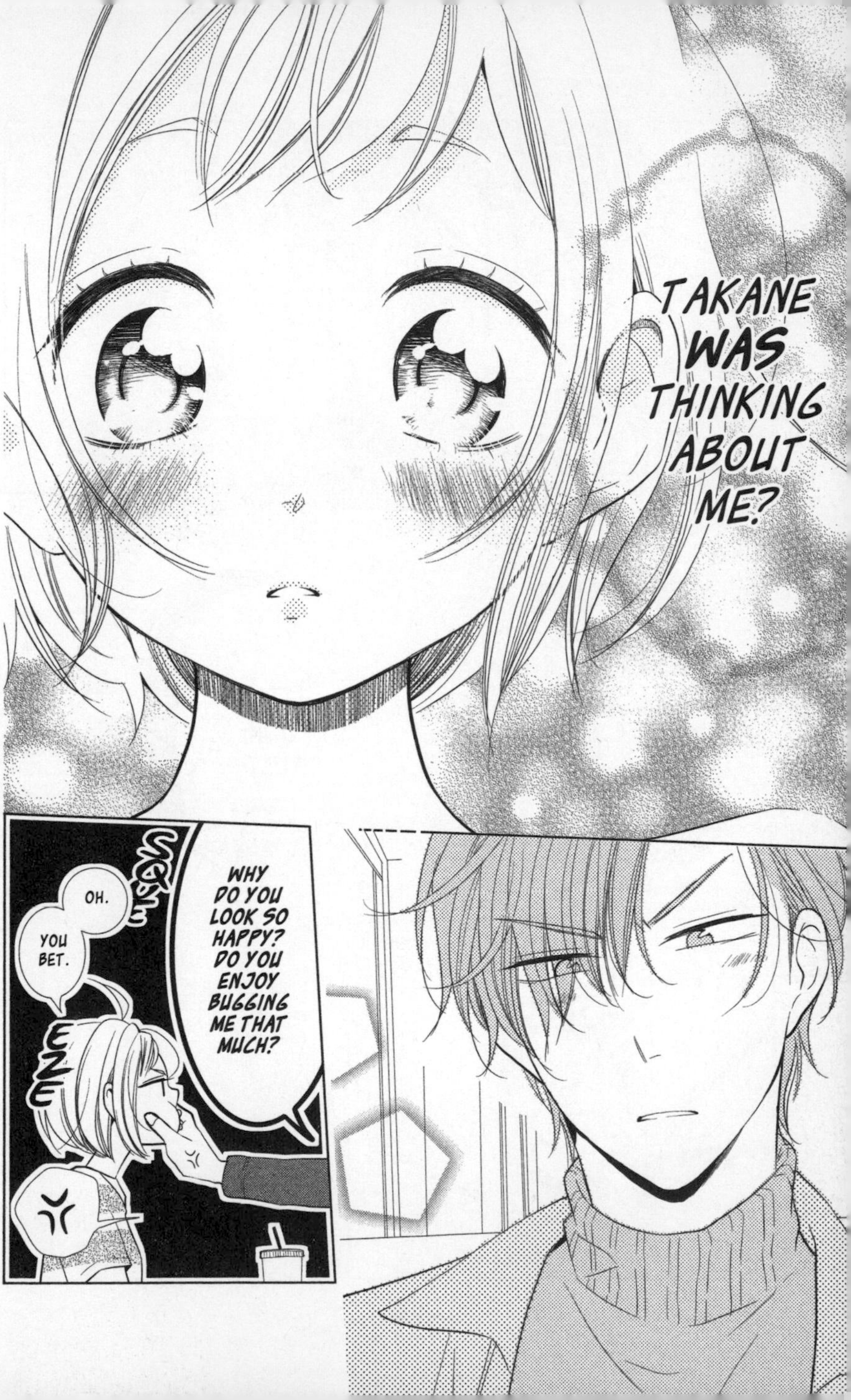
TAKANE WAS THINKING ABOUT ME?
WHY DO YOU LOOK SO HAPPY? DO YOU ENJOY BUGGING ME THAT MUCH?
OH.
YOU BET.

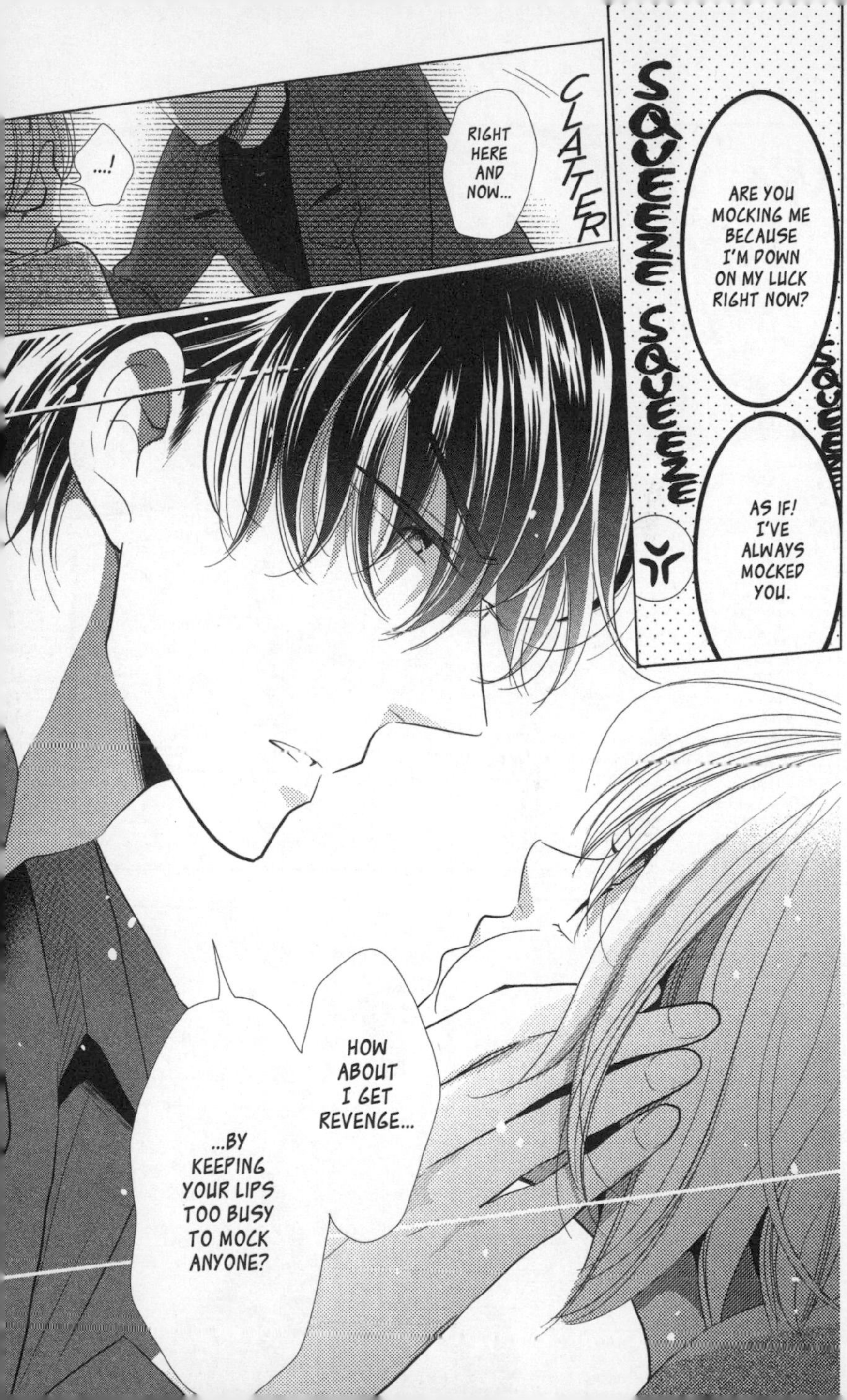
SQUEEZE SQUEEZE
ARE YOU MOCKING ME BECAUSE I'M DOWN ON MY LUCK RIGHT NOW?
AS IF! I'VE ALWAYS MOCKED YOU.
CLATTER
RIGHT HERE AND NOW...
...!
HOW ABOUT I GET REVENGE...
...BY KEEPING YOUR LIPS TOO BUSY TO MOCK ANYONE?

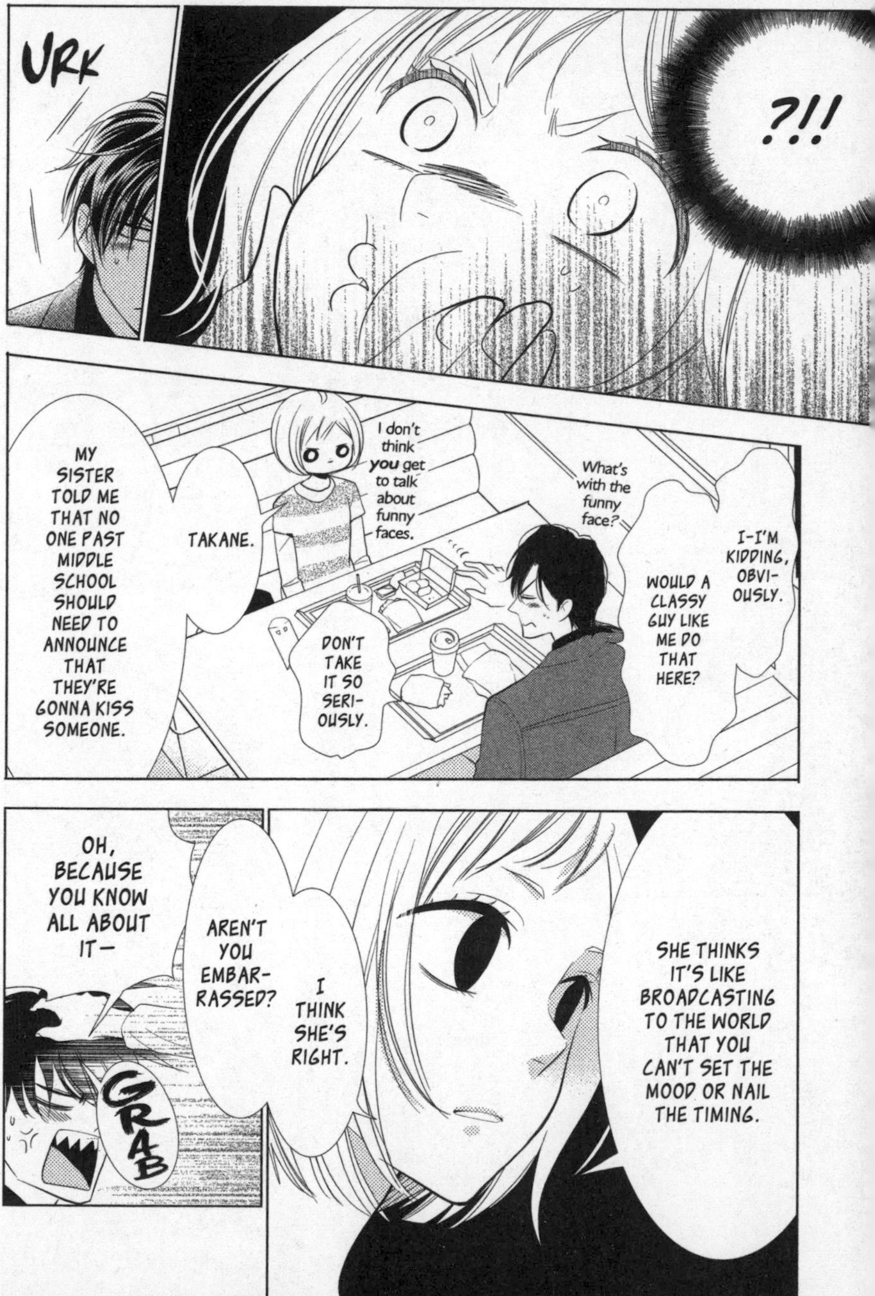
?!!
URK
What's with the funny face?
I don't think you get to talk about funny faces.
I-I'M KIDDING, OBVIOUSLY.
WOULD A CLASSY GUY LIKE ME DO THAT HERE?
DON'T TAKE IT SO SERIOUSLY.
TAKANE.
MY SISTER TOLD ME THAT NO ONE PAST MIDDLE SCHOOL SHOULD NEED TO ANNOUNCE THAT THEY'RE GONNA KISS SOMEONE.
SHE THINKS IT'S LIKE BROADCASTING TO THE WORLD THAT YOU CAN'T SET THE MOOD OR NAIL THE TIMING.
I THINK SHE'S RIGHT.
AREN'T YOU EMBARRASSED?
OH, BECAUSE YOU KNOW ALL ABOUT IT—
GRAB

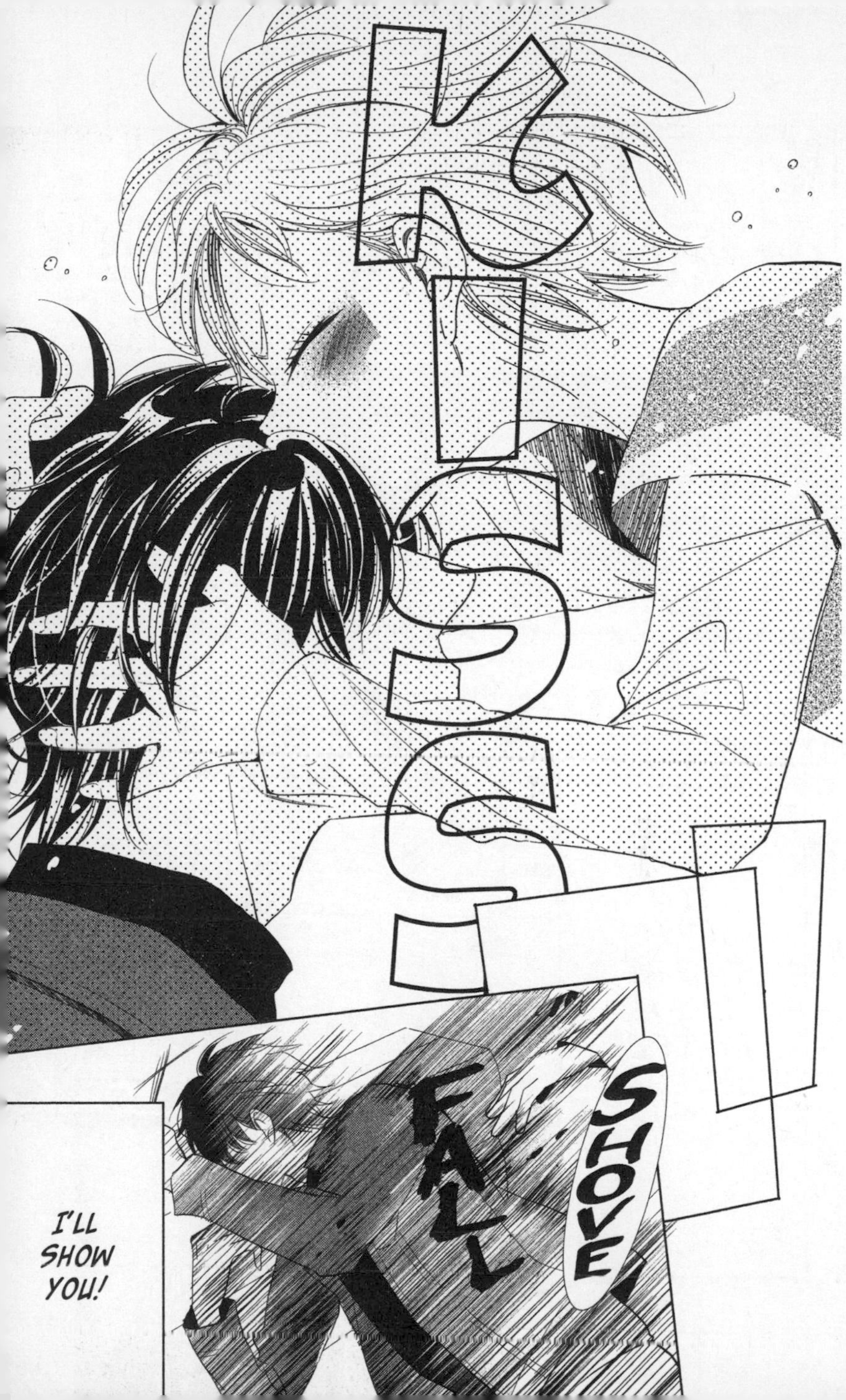
KISS!
SHOVE
FALL
I'LL SHOW YOU!

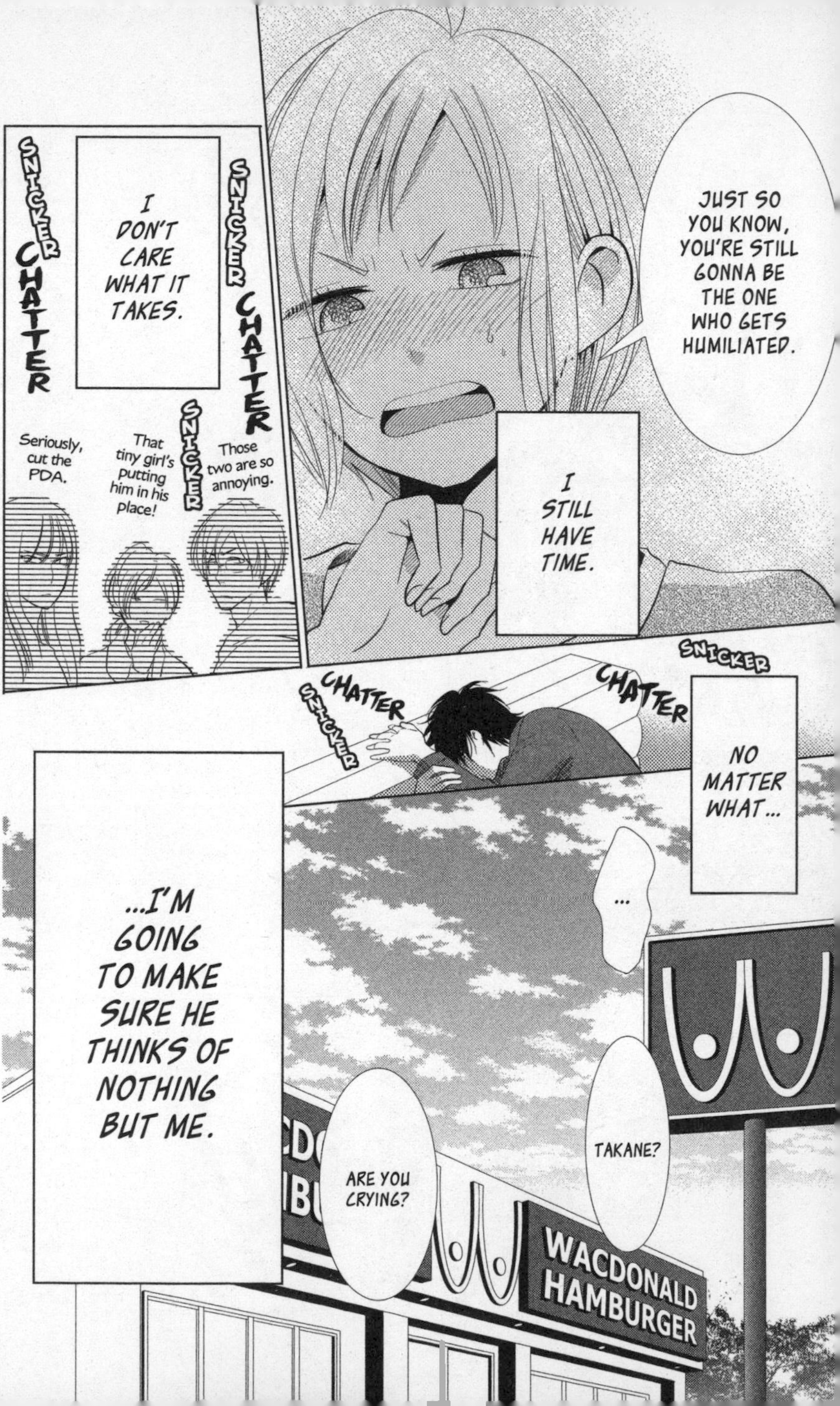
JUST SO YOU KNOW, YOU'RE STILL GONNA BE THE ONE WHO GETS HUMILIATED.
I STILL HAVE TIME.
SNICKER CHATTER
I DON'T CARE WHAT IT TAKES.
SNICKER CHATTER
SNICKER
Those two are so annoying.
That tiny girl's putting him in his place!
Seriously, cut the PDA.
SNICKER
CHATTER
CHATTER
SNICKER
NO MATTER WHAT...
...I'M GOING TO MAKE SURE HE THINKS OF NOTHING BUT ME.
...
TAKANE?
ARE YOU CRYING?
WACDONALD HAMBURGER

At the Flea Market

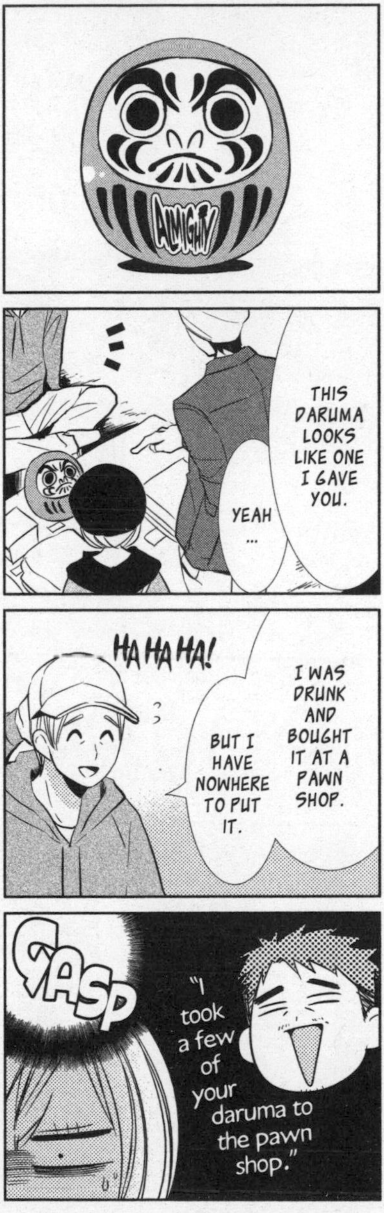
ALMIGHTY
THIS DARUMA LOOKS LIKE ONE I GAVE YOU.
YEAH...
I WAS DRUNK AND BOUGHT IT AT A PAWN SHOP.
BUT I HAVE NOWHERE TO PUT IT.
HA HA HA!
"I took a few of your daruma to the pawn shop."
GASP

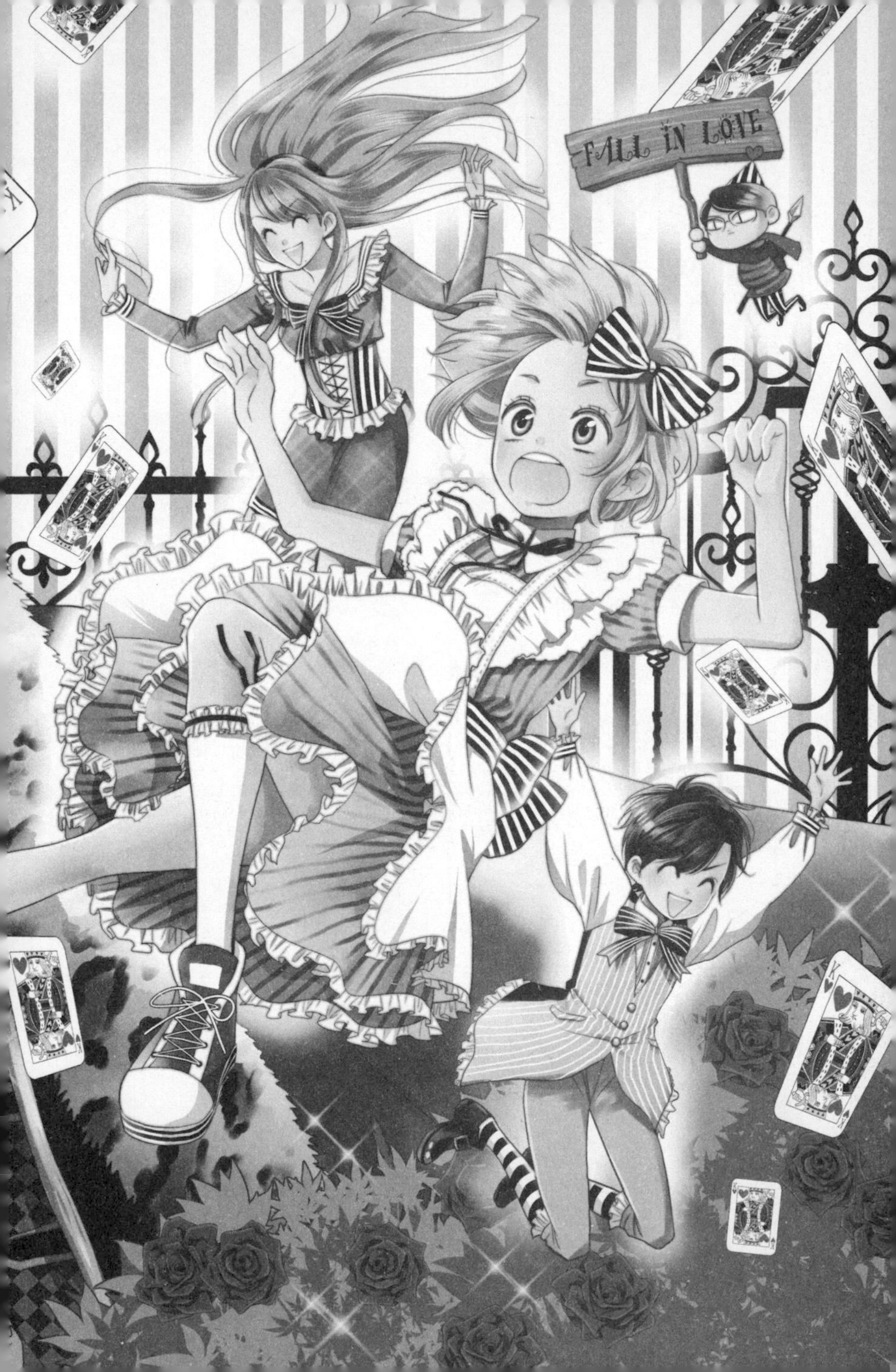
FALL IN LOVE

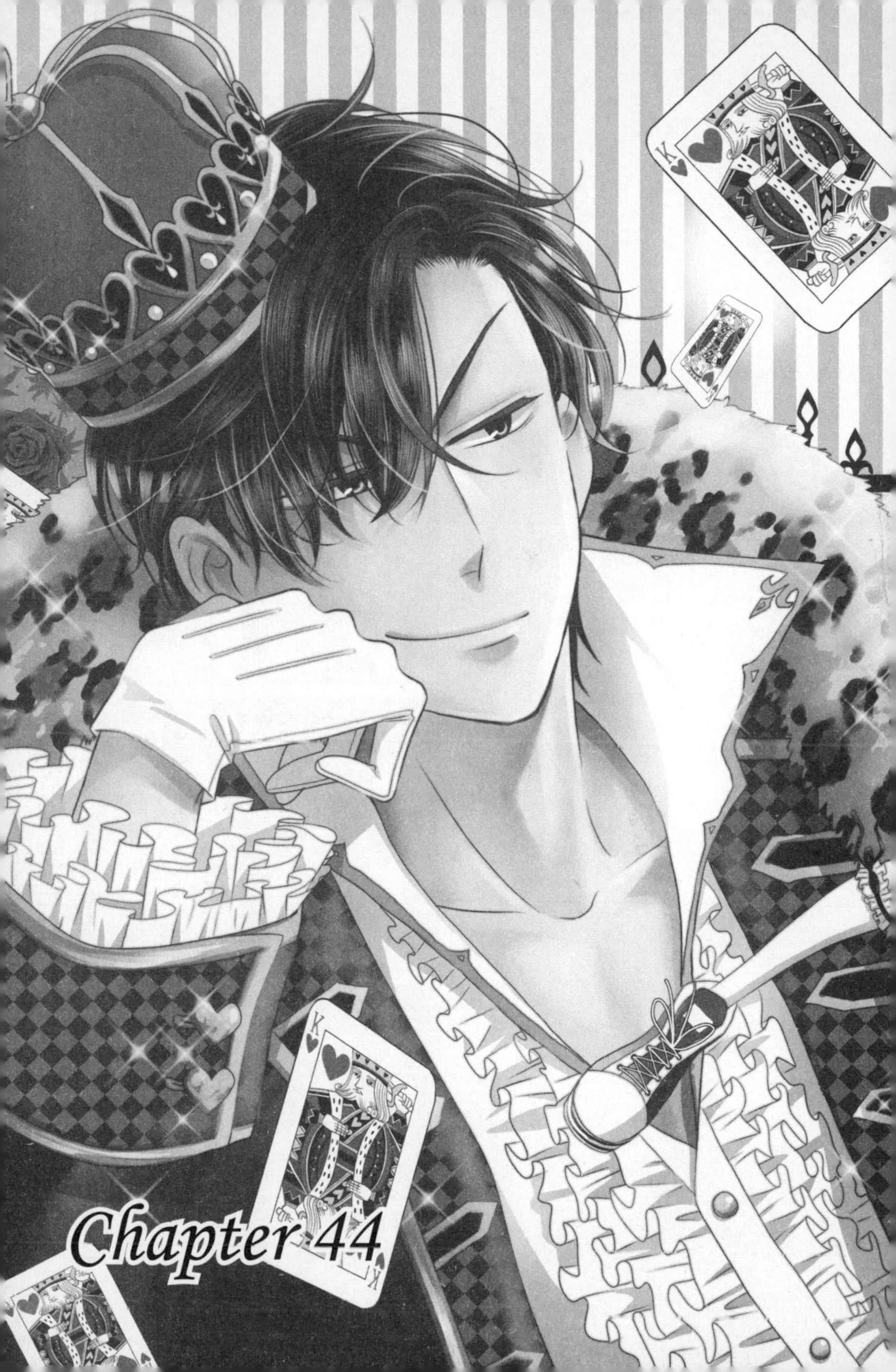
Chapter 44

At the Movies

Anger
comes
in
waves.

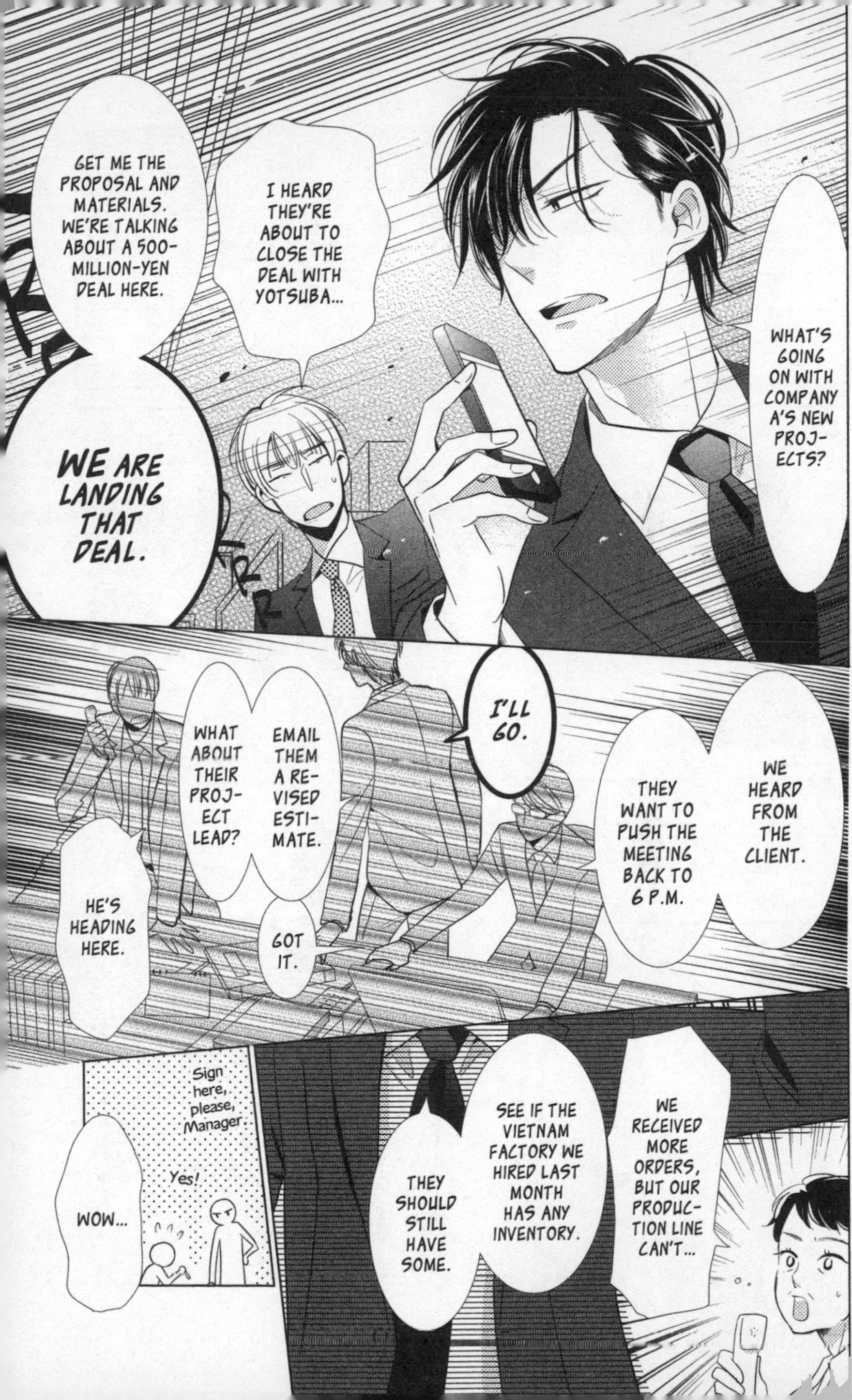
WHAT'S GOING ON WITH COMPANY A'S NEW PROJECTS?
I HEARD THEY'RE ABOUT TO CLOSE THE DEAL WITH YOTSUBA...
GET ME THE PROPOSAL AND MATERIALS. WE'RE TALKING ABOUT A 500-MILLION-YEN DEAL HERE.
WE ARE LANDING THAT DEAL.
WE HEARD FROM THE CLIENT.
THEY WANT TO PUSH THE MEETING BACK TO 6 P.M.
I'LL GO.
EMAIL THEM A REVISED ESTIMATE.
WHAT ABOUT THEIR PROJECT LEAD?
GOT IT.
HE'S HEADING HERE.
WE RECEIVED MORE ORDERS, BUT OUR PRODUCTION LINE CAN'T...
SEE IF THE VIETNAM FACTORY WE HIRED LAST MONTH HAS ANY INVENTORY.
THEY SHOULD STILL HAVE SOME.
Sign here, please, Manager.
Yes!
WOW...

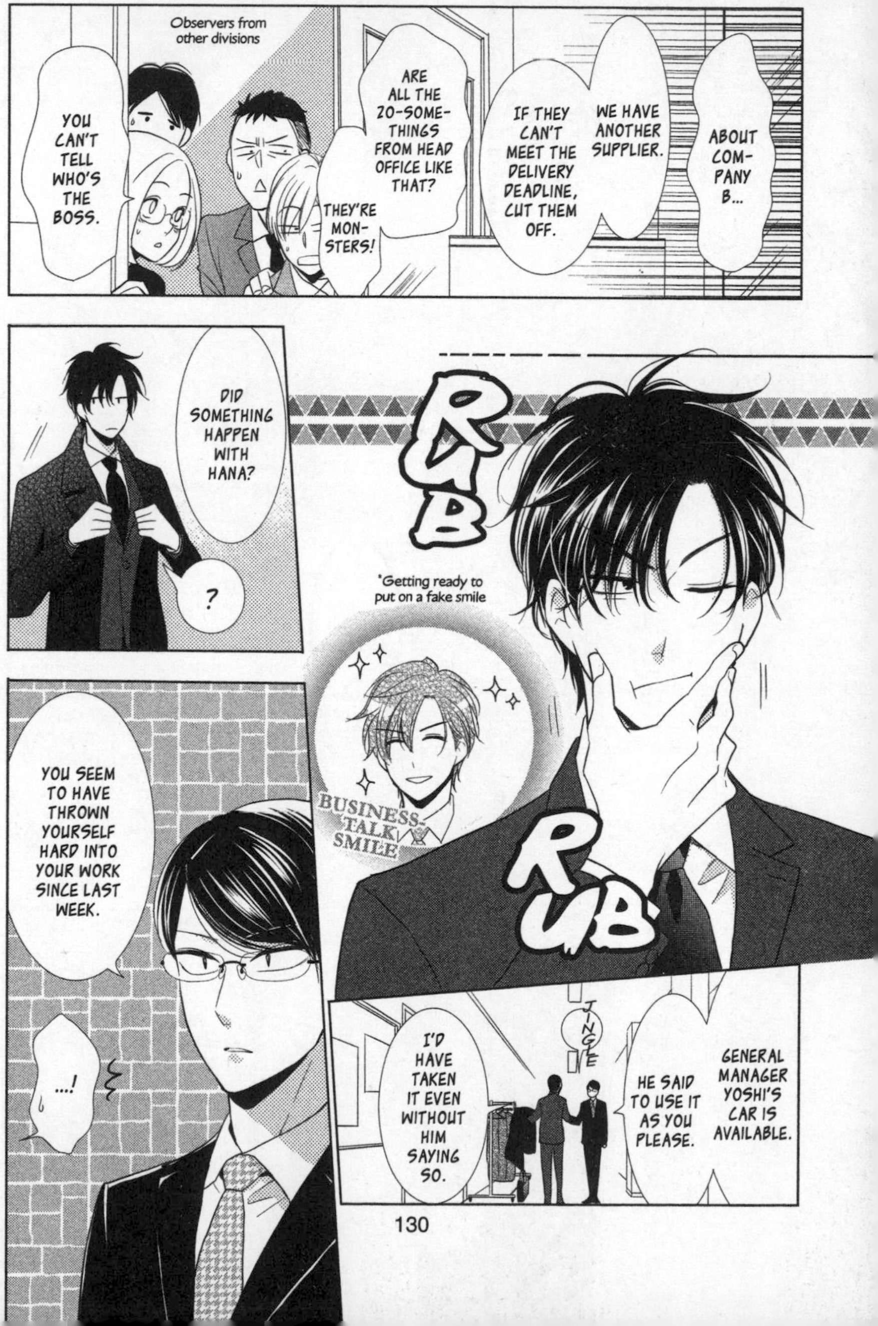
ABOUT COMPANY B...
WE HAVE ANOTHER SUPPLIER.
IF THEY CAN'T MEET THE DELIVERY DEADLINE, CUT THEM OFF.
ARE ALL THE 20-SOMETHINGS FROM HEAD OFFICE LIKE THAT?
THEY'RE MONSTERS!
Observers from other divisions
YOU CAN'T TELL WHO'S THE BOSS.
RUB
*Getting ready to put on a fake smile
BUSINESS-TALK SMILE
RUB
DID SOMETHING HAPPEN WITH HANA?
?
YOU SEEM TO HAVE THROWN YOURSELF HARD INTO YOUR WORK SINCE LAST WEEK.
...!
GENERAL MANAGER YOSHI'S CAR IS AVAILABLE.
HE SAID TO USE IT AS YOU PLEASE.
JINGLE
I'D HAVE TAKEN IT EVEN WITHOUT HIM SAYING SO.

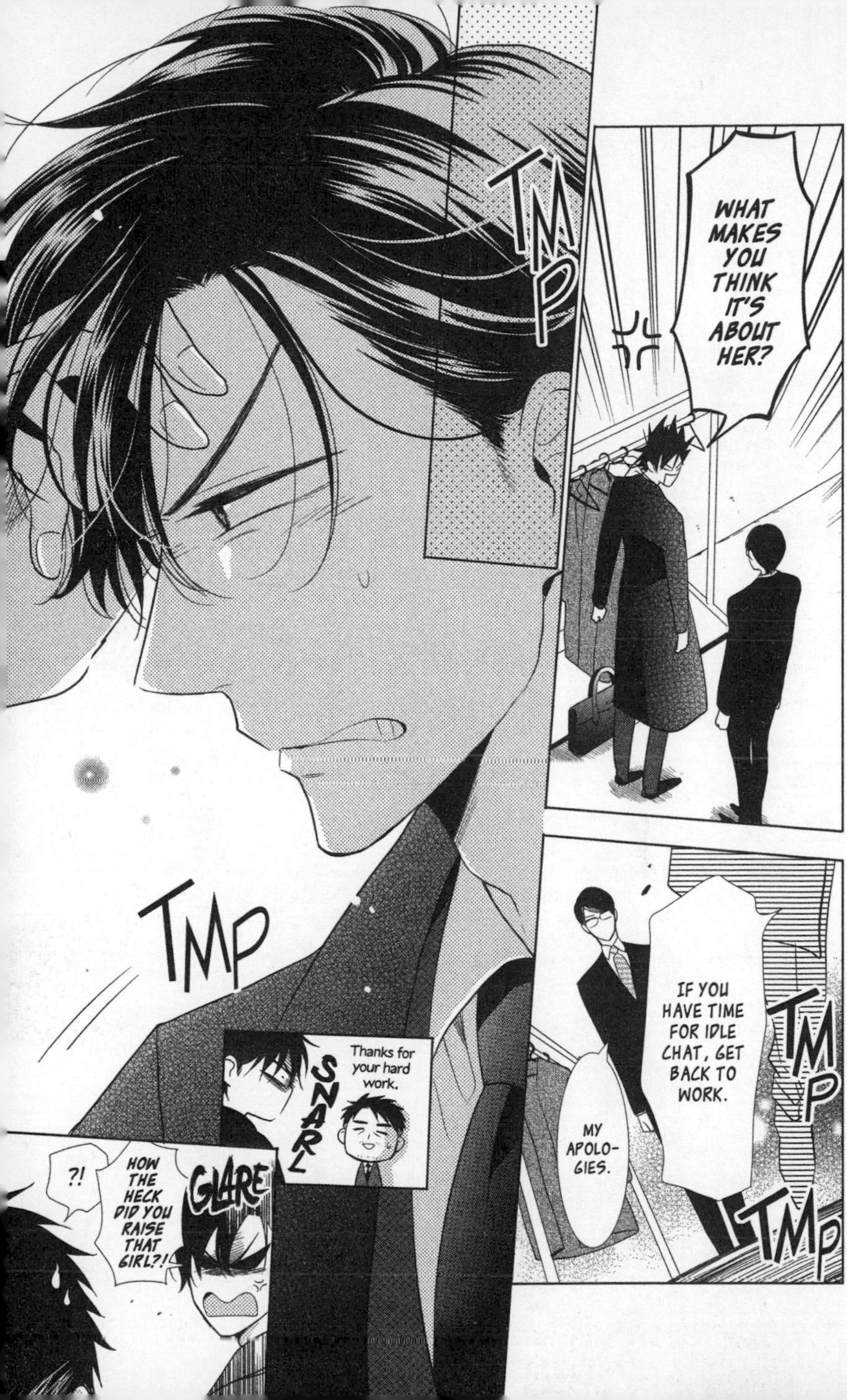
WHAT MAKES YOU THINK IT'S ABOUT HER?
IF YOU HAVE TIME FOR IDLE CHAT, GET BACK TO WORK.
MY APOLOGIES.
TMP
TMP
TMP
TMP
Thanks for your hard work.
SNARL
GLARE
?!
HOW THE HECK DID YOU RAISE THAT GIRL?!

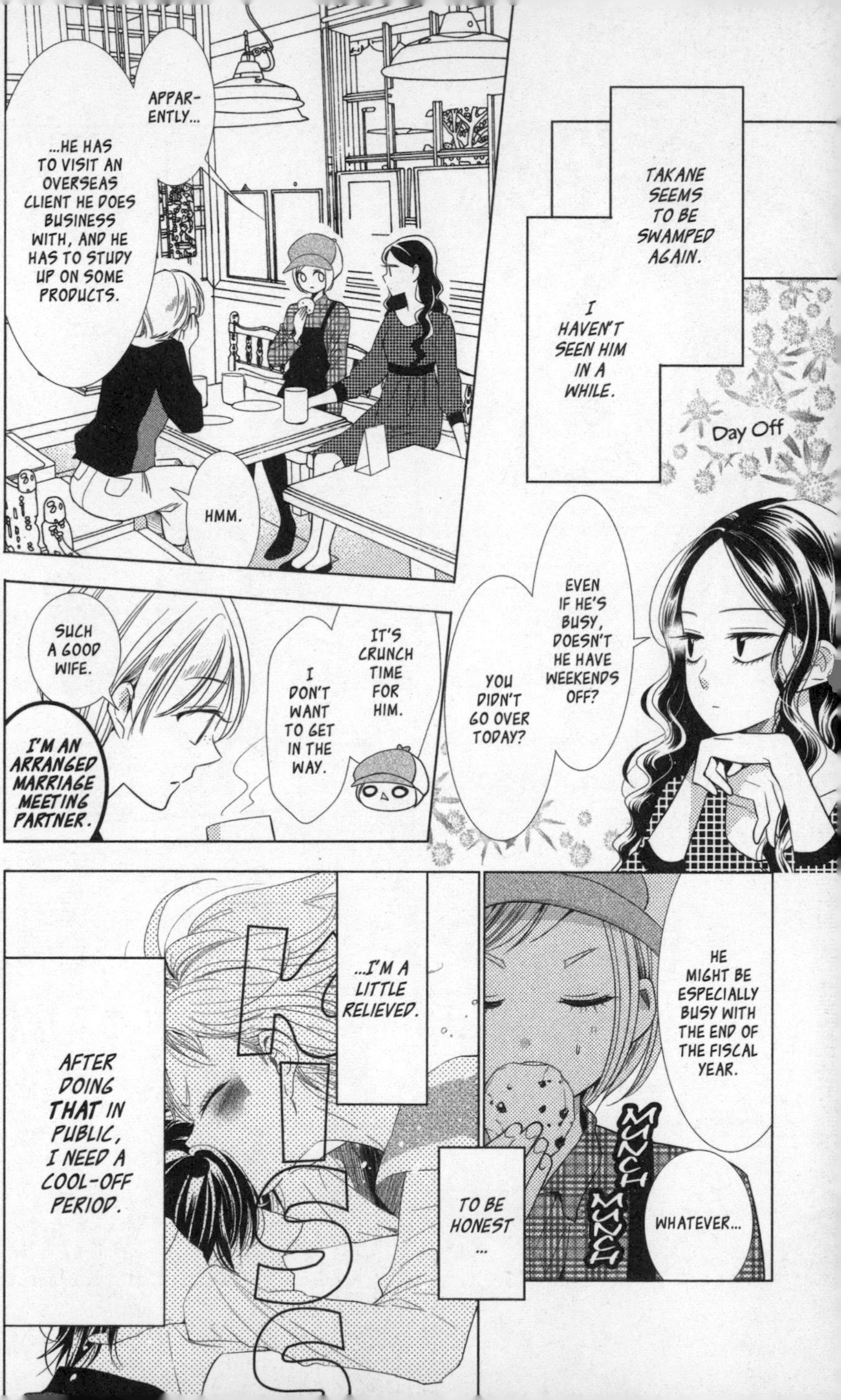

TAKANE SEEMS TO BE SWAMPED AGAIN.
I HAVEN'T SEEN HIM IN A WHILE.
Day Off
APPAR-ENTLY...
...HE HAS TO VISIT AN OVERSEAS CLIENT HE DOES BUSINESS WITH, AND HE HAS TO STUDY UP ON SOME PRODUCTS.
HMM.
EVEN IF HE'S BUSY, DOESN'T HE HAVE WEEKENDS OFF?
YOU DIDN'T GO OVER TODAY?
IT'S CRUNCH TIME FOR HIM.
I DON'T WANT TO GET IN THE WAY.
SUCH A GOOD WIFE.
I'M AN ARRANGED MARRIAGE MEETING PARTNER.
HE MIGHT BE ESPECIALLY BUSY WITH THE END OF THE FISCAL YEAR.
MUNCH MUNCH
WHATEVER...
TO BE HONEST ...
...I'M A LITTLE RELIEVED.
AFTER DOING THAT IN PUBLIC, I NEED A COOL-OFF PERIOD.

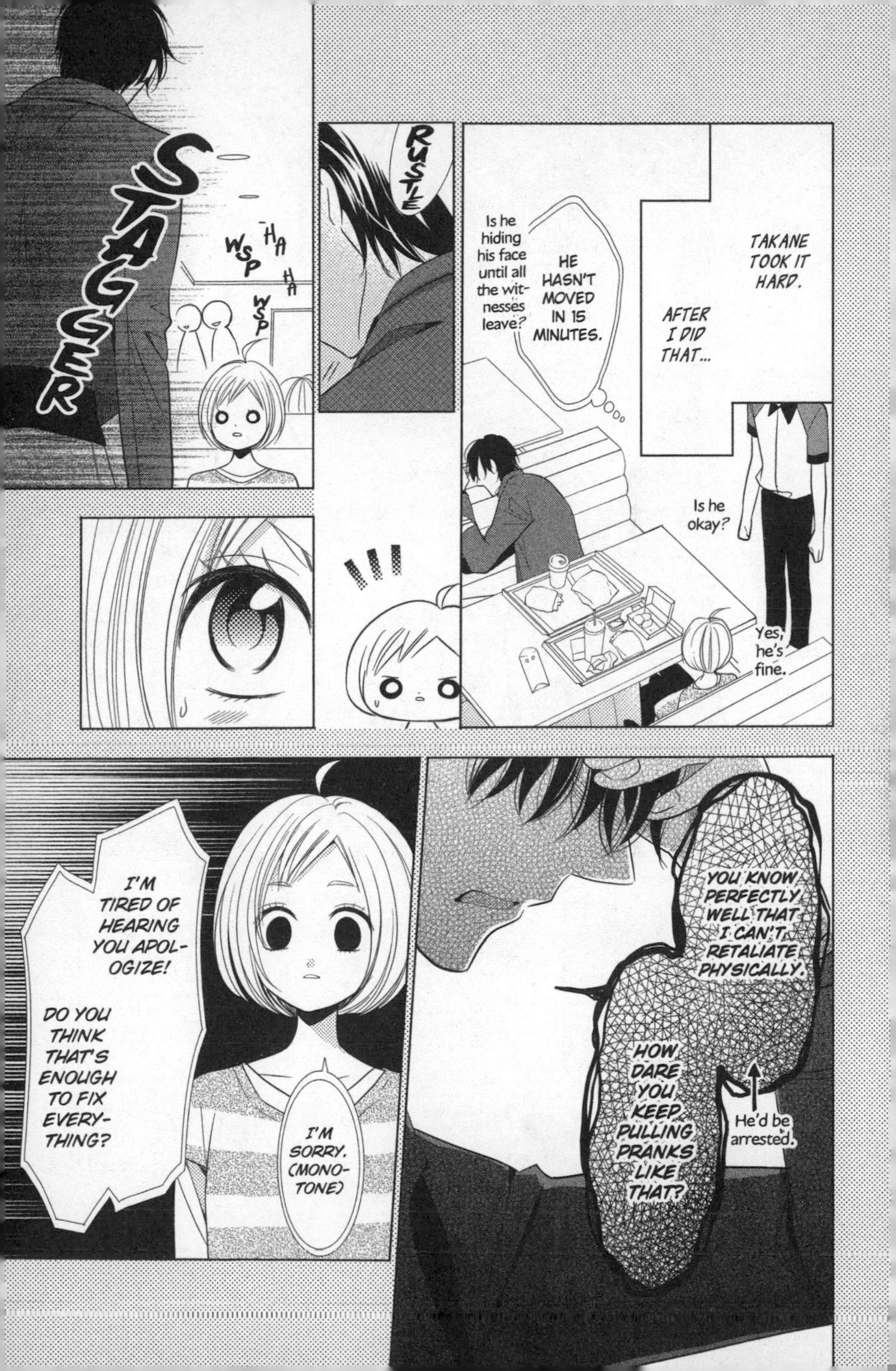

TAKANE TOOK IT HARD.
AFTER I DID THAT...
HE HASN'T MOVED IN 15 MINUTES.
Is he hiding his face until all the witnesses leave?
Is he okay?
Yes, he's fine.
RUSTLE
STAGGER
-HA HA
WSP WSP
!!!
YOU KNOW PERFECTLY WELL THAT I CAN'T RETALIATE PHYSICALLY.
HOW DARE YOU KEEP PULLING PRANKS LIKE THAT?
He'd be arrested.
I'M SORRY. (MONOTONE)
I'M TIRED OF HEARING YOU APOLOGIZE!
DO YOU THINK THAT'S ENOUGH TO FIX EVERYTHING?

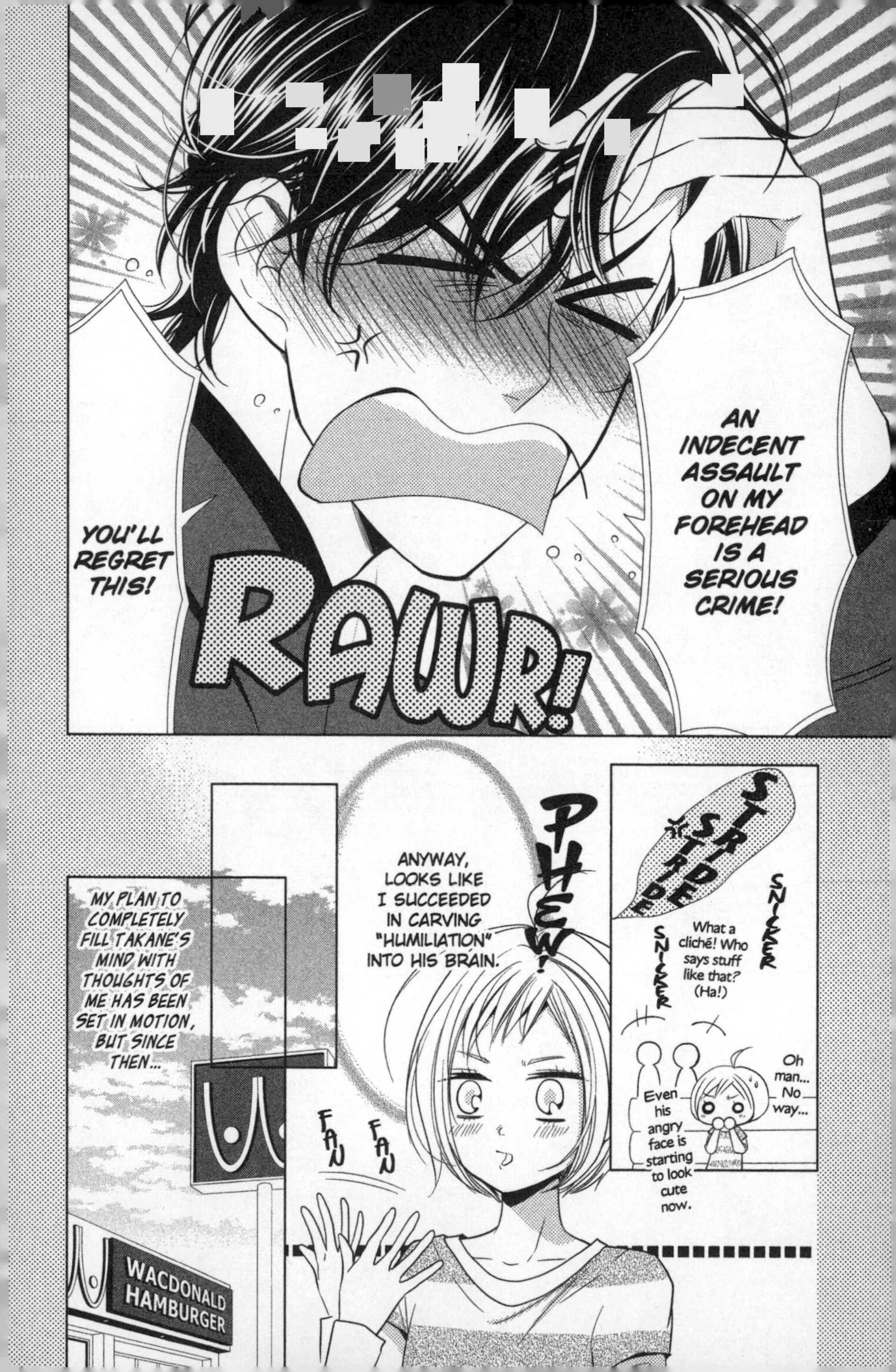
AN INDECENT ASSAULT ON MY FOREHEAD IS A SERIOUS CRIME!
YOU'LL REGRET THIS!
RAWR!
STRIDE STRIDE
SNICKER SNICKER
What a cliché! Who says stuff like that? (Ha!)
Oh man... No way...
Even his angry face is starting to look cute now.
PHEW!
ANYWAY, LOOKS LIKE I SUCCEEDED IN CARVING "HUMILIATION" INTO HIS BRAIN.
FAN FAN
MY PLAN TO COMPLETELY FILL TAKANE'S MIND WITH THOUGHTS OF ME HAS BEEN SET IN MOTION, BUT SINCE THEN...
WACDONALD HAMBURGER

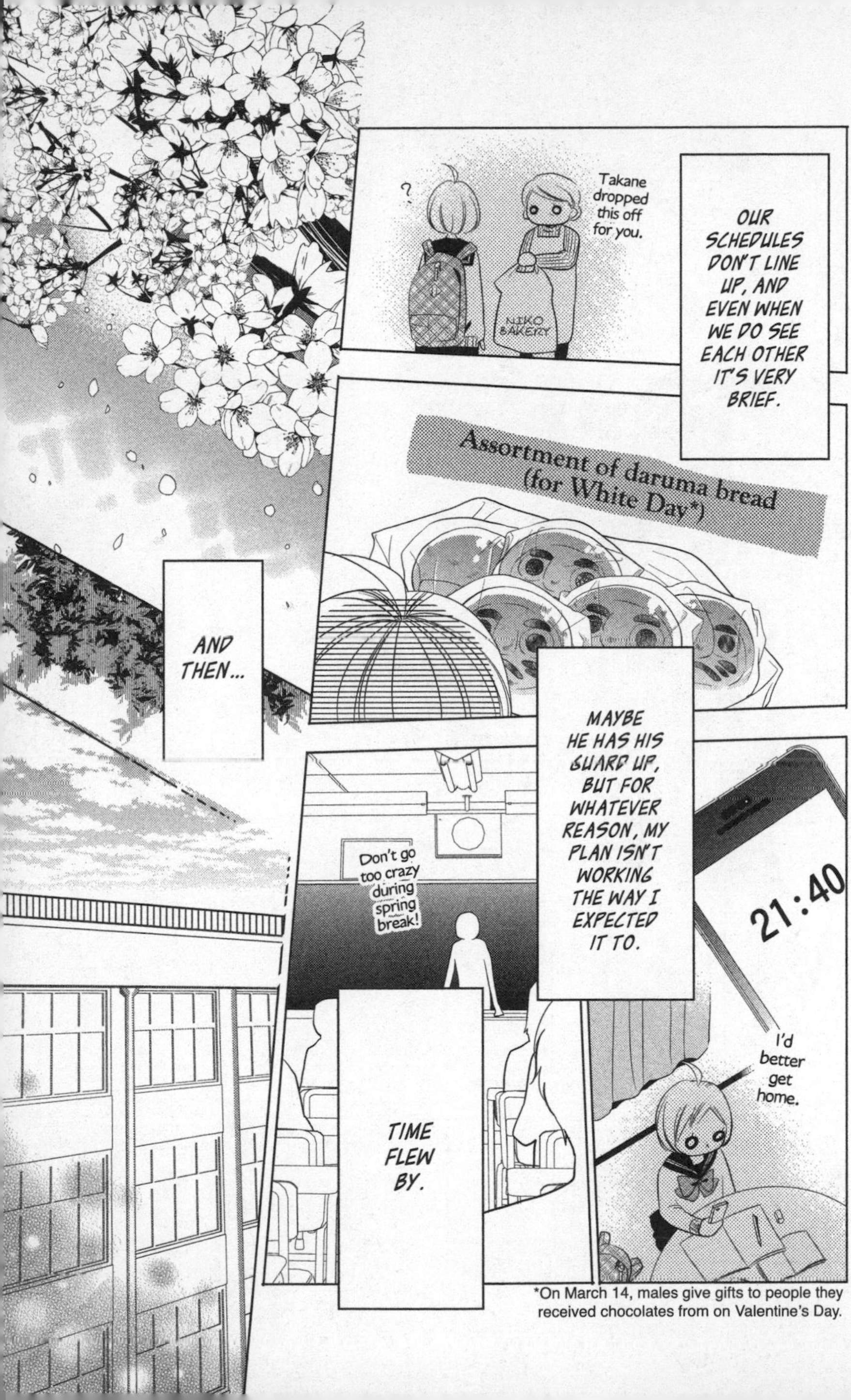
OUR SCHEDULES DON'T LINE UP, AND EVEN WHEN WE DO SEE EACH OTHER IT'S VERY BRIEF.
?
Takane dropped this off for you.
NIKO BAKERY
Assortment of daruma bread (for White Day*)
MAYBE HE HAS HIS GUARD UP, BUT FOR WHATEVER REASON, MY PLAN ISN'T WORKING THE WAY I EXPECTED IT TO.
21:40
I'd better get home.
Don't go too crazy during spring break!
TIME FLEW BY.
AND THEN...

*On March 14, males give gifts to people they received chocolates from on Valentine's Day.

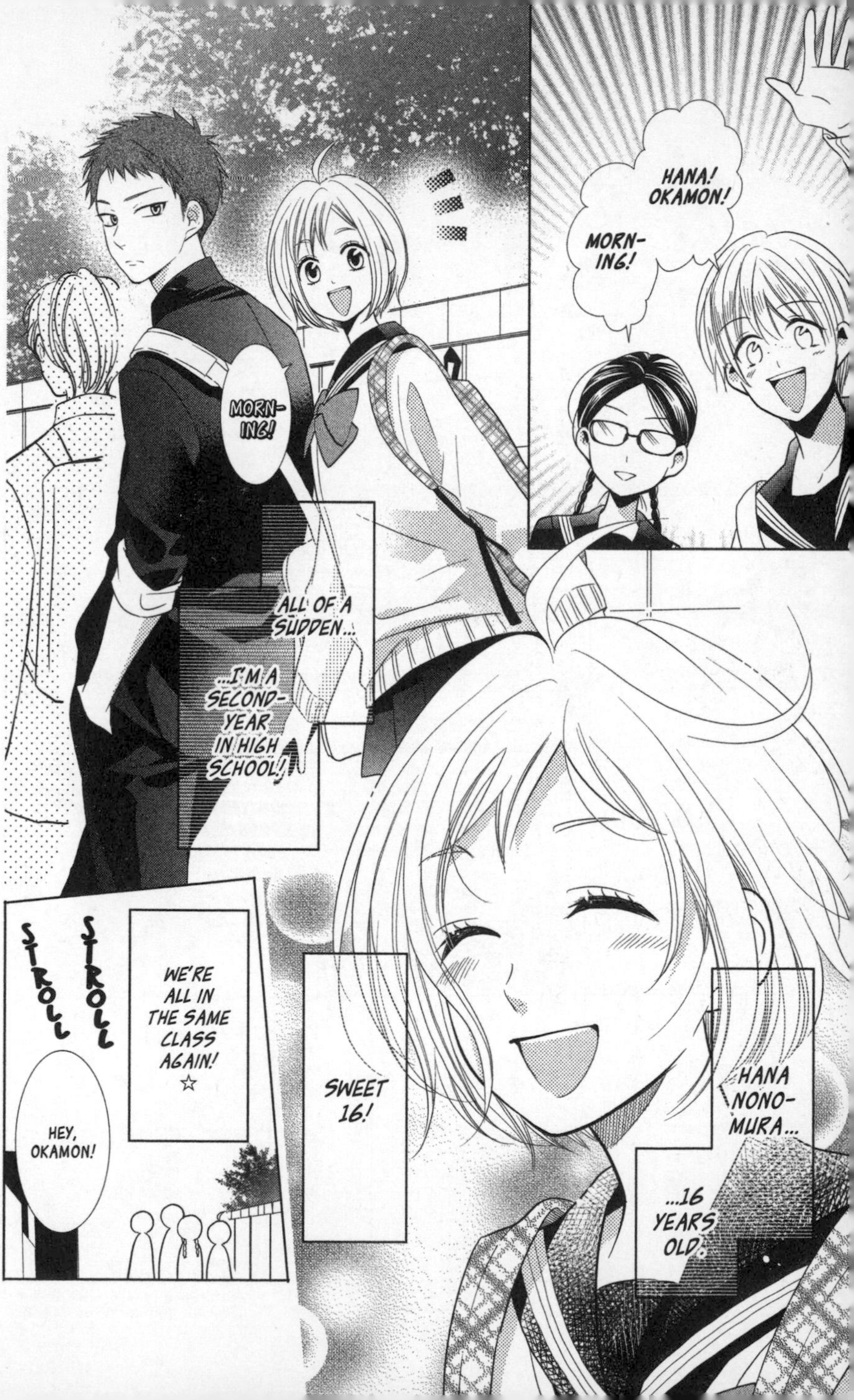
HANA! OKAMON!
MORN-ING!
MORN-ING!
ALL OF A SUDDEN...
...I'M A SECOND-YEAR IN HIGH SCHOOL!
HANA NONO-MURA...
...16 YEARS OLD.
SWEET 16!
WE'RE ALL IN THE SAME CLASS AGAIN! ☆
STROLL STROLL
HEY, OKAMON!

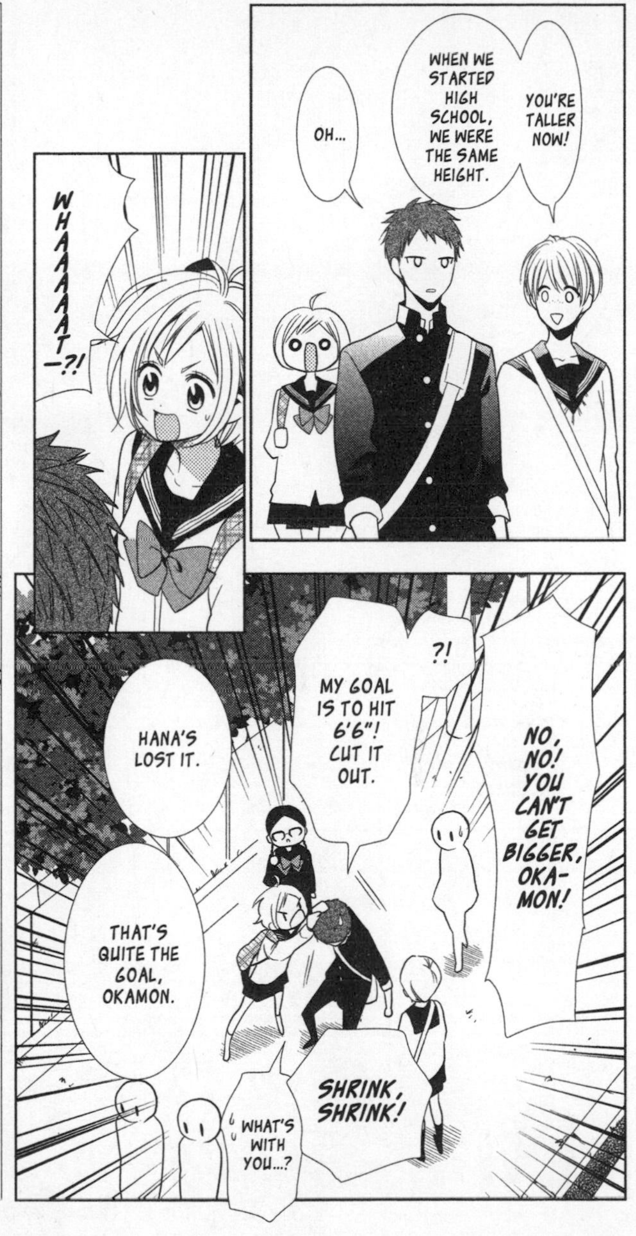
YOU'RE TALLER NOW!
WHEN WE STARTED HIGH SCHOOL, WE WERE THE SAME HEIGHT.
OH...
WHAAAAAAT—?!
NO, NO! YOU CAN'T GET BIGGER, OKAMON!
?!
MY GOAL IS TO HIT 6'6"! CUT IT OUT.
HANA'S LOST IT.
THAT'S QUITE THE GOAL, OKAMON.
SHRINK, SHRINK!
WHAT'S WITH YOU...?

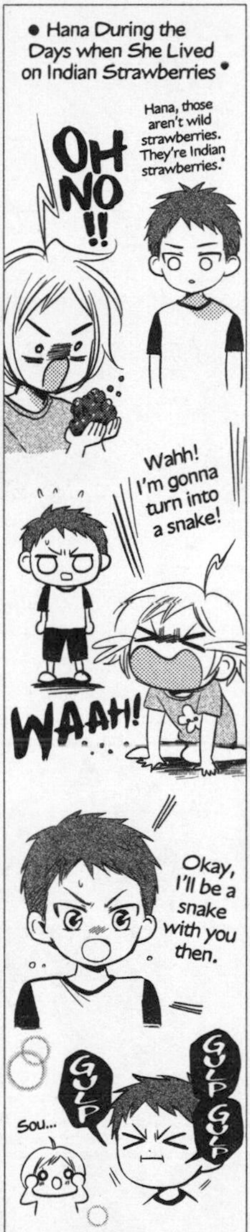
• Hana During the Days when She Lived on Indian Strawberries •
Hana, those aren't wild strawberries. They're Indian strawberries.*
OH NO!!
Wahh! I'm gonna turn into a snake!
WAAH!
Okay, I'll be a snake with you then.
GULP GULP
GULP
Sou...
They're so bland...

*Called *hebi ichigo*, with *hebi* meaning "snake"

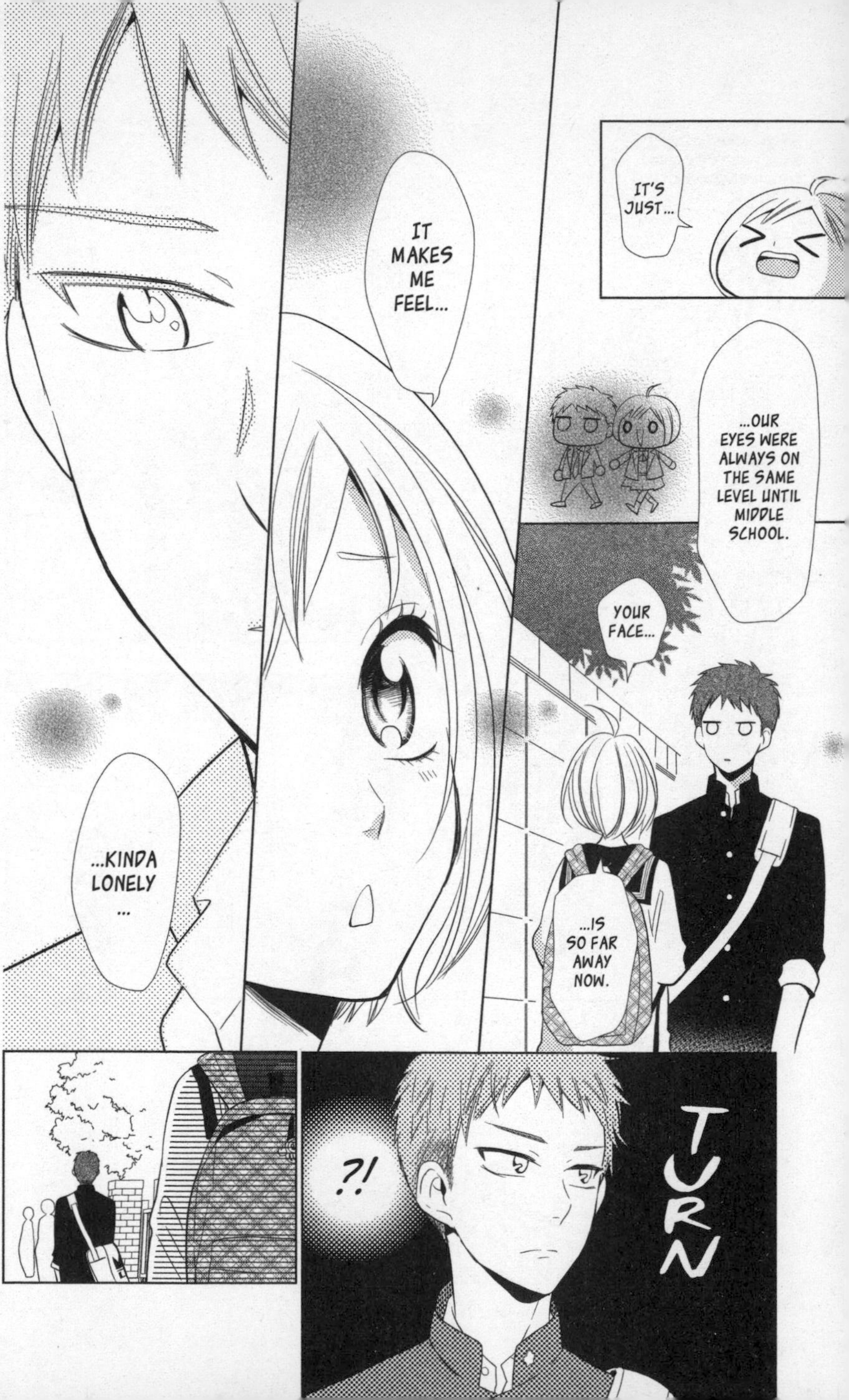
IT'S JUST...
...OUR EYES WERE ALWAYS ON THE SAME LEVEL UNTIL MIDDLE SCHOOL.
YOUR FACE...
...IS SO FAR AWAY NOW.
IT MAKES ME FEEL...
...KINDA LONELY ...
TURN
?!

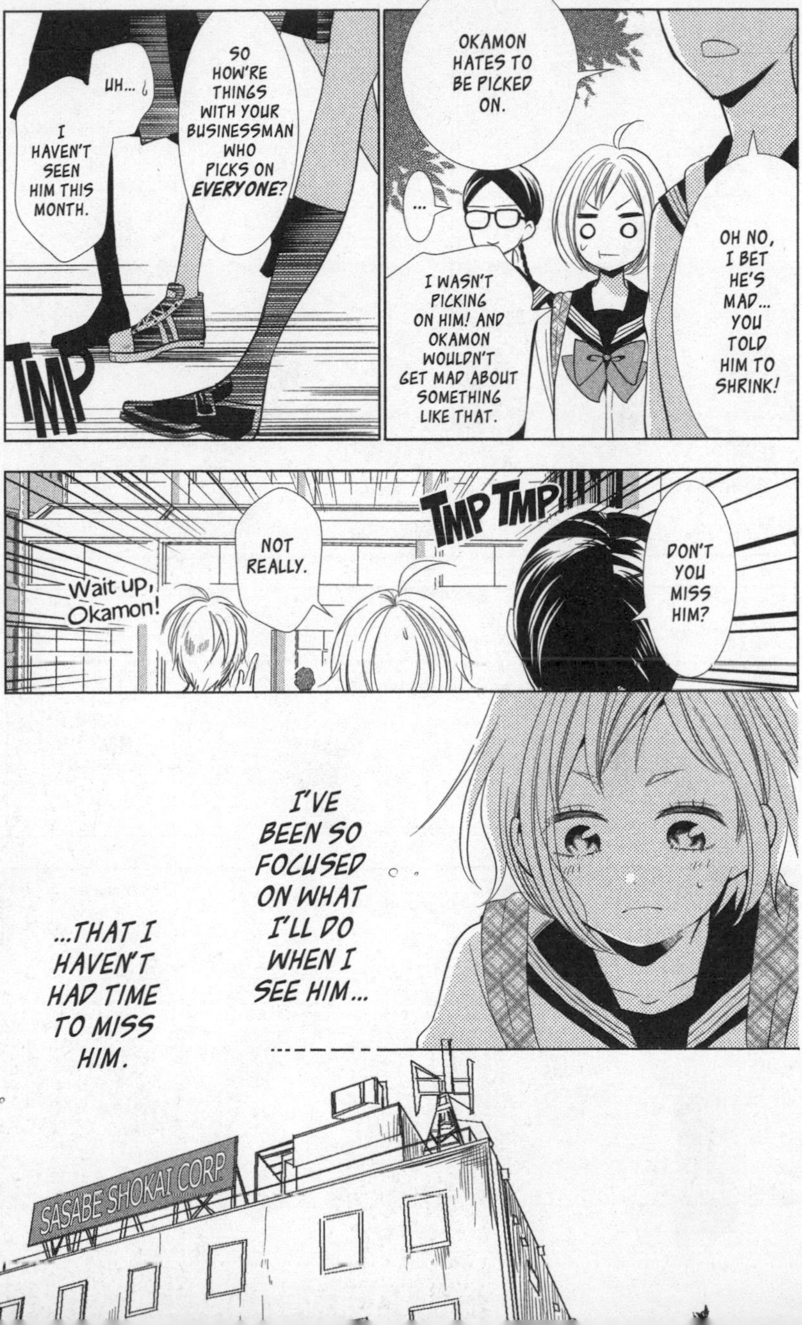
OKAMON HATES TO BE PICKED ON.
OH NO, I BET HE'S MAD... YOU TOLD HIM TO SHRINK!
...
I WASN'T PICKING ON HIM! AND OKAMON WOULDN'T GET MAD ABOUT SOMETHING LIKE THAT.
SO HOW'RE THINGS WITH YOUR BUSINESSMAN WHO PICKS ON *EVERYONE*?
UH...
I HAVEN'T SEEN HIM THIS MONTH.
TMP
DON'T YOU MISS HIM?
TMP TMP
NOT REALLY.
Wait up, Okamon!
I'VE BEEN SO FOCUSED ON WHAT I'LL DO WHEN I SEE HIM...
...THAT I HAVEN'T HAD TIME TO MISS HIM.
SASABE SHOKAI CORP.

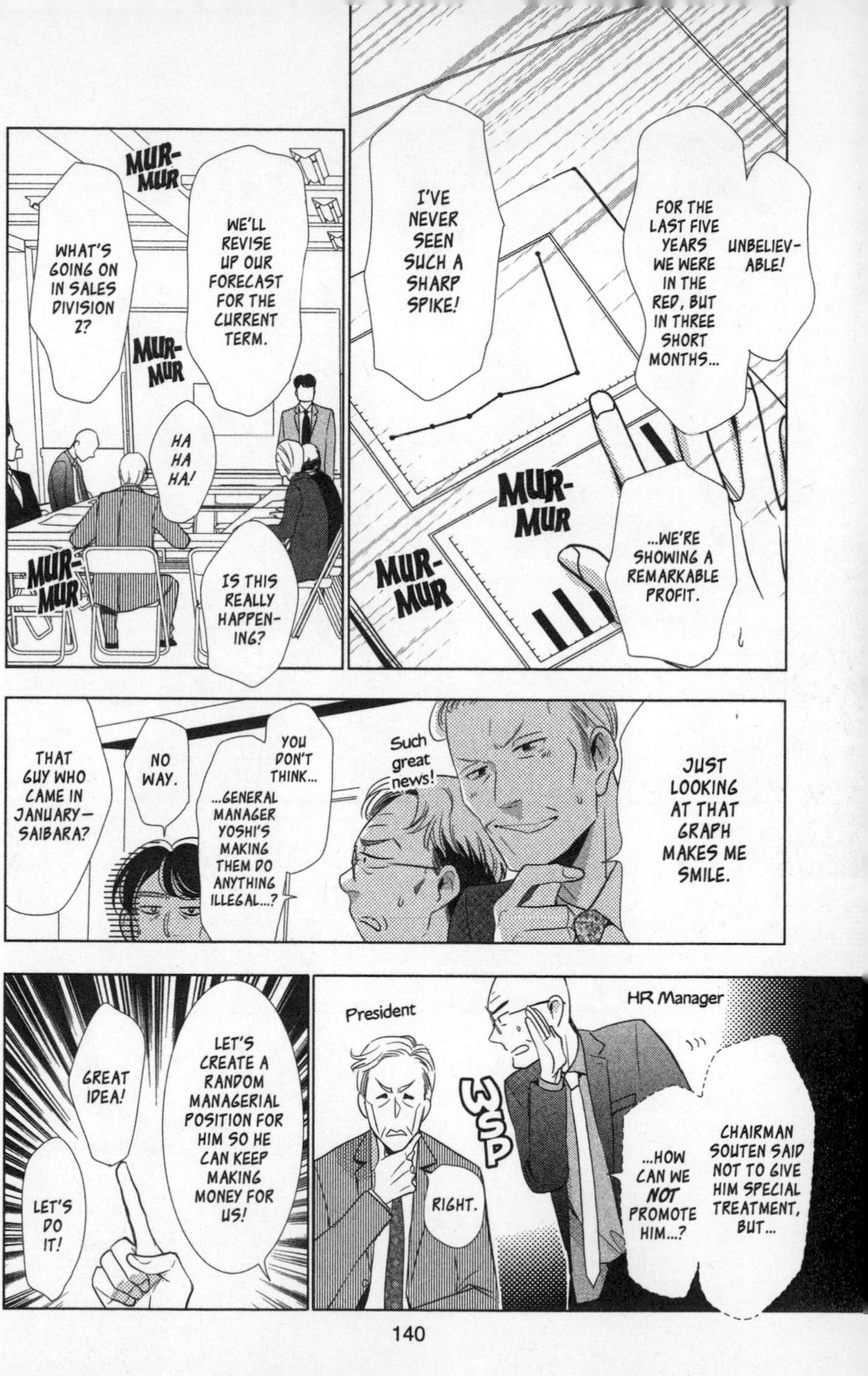
UNBELIEVABLE!
FOR THE LAST FIVE YEARS WE WERE IN THE RED, BUT IN THREE SHORT MONTHS...
I'VE NEVER SEEN SUCH A SHARP SPIKE!
MUR-MUR
...WE'RE SHOWING A REMARKABLE PROFIT.
MUR-MUR
WE'LL REVISE UP OUR FORECAST FOR THE CURRENT TERM.
MUR-MUR
WHAT'S GOING ON IN SALES DIVISION 2?
MUR-MUR
HA HA HA!
IS THIS REALLY HAPPENING?
MUR-MUR
JUST LOOKING AT THAT GRAPH MAKES ME SMILE.
Such great news!
YOU DON'T THINK...
...GENERAL MANAGER YOSHI'S MAKING THEM DO ANYTHING ILLEGAL...?
NO WAY.
THAT GUY WHO CAME IN JANUARY—SAIBARA?
HR Manager
CHAIRMAN SOUTEN SAID NOT TO GIVE HIM SPECIAL TREATMENT, BUT...
...HOW CAN WE NOT PROMOTE HIM...?
WSP
President
RIGHT.
LET'S CREATE A RANDOM MANAGERIAL POSITION FOR HIM SO HE CAN KEEP MAKING MONEY FOR US!
GREAT IDEA!
LET'S DO IT!

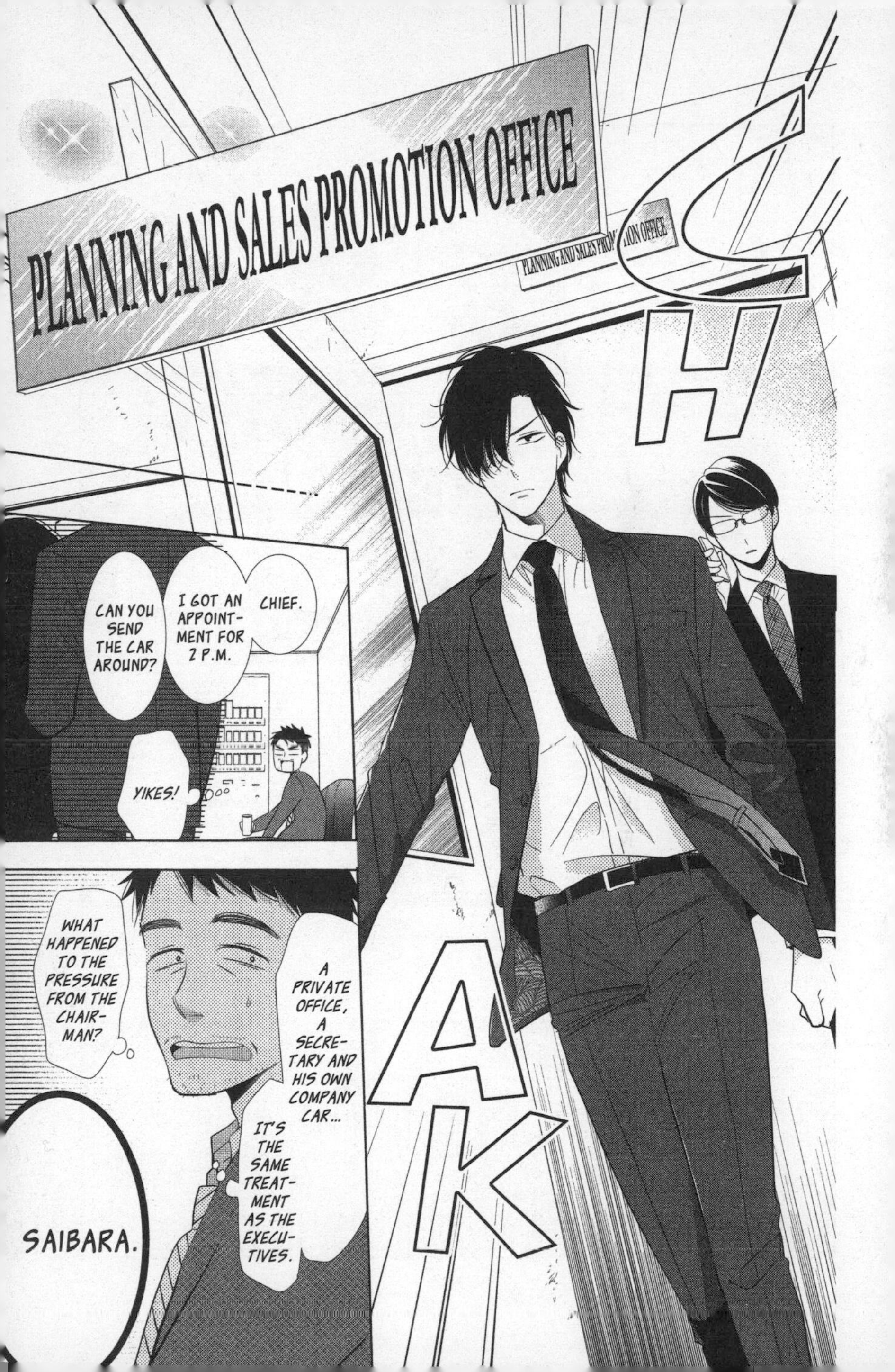
PLANNING AND SALES PROMOTION OFFICE
PLANNING AND SALES PROMOTION OFFICE
CHAK
CHIEF.
I GOT AN APPOINTMENT FOR 2 P.M.
CAN YOU SEND THE CAR AROUND?
YIKES!
A PRIVATE OFFICE, A SECRETARY AND HIS OWN COMPANY CAR...
IT'S THE SAME TREATMENT AS THE EXECUTIVES.
WHAT HAPPENED TO THE PRESSURE FROM THE CHAIRMAN?
SAIBARA.

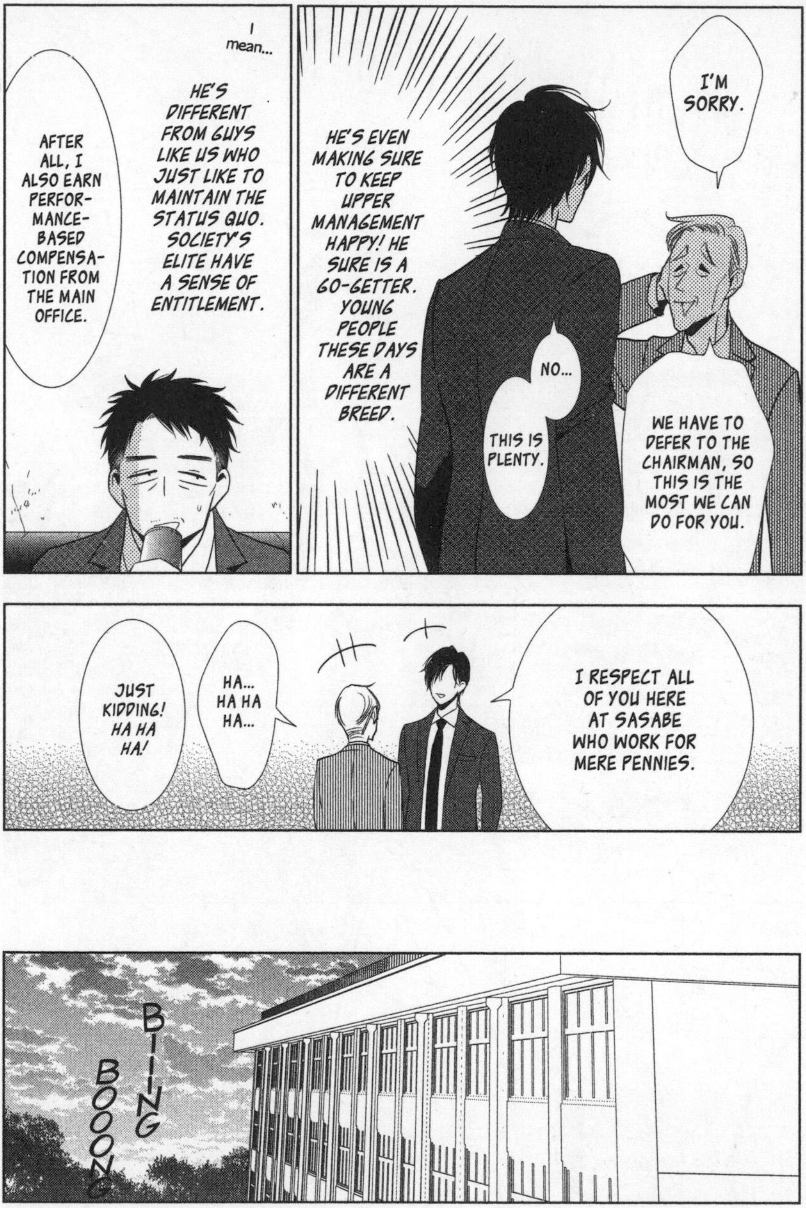
I'M SORRY.
WE HAVE TO DEFER TO THE CHAIRMAN, SO THIS IS THE MOST WE CAN DO FOR YOU.
NO...
THIS IS PLENTY.
HE'S EVEN MAKING SURE TO KEEP UPPER MANAGEMENT HAPPY! HE SURE IS A GO-GETTER. YOUNG PEOPLE THESE DAYS ARE A DIFFERENT BREED.
I mean...
HE'S DIFFERENT FROM GUYS LIKE US WHO JUST LIKE TO MAINTAIN THE STATUS QUO. SOCIETY'S ELITE HAVE A SENSE OF ENTITLEMENT.
AFTER ALL, I ALSO EARN PERFORMANCE-BASED COMPENSATION FROM THE MAIN OFFICE.
I RESPECT ALL OF YOU HERE AT SASABE WHO WORK FOR MERE PENNIES.
HA... HA HA HA...
JUST KIDDING! HA HA HA!
BING
BOOONG

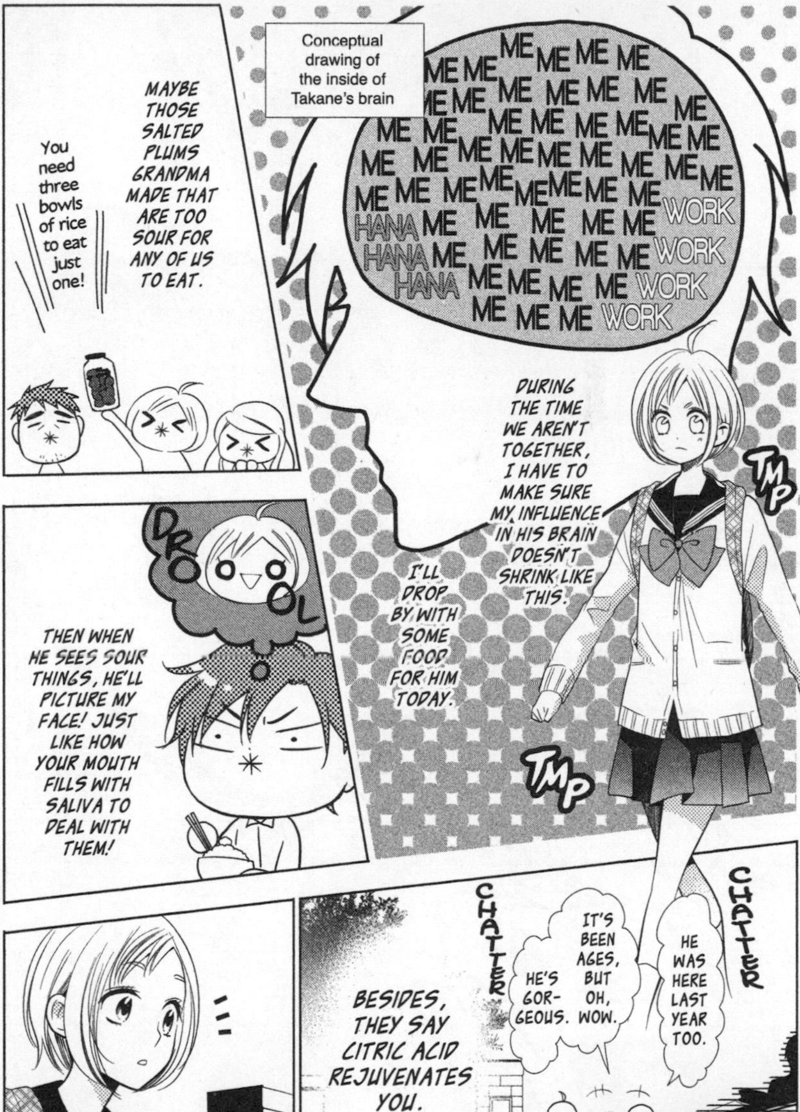

Conceptual drawing of the inside of Takane's brain
ME ME ME ME ME ME
ME ME ME ME ME ME ME
ME ME ME ME ME ME ME ME ME
ME ME ME ME ME ME ME ME ME
ME ME ME ME ME ME ME ME ME ME
HANA ME ME ME ME ME WORK
HANA ME ME ME ME ME WORK
HANA ME ME ME ME WORK
ME ME ME WORK
DURING THE TIME WE AREN'T TOGETHER, I HAVE TO MAKE SURE MY INFLUENCE IN HIS BRAIN DOESN'T SHRINK LIKE THIS.
I'LL DROP BY WITH SOME FOOD FOR HIM TODAY.
TMP
TMP
MAYBE THOSE SALTED PLUMS GRANDMA MADE THAT ARE TOO SOUR FOR ANY OF US TO EAT.
You need three bowls of rice to eat just one!
DROOOOL
THEN WHEN HE SEES SOUR THINGS, HE'LL PICTURE MY FACE! JUST LIKE HOW YOUR MOUTH FILLS WITH SALIVA TO DEAL WITH THEM!
BESIDES, THEY SAY CITRIC ACID REJUVENATES YOU.
CHATTER
HE WAS HERE LAST YEAR TOO.
IT'S BEEN AGES, BUT OH, WOW.
HE'S GOR-GEOUS.
CHATTER

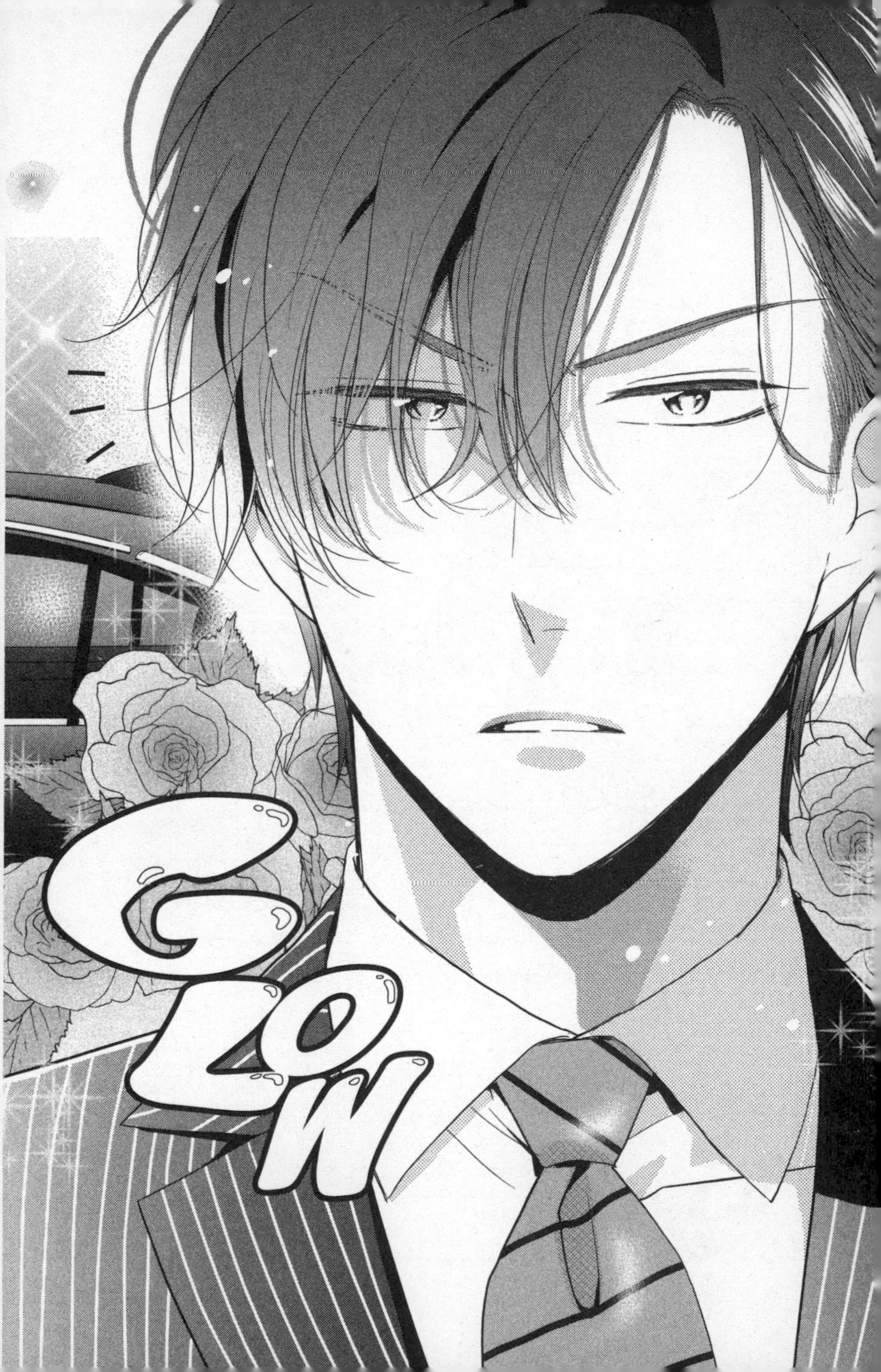
GLOW

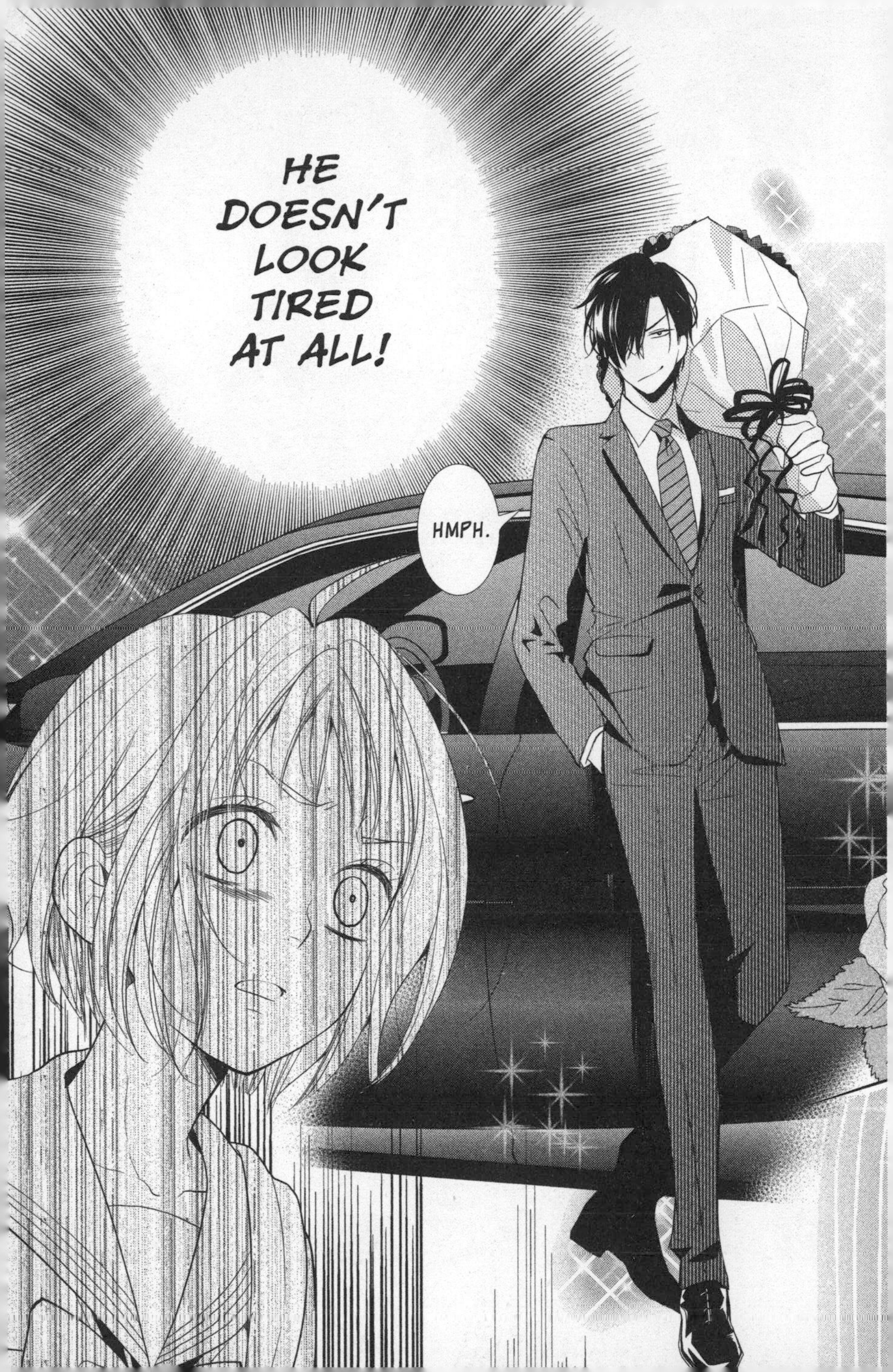
HE DOESN'T LOOK TIRED AT ALL!
HMPH.

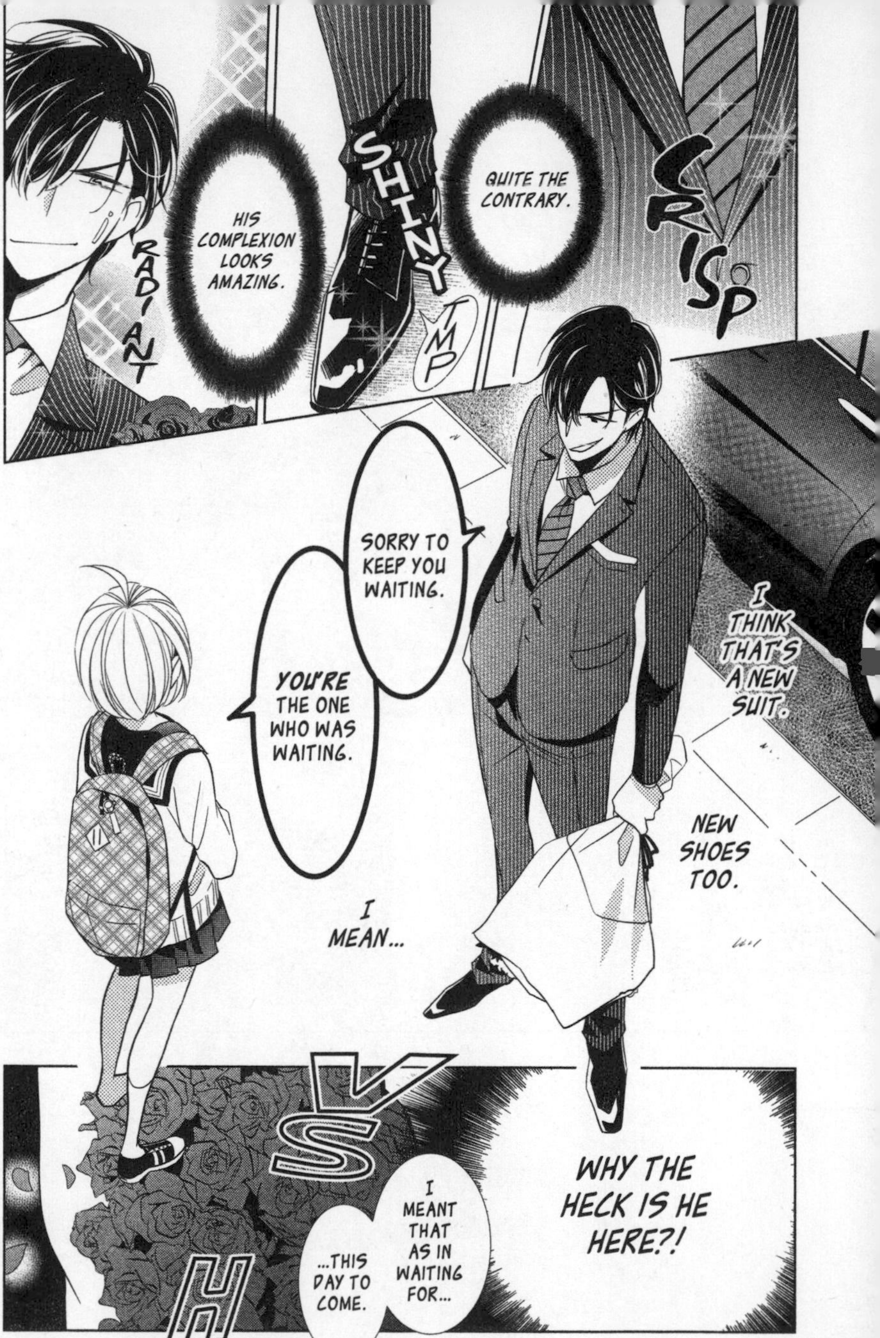
CRISP
QUITE THE CONTRARY.
SHINY
TMP
HIS COMPLEXION LOOKS AMAZING.
RADIANT
I THINK THAT'S A NEW SUIT.
NEW SHOES TOO.
SORRY TO KEEP YOU WAITING.
YOU'RE THE ONE WHO WAS WAITING.
I MEAN...
WHY THE HECK IS HE HERE?!
I MEANT THAT AS IN WAITING FOR...
...THIS DAY TO COME.
VSH

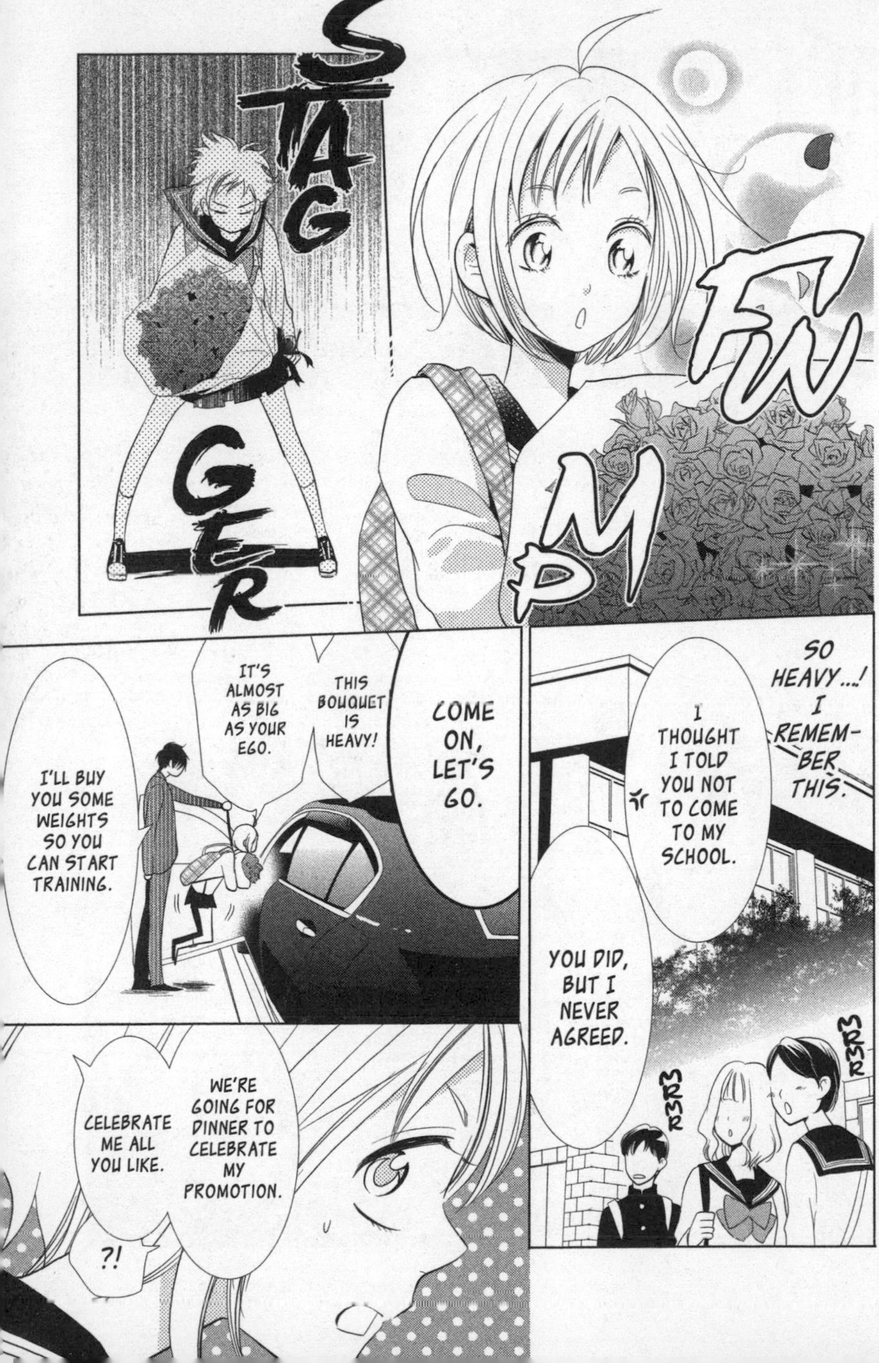
FWUMP
STAGGER
SO HEAVY...! I REMEMBER THIS.
I THOUGHT I TOLD YOU NOT TO COME TO MY SCHOOL.
YOU DID, BUT I NEVER AGREED.
MRMR
MRMR
COME ON, LET'S GO.
THIS BOUQUET IS HEAVY!
IT'S ALMOST AS BIG AS YOUR EGO.
I'LL BUY YOU SOME WEIGHTS SO YOU CAN START TRAINING.
WE'RE GOING FOR DINNER TO CELEBRATE MY PROMOTION.
CELEBRATE ME ALL YOU LIKE.
?!

THIS IS ALL HAPPENING TOO FAST FOR ME TO KEEP UP.
DID YOU BUY A NEW CAR?
IT'S A COMPANY CAR.
I'D NEVER CHOOSE A MASS-PRODUCED CAR LIKE THIS.
HE'S ALWAYS DRIVEN A FOREIGN CAR WITH THE STEERING WHEEL ON THE LEFT, SO THIS FEELS WEIRD.
HUSH
It's totally silent...
WHAT'S WRONG? YOU'RE SO QUIET.
IT'S OUR FIRST DRIVE TOGETHER IN A WHILE. ARE YOU SPEECHLESS WITH JOY?
I'M WORRIED THAT YOU'LL GET INTO AN ACCIDENT DRIVING AN UNFAMILIAR CAR.
THE THINGS YOU SAY AND DO CAUSE SO MANY ACCIDENTS.
WHAT DO YOU MEAN? I ALWAYS DRIVE SAFELY.
ALTHOUGH...
...I COULD GET TICKETED FOR THE SPEED AT WHICH I WAS PROMOTED...
...RIGHT?
TAKANE'S THE TYPE TO WORK HARD BEHIND THE SCENES, AND HE DID A GREAT JOB BACK AT THE MAIN OFFICE. I KNEW HE WOULD BE OKAY IN THE LONG RUN, BUT...
....
DON'T IGNORE ME.
...I HAD NO IDEA HE'D BE BACK ON HIS FEET SO FAST.

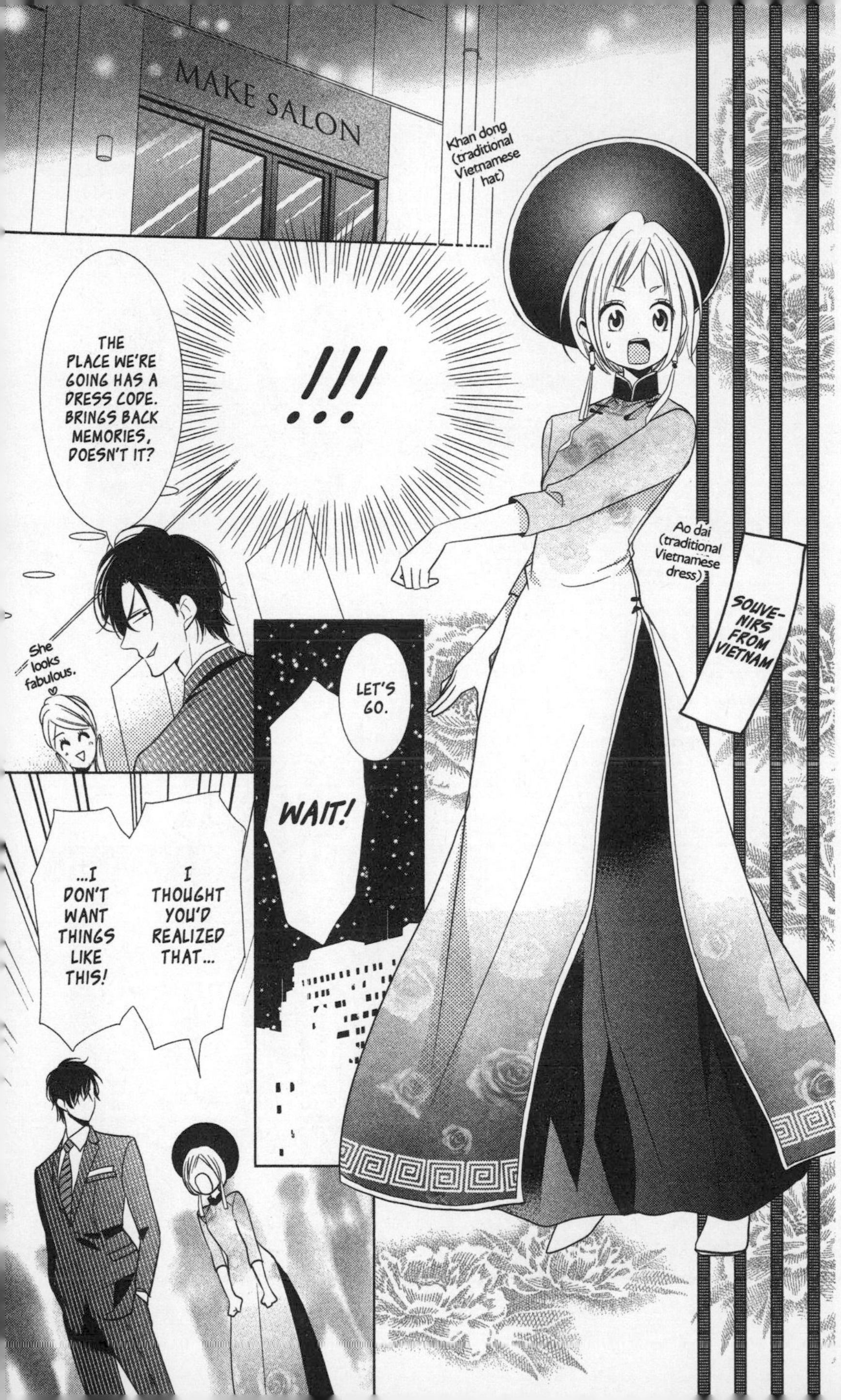
Khan dong (traditional Vietnamese hat)
Ao dai (traditional Vietnamese dress)
SOUVE-NIRS FROM VIETNAM
MAKE SALON
THE PLACE WE'RE GOING HAS A DRESS CODE. BRINGS BACK MEMORIES, DOESN'T IT?
!!!
She looks fabulous.
LET'S GO.
WAIT!
I THOUGHT YOU'D REALIZED THAT...
...I DON'T WANT THINGS LIKE THIS!

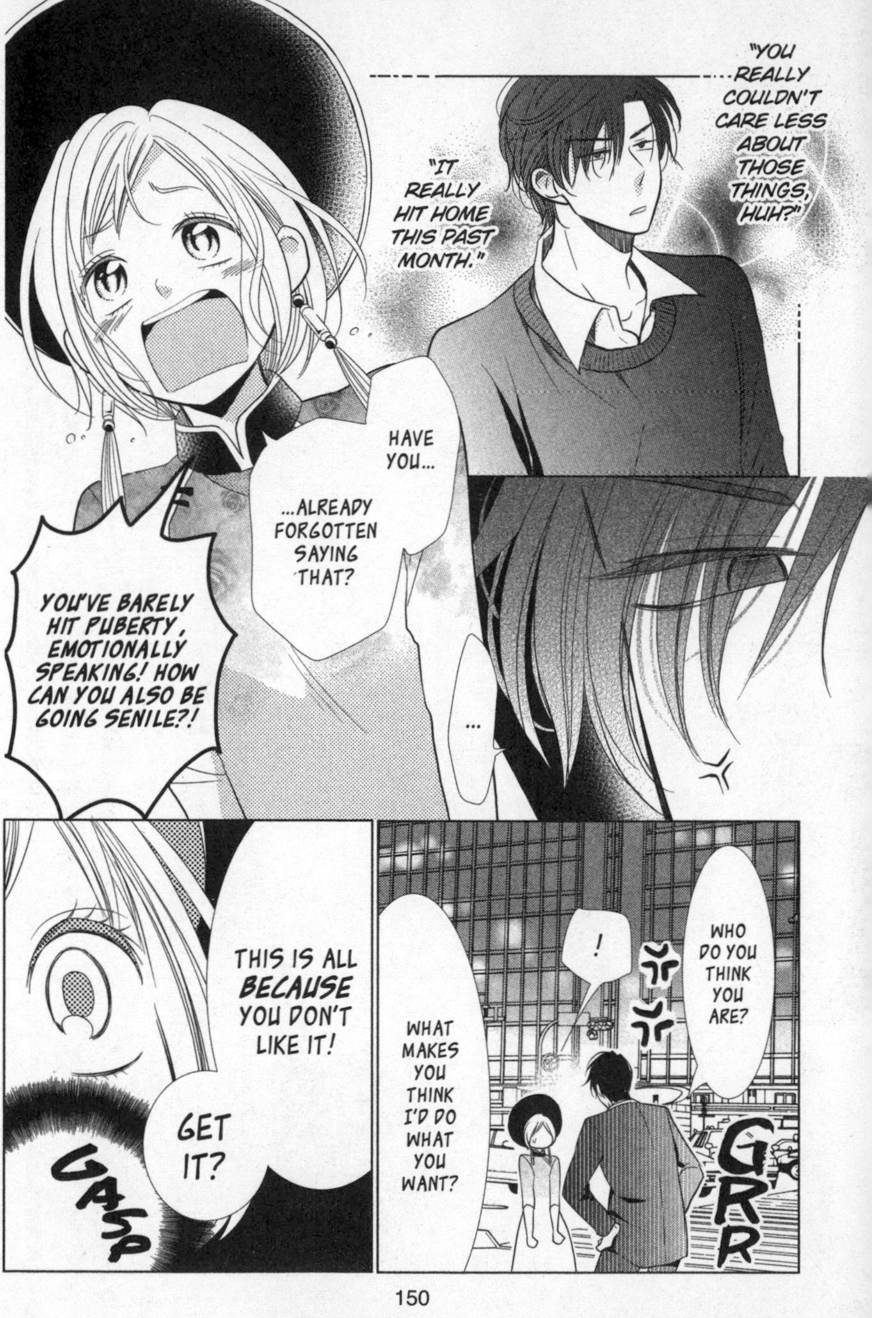
"YOU REALLY COULDN'T CARE LESS ABOUT THOSE THINGS, HUH?"
"IT REALLY HIT HOME THIS PAST MONTH."
HAVE YOU...
...ALREADY FORGOTTEN SAYING THAT?
...
YOU'VE BARELY HIT PUBERTY, EMOTIONALLY SPEAKING! HOW CAN YOU ALSO BE GOING SENILE?!
WHO DO YOU THINK YOU ARE?
!
WHAT MAKES YOU THINK I'D DO WHAT YOU WANT?
GRR
THIS IS ALL **BECAUSE** YOU DON'T LIKE IT!
GET IT?
GASP

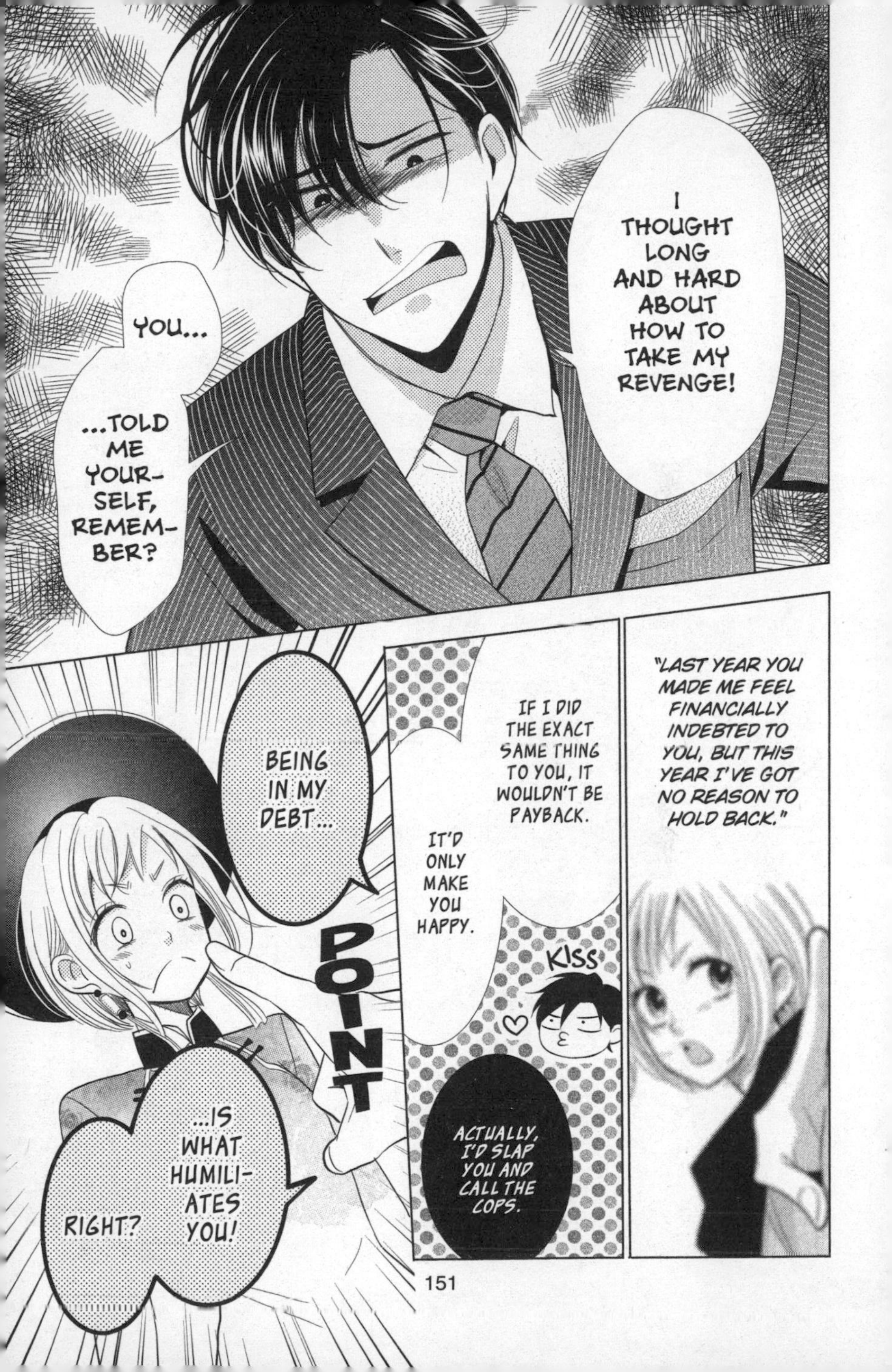
I THOUGHT LONG AND HARD ABOUT HOW TO TAKE MY REVENGE!
YOU...
...TOLD ME YOUR-SELF, REMEMBER?
"LAST YEAR YOU MADE ME FEEL FINANCIALLY INDEBTED TO YOU, BUT THIS YEAR I'VE GOT NO REASON TO HOLD BACK."
IF I DID THE EXACT SAME THING TO YOU, IT WOULDN'T BE PAYBACK.
IT'D ONLY MAKE YOU HAPPY.
KISS
ACTUALLY, I'D SLAP YOU AND CALL THE COPS.
BEING IN MY DEBT...
POINT
...IS WHAT HUMILI-ATES YOU!
RIGHT?

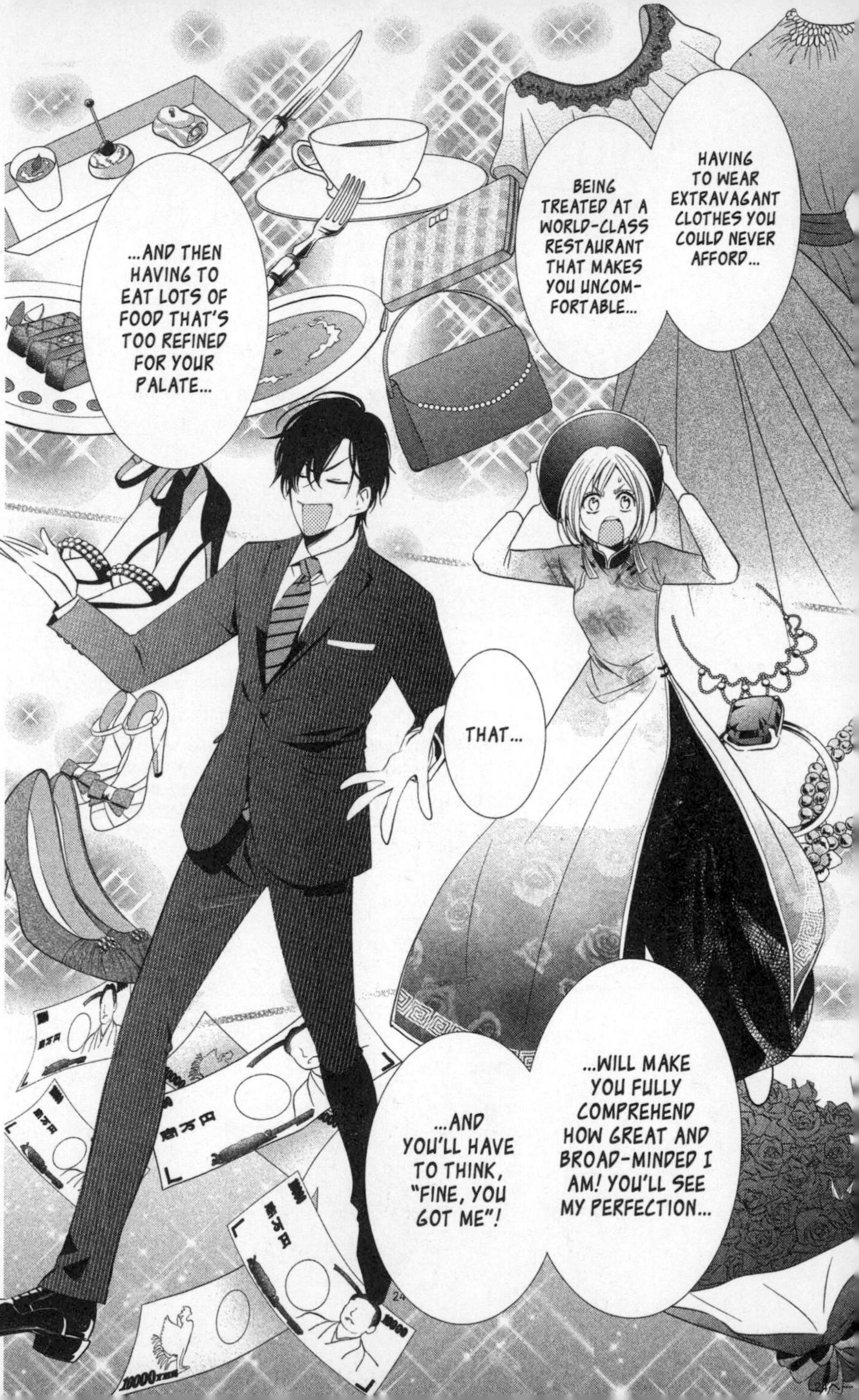
HAVING TO WEAR EXTRAVAGANT CLOTHES YOU COULD NEVER AFFORD...
BEING TREATED AT A WORLD-CLASS RESTAURANT THAT MAKES YOU UNCOM-FORTABLE...
...AND THEN HAVING TO EAT LOTS OF FOOD THAT'S TOO REFINED FOR YOUR PALATE...
THAT...
...WILL MAKE YOU FULLY COMPREHEND HOW GREAT AND BROAD-MINDED I AM! YOU'LL SEE MY PERFECTION...
...AND YOU'LL HAVE TO THINK, "FINE, YOU GOT ME"!

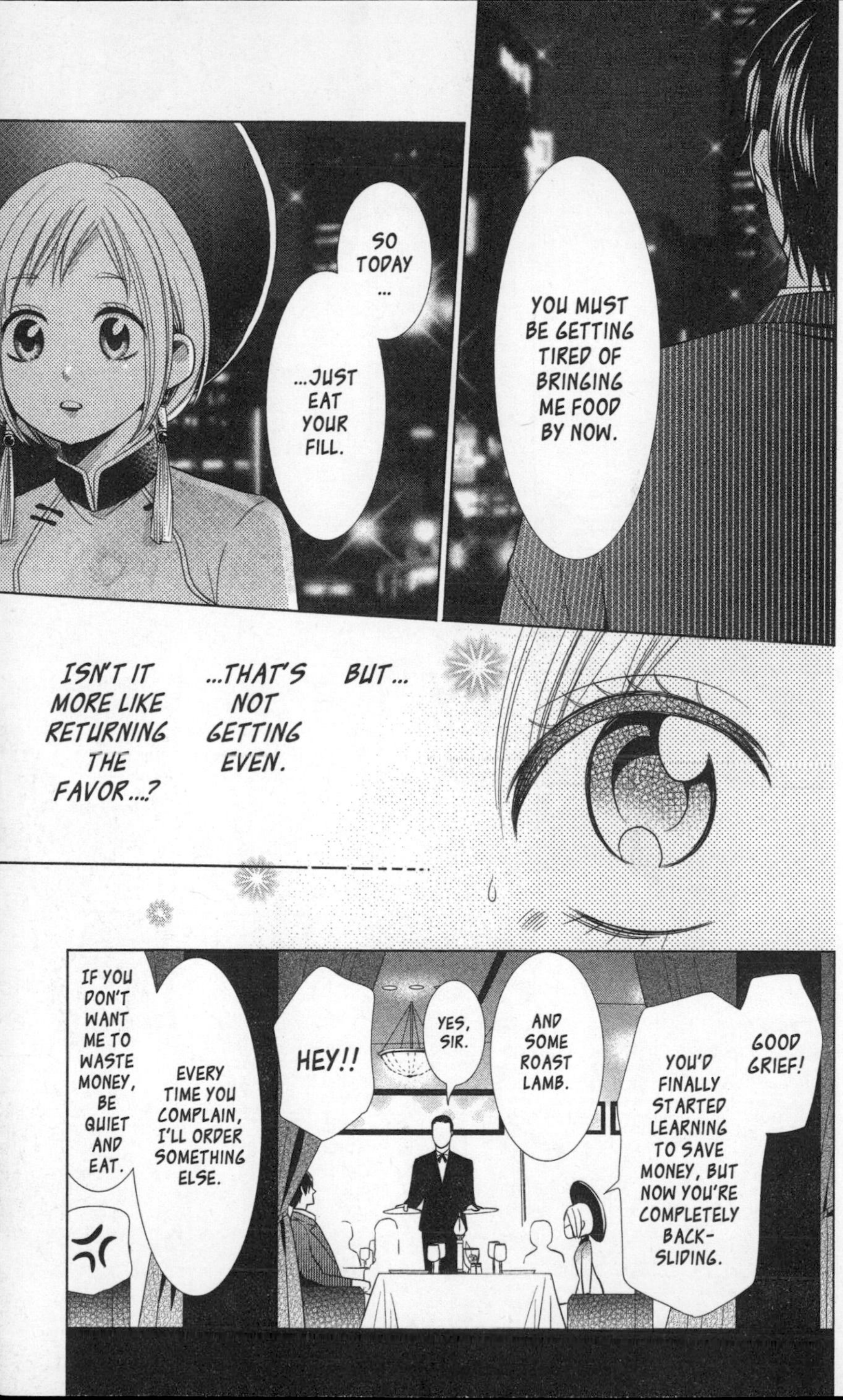
YOU MUST BE GETTING TIRED OF BRINGING ME FOOD BY NOW.
SO TODAY ...
...JUST EAT YOUR FILL.
BUT...
...THAT'S NOT GETTING EVEN.
ISN'T IT MORE LIKE RETURNING THE FAVOR...?
GOOD GRIEF!
YOU'D FINALLY STARTED LEARNING TO SAVE MONEY, BUT NOW YOU'RE COMPLETELY BACK-SLIDING.
AND SOME ROAST LAMB.
YES, SIR.
HEY!!
EVERY TIME YOU COMPLAIN, I'LL ORDER SOMETHING ELSE.
IF YOU DON'T WANT ME TO WASTE MONEY, BE QUIET AND EAT.

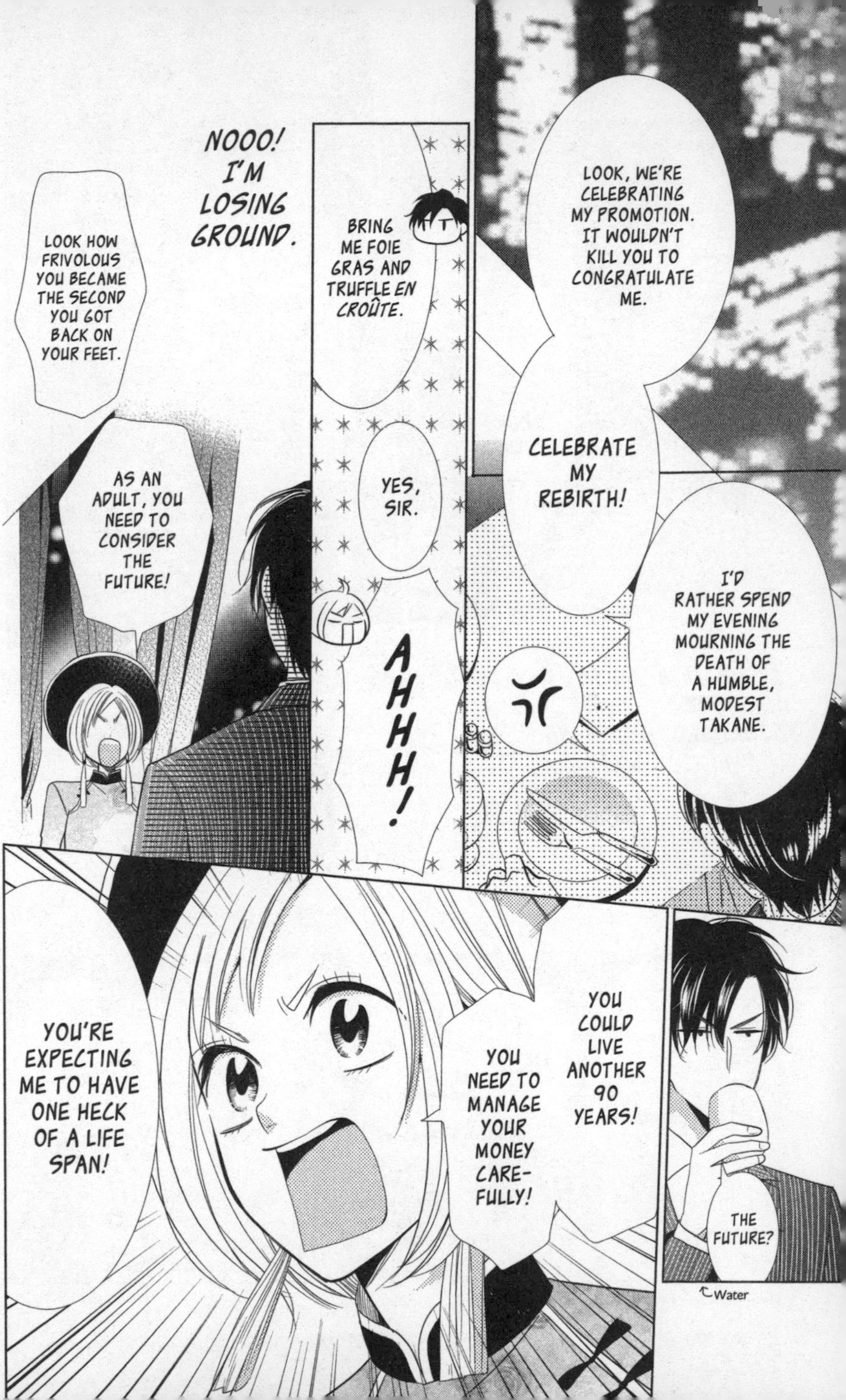
LOOK, WE'RE CELEBRATING MY PROMOTION. IT WOULDN'T KILL YOU TO CONGRATULATE ME.
I'D RATHER SPEND MY EVENING MOURNING THE DEATH OF A HUMBLE, MODEST TAKANE.
CELEBRATE MY REBIRTH!
BRING ME FOIE GRAS AND TRUFFLE *EN CROÛTE*.
YES, SIR.
AHHHH!
NOOO! I'M LOSING GROUND.
LOOK HOW FRIVOLOUS YOU BECAME THE SECOND YOU GOT BACK ON YOUR FEET.
AS AN ADULT, YOU NEED TO CONSIDER THE FUTURE!
THE FUTURE?
Water
YOU COULD LIVE ANOTHER 90 YEARS!
YOU NEED TO MANAGE YOUR MONEY CARE-FULLY!
YOU'RE EXPECTING ME TO HAVE ONE HECK OF A LIFE SPAN!

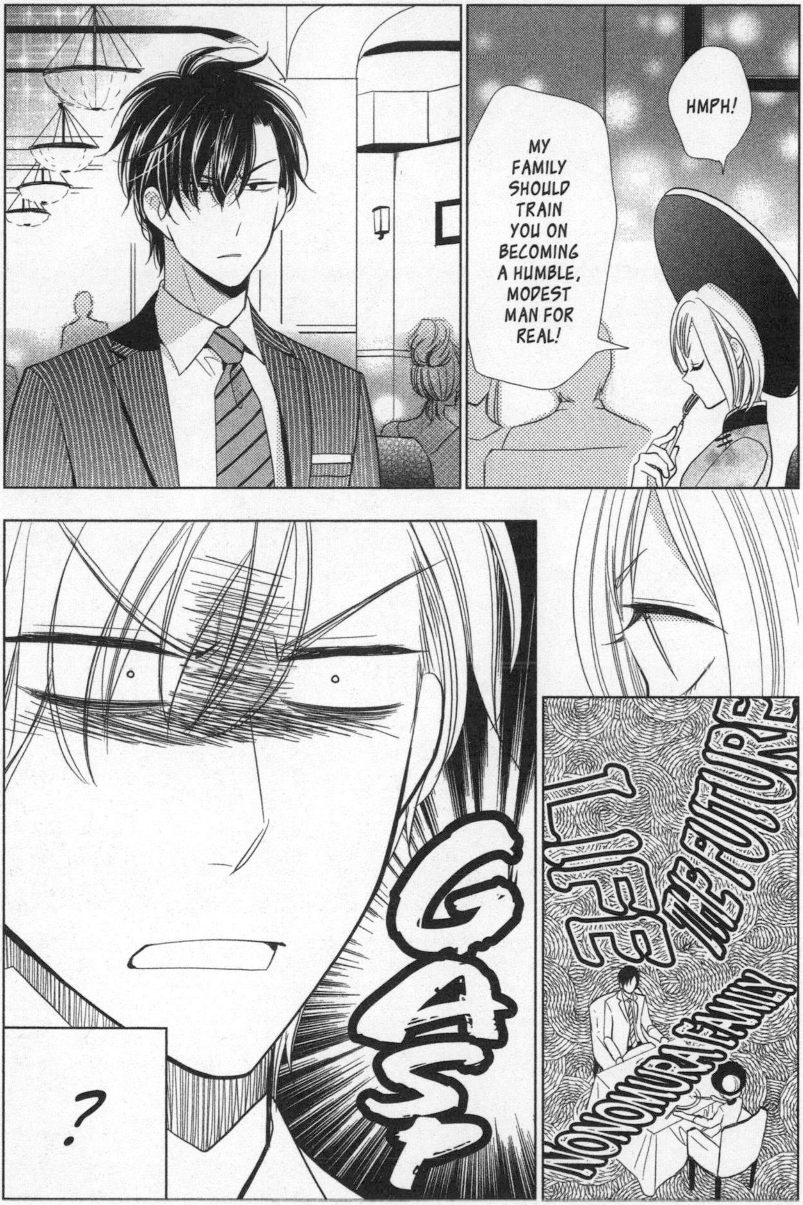
HMPH!
MY FAMILY SHOULD TRAIN YOU ON BECOMING A HUMBLE, MODEST MAN FOR REAL!
THE FUTURE
LIFE
NONONOMURA FAMILY
GASP
?

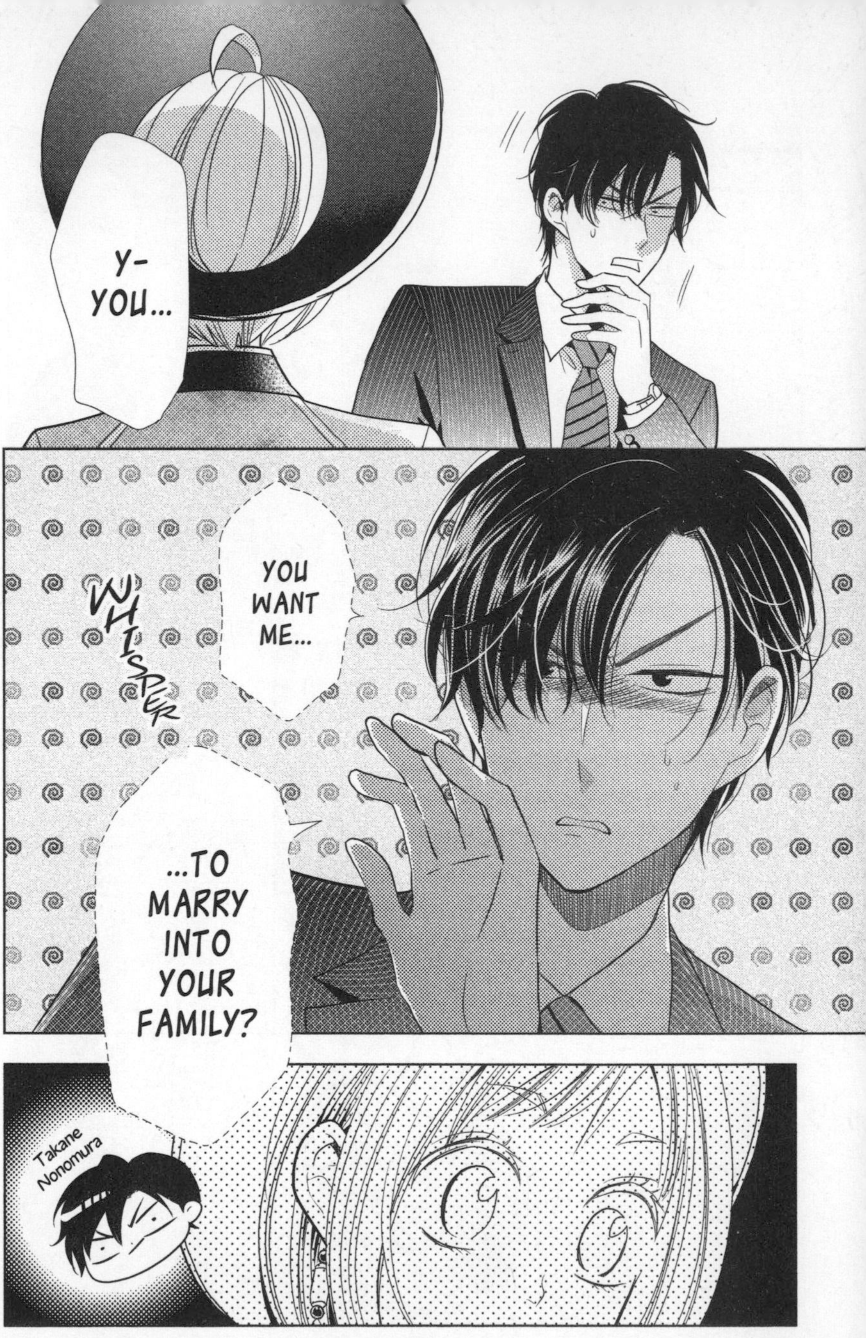
Y-
YOU...
YOU WANT ME...
WHISPER
...TO MARRY INTO YOUR FAMILY?
Takane Nonomura

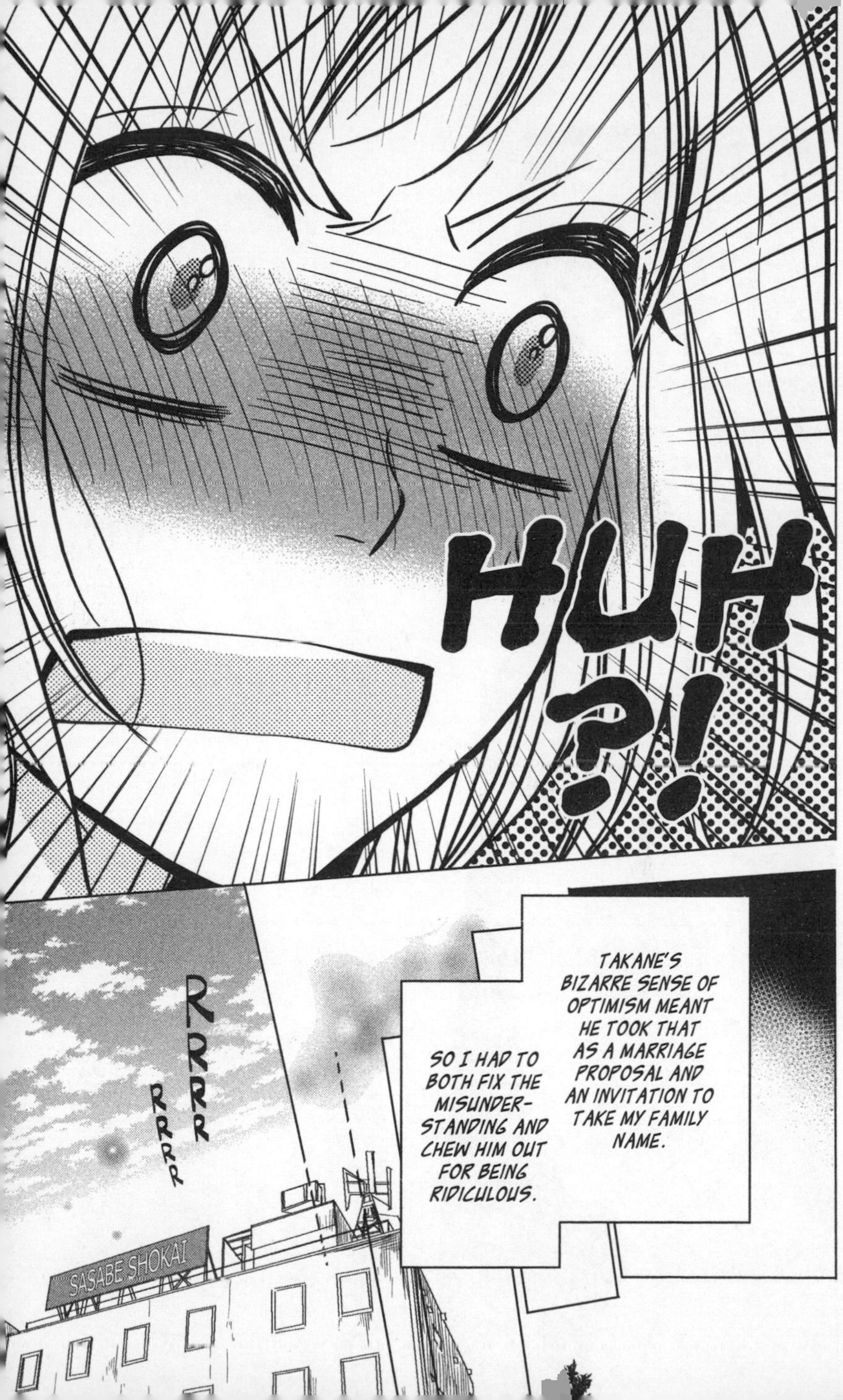
HUH?!
TAKANE'S BIZARRE SENSE OF OPTIMISM MEANT HE TOOK THAT AS A MARRIAGE PROPOSAL AND AN INVITATION TO TAKE MY FAMILY NAME.
SO I HAD TO BOTH FIX THE MISUNDER-STANDING AND CHEW HIM OUT FOR BEING RIDICULOUS.
RRRR
RRRR
SASABE SHOKAI

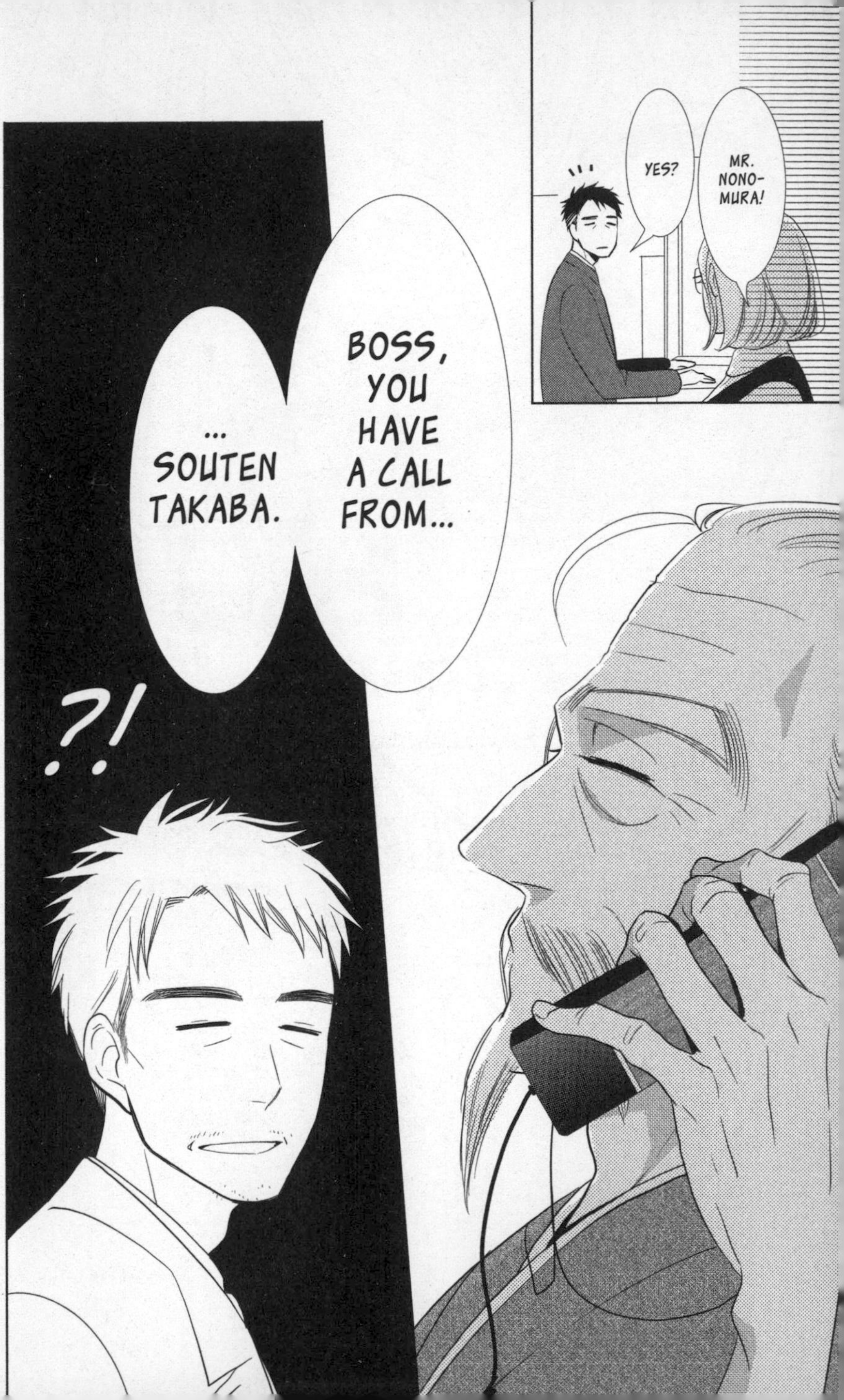
MR. NONO-MURA!
YES?
BOSS, YOU HAVE A CALL FROM...
... SOUTEN TAKABA.
?!

Chapter 45

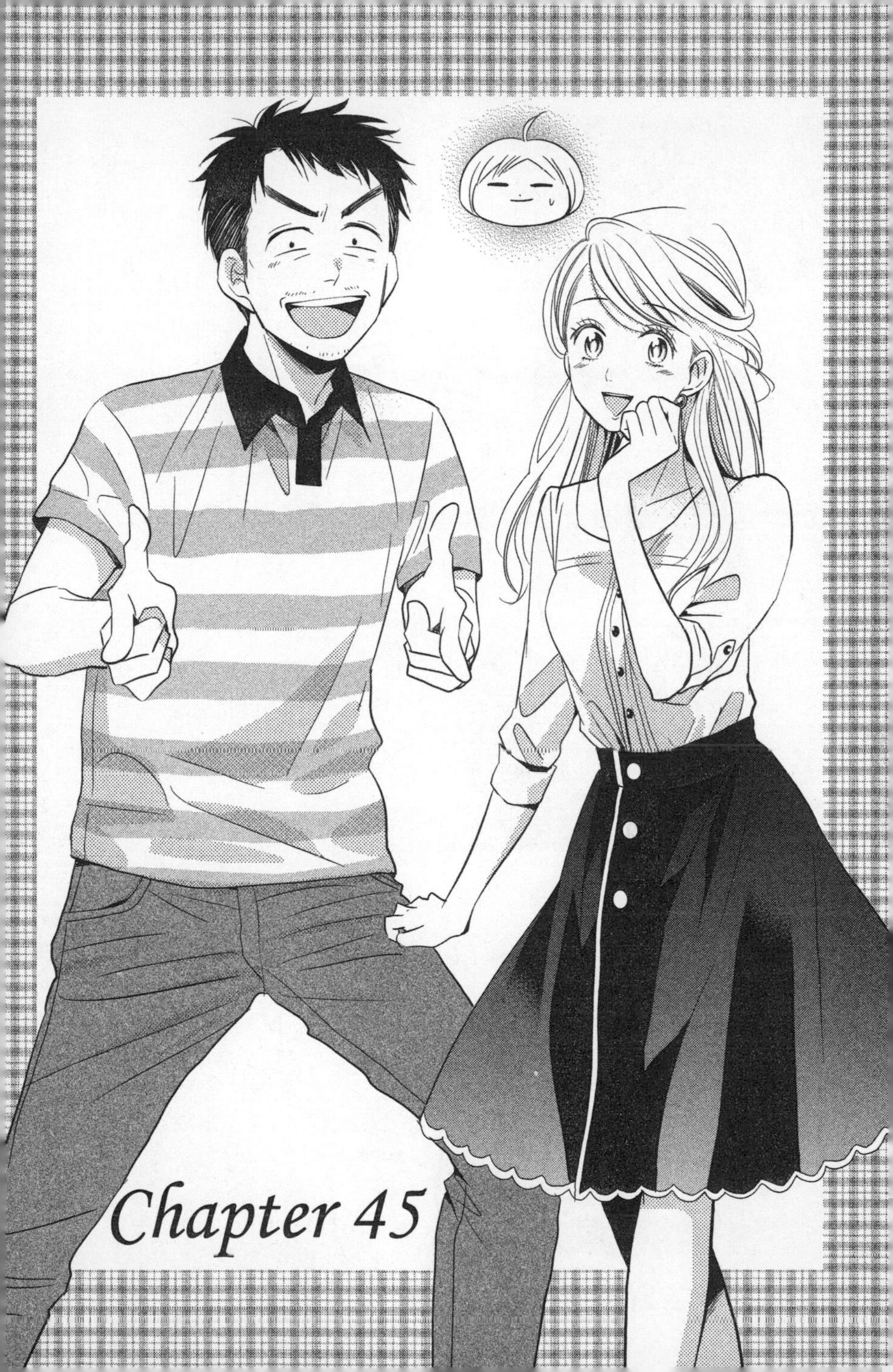

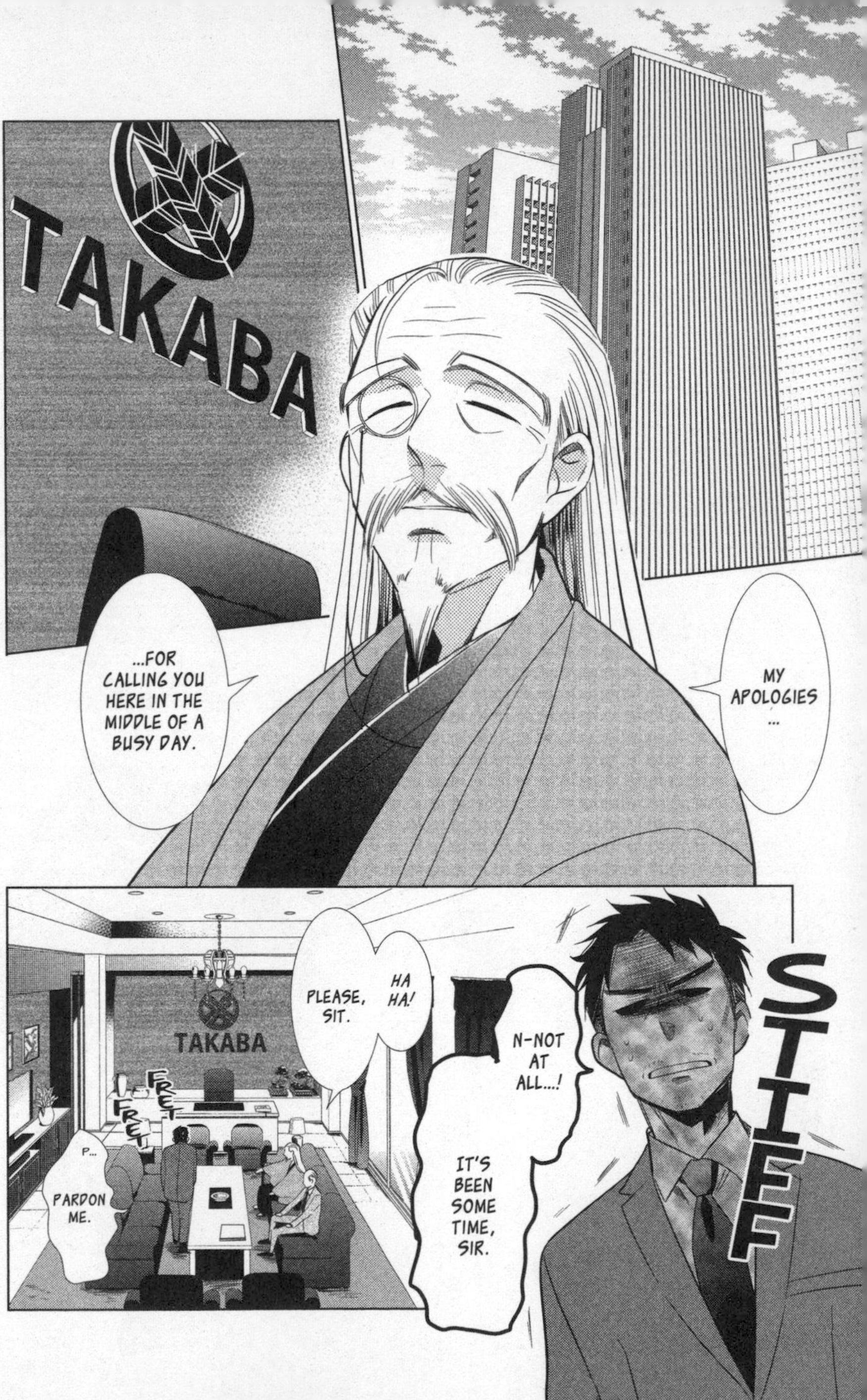
TAKABA
MY APOLOGIES ...
...FOR CALLING YOU HERE IN THE MIDDLE OF A BUSY DAY.
STIFF
N-NOT AT ALL...!
IT'S BEEN SOME TIME, SIR.
HA HA!
PLEASE, SIT.
TAKABA
FRET FRET
P... PARDON ME.

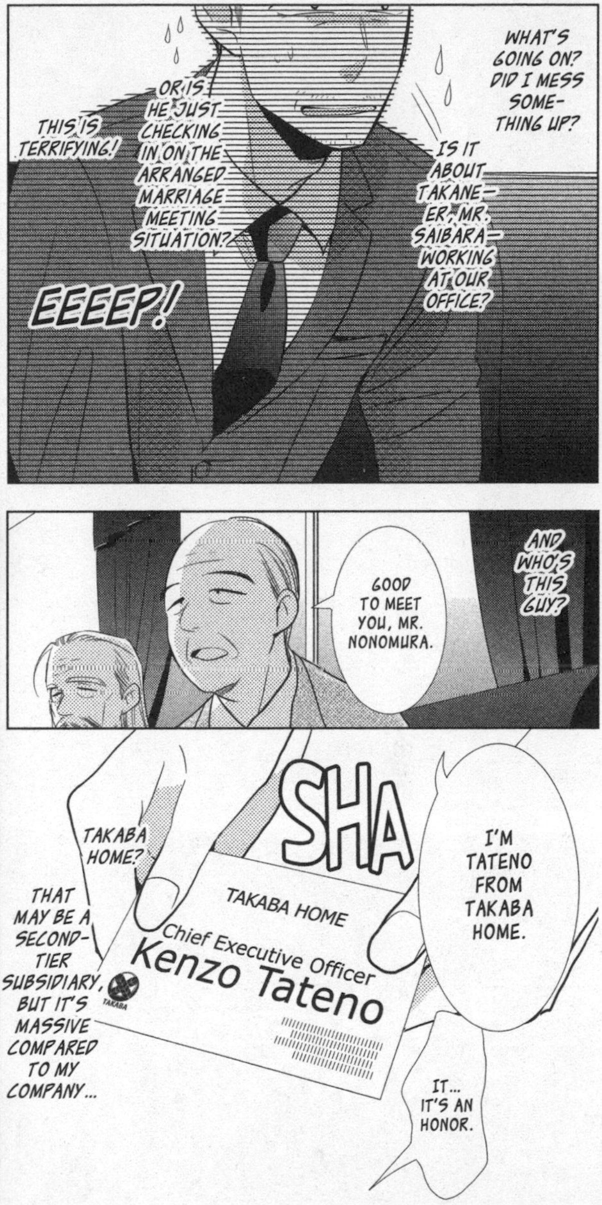
WHAT'S GOING ON? DID I MESS SOME-THING UP?
IS IT ABOUT TAKANE—ER, MR. SAIBARA—WORKING AT OUR OFFICE?
OR IS HE JUST CHECKING IN ON THE ARRANGED MARRIAGE MEETING SITUATION?
THIS IS TERRIFYING!
EEEEP!
AND WHO'S THIS GUY?
GOOD TO MEET YOU, MR. NONOMURA.
I'M TATENO FROM TAKABA HOME.
SHA
TAKABA HOME
Chief Executive Officer
Kenzo Tateno
TAKABA
IT... IT'S AN HONOR.
TAKABA HOME?
THAT MAY BE A SECOND-TIER SUBSIDIARY, BUT IT'S MASSIVE COMPARED TO MY COMPANY...

Send Us Your Feedback!

Yuki Shiwasu
c/o Takane & Hana Editor
VIZ Media
P.O. Box 77010
San Francisco, CA 94107

I look forward to hearing what you think of the story.

Please feel free to send requests too (although I might not be able to respond to all of them)!

Hana, 6 ♥ Takane, 16

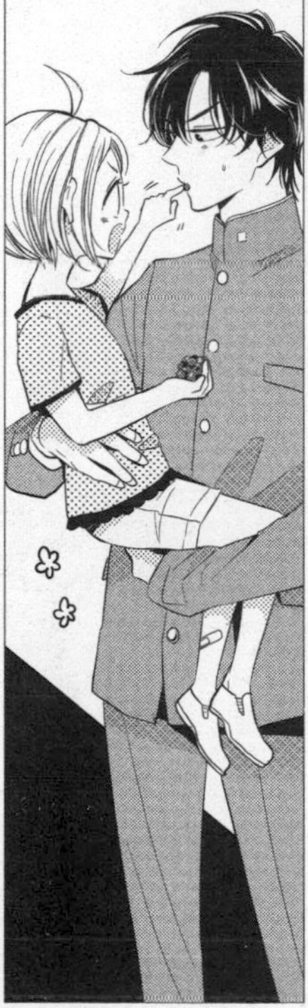

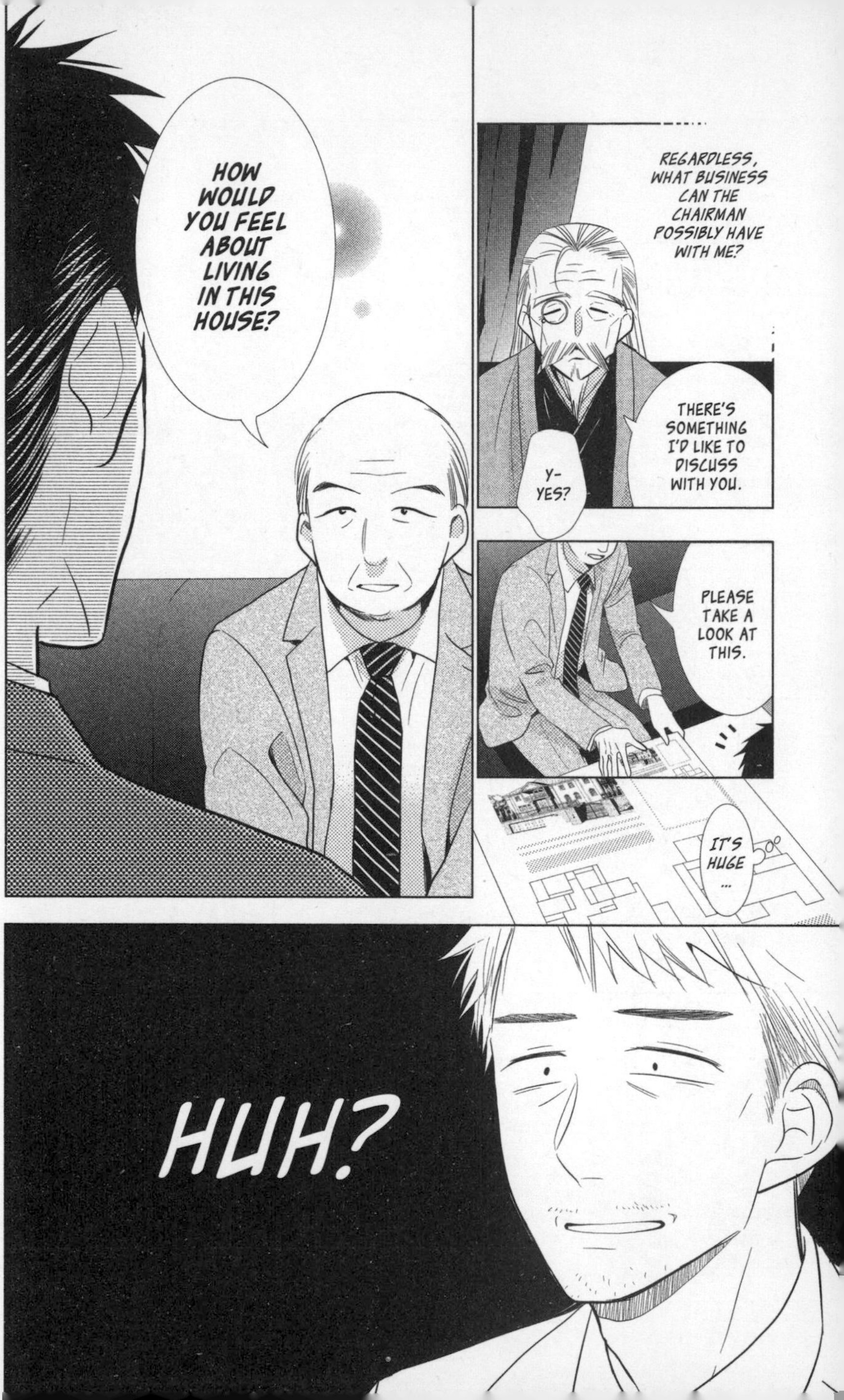
REGARDLESS, WHAT BUSINESS CAN THE CHAIRMAN POSSIBLY HAVE WITH ME?
THERE'S SOMETHING I'D LIKE TO DISCUSS WITH YOU.
Y-YES?
PLEASE TAKE A LOOK AT THIS.
IT'S HUGE ...
HOW WOULD YOU FEEL ABOUT LIVING IN THIS HOUSE?
HUH?

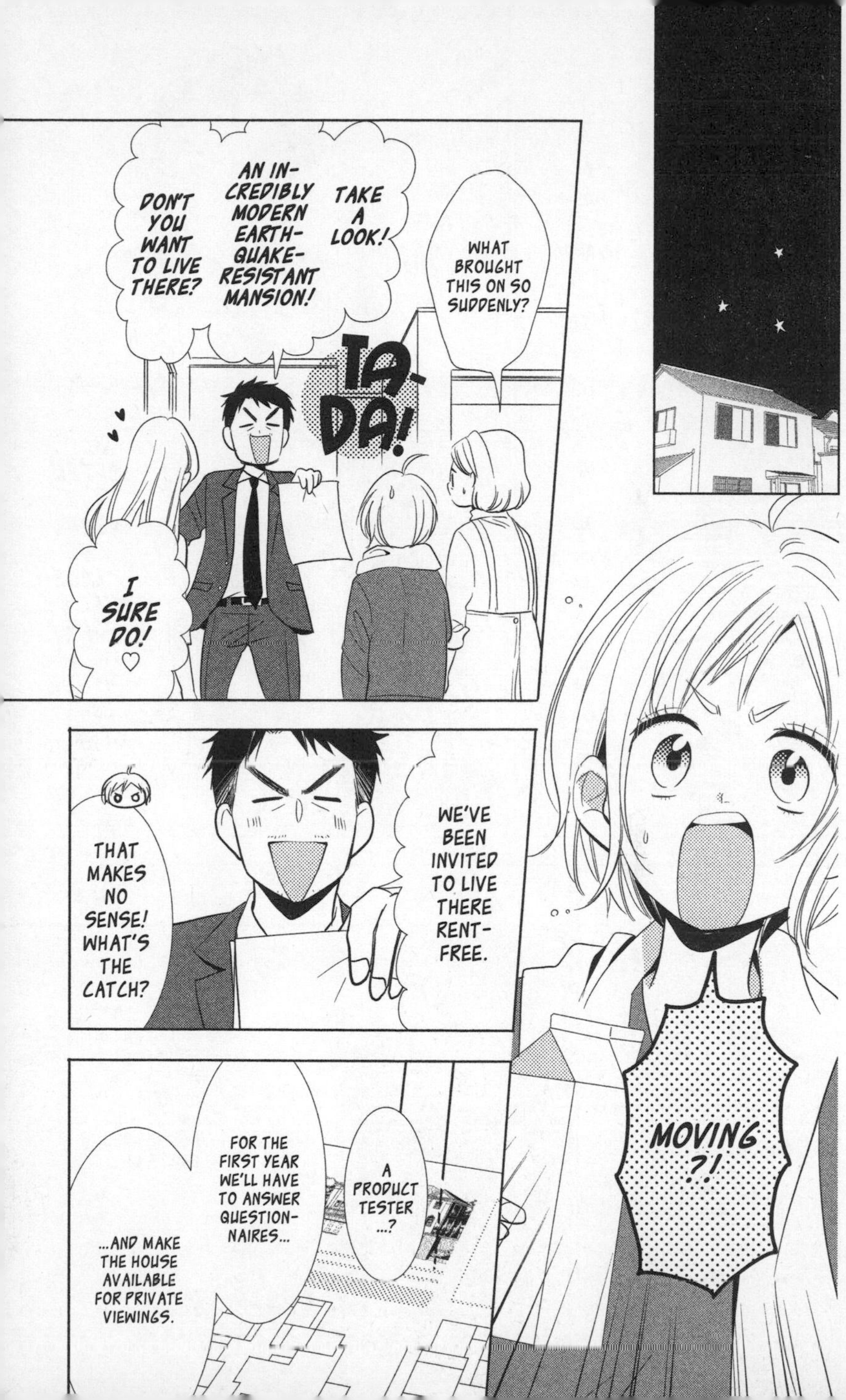
MOVING?!
WHAT BROUGHT THIS ON SO SUDDENLY?
TA-DA!
TAKE A LOOK!
AN IN-CREDIBLY MODERN EARTH-QUAKE-RESISTANT MANSION!
DON'T YOU WANT TO LIVE THERE?
I SURE DO! ♡
WE'VE BEEN INVITED TO LIVE THERE RENT-FREE.
THAT MAKES NO SENSE! WHAT'S THE CATCH?
A PRODUCT TESTER ...?
FOR THE FIRST YEAR WE'LL HAVE TO ANSWER QUESTION-NAIRES...
...AND MAKE THE HOUSE AVAILABLE FOR PRIVATE VIEWINGS.

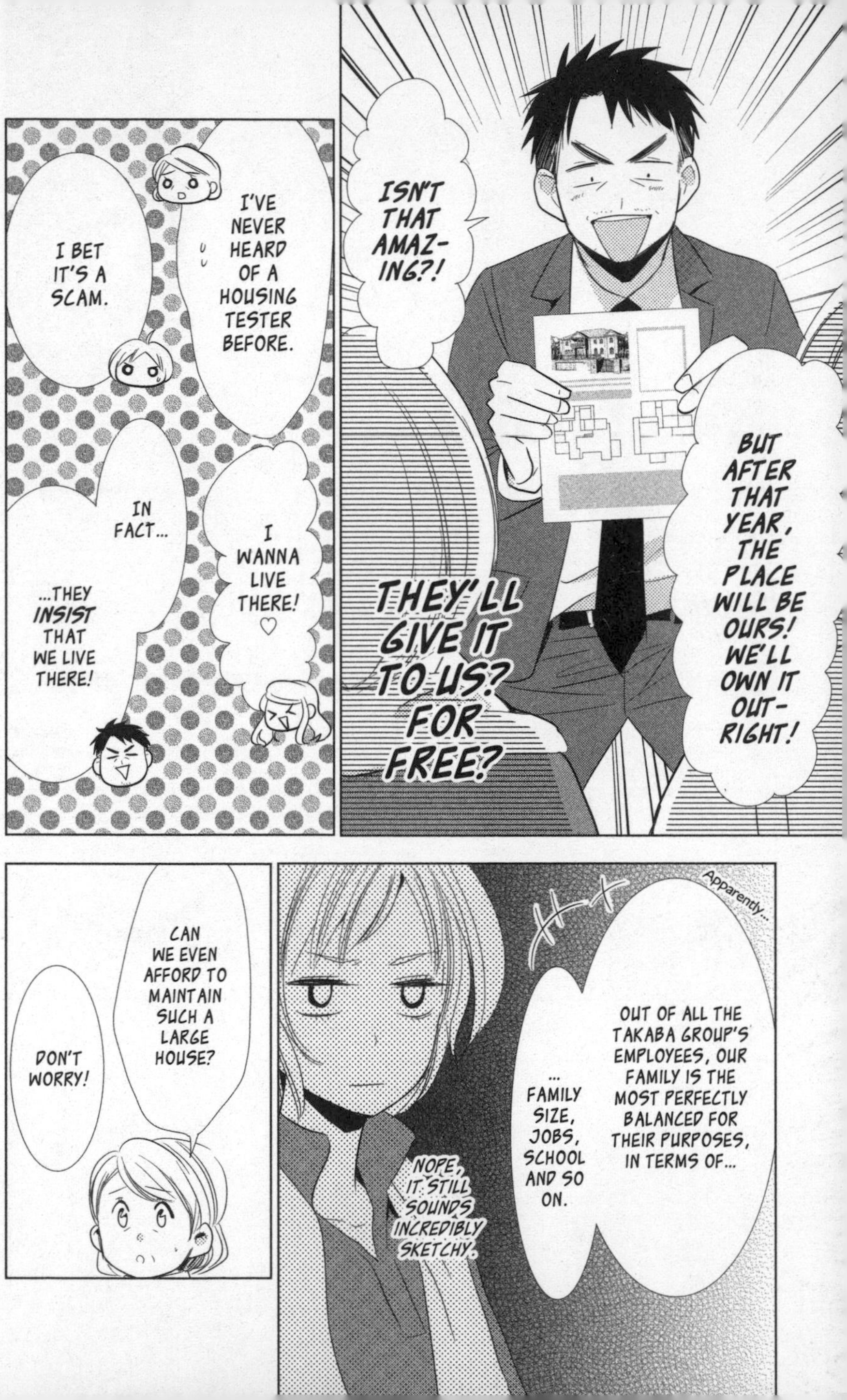
BUT AFTER THAT YEAR, THE PLACE WILL BE OURS! WE'LL OWN IT OUT-RIGHT!
ISN'T THAT AMAZ-ING?!
THEY'LL GIVE IT TO US? FOR FREE?
I'VE NEVER HEARD OF A HOUSING TESTER BEFORE.
I BET IT'S A SCAM.
I WANNA LIVE THERE! ♡
IN FACT...
...THEY INSIST THAT WE LIVE THERE!
Apparently...
OUT OF ALL THE TAKABA GROUP'S EMPLOYEES, OUR FAMILY IS THE MOST PERFECTLY BALANCED FOR THEIR PURPOSES, IN TERMS OF...
...FAMILY SIZE, JOBS, SCHOOL AND SO ON.
NOPE, IT STILL SOUNDS INCREDIBLY SKETCHY.
CAN WE EVEN AFFORD TO MAINTAIN SUCH A LARGE HOUSE?
DON'T WORRY!

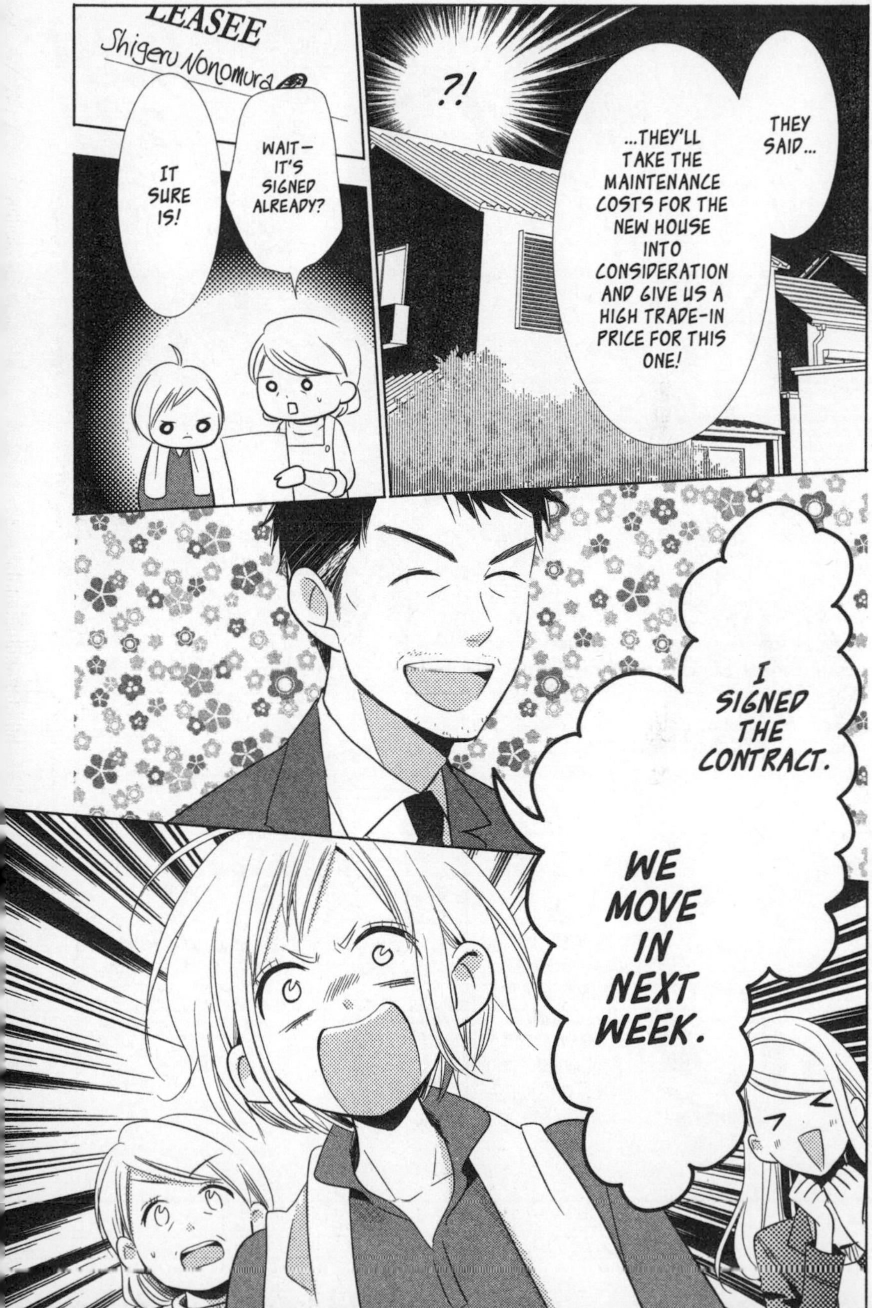
?!
THEY SAID...
...THEY'LL TAKE THE MAINTENANCE COSTS FOR THE NEW HOUSE INTO CONSIDERATION AND GIVE US A HIGH TRADE-IN PRICE FOR THIS ONE!
LEASEE
Shigeru Nonomura
WAIT—IT'S SIGNED ALREADY?
IT SURE IS!
I SIGNED THE CONTRACT.
WE MOVE IN NEXT WEEK.

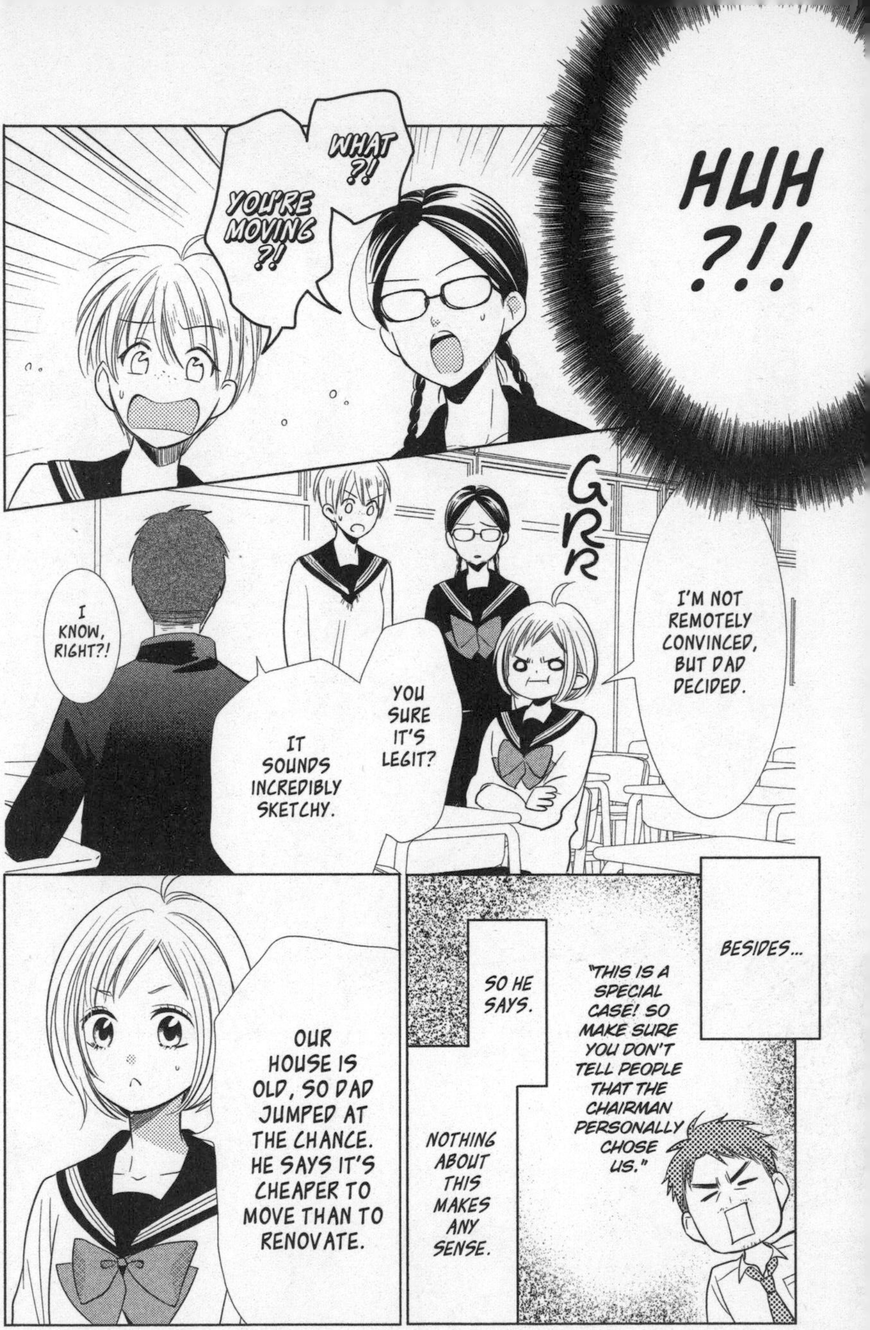
HUH ?!!
WHAT ?!
YOU'RE MOVING ?!
GRR
I'M NOT REMOTELY CONVINCED, BUT DAD DECIDED.
YOU SURE IT'S LEGIT?
IT SOUNDS INCREDIBLY SKETCHY.
I KNOW, RIGHT?!
BESIDES...
"THIS IS A SPECIAL CASE! SO MAKE SURE YOU DON'T TELL PEOPLE THAT THE CHAIRMAN PERSONALLY CHOSE US."
SO HE SAYS.
NOTHING ABOUT THIS MAKES ANY SENSE.
OUR HOUSE IS OLD, SO DAD JUMPED AT THE CHANCE. HE SAYS IT'S CHEAPER TO MOVE THAN TO RENOVATE.

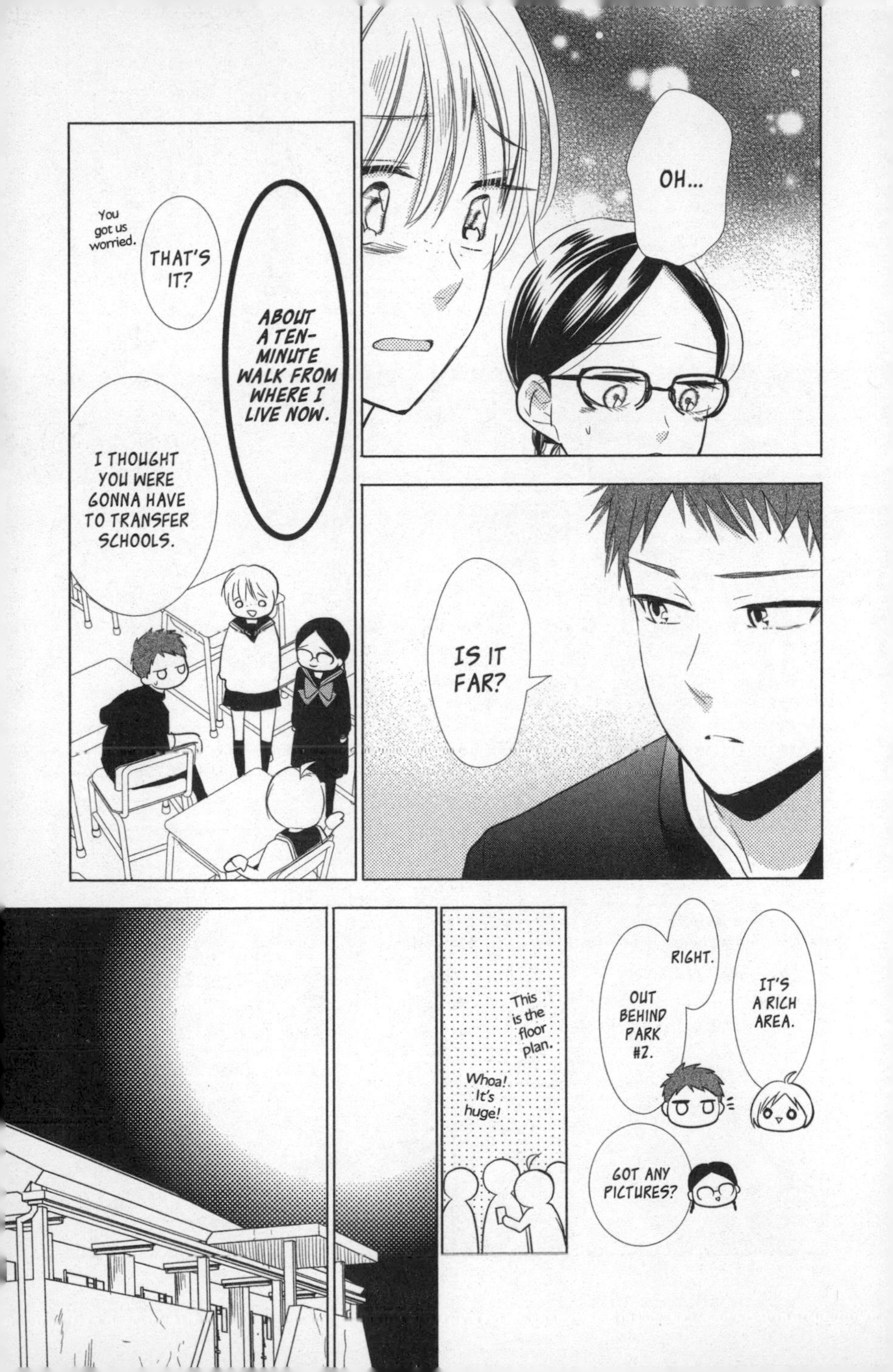
OH...
IS IT FAR?
ABOUT A TEN-MINUTE WALK FROM WHERE I LIVE NOW.
THAT'S IT?
You got us worried.
I THOUGHT YOU WERE GONNA HAVE TO TRANSFER SCHOOLS.
IT'S A RICH AREA.
RIGHT.
OUT BEHIND PARK #2.
GOT ANY PICTURES?
This is the floor plan.
Whoa! It's huge!

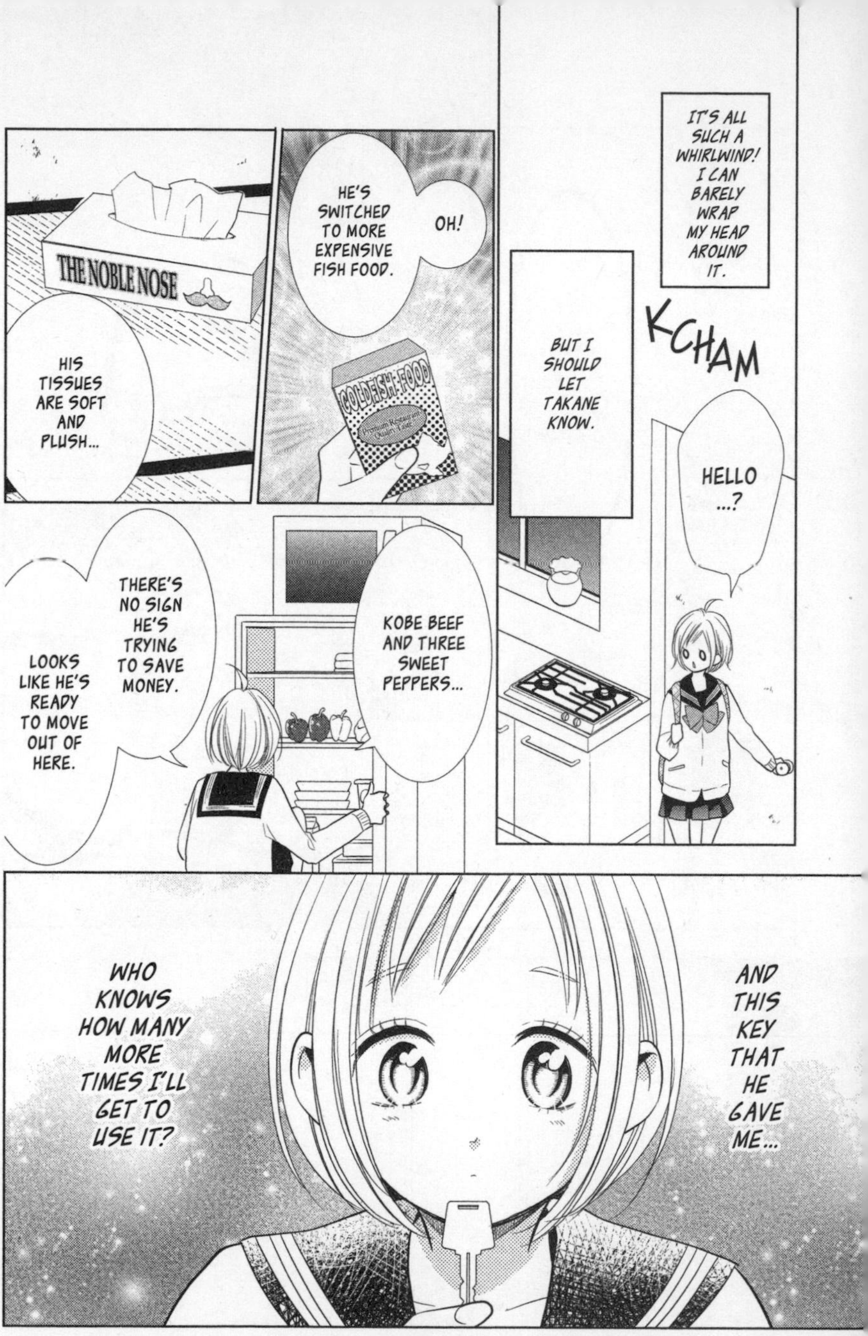
IT'S ALL SUCH A WHIRLWIND! I CAN BARELY WRAP MY HEAD AROUND IT.
BUT I SHOULD LET TAKANE KNOW.
KCHAM
HELLO ...?
OH!
HE'S SWITCHED TO MORE EXPENSIVE FISH FOOD.
GOLDFISH FOOD
Premium Restaurant Quality Taste
THE NOBLE NOSE
HIS TISSUES ARE SOFT AND PLUSH...
KOBE BEEF AND THREE SWEET PEPPERS...
THERE'S NO SIGN HE'S TRYING TO SAVE MONEY.
LOOKS LIKE HE'S READY TO MOVE OUT OF HERE.
AND THIS KEY THAT HE GAVE ME...
WHO KNOWS HOW MANY MORE TIMES I'LL GET TO USE IT?

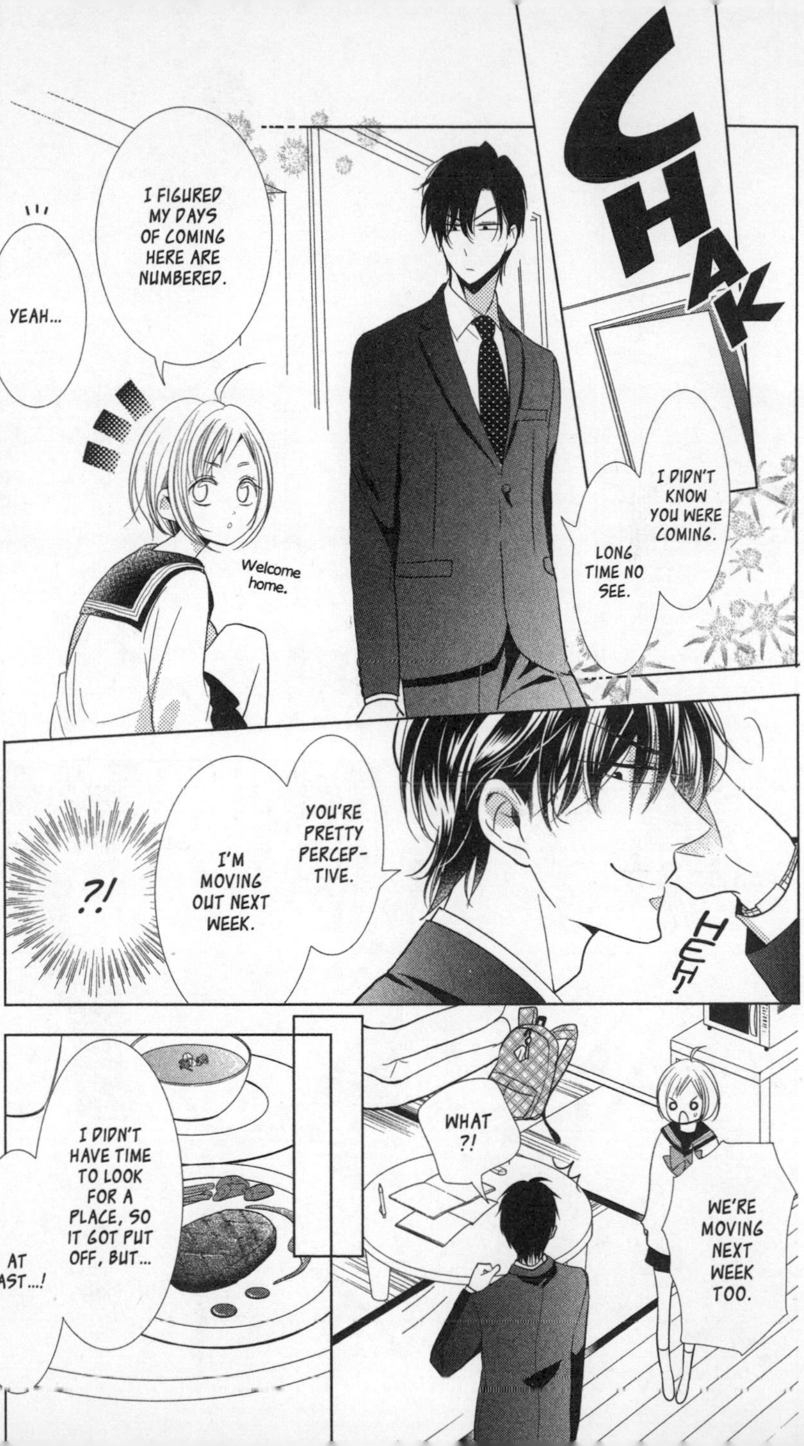
CHAK
I DIDN'T KNOW YOU WERE COMING.
LONG TIME NO SEE.
Welcome home.
I FIGURED MY DAYS OF COMING HERE ARE NUMBERED.
YEAH...
HEH!
YOU'RE PRETTY PERCEP-TIVE.
I'M MOVING OUT NEXT WEEK.
?!
WHAT?!
WE'RE MOVING NEXT WEEK TOO.
I DIDN'T HAVE TIME TO LOOK FOR A PLACE, SO IT GOT PUT OFF, BUT...
AT LAST...!

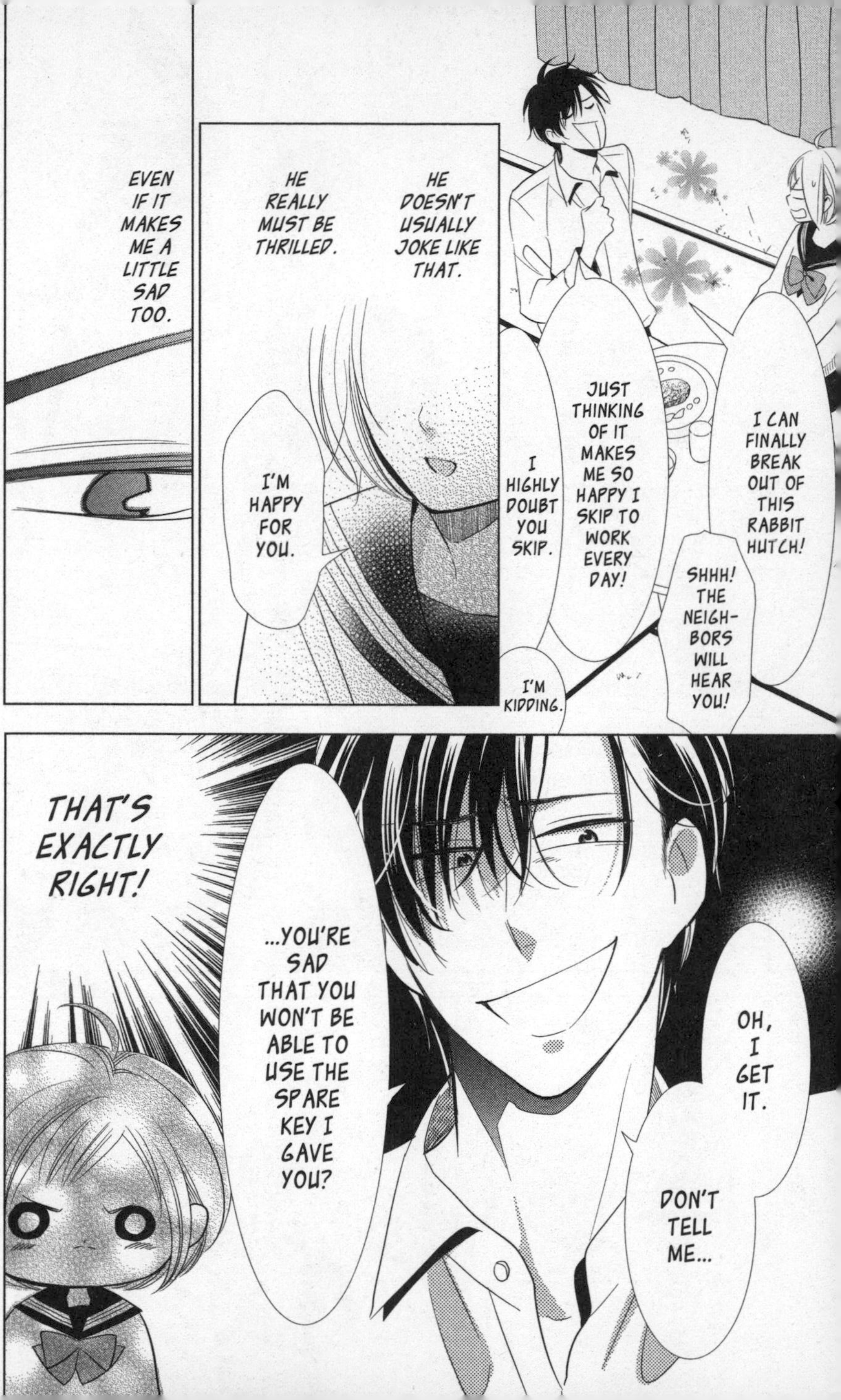

I CAN FINALLY BREAK OUT OF THIS RABBIT HUTCH!
SHHH! THE NEIGHBORS WILL HEAR YOU!
JUST THINKING OF IT MAKES ME SO HAPPY I SKIP TO WORK EVERY DAY!
I HIGHLY DOUBT YOU SKIP.
I'M KIDDING.
HE DOESN'T USUALLY JOKE LIKE THAT.
HE REALLY MUST BE THRILLED.
I'M HAPPY FOR YOU.
EVEN IF IT MAKES ME A LITTLE SAD TOO.
OH, I GET IT.
DON'T TELL ME...
...YOU'RE SAD THAT YOU WON'T BE ABLE TO USE THE SPARE KEY I GAVE YOU?
THAT'S EXACTLY RIGHT!

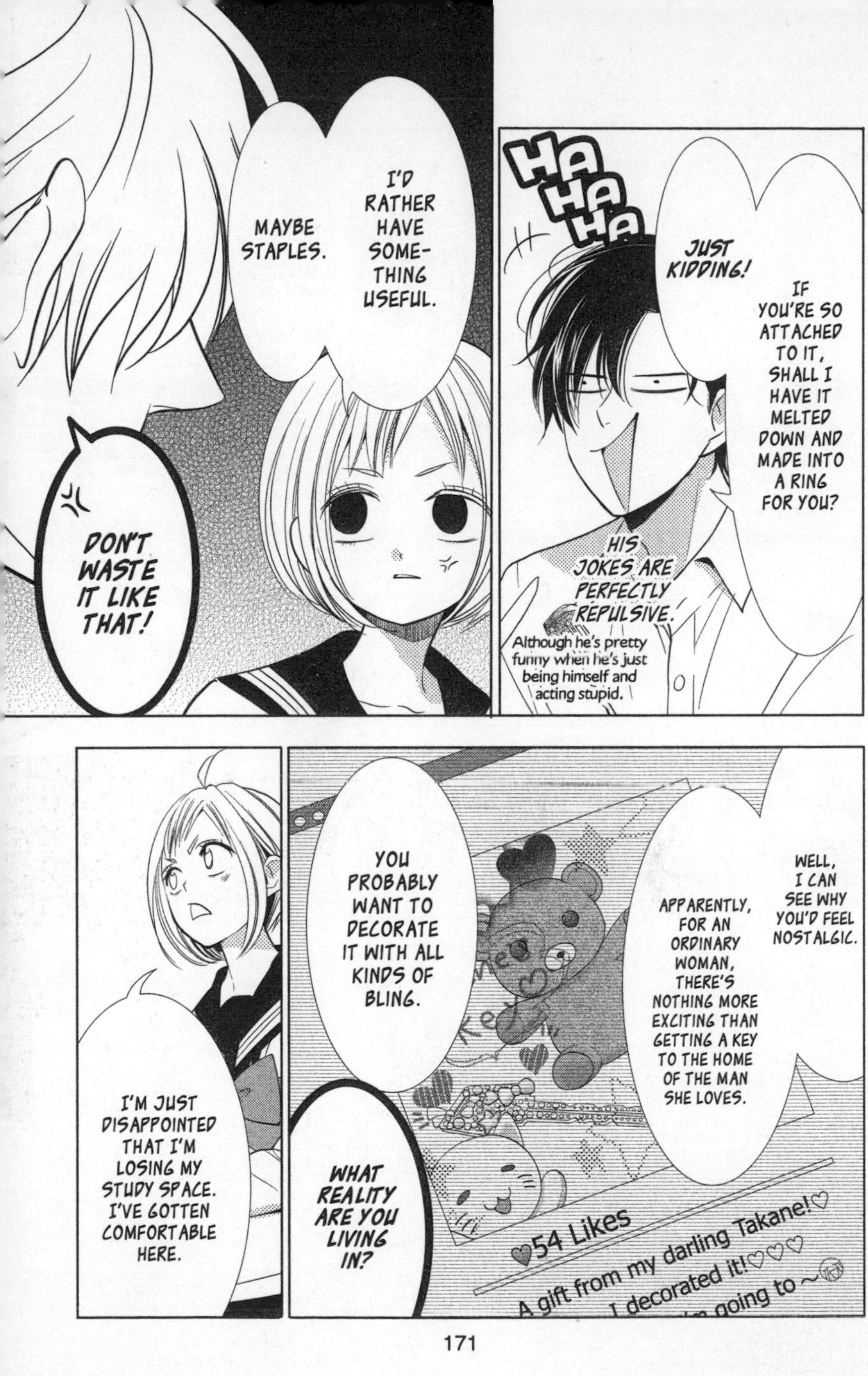
HA HA HA
JUST KIDDING!
IF YOU'RE SO ATTACHED TO IT, SHALL I HAVE IT MELTED DOWN AND MADE INTO A RING FOR YOU?
HIS JOKES ARE PERFECTLY REPULSIVE.
Although he's pretty funny when he's just being himself and acting stupid.
I'D RATHER HAVE SOME-THING USEFUL.
MAYBE STAPLES.
DON'T WASTE IT LIKE THAT!
WELL, I CAN SEE WHY YOU'D FEEL NOSTALGIC.
APPARENTLY, FOR AN ORDINARY WOMAN, THERE'S NOTHING MORE EXCITING THAN GETTING A KEY TO THE HOME OF THE MAN SHE LOVES.
YOU PROBABLY WANT TO DECORATE IT WITH ALL KINDS OF BLING.
WHAT REALITY ARE YOU LIVING IN?
♡54 Likes
A gift from my darling Takane!♡
I decorated it!♡♡♡
I'M JUST DISAPPOINTED THAT I'M LOSING MY STUDY SPACE. I'VE GOTTEN COMFORTABLE HERE.

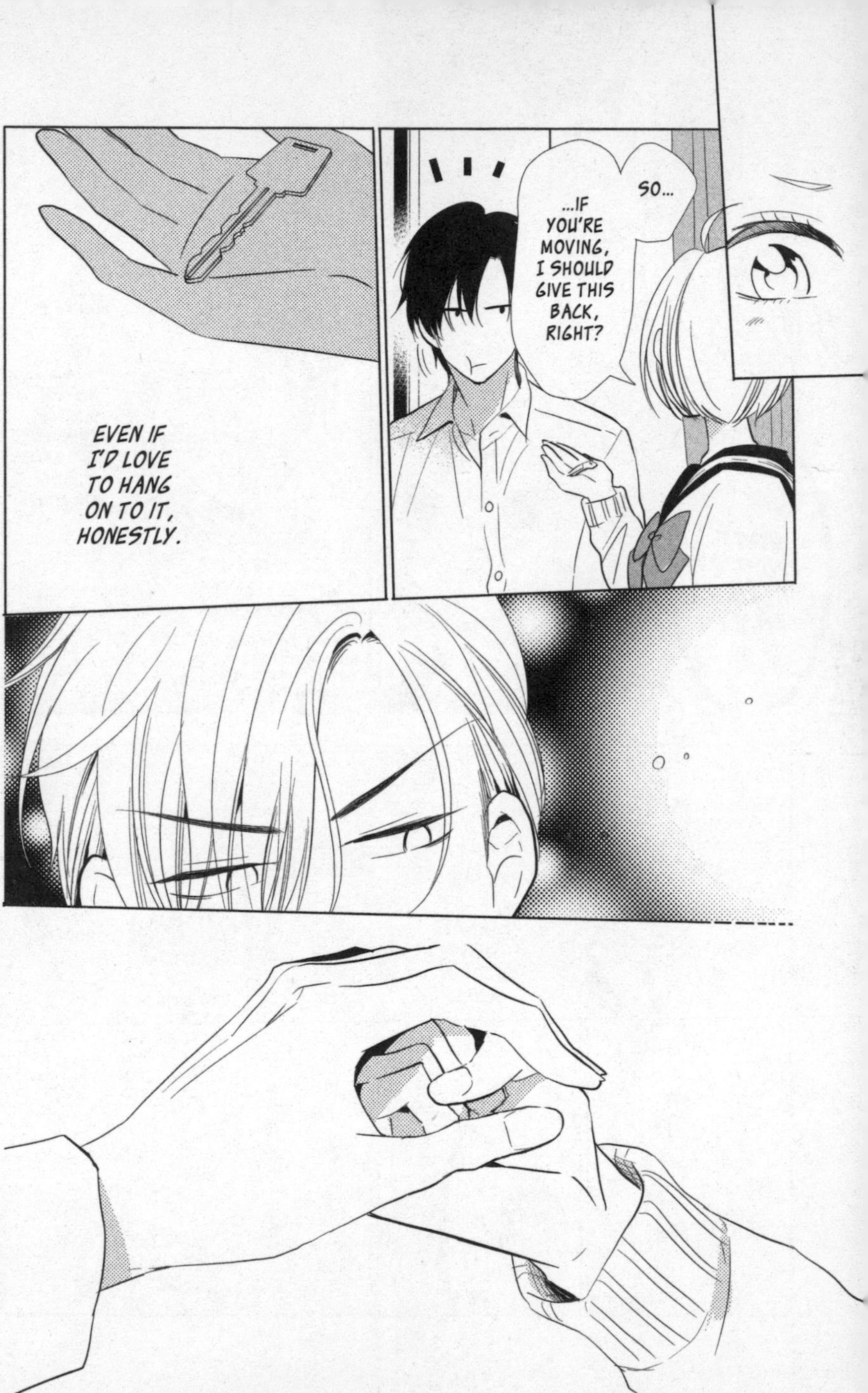
SO...
...IF YOU'RE MOVING, I SHOULD GIVE THIS BACK, RIGHT?
EVEN IF I'D LOVE TO HANG ON TO IT, HONESTLY.

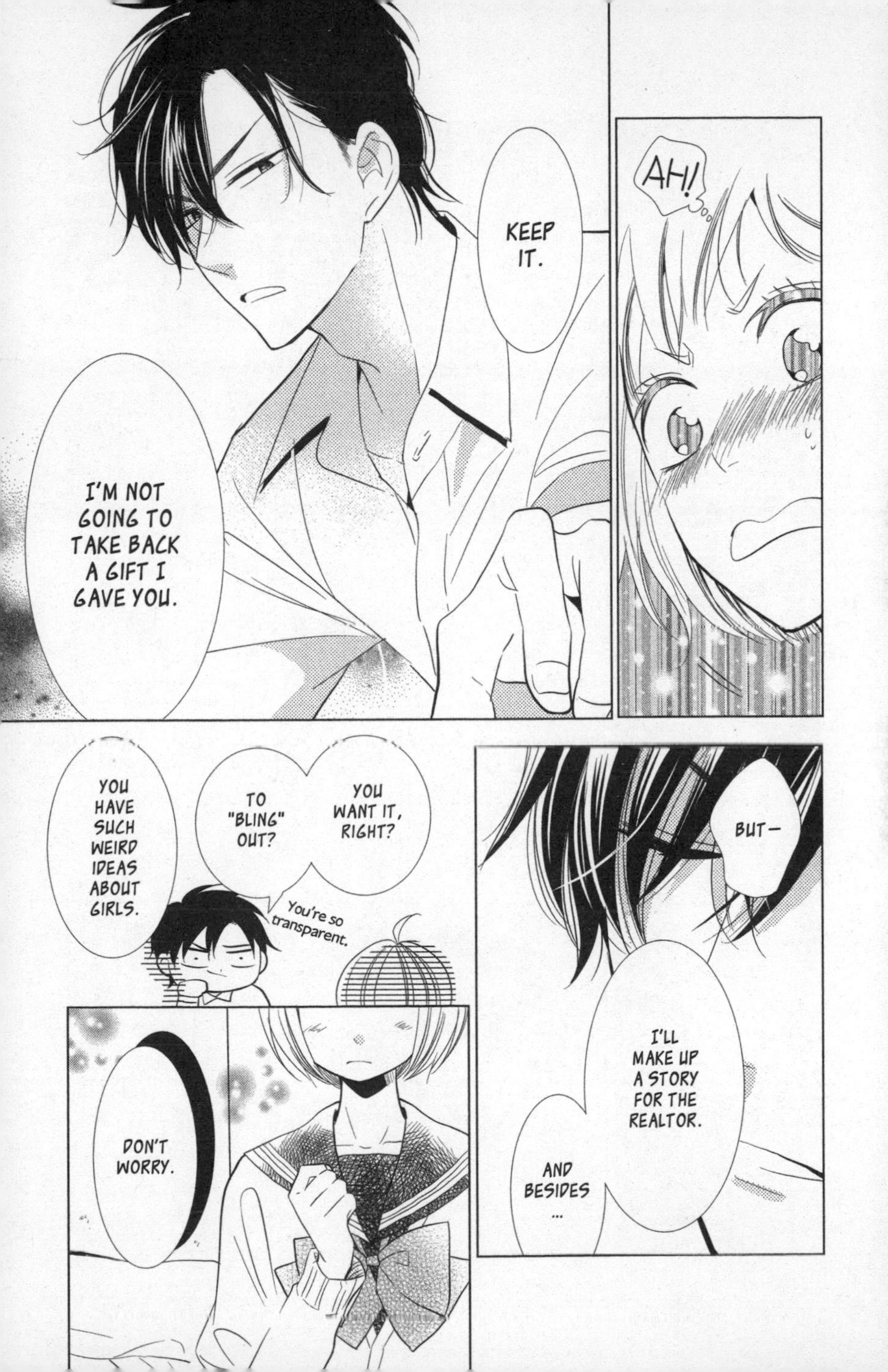
AH!
KEEP IT.
I'M NOT GOING TO TAKE BACK A GIFT I GAVE YOU.
BUT—
I'LL MAKE UP A STORY FOR THE REALTOR.
AND BESIDES ...
YOU WANT IT, RIGHT?
TO "BLING" OUT?
You're so transparent.
YOU HAVE SUCH WEIRD IDEAS ABOUT GIRLS.
DON'T WORRY.

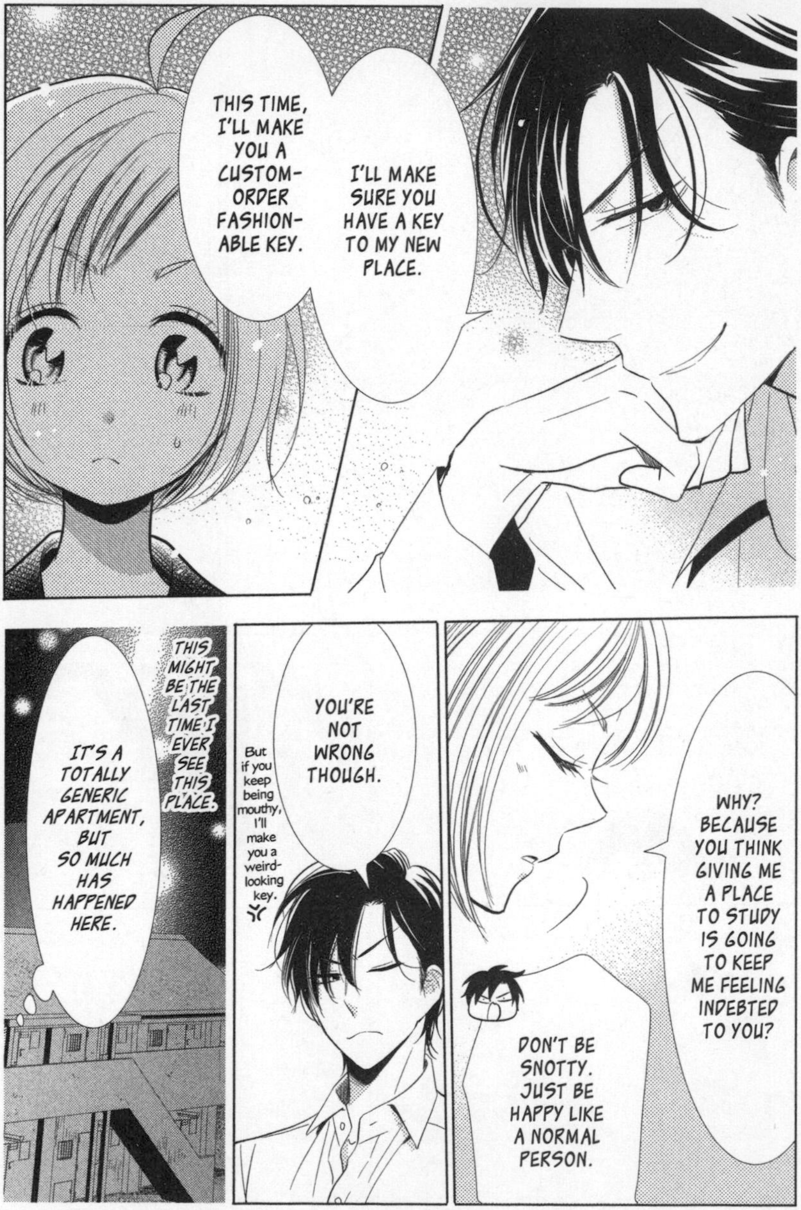
I'LL MAKE SURE YOU HAVE A KEY TO MY NEW PLACE.
THIS TIME, I'LL MAKE YOU A CUSTOM-ORDER FASHIONABLE KEY.
WHY? BECAUSE YOU THINK GIVING ME A PLACE TO STUDY IS GOING TO KEEP ME FEELING INDEBTED TO YOU?
DON'T BE SNOTTY. JUST BE HAPPY LIKE A NORMAL PERSON.
YOU'RE NOT WRONG THOUGH.
But if you keep being mouthy, I'll make you a weird-looking key.
THIS MIGHT BE THE LAST TIME I EVER SEE THIS PLACE.
IT'S A TOTALLY GENERIC APARTMENT, BUT SO MUCH HAS HAPPENED HERE.

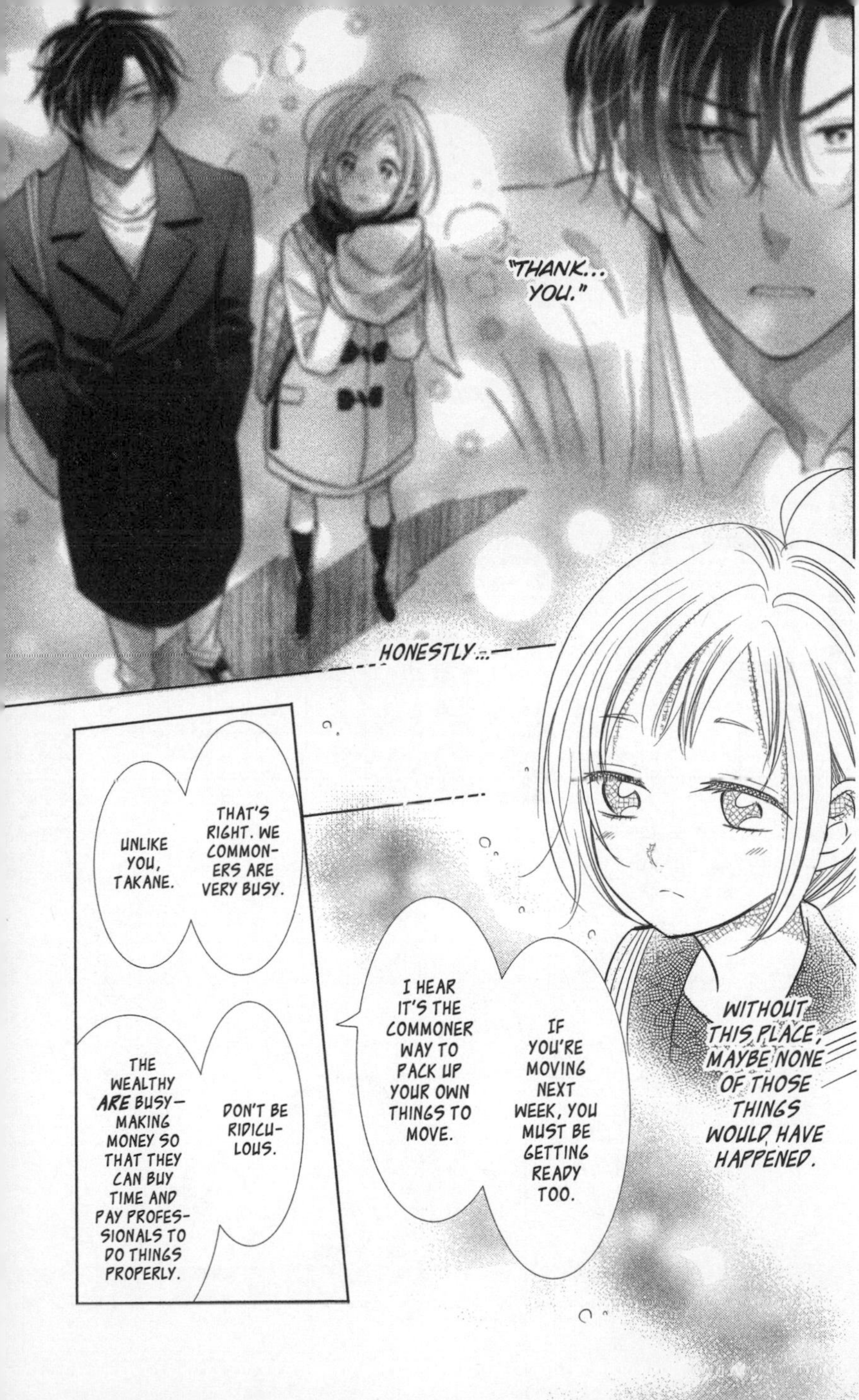
"THANK... YOU."
HONESTLY...
WITHOUT THIS PLACE, MAYBE NONE OF THOSE THINGS WOULD HAVE HAPPENED.
IF YOU'RE MOVING NEXT WEEK, YOU MUST BE GETTING READY TOO.
I HEAR IT'S THE COMMONER WAY TO PACK UP YOUR OWN THINGS TO MOVE.
THAT'S RIGHT. WE COMMONERS ARE VERY BUSY.
UNLIKE YOU, TAKANE.
DON'T BE RIDICULOUS.
THE WEALTHY *ARE* BUSY—MAKING MONEY SO THAT THEY CAN BUY TIME AND PAY PROFESSIONALS TO DO THINGS PROPERLY.

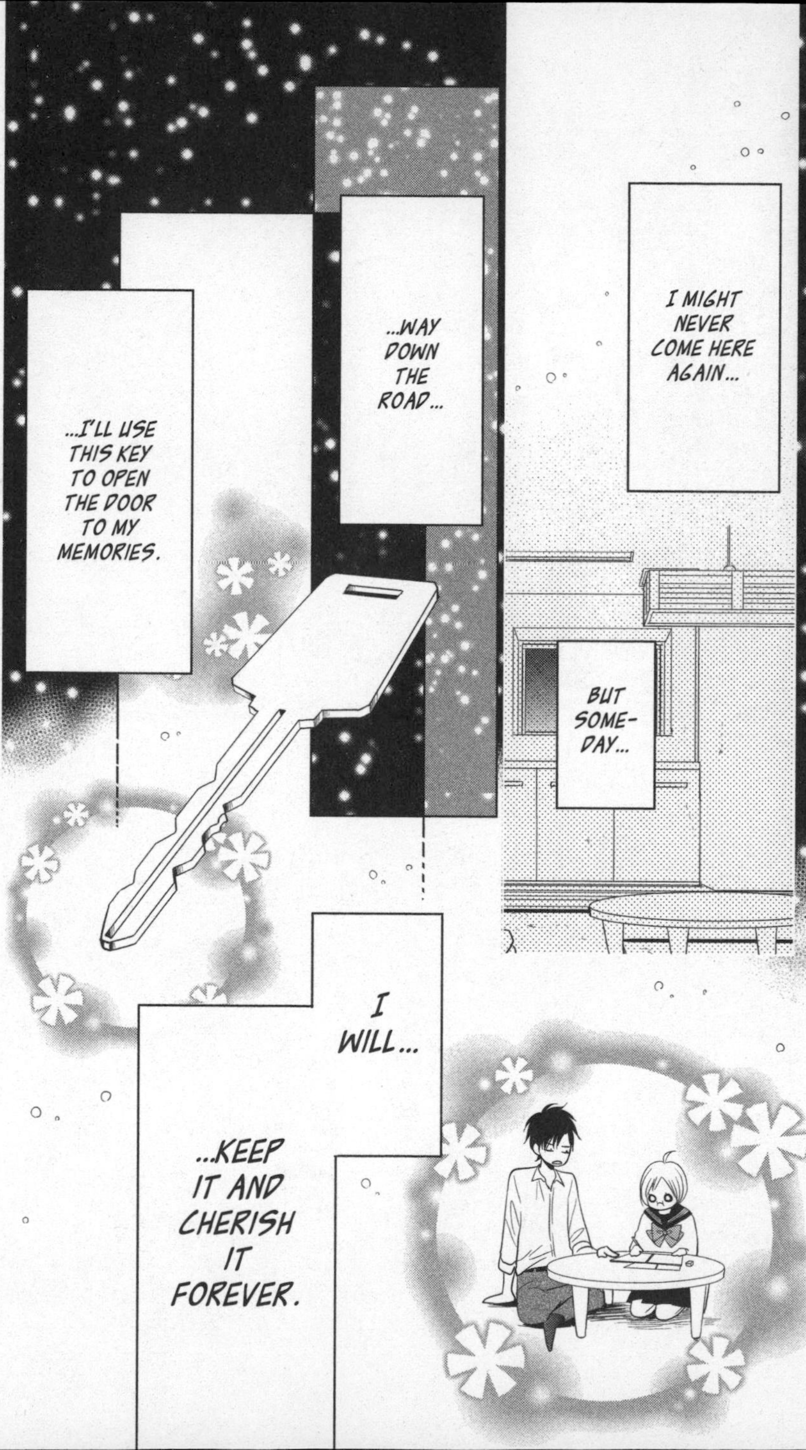
I MIGHT NEVER COME HERE AGAIN...
BUT SOME-DAY...
...WAY DOWN THE ROAD...
...I'LL USE THIS KEY TO OPEN THE DOOR TO MY MEMORIES.
I WILL...
...KEEP IT AND CHERISH IT FOREVER.

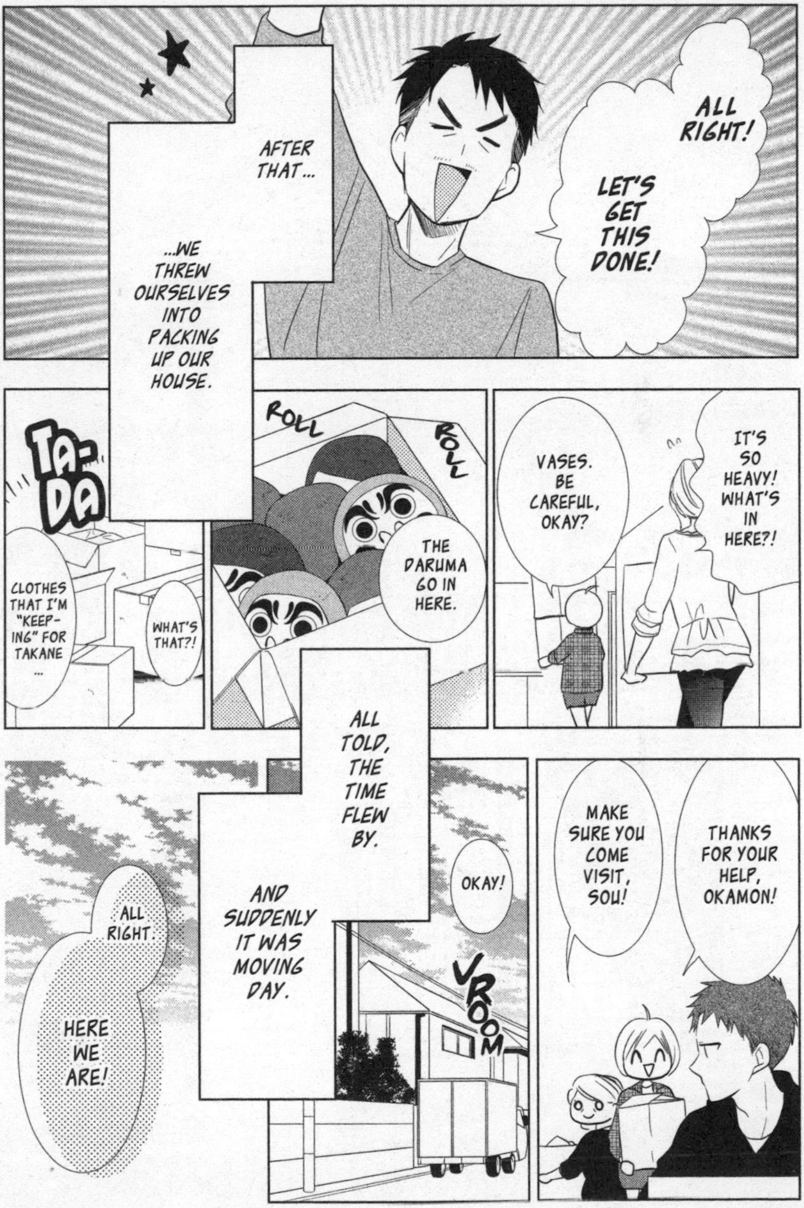
ALL RIGHT!
LET'S GET THIS DONE!
AFTER THAT...
...WE THREW OURSELVES INTO PACKING UP OUR HOUSE.
IT'S SO HEAVY! WHAT'S IN HERE?!
VASES. BE CAREFUL, OKAY?
ROLL
ROLL
THE DARUMA GO IN HERE.
TA-DA
WHAT'S THAT?!
CLOTHES THAT I'M "KEEP-ING" FOR TAKANE ...
THANKS FOR YOUR HELP, OKAMON!
MAKE SURE YOU COME VISIT, SOU!
ALL TOLD, THE TIME FLEW BY.
OKAY!
AND SUDDENLY IT WAS MOVING DAY.
VROOM
ALL RIGHT.
HERE WE ARE!

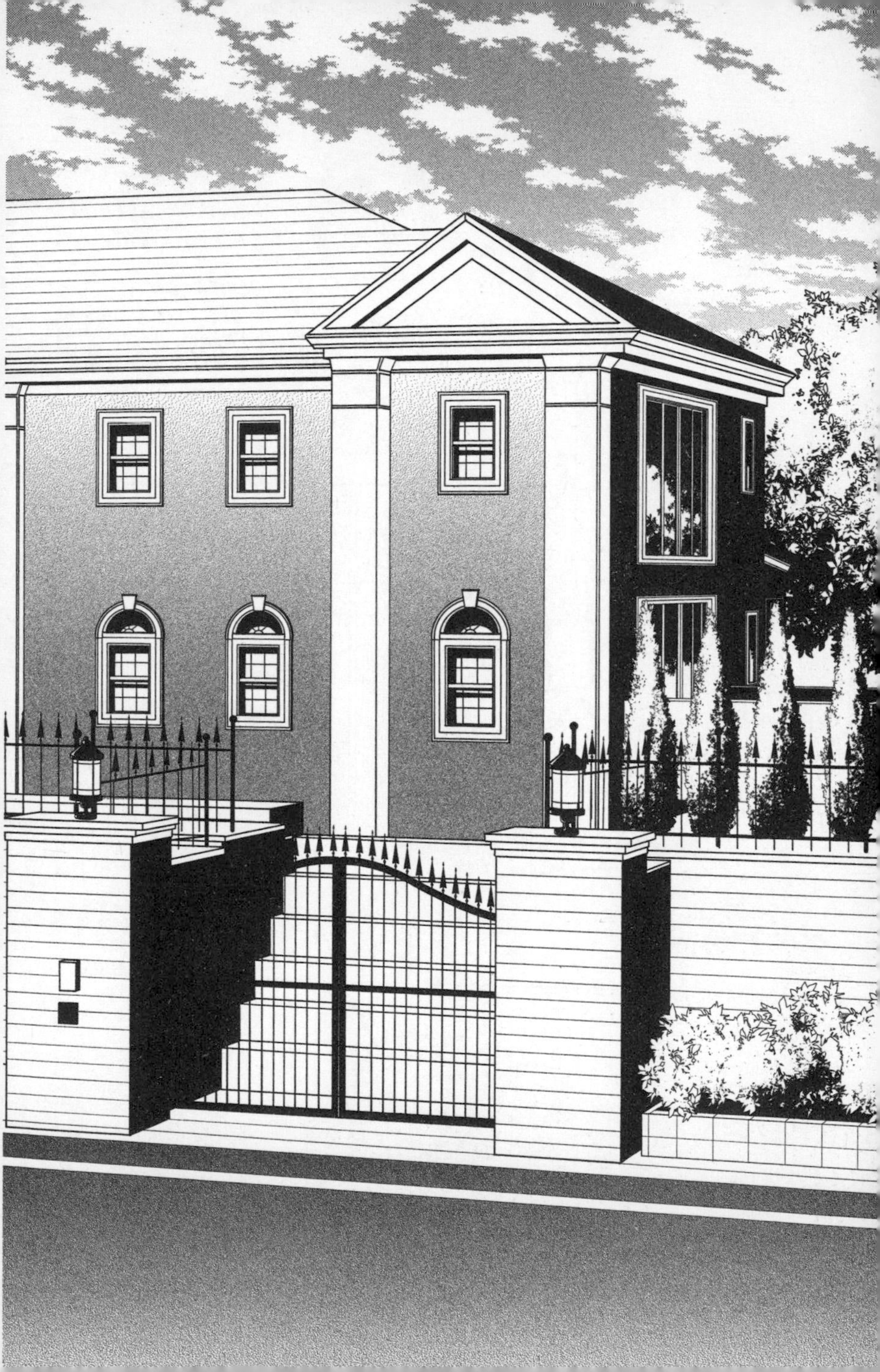

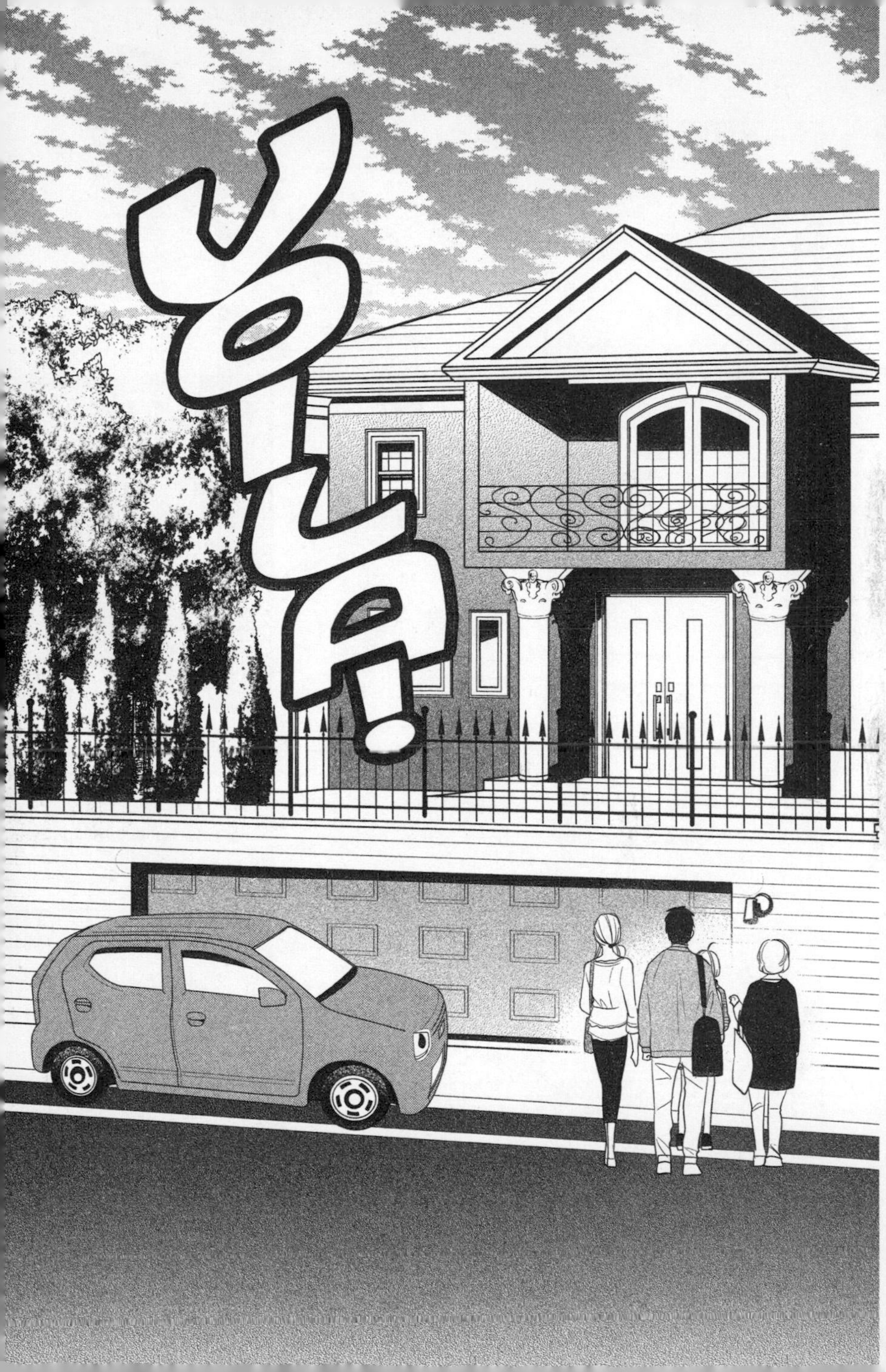
VOILA!

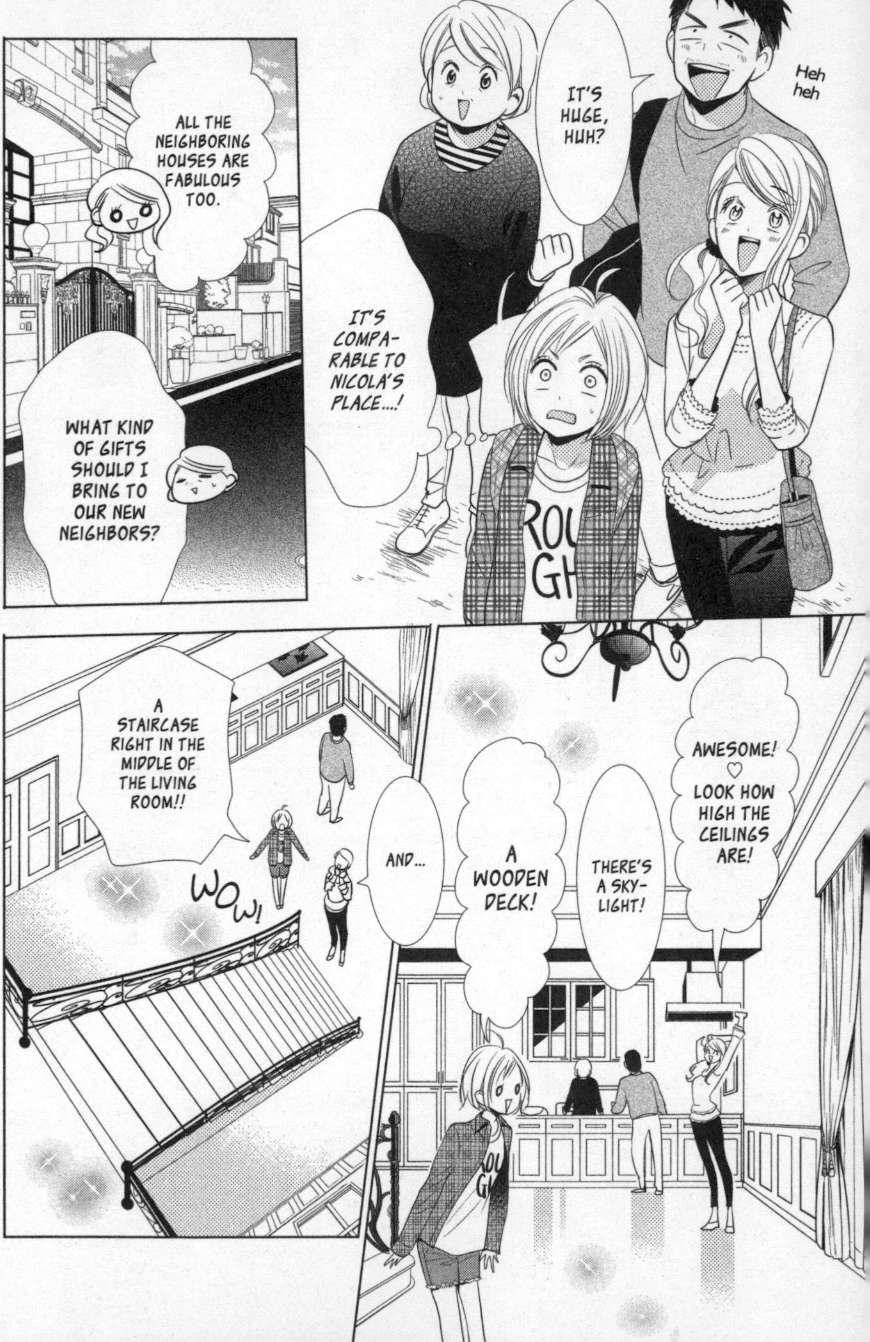

IT'S HUGE, HUH?
Heh heh
IT'S COMPARABLE TO NICOLA'S PLACE...!
ALL THE NEIGHBORING HOUSES ARE FABULOUS TOO.
WHAT KIND OF GIFTS SHOULD I BRING TO OUR NEW NEIGHBORS?
AWESOME! ♡ LOOK HOW HIGH THE CEILINGS ARE!
THERE'S A SKY-LIGHT!
A WOODEN DECK!
AND...
A STAIRCASE RIGHT IN THE MIDDLE OF THE LIVING ROOM!!
WOW!

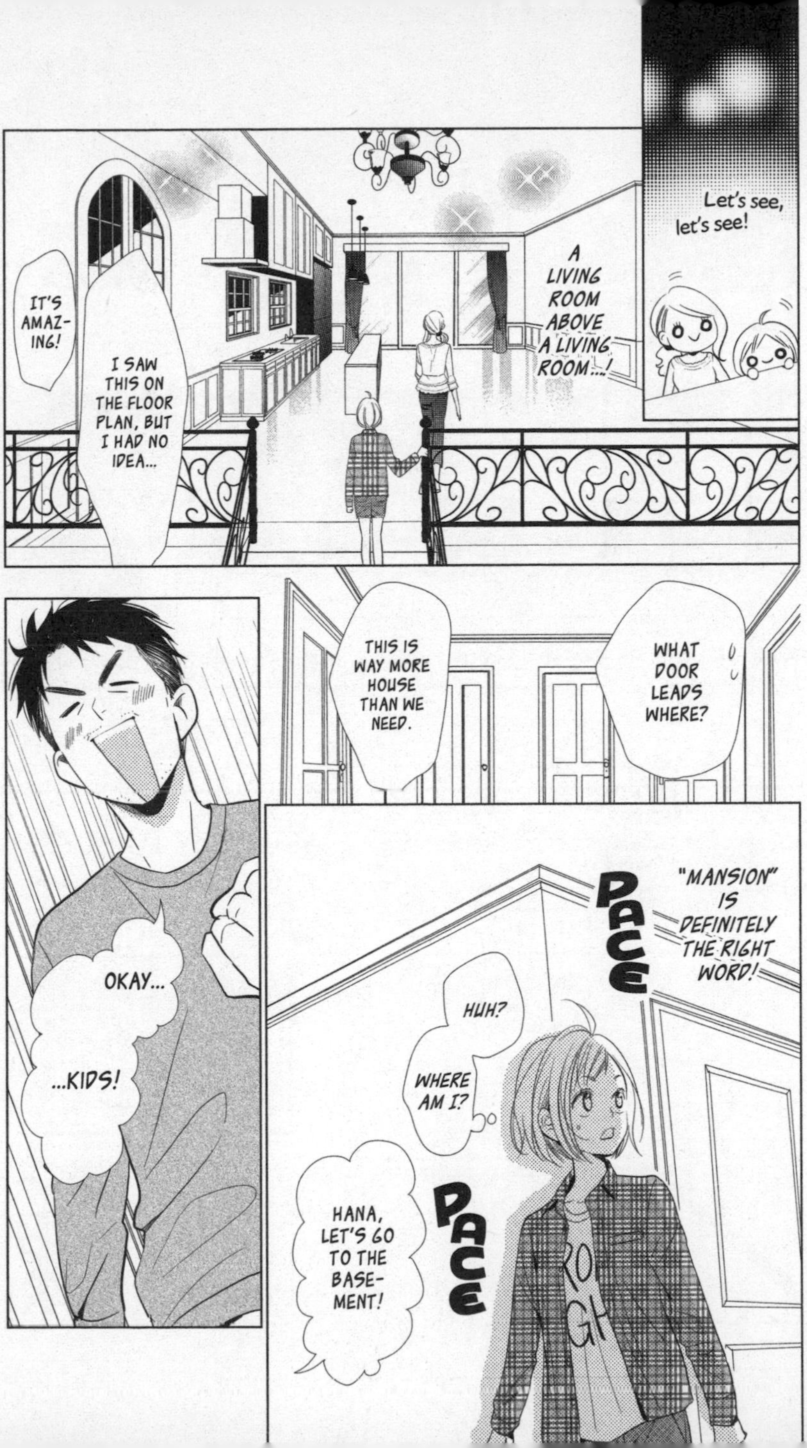
Let's see, let's see!
A LIVING ROOM ABOVE A LIVING ROOM...!
I SAW THIS ON THE FLOOR PLAN, BUT I HAD NO IDEA...
IT'S AMAZ-ING!
WHAT DOOR LEADS WHERE?
THIS IS WAY MORE HOUSE THAN WE NEED.
"MANSION" IS DEFINITELY THE RIGHT WORD!
PACE
HUH?
WHERE AM I?
PACE
HANA, LET'S GO TO THE BASE-MENT!
OKAY...
...KIDS!

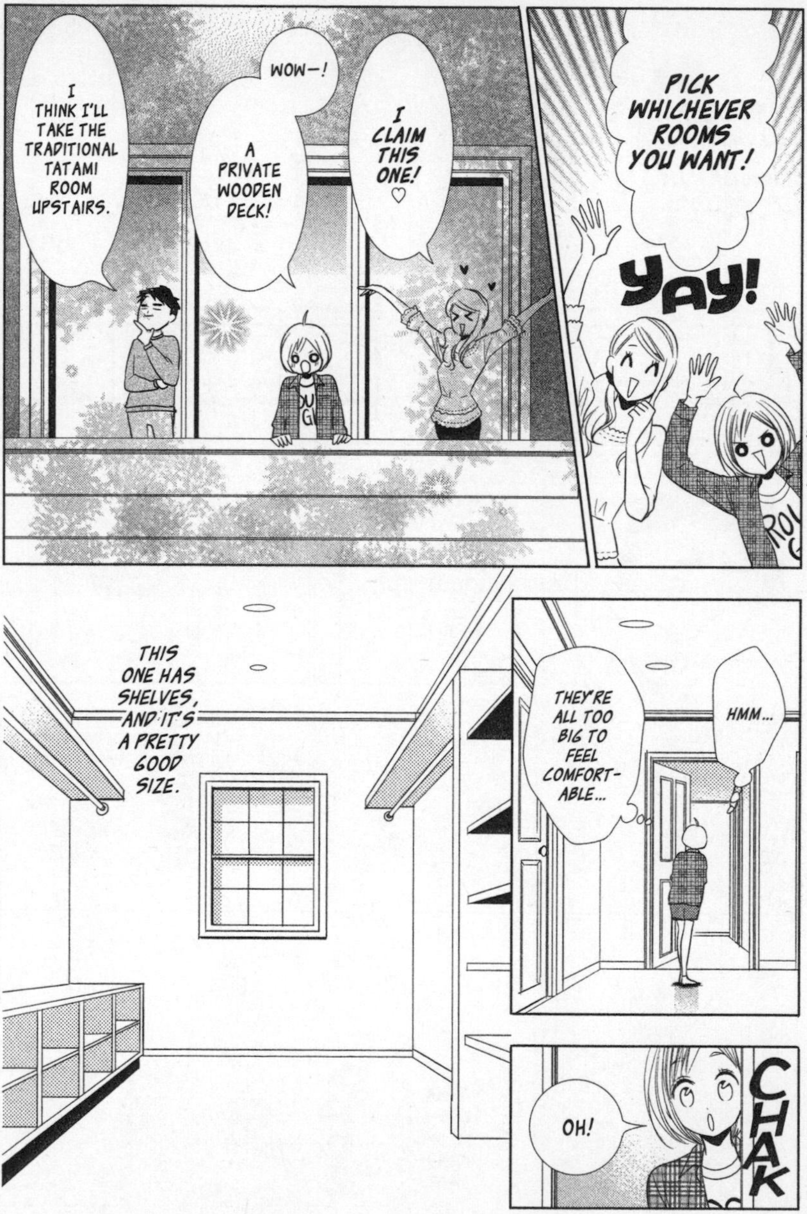
PICK WHICHEVER ROOMS YOU WANT!
YAY!
Starting to get into it!
I CLAIM THIS ONE! ♡
WOW—!
A PRIVATE WOODEN DECK!
I THINK I'LL TAKE THE TRADITIONAL TATAMI ROOM UPSTAIRS.
HMM...
THEY'RE ALL TOO BIG TO FEEL COMFORTABLE...
CHAK
OH!
THIS ONE HAS SHELVES, AND IT'S A PRETTY GOOD SIZE.

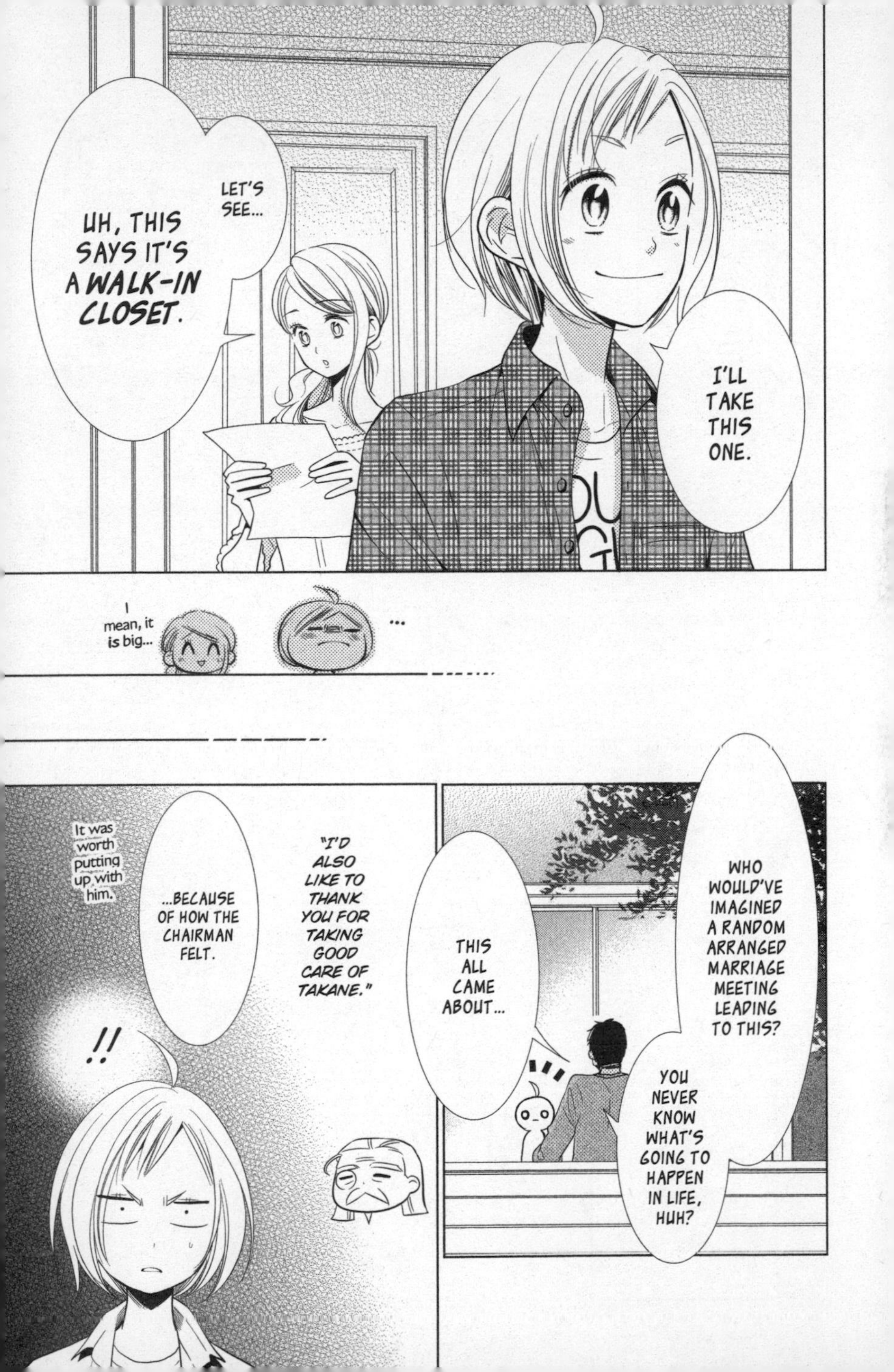
I'LL TAKE THIS ONE.
LET'S SEE...
UH, THIS SAYS IT'S A WALK-IN CLOSET.
...
I mean, it is big...
WHO WOULD'VE IMAGINED A RANDOM ARRANGED MARRIAGE MEETING LEADING TO THIS?
YOU NEVER KNOW WHAT'S GOING TO HAPPEN IN LIFE, HUH?
THIS ALL CAME ABOUT...
"I'D ALSO LIKE TO THANK YOU FOR TAKING GOOD CARE OF TAKANE."
...BECAUSE OF HOW THE CHAIRMAN FELT.
It was worth putting up with him.
!!

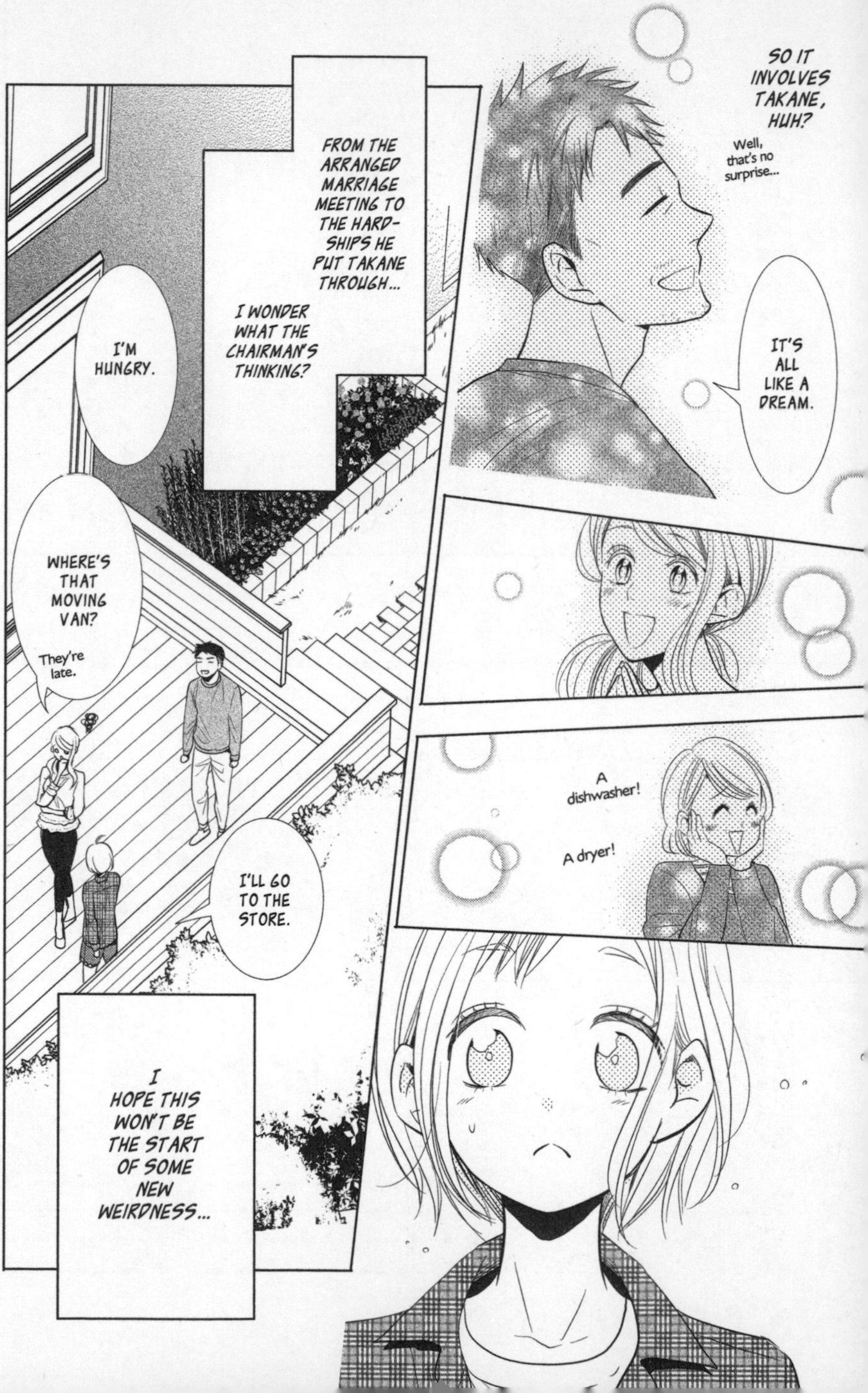
SO IT INVOLVES TAKANE, HUH?
Well, that's no surprise...
IT'S ALL LIKE A DREAM.
A dishwasher!
A dryer!
FROM THE ARRANGED MARRIAGE MEETING TO THE HARD-SHIPS HE PUT TAKANE THROUGH...
I WONDER WHAT THE CHAIRMAN'S THINKING?
I'M HUNGRY.
WHERE'S THAT MOVING VAN?
They're late.
I'LL GO TO THE STORE.
I HOPE THIS WON'T BE THE START OF SOME NEW WEIRDNESS...

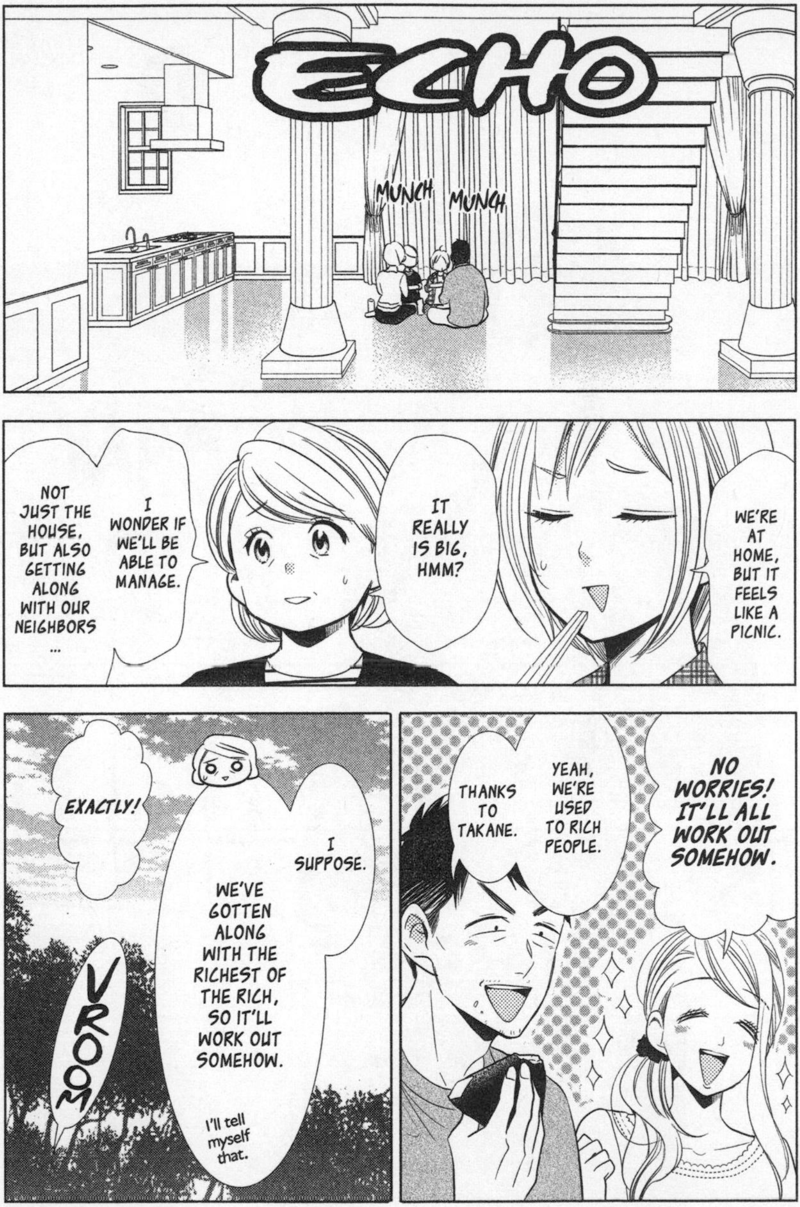
ECHO
MUNCH MUNCH
WE'RE AT HOME, BUT IT FEELS LIKE A PICNIC.
IT REALLY IS BIG, HMM?
I WONDER IF WE'LL BE ABLE TO MANAGE.
NOT JUST THE HOUSE, BUT ALSO GETTING ALONG WITH OUR NEIGHBORS ...
NO WORRIES! IT'LL ALL WORK OUT SOMEHOW.
YEAH, WE'RE USED TO RICH PEOPLE.
THANKS TO TAKANE.
I SUPPOSE.
WE'VE GOTTEN ALONG WITH THE RICHEST OF THE RICH, SO IT'LL WORK OUT SOMEHOW.
I'll tell myself that.
EXACTLY!
VROOM

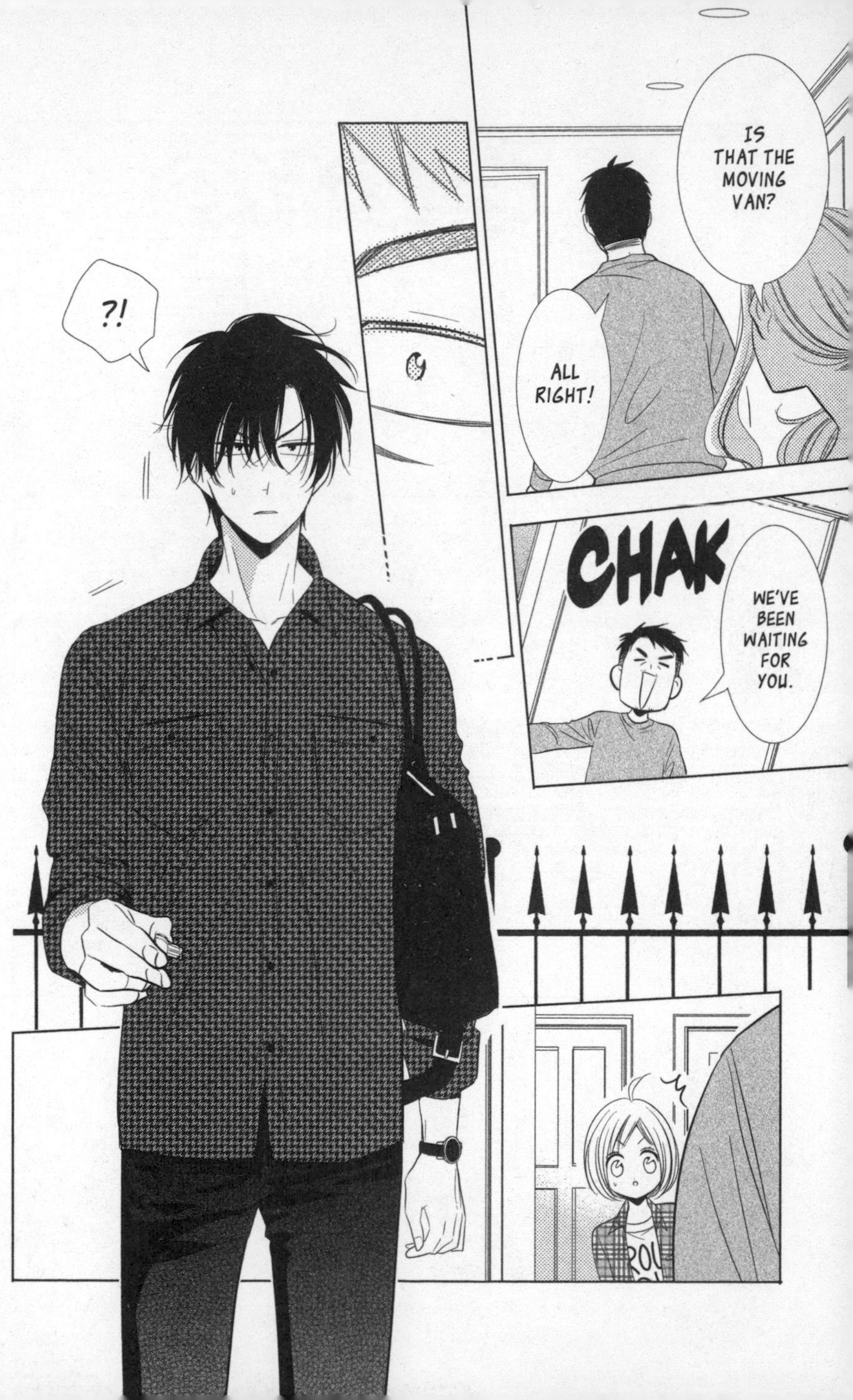
IS THAT THE MOVING VAN?
ALL RIGHT!
CHAK
WE'VE BEEN WAITING FOR YOU.
?!

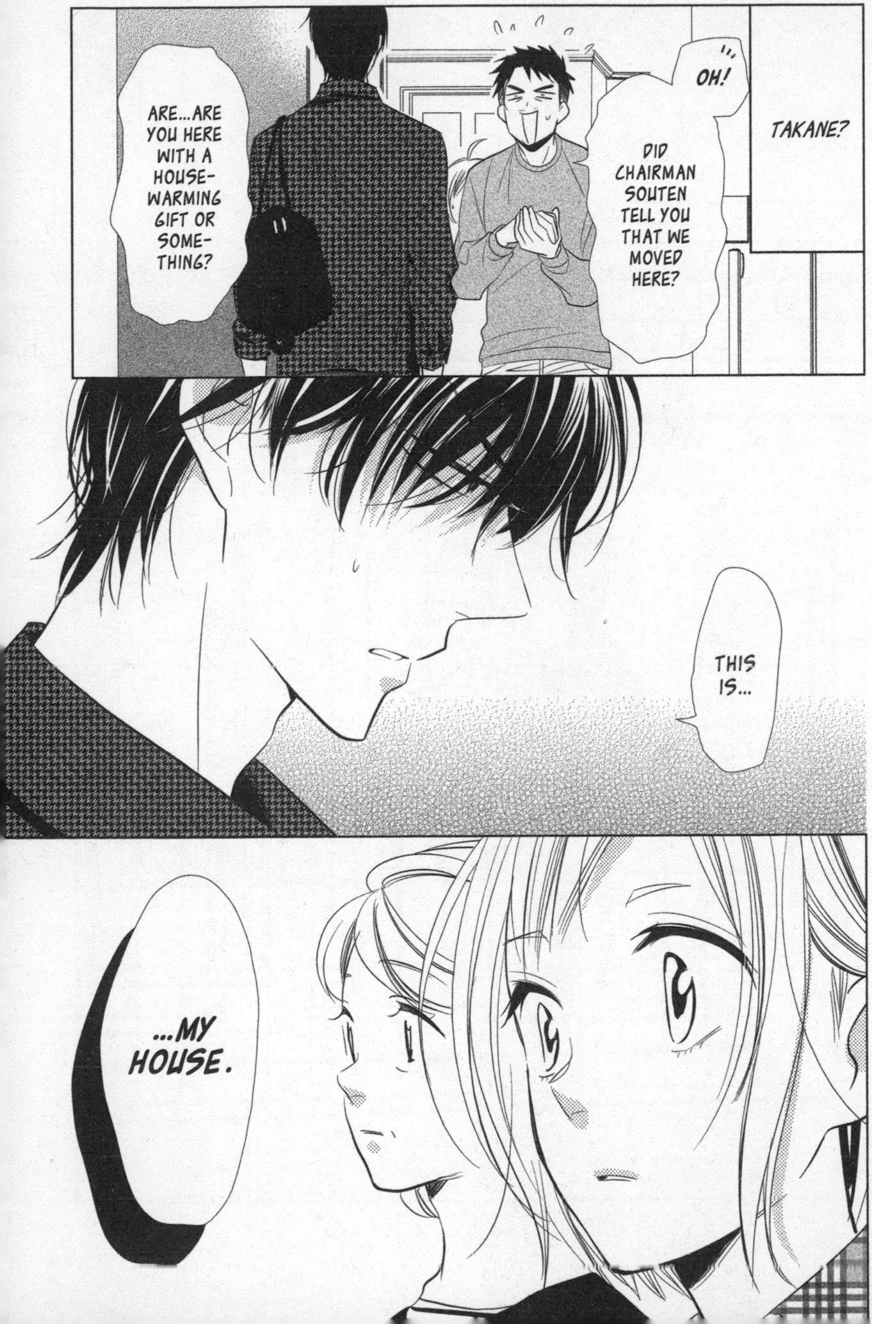
TAKANE?
OH!
DID CHAIRMAN SOUTEN TELL YOU THAT WE MOVED HERE?
ARE...ARE YOU HERE WITH A HOUSE-WARMING GIFT OR SOME-THING?
THIS IS...
...MY HOUSE.

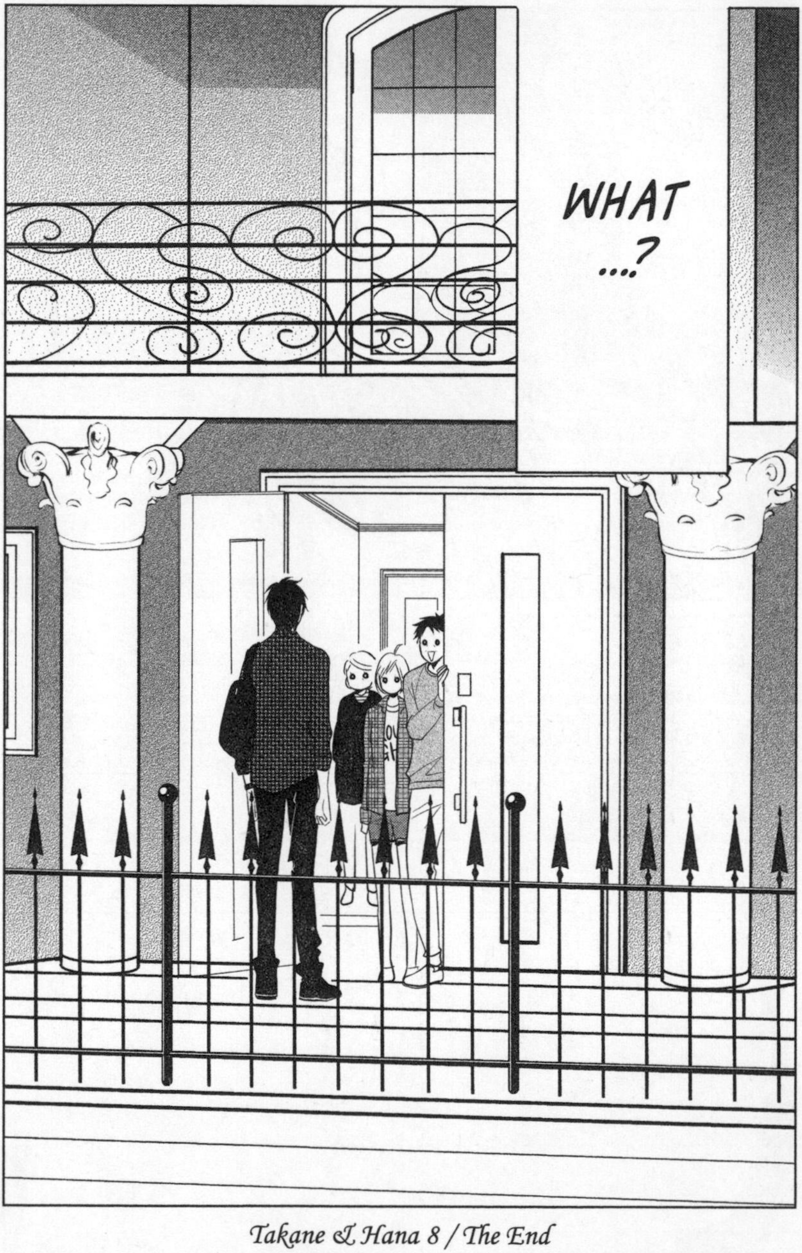
WHAT
...?

Takane & Hana 8 / The End

Bonus Story
Takane & Hana
& Jr.

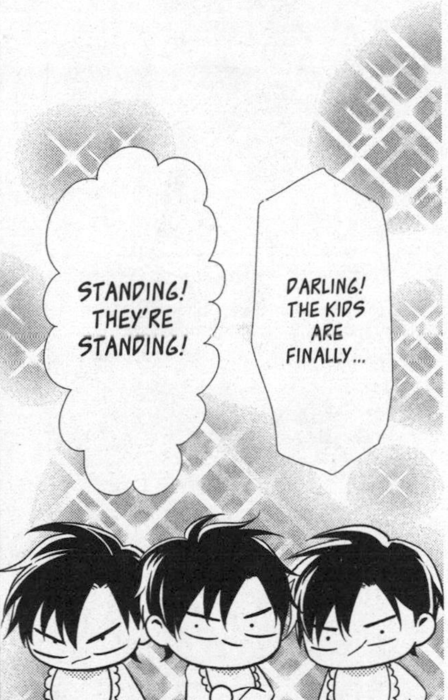
DARLING! THE KIDS ARE FINALLY...
STANDING! THEY'RE STANDING!

Growth

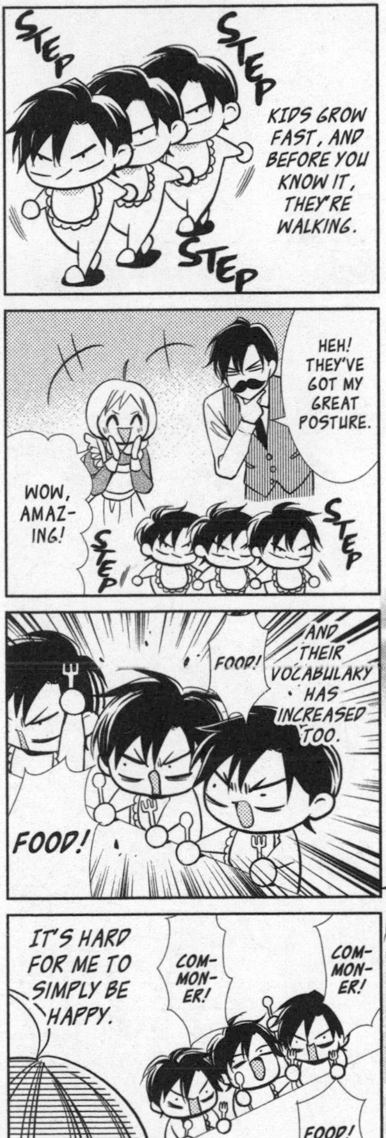
STEP
KIDS GROW FAST, AND BEFORE YOU KNOW IT, THEY'RE WALKING.
STEP
STEP
HEH! THEY'VE GOT MY GREAT POSTURE.
WOW, AMAZ-ING!
STEP
STEP
AND THEIR VOCABULARY HAS INCREASED TOO.
FOOD!
FOOD!
COM-MON-ER!
COM-MON-ER!
IT'S HARD FOR ME TO SIMPLY BE HAPPY.
FOOD!

First-Person Pronouns

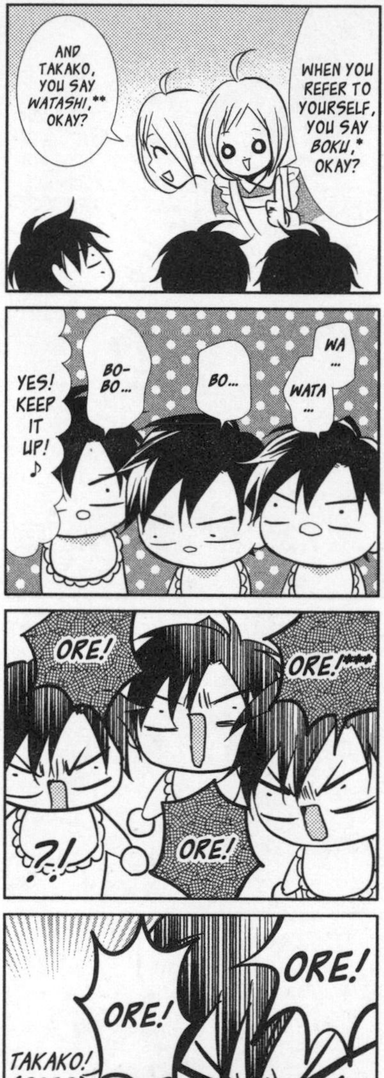
WHEN YOU REFER TO YOURSELF, YOU SAY BOKU,* OKAY?
AND TAKAKO, YOU SAY WATASHI,** OKAY?
WA ... WATA ...
BO...
BO-BO...
YES! KEEP IT UP! ♪
ORE!***
ORE!
ORE!
?!
ORE!
ORE!
TAKAKO! (SOBS)
ORE!

*Used by males, a more polite way to refer to oneself
**Used mostly by females
***Used mostly by males, a crasser way to refer to oneself

Takako

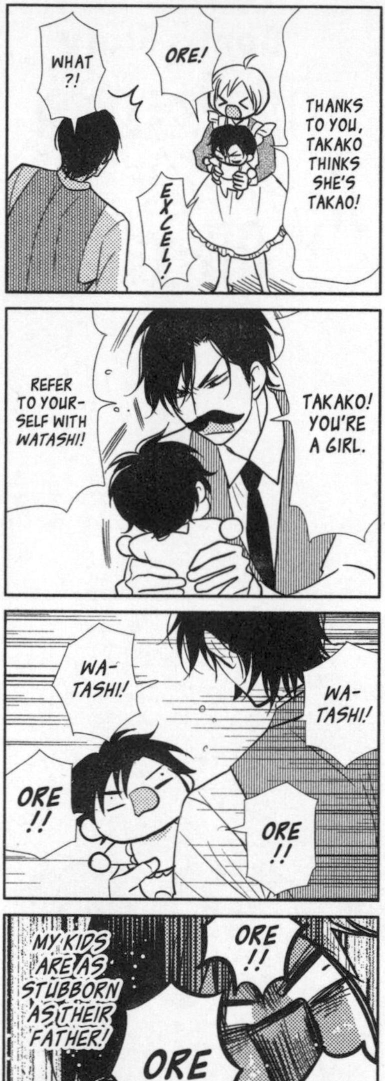
THANKS TO YOU, TAKAKO THINKS SHE'S TAKAO!
ORE!
WHAT ?!
EXCEL!
TAKAKO! YOU'RE A GIRL.
REFER TO YOURSELF WITH WATASHI!
WA-TASHI!
WA-TASHI!
ORE !!
ORE !!
ORE !!
MY KIDS ARE AS STUBBORN AS THEIR FATHER!
ORE !!
ORE !!
ORE !!

Takao

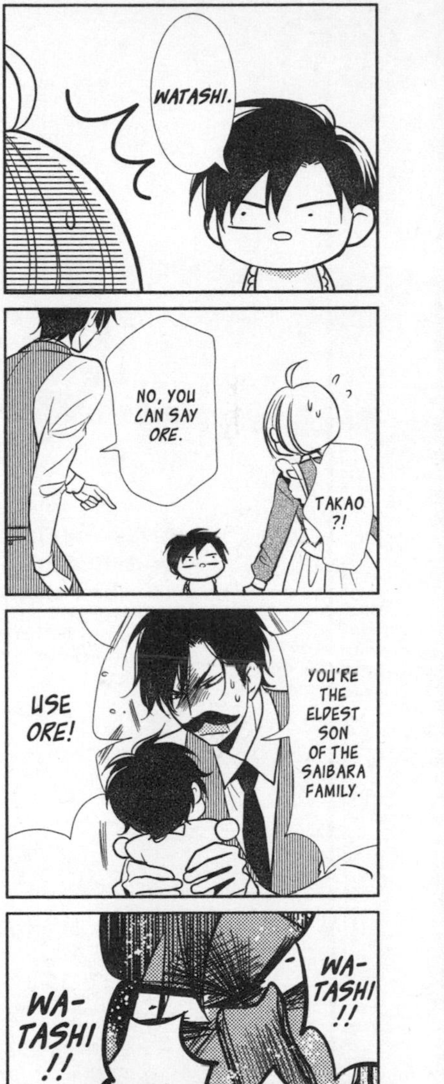
WATASHI.
TAKAO ?!
NO, YOU CAN SAY ORE.
YOU'RE THE ELDEST SON OF THE SAIBARA FAMILY.
USE ORE!
WA-TASHI !!
WA-TASHI !!
WA-TASHI !!
WA-TASHI !!

Takane

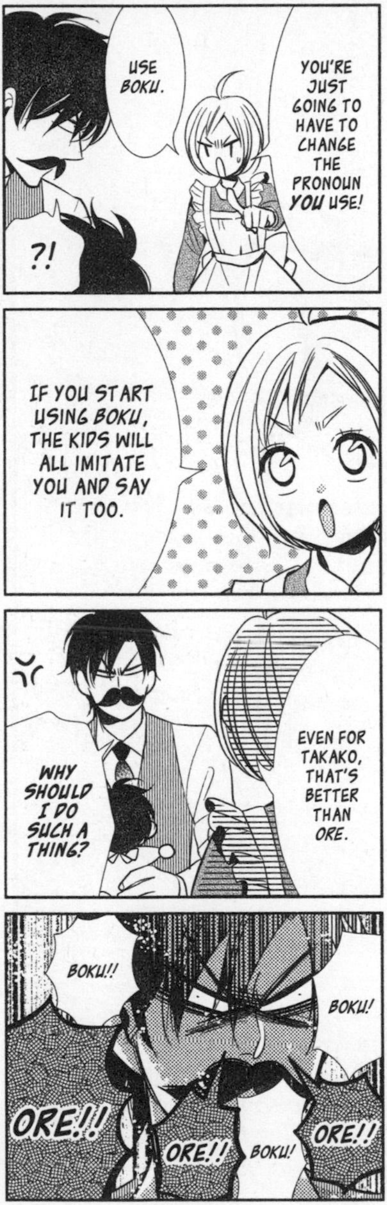
YOU'RE JUST GOING TO HAVE TO CHANGE THE PRONOUN *YOU* USE!
USE BOKU.
?!
IF YOU START USING *BOKU*, THE KIDS WILL ALL IMITATE YOU AND SAY IT TOO.
EVEN FOR TAKAKO, THAT'S BETTER THAN ORE.
WHY SHOULD I DO SUCH A THING?
BOKU!
BOKU!!
ORE!!
BOKU!
ORE!!
ORE!!

Bonus Story: Takane & Hana & Jr. / The End

I was thrilled to hear that you all loved volume 7's cover! Whenever I put those two together, somehow Hana always ends up on top.

—YUKI SHIWASU

Born on March 7 in Fukuoka Prefecture, Japan, Yuki Shiwasu began her career as a manga artist after winning the top prize in the Hakusensha Athena Newcomers' Awards from *Hana to Yume* magazine. She is also the author of *Furou Kyoudai* (Immortal Siblings), which was published by Hakusensha in Japan.

Takane & Hana

VOLUME 8
SHOJO BEAT EDITION

STORY & ART BY **YUKI SHIWASU**

ENGLISH ADAPTATION **Ysabet Reinhardt MacFarlane**
TRANSLATION **JN Productions**
TOUCH-UP ART & LETTERING **Annaliese Christman**
DESIGN **Shawn Carrico**
EDITOR **Amy Yu**

Takane to Hana by Yuki Shiwasu
© Yuki Shiwasu 2017
All rights reserved.
First published in Japan in 2017 by HAKUSENSHA, Inc., Tokyo.
English language translation rights arranged with HAKUSENSHA, Inc., Tokyo.

Printed in the U.S.A.

Published by VIZ Media, LLC
P.O. Box 77010
San Francisco, CA 94107

10 9 8 7 6 5 4 3 2 1
First printing, April 2019

viz.com   shojobeat.com

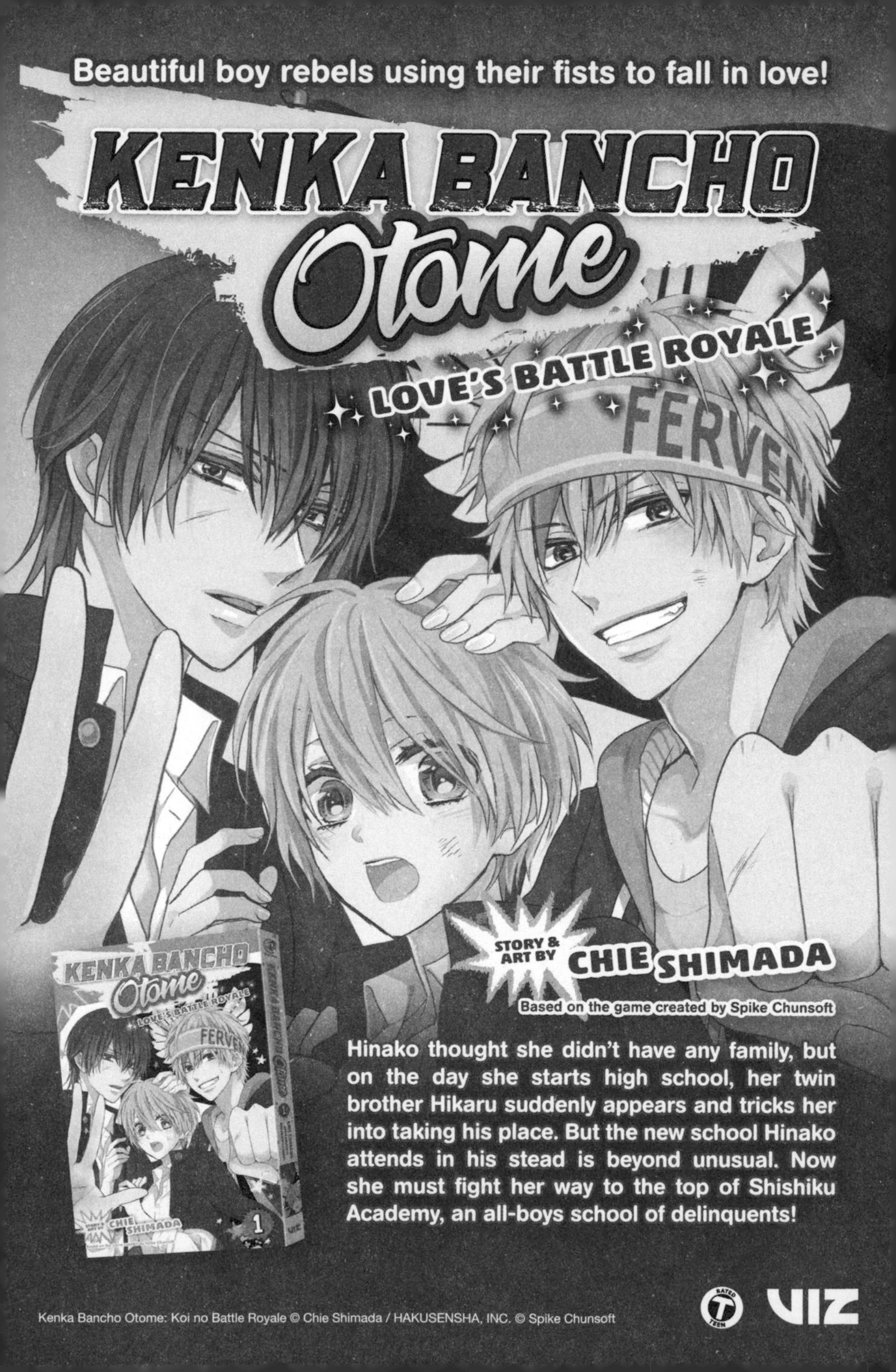

Beautiful boy rebels using their fists to fall in love!
KENKA BANCHO Otome
LOVE'S BATTLE ROYALE
FERVEN
STORY & ART BY CHIE SHIMADA
Based on the game created by Spike Chunsoft
KENKA BANCHO Otome
LOVE'S BATTLE ROYALE
FERVEN
STORY & ART BY CHIE SHIMADA
1
Hinako thought she didn't have any family, but on the day she starts high school, her twin brother Hikaru suddenly appears and tricks her into taking his place. But the new school Hinako attends in his stead is beyond unusual. Now she must fight her way to the top of Shishiku Academy, an all-boys school of delinquents!
RATED T TEEN
VIZ
Kenka Bancho Otome: Koi no Battle Royale © Chie Shimada / HAKUSENSHA, INC. © Spike Chunsoft

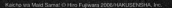

Nino Arisugawa, a girl who loves to sing, experiences her first heart-wrenching goodbye when her beloved childhood friend, Momo, moves away. And after Nino befriends Yuzu, a music composer, she experiences another sad parting! With music as their common ground and only outlet, how will everyone's unrequited loves play out?

ANONYMOUS NOISE

IDOL dreams

STORY & ART BY
ARINA TANEMURA

At age 31, office worker Chikage Deguchi feels she missed her chances at love and success. When word gets out that she's a virgin, Chikage is humiliated and wishes she could turn back time to when she was still young and popular. She takes an experimental drug that changes her appearance back to when she was 15. Now Chikage is determined to pursue everything she missed out on all those years ago—including becoming a star!

Behind the Scenes!!

STORY AND ART BY BISCO HATORI

From the creator of Ouran High School Host Club

Ranmaru Kurisu comes from a family of hardy, rough-and-tumble fisherfolk and he sticks out at home like a delicate, artistic sore thumb. It's given him a raging inferiority complex and a permanently pessimistic outlook. Now that he's in college, he's hoping to find a sense of belonging. But after a whole life of being left out, does he even know how to fit in?!

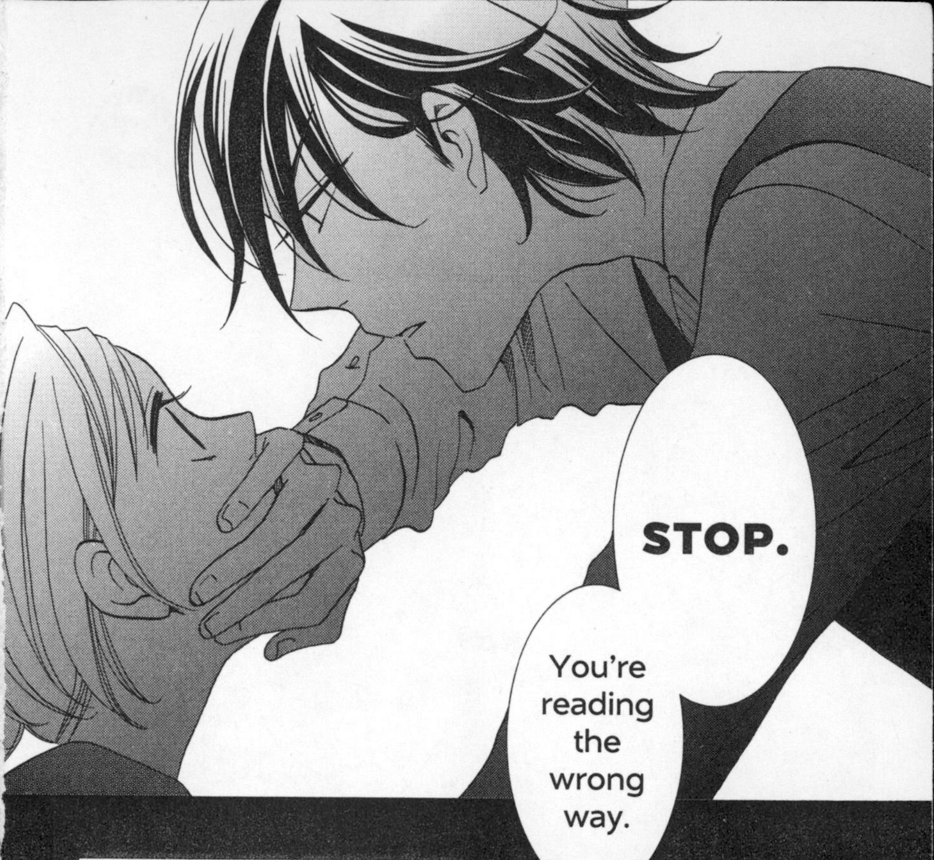
STOP.
You're reading the wrong way.

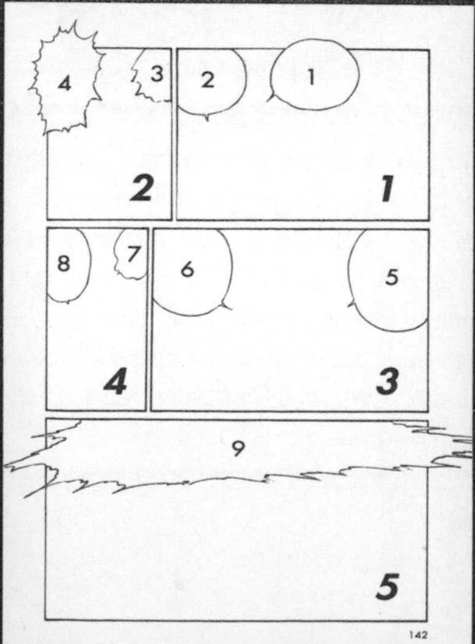
1
2
3
4
1
2
5
6
7
8
3
4
9
5
142

In keeping with the original Japanese comic format, this book reads from right to left—so action, sound effects and word balloons are completely reversed to preserve the orientation of the original artwork.

Check out the diagram shown here to get the hang of things, and then turn to the other side of the book to get started!